Cassell
Dictionary of
Humorous
Quotations

Cassell
Dictionary of
Humorous
Quotations

Nigel Rees

CASSELL

Cassell
Wellington House
125 Strand
London WC2R 0BB

www.cassell.co.uk

First published in 1998

Distributed in the United States
by Sterling Publishing Co. Inc.
387 Park Avenue South,
New York, NY 10016—8810

British Library Cataloguing-in-Publication Data
A catalogue record for this book is available
from the British Library

ISBN 0-304-35095-8

Designed and typeset by Tim Higgins

Printed and bound in Great Britain by
Mackays of Chatham PLC,
Chatham, Kent

Contents

Introduction

The first move any compiler of a dictionary of humorous quotations makes is to take a look at the work of those who have attempted the task before him. That done, he exclaims, 'But that's not humorous!' So what exactly is a humorous quotation? Does it have to raise a laugh or even a smile to qualify?

On the whole, I think, yes. The quotations selected should not just be pithy observations or critical barbs, but things said with either the warmth of humour or the cleverness of wit. But I am perfectly aware that the same test will be made of the quotations in my collection and, on occasions, I, too, am found wanting.

Nevertheless, on the whole, I should be surprised if the majority of quotations in this volume did not produce a reaction in the reader somewhere on the scale from wry amusement to outright glee, as was their authors' intention. There are also some remarks included because they are themselves risible, in the sense of being laughed *at* rather than *with*, and not because their speakers intended them to be so received.

In addition, there is a selection of quotations, not necessarily humorous in themselves but on the subject of humour, comedy and wit.

As in all my books – and, if I may say so, unlike most other compilers of dictionaries of humorous quotations – I have tried to provide some sort of source for the quotations and not just plonk down the quote with an 'attributed to …' There is, again somewhat unusually, a comprehensive index which should make it the simplest matter to find any half-remembered line that the reader might be interested in.

I have encountered the majority of quotations in this book during the more than twenty years I have spent writing and presenting the BBC Radio programme *Quote … Unquote*. My thanks to Radio 4 and World Service for maintaining their faith over what is, by anybody's standards, a very long time in broadcasting. As it happens, this dictionary appears on the twentieth anniversary of the publication of the very first *Quote … Unquote* book, so my gratitude is due to the several publishers who have helped me pursue the idea since then.

vii

My thanks go to the many faithful readers of *The 'Quote ... Unquote'*
Newsletter around the world. In asking about and contributing humorous
quotations, they have kept me up to date on the sayings that have amused
them or about which they have sought sources or further information.
In particular, I should like to acknowledge the help and interest of:
Dr J. K. Aronson; H. E. Bell; Jonathan Cecil; Denis Norden; Jaap
Engelsman; Mark English; John Fletcher; Charles G. Francis; Ian Gillies;
John Gray; W. Eric Gustafson; Raymond Harris; Donald Hickling; Roy
Hudd; W. W. Keen James; Sir Antony Jay; Oonagh Lahr; Michael R. Lewis;
R. P. W. Lewis; Leonard Miall; Professor Wolfgang Mieder; the late
Frank Muir; Michael and Valerie Grosvenor Myer; John Julius Norwich;
Derek Parker; Philip Purser; Steve Race; Claire Rayner; and many,
many others.

NIGEL REES
London, 1998

The Dictionary

A

Aardvark

1 It's aardvark, but it pays well.

Anonymous. Quoted in John S. Crosbie, *Crosbie's Dictionary of Puns* (1977).

Abdication

Within days of the abdication of King Edward VIII in December 1936 school-children were singing:

2 Hark the herald angels sing
Mrs Simpson's pinched our king .

Anonymous (British). Quoted in Kenneth Harris, *Attlee* (1982).

Abilities

To H. G. Wells:

3 It is all very well to be able to write books, but can you waggle your ears?

J. M. Barrie, Scottish playwright (1860–1937). Quoted in J. A. Hammerton, *Barrie: The Story of a Genius* (1929).

Absence

4 I was ... court-martialled in my absence, sentenced to death in my absence. So I said, right, you can shoot me in my absence.

Brendan Behan, Irish playwright (1923–64). *The Hostage* (1962 version).

5 What is better than presence of mind in a railway accident? Absence of body.

Punch Magazine, Vol. 16 (1849).

6 The more he looked inside the more Piglet wasn't there.

A. A. Milne, English children's writer (1882–1956). *The House at Pooh Corner*, Chap. 1 (1928).

Absentmindedness

Telegram to wife:

7 Am in Market Harborough. Where ought I to be?

G. K. Chesterton, English poet, novelist and critic (1874–1936). *Autobiography*, Chap. 16 (1936): 'Of those days the tale is told that I once sent a telegram to my wife in London, which ran: "Am in Market Harborough. Where ought I to be?" I cannot remember whether this story is true; but it is not unlikely or, I think, unreasonable.' Maisie Ward, in *Return to Chesterton* (1944), says that a hundred different places have been substituted for 'Market Harborough' in the telling of this story. Chesterton's wife, Frances, on this occasion cabled the answer 'Home' – because, as she exclaimed, it was easier to get him home and start him off again.

Absinthe

8 Absinthe makes the heart grow fonder.

Anonymous, but also ascribed to Oscar Wilde and to Addison Mizner, American architect (1872–1933) and so quoted in *The Treasury of Humorous Quotations*, ed. Evan Esar & Nicolas Bentley (1951).

Proposing a toast:

9 Absinthe makes the tart grow fonder.

Hugh Drummond (untraced). Quoted in Sir Seymour Hicks, *Vintage Years* (1943).

Abstention

10 If you resolve to give up smoking, drinking and loving, you don't actually live longer; it just seems longer.

(Sir) Clement Freud , English humorist and politician (1924–). Quoted in *The Observer*

(27 December 1964) and ascribed to 'a third-rate comedian in Sloane Square'.

1 Abstinence is the thin end of the pledge.

Anonymous (graffito). Quoted in *Graffiti Lives OK* (1979).

2 Abstainer: a weak person who yields to the temptation of denying himself a pleasure.

Ambrose Bierce, American journalist (1842–?1914). Quoted in *The Treasury of Humorous Quotations,* ed. Evan Esar & Nicolas Bentley (1951).

Abuse

When a man attacked him with coarse raillery:

3 Sir, your wife, *under pretence of keeping a bawdy-house*, is a receiver of stolen goods.

Samuel Johnson, English writer and lexicographer (1709–84). Quoted in James Boswell, *Life of Johnson* (1791), for 1780. Here Boswell reproduces some Johnsoniana collected by Bennet Langton. When the 'contests' in abusive language conducted between passers-by on the River Thames are mentioned, this example is adduced, though it is not clear whether Johnson himself was on the river when he uttered the squelch.

Academics

4 No academic person is ever voted into the chair until he has reached an age at which he has forgotten the meaning of the word 'irrelevant'.

Francis M. Cornford, English academic (1874–1943). *Microcosmographia Academica* (1908).

Accents

5 I have traveled more than any one else, and I have noticed that even the angels speak English with an accent.

Mark Twain, American writer (1835–1910). 'Conclusion', *Following the Equator* (1897).

Accordions

6 A gentleman knows how to play the accordion, but doesn't.

Al Cohn, American saxophonist (1925–88). Unverified.

Accountancy

7 You see, your report here says that you are an extremely dull person. You see, our experts describe you as an appallingly dull fellow, unimaginative, timid, lacking in initiative, spineless, easily dominated, no sense of humour, tedious company and irrepressibly drab and awful. And whereas in most professions these would be considered drawbacks, in chartered accountancy they are a positive boon.

BBC TV *Monty Python's Flying Circus*, First Series, Episode 10 (21 December 1969). Script by various.

8 [Accountancy is] a profession whose idea of excitement is sharpening a bundle of No. 2 pencils ...

Anonymous. Quoted in *Time* Magazine (19 April 1993).

Achievement

9 It is a sobering thought ... that when Mozart was my age he had been dead for two years.

Tom Lehrer, American songwriter and entertainer (1928–). Record album *That Was the Year That Was* (1965).

Acquaintances

When Algernon is to be sent back to London, Cecily says:

10 It is always painful to part from people whom one has known for a very brief space of time. The absence of old friends one can endure with equanimity. But even a momentary separation from anyone to whom one has just been introduced is almost unbearable.

Oscar Wilde, Irish playwright, poet and wit (1854–1900). *The Importance of Being Earnest*, Act 2 (1895).

Acting and Actors

11 An actor's a guy who, if you ain't talking about him, ain't listening.

Marlon Brando, American film actor (1924–). Quoted in *The Observer* (January 1956). In fact, according to Bob Thomas in *Brando* (1973), Brando appears to have been quoting George Glass (1910–84).

1 **When an actor has money, he doesn't send letters but telegrams.**

Anton Chekhov, Russian playwright (1860–1904). Quoted in *The Treasury of Humorous Quotations*, ed. Evan Esar & Nicolas Bentley (1951).

Of Sir Seymour Hicks, English actor-manager (1871–1949):

2 **It was said that whereas Irving and Garrick had been *tours de force*, Hicks had been forced to tour.**

Anonymous. Quoted by Sheridan Morley on BBC Radio *Quote . . . Unquote* (1989). Peter Hay, in *Theatrical Anecdotes* (1987), also finds both 'Olivier is a *tour de force* but Wolfit is forced to tour' and Mrs Patrick Campbell saying to Lilian Braithwaite, 'You are a perfect *tour de force* and here I am forced to tour.' Ned Sherrin in *Theatrical Anecdotes* (1991) has the Campbell version (reported by Emlyn Williams) said when Braithwaite was playing a role based on Campbell in Ivor Novello's *Party* (1932), when Braithwaite was in the West End but the real Campbell off to the provinces. And Sherrin has the Olivier version as a recycling by Hermione Gingold's writers for a revue in the 1940s.

Producing one of his own plays, the author was approached by a young actor who was having difficulty interpreting his part. He told him:

3 **Try and look as if you had a younger brother in Shropshire.**

J. M. Barrie, Scottish playwright (1860–1937). Quoted in Lady Cynthia Asquith, *Diaries 1915–18* (entry for 6 January 1918). The story also occurs in John Aye, *Humour in the Theatre* (1932), where the advice is, 'I should like you to convey that the man you portray has a brother in Shropshire who drinks port.' From about the same period there is said to have been a stage direction (from another dramatist): 'Sir Henry turns his back to the audience and conveys that he has a son' (quoted in Michael Holroyd, *Bernard Shaw, Vol. 3: 1918–1950*, 1991).

Of Jeanette MacDonald and Nelson Eddy:

4 **An affair between a mad rockinghorse and a rawhide suitcase.**

Noël Coward (later Sir Noël), English entertainer and writer (1899–1973). Quoted in *A Year of Stings and Squelches* (1985).

5 **Scratch an actor and you'll find an actress.**

Dorothy Parker, American writer (1893–1967). Quoted in Leslie Halliwell, *The Filmgoer's Book of Quotes* (1973), but unverified.

6 **For an actress to succeed, she must have the face of a Venus, the brains of a Minerva, the grace of Terpsichore, the memory of a Macaulay, the figure of Juno, and the hide of a rhinoceros.**

Ethel Barrymore, American actress (1879–1959). Quoted in George Jean Nathan, *The Theatre in the Fifties* (1953).

Visiting the set of the 1941 remake of Dr Jekyll and Mr Hyde *with Spencer Tracy in the title roles:*

7 **Which is he playing now?**

W. Somerset Maugham, English novelist, playwright and writer (1874–1965). Quoted in Leslie Halliwell, *The Filmgoer's Book of Quotes* (1978 edn). The point of this story is that Tracy did not use any shock make-up, other than a pair of false teeth, to show the transformation from Dr Jekyll to Mr Hyde. The effect was rather subtle – obviously for Maugham. Discussed in John Sutherland, *Can Jane Eyre Be Happy?* (1997).

Of John Hurt in the film 1984:

8 **As usual he looked just like Joan of bloody Arc – after she's been burnt at the stake.**

Anonymous. Quoted in *A Year of Stings and Squelches* (1985).

On the Burton-Taylor Private Lives *in 1964:*

9 **He's miscast and she's Miss Taylor.**

Emlyn Williams, Welsh actor and playwright (1905–87). Quoted in James Harding, *Emlyn Williams* (1987).

Of Raymond Massey's off-stage interpretation of Abraham Lincoln:

10 **Massey won't be satisfied until somebody assassinates him.**

George S. Kaufman, American playwright (1889–1961). Quoted in Howard Teichman, *George S. Kaufman* (1973).

Of Peter O'Toole's Macbeth at the Old Vic:

1 He delivers every line with a monotonous bark as if addressing an audience of Eskimos who have never heard of Shakespeare.

Michael Billington, English theatre critic (1939–). In *The Guardian* (1980). Quoted in Ned Sherrin, *Cutting Edge* (1984).

2 Actresses will happen in the best-regulated families.

Oliver Herford, American humorist (1863– 1935). Quoted in *The Treasury of Humorous Quotations*, ed. Evan Esar & Nicolas Bentley (1951).

Of an actress unable to elicit comedy from his lines:

3 She couldn't get a laugh if she pulled a kipper out of her cunt.

Noël Coward (later Sir Noël), English entertainer and writer (1899–1973). Quoted in *The Sayings of Noël Coward*, ed. Philip Hoare (1997). When the said actress got a laugh: 'She's pulled it out'– quoted in Richard Briers, *Coward and Company* (1987).

To a limp-wristed actor who was turning in a less than convincing martial performance as a soldier:

4 A little more Marshall and rather less Snelgrove, if you please!

Noël Coward. Quoted in *A Year of Stings and Squelches* (1985). Marshall and Snelgrove was the name of a prominent London store.

Of Ingrid Bergman:

5 Dear Ingrid – speaks five languages and can't act in any of them.

(Sir) John Gielgud , English actor (1904–). Quoted in Ronald Harwood, *The Ages of Gielgud* (1984).

Ehrhardt (to Tura, in disguise):

6 What he [Tura] did to Shakespeare, we are doing now to Poland.

Film, *To Be Or Not To Be* (US, 1942). Script by Edwin Justus Mayer. With Jack Benny as Joseph Tura and Sig Rumann as Colonel Ehrhardt.

Of Creston Clarke as King Lear:

7 He played the King as though under momentary apprehension that someone else was about to play the ace.

Eugene Field, American critic (1850–95). In review attributed to him in the *Denver Tribune* (c.1880).

On Crossroads*:*

8 The TV soap opera whose acting gives trees a bad name.

Tim Satchell, English critic (1946–), in the *Daily Mail*. Quoted in *A Year of Stings and Squelches* (1985).

To Dustin Hoffman during the filming of Marathon Man *(c.1975) – Hoffman having stayed up for three nights in order to portray a sleepless character:*

9 Dear boy, why not try acting?

Sir Laurence Olivier (later Lord Olivier), English actor (1907–89). Quoted in *The Times* (17 May 1982).

Of a certain actor:

10 He has delusions of adequacy.

Anonymous. Quoted in *A Year of Stings and Squelches* (1985).

Reviewing Robert Mitchum's performance in the TV mini-series The Winds of War*:*

11 Nowadays Mitchum doesn't so much act as point his suit at people.

Russell Davies, Welsh journalist (1946–). *The Sunday Times* (18 September 1983).

To an actor who wailed, 'Who do I have to fuck to get out of this show?':

12 The same person you fucked to get in!

Stephen Sondheim, American songwriter (1930–). To Larry Kert during a technical rehearsal for the London production of *Company* (1972). Quoted in Ned Sherrin, *Cutting Edge* (1984).

13 The secret of acting is sincerity – and if you can fake that, you've got it made.

George Burns, American comedian (1896– 1996). Quoted in Michael York, *Travelling Player* (1991). Fred Metcalf in *The Penguin Dictionary of Modern Humorous Quotations* (1987) has Burns saying, rather: 'Acting is about honesty. If you can fake that, you've got it made.' However, Kingsley Amis in a devastating piece about Leo Rosten in his *Memoirs* (1991) has the humorist relating 'at some stage in the 1970s' how he had given a Commencement address including the line: 'Sincerity. If you can *fake* that . . . you'll have the world at your feet.' So perhaps the saying was circulating even before Burns received the credit. Or perhaps Rosten took it from him? An advertisement in *Rolling Stone, c.*1982, offered a T-shirt with the slogan (anonymous): 'The secret of success is sincerity. Once you can fake that you've got it made.'

Activity

A vicar's wife is talking to an old, somewhat rustic gentleman who has been laid up with an injured foot. She is sympathizing with him and saying: 'Now that you can't get about, and are not able to read, how do you manage to occupy the time?' He replies:

1 Well, mum, sometimes I sits and thinks and then again I just sits.

Caption by Gunning-King, English cartoonist. *Punch* Magazine, Vol. 131 (24 October 1906).

Adaptations

On adapting Middlemarch *for television:*

2 Like getting an elephant into a suitcase.

Andrew Davies, English TV playwright and adapter (1936–). Quoted by Sue Birtwhistle in *The Guardian* (13 October 1995).

Addiction

3 Cocaine habit-forming? Of course not. I ought to know. I've been using it for years.

Tallulah Bankhead, American actress (1903–68). *Tallulah* (1952).

4 Giving up smoking is easy. I've done it hundreds of times.

Mark Twain, American writer (1835–1910). Attributed but not verified. Quoted in *The Sayings of Mark Twain*, ed. James Munson (1992).

Adjectives

5 As to the Adjective: when in doubt strike it out.

Mark Twain, American writer (1835–1910). *Pudd'nhead Wilson* (1894).

Adolescence

6 Adolescence is the stage between puberty and adultery.

Anonymous. Quoted in John S. Crosbie, *Crosbie's Dictionary of Puns* (1977).

Advertising

A grubby tramp is writing a testimonial:

7 GOOD ADVERTISEMENT. I used your soap two years ago; since then I have used no other.

Caption by Harry Furniss, Irish cartoonist (1854–1925). *Punch* Magazine, Vol. 86 (26 April 1884). This was taken up, with permission, by Pears' Soap and widely used in advertisements during the 1880s and 1890s. The slogan was changed slightly to: 'Two years ago I used your soap since when I have used no other!'

Two women are being served in a chemist's shop and one called 'Sweet Simplicity' says:

8 And I'll have a bottle of that Dentifrine – I *must* try some of that. All the advertisements speak so well of it.

Caption by unidentified cartoonist. *Punch Almanack* (1911).

9 I think that I shall never see
A billboard lovely as a tree.
Perhaps unless the billboards fall,
I'll never see a tree at all.

Ogden Nash, American poet (1902–71). 'Song of the Open Road', *Happy Days* (1933).

Suggesting a slogan:

10 Everybody sat around thinking about Panasonic, the Japanese electronics account. Finally I decided what the hell, I'll throw a line to loosen them up ... 'The headline is, the headline is: From Those Wonderful Folks Who Gave You Pearl Harbor.' Complete silence.

Jerry Della Femina, American advertising executive (1936–). *From Those Wonderful Folks Who Gave You Pearl Harbor* (1970).

11 Advertising is the most fun you can have with your clothes on.

Jerry Della Femina, in *ibid.*

Suggested all-purpose advertising line:

1 It's what it's not that makes it what it is.

Anonymous. Quoted in Nigel Rees, *Slogans* (1982). In 1997, the Guernsey Tourist Board actually ran advertisements with the slogan, 'It's what it isn't that makes it what it is.'

2 Advertising may be described as the science of arresting the human intelligence long enough to get money from it.

Stephen Leacock, Canadian humorist (1869– 1944). Quoted in Herbert V. Prochnow, Snr & Jnr, *A Treasury of Humorous Quotations* (1969).

3 Advertising is 85 percent confusion and 15 percent commission.

Fred Allen, American comedian (1894–1956). Quoted in Herbert V. Prochnow, Snr & Jnr, *A Treasury of Humorous Quotations* (1969).

4 When the client moans and sighs
Make his logo twice the size.
If he still should prove refractory,
Show a picture of a factory.
Only in the gravest cases
Should you show the clients' faces.

Anonymous. Quoted in David Ogilvy, *Ogilvy on Advertising* (1983).

5 Advertising is the rattling of a stick inside a swill bucket.

George Orwell, English novelist and journalist (1903–50). Quoted in Laurence J. Peter, *Quotations for Our Time* (1977).

6 Doing business without advertising is like winking at a girl in the dark: you know what you are doing, but nobody else does.

Edgar Watson Howe, American journalist and author (1853–1937). Quoted in *The Penguin Dictionary of Modern Humorous Quotations*, ed. Fred Metcalf (1987).

7 Half the money I spend on advertising is wasted, and the trouble is I don't know which half.

William Hesketh Lever (1st Viscount Lever-hulme), English soapmaker and philanthropist (1851–1925). Quoted by David Ogilvy in *Confessions of an Advertising Man* (1963). This observation has also been fathered on John Wanamaker and, indeed, on Ogilvy himself. Ogilvy says 'as the first Lord Leverhulme (and John Wanamaker after him) complained . . .' Leverhulme remains the most likely originator – he made his fortune through the manufacture of soap from vegetable oils instead of from tallow. Ogilvy had Lever Brothers as a client and could presumably have picked up the remark that way. However, Wanamaker, who more or less invented the modern department store in the US, was active by the 1860s and so possibly could have said it first.

Advice

8 Never eat at a place called Mom's.
Never play cards with a man called Doc.
Never go to bed with a woman whose troubles are greater than your own.

Nelson Algren, American novelist and short-story writer (1909–81). *A Walk on the Wild Side* (1956).

9 The first rule for a young playwright to follow is not to write like Henry Arthur Jones . . . The second and third rules are the same.

Oscar Wilde, Irish playwright, poet and wit (1854–1900). Quoted in *A Year of Stings and Squelches* (1985).

Advice to all actors:

10 Always remember before going on stage, wipe your nose and check your flies.

(Sir) Alec Guinness, English actor (1914–). No source. Quoted in *Time* Magazine (11 May 1987) as: 'Blow your nose and check your fly.' Michael Freedland in *Kenneth Williams* (1990) has it as a comment to Williams after Guinness had apparently tried to jostle Williams out of public view and behind a potted palm during *Hotel Paradiso* (Williams's flies being undone). As this incident is not recorded in *The Kenneth Williams Diaries* (1993), it may not be true.

11 Treat a whore like a lady and a lady like a whore.

Wilson Mizner, American playwright (1876–1933). Quoted in Bob Chieger, *Was It Good For You Too?* (1983).

12 Treat every woman as if you have slept with her and you soon will.

Anonymous. Quoted in the author's diary (17 April 1966).

To a man struggling under the weight of a grandfather clock:

1 My poor fellow, why not carry a watch?

Sir Herbert Beerbohm Tree, English actor-manager (1853–1917). Quoted in Hesketh Pearson, *Beerbohm Tree* (1956).

2 1. Never hunt south of the Thames.
2. Never drink port after champagne.
3. Never have your wife in the morning lest something better should turn up during the day.

Anonymous (British). Quoted in Laurence Olivier, *Confessions of an Actor* (1982).

3 1. Never drink claret in an East wind.
2. Take your pleasures singly, one by one.
3. Never sit on a hard chair after drinking port.

Revd H. J. Bidder (untraced), English clergyman. Quoted in *Geoffrey Madan's Notebooks* (1981): 'Three pieces of earnest advice from the Revd H. J. Bidder, aged 86, after sitting silent, with a crumpled face, all through dinner.'

4 I long ago associated with the Chinese doctrine that it is foolish to do anything standing up that can be done sitting down, or anything sitting down that can be done lying down.

H. L. Mencken, American journalist and linguist (1880–1956). *Happy Days* (1940).

Advice to actors:

5 Just know your lines and don't bump into the furniture.

Noël Coward (later Sir Noël), English entertainer and writer (1899–1973). This was attributed to Spencer Tracy in *Bartlett's Familiar Quotations* (1980) but to Coward in the 1992 edition. In Leslie Halliwell, *The Filmgoer's Book of Quotes* (1973), Alfred Lunt is credited with the line: 'The secret of my success? I speak in a loud clear voice and try not to bump into the furniture.' In *Time* Magazine (16 June 1986), it was reported that President Reagan had offered a few hints on appearing before the cameras to a White House breakfast for Senators: 'Don't bump into the furniture,' he said, 'and in the kissing scenes, keep your mouth closed.' Coward seems to be the originator and Dick Richards,

The Wit of Noël Coward (1968), has it that he said it during the run of his play *Nude With Violin* (1956–57). *The Sayings of Noël Coward*, ed. Philip Hoare (1997), has this from a 'speech to the Gallery First-Nighter's Club, 1962': 'Speak clearly, don't bump into people, and if you must have motivation think of your pay packet on Friday.'

6 Never miss an opportunity to relieve yourself; never miss a chance to sit down and rest your feet.

George V, British King (1865–1936). His son, the Duke of Windsor, was later to ascribe this remark to 'an old courtier' – quoted in Herbert V. Prochnow, Snr & Jnr, *A Treasury of Humorous Quotations* (1969) – but it seems likely that it was said by George V himself. A correspondent who wished to remain anonymous wrote in 1981 that a naval officer of her acquaintance who was about to accompany Prince George, Duke of Kent, on a cruise was asked by George V to make sure that the Prince was properly dressed before going ashore. He also advised: 'Always take an opportunity to relieve yourselves.' Another correspondent suggests that it was an equerry's first advice to the new King George V; yet another that Edward VII was the first to say this when he was Prince of Wales. On the other hand, more than a century earlier, the Duke of Wellington had said: 'Always make water when you can.'

Compare also the remark of Samuel Freeman, who served in the US Supreme Court from 1862 to 1890. He advised: 'Never walk when you can ride, never sit when you can lie down.' Winston Churchill is reported to have said: 'Never stand when you can sit and never sit when you can lie down.' Claire Rayner has an even longer version culled from the Sister Tutor who trained her as a nurse in the 1950s: 'Nurse, never stand when you can sit, never sit when you can lie down, and never lie if there's any chance they might find you out.' Quoted in *The 'Quote ... Unquote' Newsletter* (October 1993).

7 While grace is saying after meat, do you and your brethren take the chairs from behind the company, so that when they go to sit again, they may fall backwards, which will make them all merry; but be you so discreet as to hold your laughter till you get to the kitchen,

and then divert your fellow-servants.

Jonathan Swift, Anglo-Irish writer and clergy-man (1667–1745). *Directions to Servants* (1745).

Age

On his challenger, Walter Mondale, during the 1984 election:

1 I will not make age an issue of this campaign. I am not going to exploit for political purposes my opponent's youth and inexperience.

Ronald Reagan, American actor and President (1911–). TV debate (22 October 1984). At that time, Reagan was 73 and Mondale 56.

2 'Someone who Must Not be Contra-dicted said that a man must be a success by the time he's thirty, or never.'

'To have reached thirty,' said Regi-nald, 'is to have failed in life.'

'Saki' (H. H. Munro), English writer (1870–1916). 'Reginald on the Academy', *Reginald* (1904).

Lady Bracknell:

3 Thirty-five is a very attractive age. London society is full of women of the very highest birth who have, of their own free choice, remained thirty-five for years.

Oscar Wilde, Irish playwright, poet and wit (1854–1900). *The Importance of Being Earnest*, Act 3 (1895).

4 She may very well pass for forty-three In the dusk with a light behind her!

W. S. Gilbert, English writer and lyricist (1836–1911). *Trial by Jury* (1875). Ian Bradley writes in *The Annotated Gilbert and Sullivan*, Vol. 2 (1984): 'Gilbert had a thing about women in their forties. Poor Ruth in *The Pirates of Penzance* is mocked by Frederic for being forty-seven ... while Marco is warned by Gianetta in *The Gondoliers* not to address any lady less than forty-five.'

5 I am 46, and have been for some time past.

Anita Brookner, English novelist (1928–). Letter to *The Times* (5 November 1984) when she considered it had drawn too much atten-tion to her actual age. In *Hotel du Lac*, Chap. 4 (published that same year), she had written: 'She was a handsome woman of forty-five and would remain so for many years.'

6 When I was young, I was told: 'You'll see, when you're fifty.' I am fifty and I haven't seen a thing.

Erik Satie, French composer (1866–1925). In a letter to his brother, quoted in Pierre-Daniel Templier, *Erik Satie* (1932).

Accepting an award:

7 I recently turned sixty. Practically a third of my life is over.

Woody Allen, American film actor, writer and director (1937–). Quoted in *The Observer*, 'Sayings of the Week' (10 March 1996).

8 At sixty-six I am entering ... the last phase of my active physical life. My body, on the move, resembles in sight and sound nothing so much as a bin-liner full of yoghourt.

Stephen Fry, English writer and actor (1957–). *The Hippopotamus* (1994).

At the age of 76:

9 Three things happen when you get to my age. First your memory starts to go ... and I have forgotten the other two.

Denis Healey (later Lord Healey), English politician (1917–). Quoted in *The Independent*, 'Quote Unquote' (23 July 1994).

10 They say a man is as old as the woman he feels. In that case I'm eighty five.

Groucho Marx, American comedian (1895–1977). *The Secret Word Is Groucho* (1976).

At age eighty-seven:

11 I'm very uncomfortable living in a world where the Pope is twenty-five years younger than I am.

Billy Wilder, American film director and writer (1906–). Quoted in *The Independent*, 'Quote Unquote' (17 July 1993).

12 The old believe everything: the middle-aged suspect everything: the young know everything.

Oscar Wilde, Irish playwright, poet and wit

(1854–1900). *Phrases and Philosophies for the Use of the Young* (1894).

Ageing

On being asked his age when he was 77:

1 I am just turning forty and taking my time about it.

Harold Lloyd, American film comedian (1893–1971). Quoted in *The Times* that same year (1970).

The distinguished actress had been so impressed by the flattering work of this particular photographer that she engaged him again to take her picture. 'Oh dear,' she remarked, looking at the new prints when they were finished, 'you make me look older than last time.' The photographer was the quintessence of tact. Said he:

2 Ah yes, but I was much younger in those days.

Anonymous. Who were the original participants? Possibly Marlene Dietrich and the cinematographer Hal Mohr. When they were working together on the film *Rancho Notorious* (US, 1952), Dietrich asked why she wasn't looking as good on the film as when the same cinematographer had shot her in *Destry Rides Again* thirteen years before. Mohr replied that he was, of course, thirteen years older.

3 One should never trust a woman who tells one her real age. A woman who would tell one that, would tell one anything.

Oscar Wilde, Irish playwright, poet and wit (1854–1900). *A Woman of No Importance*, Act 1 (1893).

Agents

When a Hollywood agent told him how he had been swimming unscathed in shark-infested waters:

4 I think that's what they call professional courtesy.

Herman J. Mankiewicz, American screenwriter (1897–1953). Quoted by Dick Vosburgh on BBC Radio *Quote . . . Unquote* (31 July 1979).

5 The trouble with this business is that the stars keep 90% of the money.

Lew Grade (later Lord Grade), Russian-born

English media tycoon (1906–). Quoted in A. Andrews, *Quotations for Speakers and Writers* (1969).

6 Then there was the actor who put in his will that he wanted to be cremated and ten per cent of his ashes thrown in his agent's face.

Anonymous. Quoted by Larry Adler on BBC Radio *Quote . . . Unquote* (25 January 1976).

Alimony

7 Alimony is like buying oats for a dead horse.

Arthur ('Bugs') Baer, American columnist and writer (1897?–1969). Quoted in *The Treasury of Humorous Quotations*, ed. Evan Esar & Nicolas Bentley (1951).

Amateurs

8 The Arts Council doesn't believe in supporting amateurs, except in its own ranks.

Sir John Drummond, English arts administrator (1934–). Quoted in *The Observer* (29 March 1998).

Ambassadors

9 An ambassador is an honest man sent to lie abroad for the good of his country.

Sir Henry Wotton, English diplomat and poet (1568–1639). Quoted in Izaak Walton, *Life of Sir Henry Wotton* (1651).

Ambition

When a child:

10 I should like to be a horse.

Elizabeth II, British Queen (1926–). Quoted in *Handbook of 20th Century Quotations*, ed. Frank S. Pepper (1984).

At the time of the Profumo scandal in 1963:

11 I want to be another Emma Hamilton. I'm looking for another Lord Nelson, only taller.

Mandy Rice-Davies, English 'model and showgirl' (1944–). Quoted in *Handbook of 20th Century Quotations*, ed. Frank S. Pepper (1984).

America and the Americans

12 America is a nation that conceives many

odd inventions for getting somewhere but can think of nothing to do when it gets there.

Will Rogers, American humorist (1879–1935). Quoted in *The Treasury of Humorous Quotations*, ed. Evan Esar & Nicolas Bentley (1951).

1 *October 12, the Discovery.* It was wonderful to find America, but it would have been more wonderful to miss it.

Mark Twain, American writer (1835–1910). 'Conclusion', *Following the Equator* (1897).

2 God protects fools, drunks and the United States of America.

Otto von Bismarck, Prusso-German statesman (1815–98). Unverified.

3 Of course America had often been discovered before Columbus, but it had always been hushed up.

Oscar Wilde, Irish playwright, poet and wit (1854–1900). Quoted in *The Treasury of Humorous Quotations*, ed. Evan Esar & Nicolas Bentley (1951).

4 MRS ALLONBY: They say, Lady Hunstanton, that when good Americans die they go to Paris.
LADY HUNSTANTON: Indeed? And when bad Americans die, where do they go to?
LORD ILLINGWORTH: Oh, they go to America.

Oscar Wilde. *A Woman of No Importance*, Act 1 (1893). Earlier, this exchange had appeared in *The Picture of Dorian Gray*, Chap. 3 (1891). The originator of the remark 'Good Americans, when they die, go to Paris' was Thomas Gold Appleton (1812–84). He was so quoted by Oliver Wendell Homes in *The Autocrat of the Breakfast Table* (1858).

5 No one ever went broke underestimating the intelligence of the American people.

H. L. Mencken, American journalist and linguist (1880–1956). What, in fact, he said on the subject of journalism in the *Chicago Tribune* (19 September 1926), was: 'No one in this world, so far as I know – and I have searched the records for years, and employed agents to help me – has ever lost money by underestimating the intelligence of the great masses of the plain people. Nor has anyone ever lost public office thereby.'

6 I've been around a bit
But I must admit
That I didn't know the half of it
Till I hit the U.S.A.

Noël Coward (later Sir Noël), English entertainer and writer (1899–1973). Song, 'I Like America', *Ace of Clubs* (1949).

7 I've roamed the Spanish Main
Eaten sugar-cane
But I never tasted cellophane
Till I struck the U.S.A.

Noël Coward, in *ibid.*

Amity

8 The lion and the calf shall lie down together, but the calf won't get much sleep.

Woody Allen, American film actor, writer and director (1937–). In *The New Republic* (31 August 1974).

Amnesty

9 Amnesty, *n.* The state's magnanimity towards those offenders whom it would be too expensive to punish.

Ambrose Bierce, American journalist (1842–?1914). *The Cynic's Word Book* (later retitled *The Devil's Dictionary*) (1906).

An

10 As soon as the Jubilee [of 1897] was over we went to what is called in England 'an hotel'. If we could have afforded an horse and an hackney cab we could have had an heavenly time flitting around.

Mark Twain, American writer (1835–1910). In *Europe and Elsewhere*, ed. James Brander (1923).

Andrews, Julie
English-born actress (1935–)

After they had made The Sound of Music *(1965):*

11 Working with her is like being hit over the head by a Valentine's Day card.

Christopher Plummer, Canadian actor (1927–). Quoted in Leslie Halliwell, *The Filmgoer's Book of Quotes* (1973).

1 Julie Andrews is like a nun with a switchblade.

Anonymous. Quoted in Leslie Halliwell, *The Filmgoer's Book of Quotes* (1973).

After her great stage success as Eliza Doolittle in My Fair Lady, *Julie Andrews was rejected in favour of Audrey Hepburn in the Warner Bros. film version of the musical. And this despite the fact that Hepburn's singing voice had to be dubbed. Andrews was thus available to go on and star in* Mary Poppins, *for which she duly won an Academy Award. Collecting her Oscar she said:*

2 I'd like to thank all those who made this possible – especially Jack L. Warner.

Julie Andrews. Quoted in Leslie Halliwell, *The Filmgoer's Book of Quotes* (1973).

Anecdotage

3 When a man fell into his anecdotage it was a sign for him to retire from the world.

Benjamin Disraeli (later 1st Earl of Beaconsfield), English politician and writer (1804–81). *Lothair*, Chap. 28 (1870). Earlier, however, his father, Isaac Disraeli, had noted in *Curiosities of Literature* (1839): 'Among my earliest literary friends, two distinguished themselves by their anecdotical literature: James Petit Andrews, by his "Anecdotes, Ancient and Modern", and William Seward, by his "Anecdotes of Distinguished Persons". These volumes were favourably received, and to such a degree, that a wit of that day, and who is still a wit as well as poet, considered that we were far gone in our "Anecdotage".' The word 'anecdotage' in a less critical sense had been used by De Quincey in 1823 simply to describe anecdotes collectively.

Anglo-Irish

4 PAT: He was an Anglo-Irishman.
MEG: In the blessed name of God what's that?
PAT: A Protestant with a horse.

Brendan Behan, Irish playwright (1923–64). *The Hostage* (1958).

Anglo-Saxon

5 The Anglo-Saxon conscience does not prevent the Anglo-Saxon from sinning; it merely prevents him from enjoying his sin.

Salvador de Madariaga, Spanish diplomat and writer (1886–1978). Quoted in *The Treasury of Humorous Quotations*, ed. Evan Esar & Nicolas Bentley (1951).

Animals

6 Odd things animals. All dogs look up at you. All cats look down at you. Only a pig looks at you as an equal.

Winston S. Churchill (later Sir Winston), British Conservative Prime Minister and writer (1874–1965). Quoted in *The Sayings of Winston Churchill*, ed. J. A. Sutcliffe (1992). Martin Gilbert, in *Never Despair* (1988), has the version: 'I am fond of pigs. Dogs look up to us. Cats look down on us. Pigs treat us as equals.'

Anniversaries

7 Sent a complimentary (sic) copy of Waterstone's Literary Diary which records the birthdays of various contemporary figures. Here is Dennis Potter on 17 May, Michael Frayn on 8 September, Edna O'Brien on 15 December, so naturally I turn to my own birthday. May 9 is blank except for the note: first British Launderette is opened on Queensway, London 1949.

Alan Bennett, English playwright and actor (1934–). Published diary entry for 2 January 1977, quoted in *The Oxford Dictionary of Literary Quotations*, ed. Peter Kemp (1997).

Anomalies

When asked if, in view of certain anomalies, he would examine alternatives:

8 We are examining alternative anomalies.

William Whitelaw (later Viscount Whitelaw), English politician (1918–). Speaking in the House of Commons (1 December 1981).

Anticipation

9 What we anticipate seldom occurs; what

we least expected generally happens.

Benjamin Disraeli (later 1st Earl of Beacons-field), English politician and writer (1804–81). *Henrietta Temple* (1837).

Anticlimax

A crossword clue in The New York Times *for one word of nine letters was a quote from Yale University's song 'For God, for Country, and for Yale'. The answer:*

1 Anticlimax.

Anonymous. Quoted in *A Year of Stings and Squelches* (1985).

Apathy

Of the British Prime Minister during the 1970 General Election:

2 Harold Wilson is going around the country stirring up apathy.

William Whitelaw (later Viscount Whitelaw), English politician (1918–). Discussed by him in *The Independent* (14 July 1992).

Appearance

On Sir Arthur Wing Pinero's eyebrows:

3 [Like] the skins of some small mammal just not large enough to be used as mats.

Sir Max Beerbohm, English writer and carica-turist (1872–1956). Quoted in Christopher Hassall, *Edward Marsh* (1959).

Of a fellow female:

4 Her heart's in the right place– what a pity the other thirteen stone aren't!

Anonymous. Quoted in *A Year of Stings and Squelches* (1985).

One woman in society to another:

5 You're looking nicer than usual, but that's so easy for you.

'Saki' (H. H. Munro), English writer (1870–1916). Quoted in *A Year of Stings and Squelches* (1985).

Of an American general:

6 An imitation rough diamond.

Margot Asquith (later Countess of Oxford and Asquith) (1864–1945). Quoted by her step-daughter Baroness Asquith in BBC TV programme *As I Remember* (30 April 1967).

Of himself:

7 Looking like a balding salmon.

Philip Larkin, English poet (1922–85). Quoted in *The Times* (3 December 1985). On another occasion he told Andrew Motion, author of *Philip Larkin: A Writer's Life* (1993), that a photo-graph showed him like 'an intellectual Eric More-cambe' rather than a 'bald, pregnant salmon'.

Of Evelyn Waugh:

8 He looked, I decided, like a letter delivered to the wrong address.

Malcolm Muggeridge, English writer and broad-caster (1903–90). 'My Fair Gentleman', *Tread Softly For You Tread on My Jokes* (1966).

Appeasement

9 An appeaser is one who feeds a crocodile hoping it will eat him last.

Winston S. Churchill (later Sir Winston), British Conservative Prime Minister and writer (1874–1965). Speech, House of Commons (January 1940).

Appetite

10 On the bus the other day a woman with a baby sat opposite, the baby bawled, and the woman at once began to unlace herself, exposing a large red udder, which she swung into the baby's face. The infant, however, continued to cry and the woman said, 'Come on, there's a good boy – if you don't, I shall give it to the gentleman opposite.'

W. N. P. Barbellion, English essayist and diarist (1889–1919). *The Journal of a Disappointed Man* (1919). Compare, however, a cartoon caption from *Punch* Magazine, Vol. 126 (11 May 1904). 'THE UNPROTECTED MALE' shows a man in an omnibus being addressed thus: *'Mother (after vainly offering a bottle to refractory infant)* "'ERE, TIKE IT, WILL YER! IF YER DON'T 'URRY UP, I'LL GIVE IT TO THE GENTLEMAN OPPOSITE!"'

Applause

11 Don't clap too hard – it's a very old building.

John Osborne, English playwright (1929–94). *The Entertainer* (1957) – but an old music-hall joke.

Arabs

1 The Arabs are only Jews upon horseback.

Benjamin Disraeli (later 1st Earl of Beaconsfield), English politician and writer (1804–81).
Tancred, Bk 4, Chap. 3 (1847).

2 I come from a land, from a faraway place
   where the caravan camels roam.
Where they cut off your ear if they don't
   like your face.
It's barbaric, but – hey – it's home.

Howard Ashman, American lyricist (d.1991).
From the opening song 'Arabian Nights' in the
Disney cartoon film *Aladdin* (US, 1993).
When the film opened in Britain, in order not to
offend Arab sensibilities, the lyrics had become:
'Where it's flat and immense and the heat is
intense/It's barbaric but hey it's home.'
The amended version was by Peter Schneider.

Archaeologists

3 An archaeologist is the best husband any
woman can have; the older she gets, the
more interested he is in her.

Agatha Christie (later Dame Agatha), English
detective novelist (1890–1976). Quoted in a
news report (8 March 1954), also in *The
Observer* (2 January 1955). However, according
to G. C. Ramsey, *Agatha Christie: Mistress of
Mystery* (1967), she vehemently denied having said
it, insisting that it would have been a very
silly remark for anyone to make, and neither
complimentary nor amusing.

Archer, Jeffrey (later Lord Archer)
English novelist and politician (1940–)

To Jeffrey Archer:

4 Is there no beginning to your talents?

Clive Anderson, English broadcaster (1952–).
On Channel 4 TV series *Clive Anderson Talks
Back*. Quoted in *The Independent* (1 December
1991).

Architects

5 The physician can bury his mistakes, but
the architect can only advise his client
to plant vines.

Frank Lloyd Wright, American architect
(1867–1959). Quoted in *The New York Times*
(4 October 1953).

Architectural criticism

*Of Chiswick House, London – a Palladian
villa built by the 3rd Earl of Burlington in
1725–29:*

6 Too small to live in and too large to
hang on a watch-chain.

Anonymous. Quoted in Cecil Roberts, *And So
to Bath* (1940). In Richard Hewlings, *Chiswick
House and Gardens* (1989), 'too little to live in
and too large to hang to one's watch' is ascribed
to Lord Hervey.

*On the Gilbert Scott belfry at Christ Church,
Oxford:*

7 The advantage of having been born in
the reign of Queen Anne, and of having
died in that or the subsequent reign,
has never been so painfully apparent as
it is now.

Lewis Carroll (Revd C. L. Dodgson), English
writer (1832–98). Quoted in *The Works of
Lewis Carroll* (1965).

Of the Albert Memorial, London:

8 It has all the earmarks of an eyesore.

Anonymous (American tourist). Quoted in
Handbook of 20th Century Quotations, ed.
Frank S. Pepper (1984).

Of London's National Theatre building:

9 The best view of London is from the
National Theatre, because from there
you can't see the National Theatre.

Anonymous. Quoted in *A Year of Stings and
Squelches* (1985).

Of the Royal Pavilion at Brighton:

10 As if St Paul's had come down and
littered.

Revd Sydney Smith, English clergyman, essayist and wit (1771–1845). Quoted in Peter
Virgin, *Sydney Smith* (1994). 'It was as though
St Paul's had gone down to the sea and pupped'
is another version.

*Of the clock over the entrance to Worcester
College, Oxford:*

11 *C'est magnifique mais ce n'est pas la gare.*

Anonymous. 'Oh, I thought that was the railway station' is quoted as said by a 'bright
young man' in a 'novel' in Dacre Balsdon,
Oxford Life (1957). It had earlier been applied
to Waterhouse Tree Court at Caius College,

Cambridge, so it may be a very old critical format indeed.

On being shown round Moss Hart's elegant country house and grounds:

1 Just what God would have done if he had the money.

Alexander Woollcott, American writer and critic (1887–1943). Quoted in Moss Hart, *Act One* (1959).

Describing the proposed design for a new wing of the National Gallery in London:

2 A kind of vast municipal fire station … I would understand better this type of high-tech approach if you demolished the whole of Trafalgar Square, but what is proposed is like a monstrous car-buncle on the face of a much-loved and elegant friend.

Charles, Prince of Wales (1948–). Speech to the Royal Institute of British Architects (30 May 1984). It had an effect: the design was scrapped and replaced by another one.

3 You have to give this much to the Luftwaffe – when it knocked down our buildings it didn't replace them with anything more offensive than rubble. We did that.

Charles, Prince of Wales. Speech to the Corporation of London Planning and Communications Committee (2 December 1987)

4 Look at the National Theatre! It seems like a clever way of building a nuclear power station in the middle of London without anyone objecting.

Charles, Prince of Wales. TV film, *A Vision of Britain* (October 1988).

5 In my experience, if you have to keep the lavatory door shut by extending your left leg, it's modern architecture.

Nancy Banks-Smith, English journalist and critic (1929–). In *The Guardian* (20 February 1979).

Argument

6 There are three sides to every argument: my side, your side and the truth.

Anonymous. Modern proverbial saying, variously ascribed: '… to every case' is said to be 'an old lawyer' advising his pupil; '… to every

argument' was 'a quote from a bloke in the pub'; from the *Financial Times* (25 October 1986): 'As everyone knows there are always three sides to the story of any marriage: His, Hers and the Truth. Here we have Hers [Dylan Thomas's widow's] with nothing kept back this time.'

Army

7 The Army works like this: if a man dies when you hang him, keep hanging him until he gets used to it.

Spike Milligan, Irish entertainer and writer (1918–). Attributed by Richard Ingrams on BBC Radio *Quote … Unquote* (4 May 1977).

Art and Artists

8 We must remember that art is art. Still, on the other hand, water is water – and east is east and west is west, and if you take cranberries and stew them like apple sauce, they taste much more like prunes than rhubarb does.

Groucho Marx, American comedian (1895–1977). Film, *Animal Crackers* (US, 1930). Script by Morrie Ryskind, from a musical by himself and George S. Kaufman.

9 Art, like morality, consists in drawing the line somewhere.

G. K. Chesterton, English poet, novelist and critic (1874–1936). Quoted in *The Treasury of Humorous Quotations*, ed. Evan Esar & Nicolas Bentley (1951).

To a woman who told him a landscape reminded her of his work:

10 Yes, madam, Nature is creeping up.

James McNeill Whistler, American painter (1834–1903). Quoted in D. C. Seitz, *Whistler Stories* (1913).

11 Any fool can paint a picture, but it takes a wise man to be able to sell it.

Samuel Butler, English author (1835–1902). Quoted in *The Treasury of Humorous Quotations*, ed. Evan Esar & Nicolas Bentley (1951).

Art criticism

On his portrait painted by Graham Sutherland:

12 The portrait is a remarkable example of modern art. It certainly combines force

and candour. These are qualities which no active member of either house can do without or should fear to meet.

Winston S. Churchill (later Sir Winston), British Conservative Prime Minister and writer (1874–1965). Speech, Westminster Hall, London (30 November 1954). For his birthday, both Houses of Parliament presented Churchill with the portrait. He did not like it but accepted the picture with a gracefully double-edged compliment. Lady Churchill's dislike of the portrait took a more practical form: she had it destroyed.

1 I look as if I was having a difficult stool.

Winston S. Churchill. Remark on the same portrait, quoted in *The Lyttelton Hart-Davis Letters* (1978) – for 20 November 1955. Other versions of this criticism are: 'How do they paint one today? Sitting on a lavatory!' (said to Charles Doughty, secretary of the committee which organized the tribute), and 'Here sits an old man on his stool, pressing and pressing.'

At the unveiling of an unlifelike statue of Nurse Edith Cavell outside the National Portrait Gallery in London (1920):

2 My god, they've shot the wrong person!

James Pryde, English artist (1866–1941). Quoted on BBC *Radio Quote . . . Unquote* (6 July 1977).

Aspirates

When J. H. Thomas, the Labour MP, complained he "ad a 'eadache':

3 Try taking a couple of aspirates.

F. E. Smith (1st Earl of Birkenhead), English politician and lawyer (1872–1930). Quoted in John Campbell, *F. E. Smith, First Earl of Birkenhead* (1983), in a form which has Thomas saying, 'Ooh, Fred, I've got an 'ell of an 'eadache' (told to the author by Lady Gaselee).

Aspiration

4 We are all in the gutter, but some of us are looking at the stars.

Oscar Wilde, Irish playwright, poet and wit (1854–1900). *Lady Windermere's Fan*, Act 3 (1892).

Assertion

5 I am not arguing with you – I am telling you.

James McNeill Whistler, American painter (1834–1903). *The Gentle Art of Making Enemies* (1890).

Assumptions

One elderly person was overheard saying to another:

6 If anything should happen to either of us, you may take it that I'm definitely going to live in Bournemouth.

Anonymous. Quoted in *Pass the Port Again* (1980). In *Eavesdroppings* (1981), it is given as said on a park bench: 'When one of us passes on, I shall move south to live with my daughter.' There is nothing new, etc.: in *Samuel Butler's Notebooks* (which covered the years 1874–1902) there appeared the entry: 'Warburg's old friend . . . said to Warburg one day, talking about his wife, who was ill, "If God were to take one or other of us, I should go and live in Paris."'

Astrology

7 I don't believe in astrology; I'm a Sagittarian and we're sceptical.

(Sir) Arthur C. Clarke, English science fiction writer (1917–). Quoted by Paul Heskett in *Astronomy Now* Magazine (undated).

Atheists

8 I am still an atheist, thank God.

Luis Buñuel, Spanish film director (1900–83). Quoted in *Le Monde* (16 December 1959).

9 An atheist is a man who has no invisible means of support.

John Buchan (Lord Tweedsmuir), Scottish politician and writer (1875–1940). Quoted in H. E. Fosdick, *On Being a Real Person* (1943).

10 God can stand being told by Professor Ayer and Marghanita Laski that he doesn't exist.

J. B. Priestley, English novelist and playwright (1894–1984). Quoted in *The Listener* (1 July 1965).

Attlee, Clement (1st Earl Attlee)
**British Labour Prime Minister
(1883–1967)**

Of himself:

1 Few thought he was even a starter
There were many who thought them-
   selves smarter
But he ended PM, CH and OM
An Earl and a Knight of the Garter.

Lines written by Attlee on 8 April 1956.
Quoted in Kenneth Harris, *Attlee* (1982).

*On Clement Attlee's reluctance to fly to
Moscow and speak plainly to Stalin:*

2 He dare not absent himself from his
Cabinet at home. He knows full well
that when the mouse is away the
cats will play.

Winston S. Churchill (later Sir Winston),
British Conservative Prime Minister and writer
(1874–1965). Quoted in Harold Nicolson,
Diaries and Letters (1968) – entry for
12 December 1946.

3 A sheep in sheep's clothing.

Winston S. Churchill. Quoted in Willans &
Roetter, *The Wit of Winston Churchill* (1954).
However, according to William Safire, in
Safire's Political Dictionary (1980), Churchill
told Sir Denis Brogan that he had said it not
about Attlee but about Ramsay MacDonald,
with rather more point. If so, it would appear
that he was quoting a joke made by the humorous columnist 'Beachcomber' *c.*1936. Aneurin
Bevan alluded to this same source *c.*1937 –
'Beachcomber once described Mr Ramsay
MacDonald as ... It applies to many of the
front-bench men with whom the Parliamentary Labour Party is cursed' (quoted in
Michael Foot, *Aneurin Bevan*, Vol. 1, 1962).
Sir Edmund Gosse is supposed to have said the
same of T. Sturge Moore, the 'woolly-bearded
poet', *c.*1906 – and was quoted as such by
Ferris Greenslet in *Under the Bridge* (1943).

4 An empty taxi arrived at 10 Downing
Street, and when the door was opened
Attlee got out.

Winston S. Churchill. When John Colville
told Churchill this remark was being attributed
to him, he commented gravely, 'after an awful
pause': 'Mr Attlee is an honourable and gallant
gentleman, and a faithful colleague who served

his country well at the time of her greatest
need. I should be obliged if you would make it
clear whenever an occasion arises that I never
would make such a remark about him, and
that I strongly disapprove of anybody who
does.' This denial was reported in Kenneth
Harris, *Attlee* (1982).

5 A modest man who has a good deal to
be modest about.

Winston S. Churchill. Quoted in the *Chicago
Sunday Tribune Magazine of Books* (27 June
1954) – perhaps in a review of Willans &
Roetter, *The Wit of Winston Churchill* (1954).

6 Reminds me of nothing so much as a
recently dead fish before it has had time
to stiffen.

George Orwell, English novelist and journalist
(1903–50). Diary entry for 19 May 1942,
quoted in *The Collected Essays, Journalism and
Letters of George Orwell*, Vol. 2 (1968).

Attraction

7 MAE: How tall are you, son?
MAN: Ma-am, I'm six feet seven inches.
MAE: Let's forget the six feet and talk
   about the seven inches.

Mae West, American vaudeville and film
actress (1893–1980). Quoted in Leslie
Halliwell, *The Filmgoer's Book of Quotes*
(1973).

8 Is that a gun in your pocket or are you
just pleased to see me?

Mae West. Quoted in Joseph Weintraub, *Peel
Me a Grape* (1975). Sometimes remembered as
'pistol' and also in connection with her play
Catherine Was Great (1944) in the form:
'Lieutenant, is that your sword, or are you just
glad to see me?' Leslie Halliwell in *The Filmgoer's Book of Quotes* (1978 edn), has this last as
West's reaction in a Broadway costume play,
when the romantic lead got his sword tangled
in his braid so that it stuck up at an unfortu-
nate angle.

Auden, W. H.
Anglo-American poet (1907–73)

9 He didn't love God, he just fancied him.

Anonymous. Quoted in the book *Quote ...
Unquote 3* (1983). Also in John Mortimer,
In Character (1983).

Of himself:

1 My face looks like a wedding-cake left out in the rain.

No, it was not said *by someone else* about Auden (as stated, for example, in L. Levinson, *Bartlett's Unfamiliar Quotations*, 1972). The poet himself said to a reporter: 'Your cameraman might enjoy himself, because my face looks like a wedding-cake left out in the rain' (cited in Humphrey Carpenter, *W. H. Auden*, 1981). However, according to Noël Annan in *Maurice Bowra: a celebration* (1974), Bowra once referred to E. M. Forster's work as a wedding-cake left out in the rain.

Of his face:

2 If a fly walked over it, it would break its leg.

Anonymous. Quoted on BBC Radio *Quote … Unquote* (5 June 1980).

Audiences

Throwing a sea-bass to a noisily-coughing audience:

3 Busy yourselves with *this*, you damned walruses, while the rest of us proceed with the libretto.

John Barrymore, American actor (1882–1942). Quoted in Bennett Cerf, *Try and Stop Me* (1944). Cerf has it that the incident occurred when Barrymore was playing Fedor in *The Living Corpse*, a version of Tolstoy's *Redemption*, in 1918.

On playing to matinée audiences at Bridlington:

4 You could see the dampness rising from the wet raincoats like mist on the marshes.

Les Dawson, English comedian (1934–93). Quoted in *The Independent on Sunday* (10 July 1993).

5 Would the people in the cheaper seats clap your hands. And the rest of you – if you'd just rattle your jewellery.

John Lennon, English singer and songwriter (1940–80). To audience at the Royal Variety Performance (4 November 1963). From the soundtrack of the TV recording.

Austen, Jane
English novelist (1775–1817)

6 To me his [Edgar Allan Poe's] prose is unreadable – like Jane Austen's. No, there is a difference. I could read his prose on a salary, but not Jane's.

Mark Twain, American writer (1835–1910). In *Mark Twain's Letters*, ed. A. B. Paine (1917).

Accepting an Oscar for her screenplay of Sense and Sensibility *(1995):*

7 I hope she knows how big she is in Uruguay.

Emma Thompson, English actress and writer (1959–). Speech in Los Angeles (26 March 1996).

Austerity

On the National Health Service and continuing austerity:

8 Here is a pretty prospect – an endless vista of free false teeth with nothing to bite.

Robert Boothby (later Lord Boothby), English Conservative politician (1900–86). Quoted in Herbert V. Prochnow, Snr & Jnr, *A Treasury of Humorous Quotations* (1969).

Australia and the Australians

Of Australia:

9 It must be so pretty with all the dear little kangaroos flying about. Agatha has found it on the map. What a curious shape it is! Just like a large packing case.

Oscar Wilde, Irish playwright, poet and wit (1854–1900). *Lady Windermere's Fan*, Act 2 (1892). Later the Duchess of Berwick calls it 'that dreadful vulgar place'.

10 We had intended you to be
The next Prime Minister but three:
The stocks were sold; the Press was
  squared;
The Middle Class was quite prepared.
But as it is! … My language fails!
Go out and govern New South Wales!

Hilaire Belloc, French-born English poet and writer (1870–1953). 'Lord Lundy', *Cautionary Tales* (1907).

1 In Australia
Inter alia,
Mediocrities
Think they're Socrates.

Peter Porter, Australian-born poet
(1929–). Unpublished clerihew, quoted in
The Dictionary of Australian Quotations
(1984). Porter commented on BBC Radio
Quote . . . Unquote (28 November 1989) that
writing these lines meant he had recently been
denied a grant by the Australian government.

2 Australia is a huge rest home, where
no unwelcome news is ever wafted on to
the pages of the worst newspapers in
the world.

Germaine Greer, Australian-born feminist
writer (1939–). In *The Observer* (1 August
1982).

Autobiography

3 Autobiography is now as common as
adultery and hardly less reprehensible.

John Grigg (formerly Lord Altrincham),
English writer (1924–). Quoted in *The Fine
Art of Political Wit*, ed. Leon Harris (1965).

Autographs

*Said to an imposing gentleman, after bowing
low to him:*

4 I beg your pardon, sir, are you anyone in
particular?

Theodore Hook, English writer, hoaxer
and joker (1788–1841). Quoted in
W. D. Adams, *Treasury of Modern Anecdote*
(1886). Hook or not, 'Please, are you
anybody?' was the caption to a cartoon
by Lewis Baumer in *Punch* Magazine
(16 February 1938). It showed a little girl
with an autograph book approaching an
impressive gentleman.

*On Neville Chamberlain and the Munich
agreement (1938):*

5 Well, he seemed such a nice old gentleman, I thought I would give him my
autograph as a souvenir.

Adolf Hitler, German Nazi leader (1889–
1945). Attributed remark in *The Penguin
Dictionary of Modern Quotations*
(1971).

6 Gather ye autographs while ye may.

Cole Porter, American composer and lyricist
(1891–1964). Title of song in *Jubilee* (1935),
but dropped from the show.

Awards

On receiving an award:

7 I don't deserve this, but I have arthritis,
and I don't deserve that either.

Jack Benny, American comedian (1894–
1974). Quoted in *Quote and Unquote*, ed.
Peter and Josie Holtom (1973).

B

Babies

Definition of a baby:

1 A loud voice at one end and no sense of responsibility at the other.

Ronald Knox, English priest and writer (1888–1957). So ascribed in the 1976 BBC Reith Lectures, though Frank S. Pepper's *Handbook of 20th Century Quotations* (1984) gives it to 'E. Adamson'. *Bartlett's Familiar Quotations* (16th edn, 1992) ascribes 'Government is like a big baby – an alimentary canal with a big appetite at one end and no responsibility at the other' to Ronald Reagan 'while campaigning for governor of California (1965).'

Bachelors

2 Somehow a bachelor never quite gets over the idea that he is a thing of beauty and a boy forever.

Helen Rowland, American columnist and writer (1875–1950). *A Guide to Men* (1922).

3 A bachelor gets tangled up with a lot of women in order to avoid getting tied up by one.

Helen Rowland. Quoted in *The Treasury of Humorous Quotations*, ed. Evan Esar & Nicolas Bentley (1951).

4 Bachelor's fare: bread and cheese and kisses.

Jonathan Swift, Anglo-Irish writer and clergyman (1667–1745). *Polite Conversation*, Dialogue 1 (1738) – a work made up of well-established sayings and expressions.

5 'Home, Sweet Home' must surely have been written by a bachelor.

Samuel Butler, English author (1835–1902). Quoted in *The Treasury of Humorous Quotations*, ed. Evan Esar & Nicolas Bentley (1951).

Bad

Of an inn at Bristol:

6 Describe it, Sir? – Why, it was so bad that Boswell wished to be in Scotland.

Samuel Johnson, English writer and lexicographer (1709–84). In James Boswell, *Life of Johnson* (1791) – for 29 April 1776.

7 The reason Michael Jackson entitled his album *Bad* was because he couldn't spell *Indescribable*.

Anonymous – shortly after the album was released in 1987.

Bagpipes

8 A true gentleman is a man who knows how to play the bagpipes – but doesn't.

Anonymous. Quoted in *Reader's Digest* (March 1976) as from *The Wall Street Journal*. This has also been ascribed to G. K. Chesterton.

9 The bagpipes sound exactly the same when you have finished learning them as when you start.

Sir Thomas Beecham, English conductor (1879–1961). Quoted in Harold Atkins & Archie Newman, *Beecham Stories* (1978).

Baldness

10 The most delightful advantage of being bald – one can *hear* snowflakes.

R. G. Daniels, English magistrate (1916–). Quoted in *The Observer* (11 July 1976).

11 There is more felicity on the far side of baldness than young men can possibly imagine.

Logan Pearsall Smith, American writer (1865–1946). *Afterthoughts* (1931).

Baldwin, Stanley
(1st Earl Baldwin of Bewdley)
English Conservative Prime Minister (1867–1947)

1 Stanley Baldwin always hits the nail on the head, but it doesn't go in any further.

G. M. Young, English historian (1882–1959). Unverified.

Ballet

2 My own personal reaction is that most ballets would be perfectly delightful if it were not for the dancing.

Anonymous. Quoted in Michael Bateman, *This England: Selections from the New Statesman column 1934–1968*, Pt 1 (1969).

Bananas

When asked whether he thought Mrs Thatcher would face any more banana skins:

3 I think there will be banana skins as long as there are bananas.

William Whitelaw (later Viscount Whitelaw), English politician (1918–). Quoted in *The Observer* (22 April 1984).

Banana republics

On the state of Britain in 1978:

4 If you subtracted the North Sea oil revenues you would realise that present policies are leading us to the status of a banana republic that has run out of bananas.

Sir Richard Marsh (later Lord Marsh), English politician (1928–). Quoted in *The Daily Telegraph* (6 September 1978).

5 Had the Conservative elite of the immediate post-war era shown half the energy and enterprise in peacetime as it had in war, it is hard to believe that Britain would have been reduced to her present stature of Italy with rockets.

Andrew Roberts, English historian (1963–). *Eminent Churchillians* (1994).

Bankers

6 A banker is a fellow who lends you his umbrella when the sun is shining and wants it back the minute it begins to rain.

Mark Twain, American author (1835–1910). Quoted in *The Treasury of Humorous Quotations*, ed. Evan Esar & Nicolas Bentley (1951).

Bankhead, Tallulah
American actress (1903–68)

7 I've just spent an hour talking to Tallulah for a few minutes.

Fred Keating (unidentified). Quoted in Ned Sherrin, *Cutting Edge* (1984).

8 Watching Tallullah on stage is like watching somebody skating on thin ice. Everyone wants to be there when it breaks.

Mrs Patrick Campbell, English actress (1865–1940). Quoted in Bankhead's obituary in *The Times* (13 December 1968).

9 A day away from Tallulah is like a month in the country.

Howard Dietz, American writer and film executive (1896–1983). Recalled in *Dancing in the Dark* (1974). This remark has also been attributed to all the usual suspects – Parker, Ace, Kaufman, Woollcott and Benchley – but Dietz said he said it and Bankhead herself wrote in *Tallulah* (1952): 'How Dietz once remarked, "A day away from Tallulah is like a month in the country." Ever since he's enjoyed the reputation of a great wit.' Ouch.

When asked towards the end of her life if she was the famous Tallulah, the actress replied:

10 What's left of her.

Quoted in *A Year of Stings and Squelches* (1985).

Banquets

11 A Banquet is probably the most fatiguing thing in the world except ditch digging. It is the insanest of all recreations. The inventor of it overlooked no detail that could furnish weariness, distress, harassment, and acute and long-sustained misery of mind and body.

Mark Twain, American writer (1835–1910). Quoted in *Mark Twain in Eruption*, ed. Bernard de Vote (1940).

Barrie, Sir James
Scottish playwright (1860–1937)

1 The cheerful clatter of Sir James Barrie's cans as he went round with the milk of human kindness.

Philip Guedalla, English writer (1889–1944). 'Some Critics', *Supers and Supermen* (1920).

Bathing

2 Two Jews were conversing about bathing. 'I take a bath once a year,' said one, 'whether I need one or not.'

Sigmund Freud, Austrian psychiatrist (1856–1939). Discussing an anti-Semitic joke in *Jokes and their Relation to the Unconscious* (1905). He adds, helpfully, 'It is clear that this boastful assurance of his cleanliness only betrays his sense of uncleanliness.' Sometimes told concerning Queen Elizabeth I – that she would take a bath once a month 'whether she need it or no'.

3 My grandmother took a bath every year, whether she was dirty or not.

Brendan Behan, Irish playwright (1923–64). *Brendan Behan's Island* (1962).

Bavarians

4 A Bavarian is half-way between an Austrian and a human being.

Otto von Bismarck, Prusso-German statesman (1815–98). Unconfirmed. R. P. W. Lewis recalled this, however, from Edward Teller's obituary of the physicist Werner Heisenberg – a Bavarian – in *Nature* (15 April 1976): 'On the 800th anniversary of the Bavarian state, he appeared on television and said, "The Bavarian unites the discipline of the Austrian with the charm of the Prussian."'

BBC (British Broadcasting Corporation)

5 Its atmosphere is something halfway between a girls' school and a lunatic asylum.

George Orwell, English novelist and journalist (1903–50). Diary entry for 14 March 1942, quoted in *The Collected Essays, Journalism and Letters of George Orwell*, Vol. 2 (1968).

Beards

6 Christlike in my behaviour,
Like every good believer,
I imitate the Saviour,
And cultivate a beaver.

Aldous Huxley, English novelist and writer (1894–1963). *Antic Hay* (1923).

Beauty

7 None but the brave can live with the fair.

Frank McKinney ('Kin') Hubbard, American humorist (1868–1930). Quoted in Herbert V. Prochnow, Snr & Jnr, *A Treasury of Humorous Quotations* (1969).

Bed

8 Believe me, you have to get up early if you want to get out of bed.

Groucho Marx, American comedian (1895–1977). Soundtrack of *The Cocoanuts* (film US, 1929). Written by George S. Kaufman and Morrie Ryskind.

9 It's not the wild, ecstatic leap across that I deplore. It is the weary trudge home.

Anonymous. 'Double Beds versus Single Beds', quoted in *Penguin Dictionary of Modern Quotations* (1971). Derek Parker recalled (1996) the comedian Derek Roy saying something similar in his act at the Palace Theatre, Plymouth in 1957: 'It's not the quick dash over – it's the slow drag back.'

Beethoven, Ludwig van
German composer (1770–1827)

On being asked what he thought of Beethoven:

10 I love him, especially his poems.

Ringo Starr, English pop musician (1940–). Quoted in Hunter Davies, *The Beatles* (1968). At a press conference during The Beatles' first American tour in 1964.

On the third movement of the 7th Symphony:

11 What can you do with it? – it's like a lot of yaks jumping about.

Sir Thomas Beecham, English conductor (1879–1961). Quoted in Harold Atkins & Archie Newman, *Beecham Stories* (1978).

1 Beethoven was so deaf, he thought he was a painter.

Anonymous (graffito) on Intercity train between Newcastle and Sheffield. Contributed to BBC Radio *Quote ... Unquote* (19 February 1979) by Pete and Kathy Weslowski of South Gosforth.

Beggars

When asked why he constantly gave money to beggars:

2 Madam, to enable them to beg on.

Samuel Johnson, English writer and lexicographer (1709–84). Quoted in *Johnsonian Miscellanies*, ed. Hill (1897).

Beginning

3 'Where shall I begin, please, your Majesty?' he [the White Rabbit] asked. 'Begin at the beginning,' the King said, gravely, 'and go on till you come to the end: then stop.'

Lewis Carroll (C. L. Dodgson), English writer (1832–98). *Alice's Adventures in Wonderland*, Chap. 12 (1865).

Belief

4 My dear child, you must believe in God in spite of what the clergy tell you.

Benjamin Jowett, English scholar (1817–93). Quoted in Margot Asquith, *Autobiography* (1920–22).

5 Believe only half of what you see and nothing that you hear.

Anonymous. Quoted in Mrs (Dinah) Craik, *A Woman's Thoughts* (1858).

6 All in all there is much to suggest that the Established Church is in a state of bewilderment and has lost its way. As a wag put it when writing to *The Times*: 'There doesn't seem very much left for us agnostics not to believe in.'

Anonymous. Quoted in *Faith and Heritage* (Summer 1995).

7 When men cease to believe in God, they will not believe in nothing, they will believe in anything.

G. K. Chesterton, English poet, novelist and critic (1874–1936). Attributed but unverified. The earliest citation appears in Emile Cammaerts, *Chesterton: The Laughing Prophet* (1937) where, in the middle of some direct quotation, there is the paraphrase, 'The first effect of not believing in God is to believe in anything.'

8 I can believe in anything, provided that it is quite incredible.

Oscar Wilde, Irish playwright, poet and wit (1854–1900). *The Picture of Dorian Gray*, Chap. 1 (1891).

9 Lord, I do not believe; help thou my unbelief.

Samuel Butler, English author (1835–1902). Quoted in *The Treasury of Humorous Quotations*, ed. Evan Esar & Nicolas Bentley (1951).

When asked by a small Commonwealth person whether she believed in Father Christmas:

10 I like to believe in Father Christmas.

Elizabeth II, British Queen (1926–). In Christmas TV broadcast (25 December 1989).

Benn, Tony
English Labour politician (1925–)

11 Tony Benn is the Bertie Wooster of Marxism.

Anonymous. Quoted in Matthew Parris, *Scorn* (1995). This remark was contributed by Malcolm Bradbury to BBC Radio *Quote ... Unquote* (11 September 1979) and might well have been of his own manufacture.

12 He immatures with age.

Harold Wilson (later Lord Wilson) (1916–95), British Labour Prime Minister. In 1981. Quoted in Anthony Sampson, *The Changing Anatomy of Britain* (1982).

Best

13 It is a funny thing about life: if you refuse to accept anything but the best you very often get it.

W. Somerset Maugham, English writer (1874–1965). Quoted in *The Treasury of Humorous Quotations*, ed. Evan Esar & Nicolas Bentley (1951).

Best-sellers

1 A best-seller is the gilded tomb of a mediocre talent.

Logan Pearsall Smith, American writer (1865–1946). *Afterthoughts* (1931).

2 A best-seller was a book which somehow sold well simply because it was selling well.

Daniel J. Boorstin, American writer (1914–). *Images* (1961).

Bible

The actor Thomas Mitchell visited W. C. Fields in a sanatorium during his last illness and was amazed to see the comedian thumbing through the Bible. When he asked, 'What are you doing?', Fields replied:

3 Looking for loopholes.

W. C. Fields, American comedian (1879–1946). Quoted in the book *Quote ... Unquote* (1978) – source unknown.

4 The total absence of humour from the Bible is one of the most singular things in all literature.

Alfred North Whitehead, English philosopher and mathematician (1961–1947). Quoted in *The 'Quote ... Unquote' Book of Love, Death and the Universe* (1980), but otherwise untraced.

5 He swalloweth the ground with fierceness and rage: neither believeth he that it is the sound of the trumpet. He saith among the trumpets, Ha, ha; and he smelleth the battle afar off, the thunder of the captains, and the shouting.

Job 39:24–25. It is a *horse* that is being talked about.

6 The Book of Life begins with a man and a woman in a garden. It ends with Revelations.

Oscar Wilde, Irish playwright, poet and wit (1854–1900). *A Woman of No Importance*, Act 1 (1893).

Bidets

Cabled response to his wife's complaint from Paris just after the war that her accommodation did not have a bidet and would he send her one:

7 UNABLE OBTAIN BIDET. SUGGEST HAND-STAND IN SHOWER.

Billy Wilder, American film director and writer (1906–). Quoted in Leslie Halliwell, *The Filmgoer's Book of Quotes* (1973).

Billiards

8 To play billiards well is the sign of an ill-spent youth.

Charles Roupell, legal official (undated). Attributed in David Duncan, *Life of Herbert Spencer* (1908). Often misascribed to Herbert Spencer and to Robert Louis Stevenson. 'Snooker', 'bridge' and 'misspent youth' are included in other versions.

Biography

9 The Art of Biography
Is different from Geography.
Geography is about Maps,
But Biography is about Chaps.

E. C. Bentley, English journalist and novelist (1875–1956). *Biography for Beginners* (1905).

10 Every great man nowadays has his disciples, and it is always Judas who writes the biography.

Oscar Wilde, Irish playwright, poet and wit (1854–1900). 'The Critic as Artist', *Intentions* (1891).

Birds

11 Der spring is sprung
Der grass is riz
I wonder where dem boidies is?
Der little boids is on der wing,
Ain't dat absoid?
Der little wings is on der boid!

Anonymous (New York). 'The Budding Bronx', quoted in Arnold Silcock, *Verse and Worse* (1952).

Birmingham (England)

12 They came from Birmingham, which is not a place to promise much, you know ... One has not great hopes from Birmingham. I always say there is something direful in the sound.

Jane Austen, English novelist (1775–1817). *Emma*, Chap. 36 (1816). Mrs Elton speaking.

Birth

When asked why he had been born in such an unfashionable place as Lowell, Massachussetts:

1 The explanation is quite simple. I wished to be near my mother.

James McNeill Whistler, American painter (1834–1903). Quoted in *Medical Quotations* (1989).

On being chaffed for being an Irishman:

2 Because a man is born in a stable that does not make him a horse.

Arthur Wellesley, 1st Duke of Wellington, Irish-born soldier and politician (1769–1852). Quoted in Elizabeth Longford, *Wellington: The Years of the Sword* (1969). Compare the proverbial 'The man who is born in a stable is a horse' (known by 1833).

3 It occurred to me that I would like to be a poet. The chief qualification, I understand, is that you must be born. Well, I hunted up my birth certificate, and found that I was all right on that score.

'Saki' (H. H. Munro), English writer (1870–1916). 'Reginald's Rubaiyat', *Reginald* (1904).

Bisexuality

4 It immediately doubles your chances for a date on Saturday night.

Woody Allen, American film actor, writer and director (1937–). Quoted in *The New York Times* (1 December 1975).

Bishops

5 How can a bishop marry? How can he flirt? The most he can say is, 'I will see you in the vestry after service.'

Revd Sydney Smith, English clergyman, essayist and wit (1771–1845). Quoted in Lady Holland, *A Memoir of Sydney Smith* (1855).

On being told by a bishop that his palace had no less than forty bedrooms in it:

6 Oh dear – and only Thirty-Nine Articles to put in them.

Winston S. Churchill (later Sir Winston), British Conservative Prime Minister and writer (1874–1965). Quoted on BBC Radio *Quote … Unquote* (1979).

Bishops and Actresses

7 'More than ever,' answered the Saint cheerfully. 'This is my idea of a night out – as the bishop said to the actress.'

Leslie Charteris, English-born American writer (1907–93). *Enter the Saint* (1930).

8 'I should be charmed to oblige you – as the actress said to the bishop,' replied the Saint.

Ibid.

9 'Let's see what you've got– as the actress said to the bishop,' murmured Simon.

Ibid.

10 'There's something I particularly want to do to-night.'
'As the bishop said to the actress,' murmured the girl.

Ibid.

11 'You're getting on – as the actress said to the bishop,' he murmured.

Ibid.

Bitchery

Of a woman journalist he disliked:

12 She missed the last lobby briefing, I hear. At the vet's with hardpad, no doubt.

Harold Wilson (later Lord Wilson of Rievaulx), English Labour Prime Minister (1916–95). Quoted in James Margach, *The Abuse of Power* (1981).

To another woman:

13 Oh, what a pretty dress – and so cheap!

Zsa Zsa Gabor, Hungarian-born film actress (1919–). Quoted in *A Year of Stings and Squelches* (1985).

To Judy, wife of Liberal politician David Steel:

14 Tell me the history of that frock, Judy. It's obviously an old favourite. You were wise to remove the curtain rings.

'Dame Edna Everage' (Barry Humphries, Australian entertainer, 1934–). TV show, *Another Audience with Dame Edna* (1984).

On novelist Ethel Mannin:

1 I do not want Miss Mannin's feelings to be hurt by the fact that I have never heard of her ... At the moment I am debarred from the pleasure of putting her in her place by the fact that she has not got one.

Dame Edith Sitwell, English poet (1887–1964). Quoted in John Pearson, *Façades* (1978) after a report in *The Yorkshire Evening News* (8 August 1930). By 13 March 1940, James Agate appears to have been reascribing this (in his *Ego 4*): 'About an American woman novelist [Mannin was English] who had been rude to her in print, Lady Oxford [i.e. Margot Asquith] is reported to have said, "I would put Miss B. in her place if she had a place."'

On Virginia Woolf:

2 I enjoyed talking to her, but thought nothing of her writing. I considered her 'a beautiful little knitter'.

Edith Sitwell. Letter to G. Singleton (11 July 1955).

Of Edith Sitwell and her two brothers, Osbert and Sacheverell:

3 Two wiseacres and a cow.

Noël Coward (later Sir Noël), English entertainer and writer (1899–1973). Quoted in John Pearson, *Façades* (1978).

On a starlet:

4 I see – she's the original good time that was had by all.

Bette Davis, American film actress (1908–89). Quoted in Leslie Halliwell, *The Filmgoer's Book of Quotes* (1973). In the form, 'There, standing at the piano, was the original good time who had been had by all', it has also been attributed to Kenneth Tynan at an Oxford Union debate in the late 1940s.

Passing a Leicester Square movie poster which proclaimed 'Michael Redgrave and Dirk Bogarde in The Sea Shall Not Have Them'*:*

5 I don't see why not: everyone else has.

Noël Coward (later Sir Noël), English entertainer and writer (1899–1973). Quoted by Sheridan Morley in the *Independent on Sunday* Magazine (12 November 1995). The film was released in 1954.

On being told that Maud Cunard was 'absolutely wonderful, she never changes':

6 I am sorry to hear that.

Sir Max Beerbohm, English writer and caricaturist (1872–1956). Quoted in Daphne Fielding, *Emerald and Nancy* (1968).

The film actress Jean Harlow inquired whether the name Margot was pronounced 'Margo' or 'Margott':

7 'Margo'– the 'T' is silent– as in 'Harlow'.

Margot Asquith (later Countess of Oxford and Asquith) (1864–1945). This story did not appear in print until T. S. Matthews' *Great Tom* in 1973. Then, in about 1983, a much more convincing version of its origin was given. Margot Grahame (1911–82) was an English actress who, after stage appearances in Johannesburg and London, went to Hollywood in 1934. Her comparatively brief career as a film star included appearances in *The Informer, The Buccaneer* and *The Three Musketeers* in the mid-1930s. It was when she was being built up as a rival to the likes of Harlow (who died in 1937) that Grahame herself claimed the celebrated exchange had occurred. She added that it was not intended as a putdown. She did not realize what she had said until afterwards. Grahame seems a convincing candidate for speaker of the famous line. When her star waned people attributed the remark to the other, better known and more quotable source.

Of a London actress who had broken a leg:

8 Oh, how terrible. She must have done it sliding down a barrister.

Dorothy Parker, American writer (1893–1967). Quoted in *The Sayings of Dorothy Parker*, ed. S. T. Brownlow (1992).

Blessings

On his defeat in the 1945 General Election, to his wife who had told him it might be a blessing in disguise:

9 At the moment it seems quite effectively disguised.

Winston S. Churchill (later Sir Winston), British Conservative Prime Minister and writer (1874–1965). Quoted in his *The Second World War*, Vol. 6 (1954).

Blondes

1 She was a blonde – with a brunette past.

Gwyn Thomas, Welsh novelist, playwright and humorist (1913–81). In BBC2 TV *Line-Up* (25 October 1969).

2 It was a blonde. A blonde to make a bishop kick a hole in a stained-glass window.

Raymond Chandler, American novelist (1888–1959). *Farewell, My Lovely* (1940).

Blood

3 I came in here in all good faith to help my country. I don't mind giving a reasonable amount [of blood], but a pint … why that's very nearly an armful. I'm sorry. I'm not walking around with an empty arm for anybody.

Tony Hancock, English comedian (1924–68). 'The Blood Donor', *Hancock* (BBC TV, 23 June 1961). Script by Alan Simpson and Ray Galton.

Bogart, Humphrey
American film actor (1899–1957)

4 Bogart's a helluva nice guy till 11.30 p.m. After that he thinks he's Bogart.

Dave Chasen, American restaurateur (1899–1973). Quoted in Leslie Halliwell, *The Filmgoer's Book of Quotes* (1973).

Booing

Responding to a solitary boo amongst the mid-act applause at the first performance of Arms and the Man *(1894):*

5 I quite agree with you, sir, but what can two do against so many?

Bernard Shaw, Irish playwright and critic (1856–1950). Quoted in St John Irvine, *Bernard Shaw: His Life, Work and Friends* (1956).

Books

6 The proper study of mankind is books.

Aldous Huxley, English novelist and writer (1894–1963). *Crome Yellow* (1921).

7 No furniture so charming as books, even if you never open them, or read a single word.

Revd Sydney Smith, English clergyman, essayist and wit (1771–1845). Quoted in Lady Holland, *A Memoir of Sydney Smith* (1855).

8 Never lend a book; never give a book away; never read a book.

John Sparrow, English scholar (1906–92). The 'book collector's caveat', which Sparrow was fond of quoting, according to his obituary in *The Independent* (4 February 1992).

On his hobby of growing trees:

9 I'm replacing some of the timber used up by my books. Books are just trees with squiggles on them.

Hammond Innes, English novelist (1913–98). Interview, *Radio Times* (18–24 August 1984).

10 Of a certain author it was said, 'A first edition of his work is a rarity but a second is rarer still.'

Franklin P. Adams, American humorist (1881–1960). Quoted in *The Treasury of Humorous Quotations*, ed. Evan Esar & Nicolas Bentley (1951).

11 There is a good saying to the effect that when a new book appears one should read an old one. As an author I would not recommend too strict adherence to this saying.

Winston S. Churchill (later Sir Winston), British Conservative Prime Minister and writer (1874–1965). Quoted in *The Sayings of Winston Churchill*, ed. J. A. Sutcliffe (1992).

12 I have known her pass the whole evening without mentioning a single book, or *in fact anything unpleasant, at all.*

Henry Reed, English poet and playwright (1914–86). Radio play, *A Very Great Man Indeed* (1953).

Bores

13 Bore, *n.* A person who talks when you wish him to listen.

Ambrose Bierce, American journalist (1842–?1914). *The Cynic's Word Book* (later retitled *The Devil's Dictionary*) (1906).

On Sir Anthony Eden:

14 He was not only a bore; he bored for England.

Malcolm Muggeridge, English writer and broadcaster (1903–90). 'Boring for England', *Tread Softly For You Tread on My Jokes* (1966).

Of Israel Zangwill:

1 He is an old bore; even the grave yawns for him.

Sir Herbert Beerbohm Tree, English actor-manager (1853–1917). Quoted in Max Beerbohm, *Herbert Beerbohm Tree* (1920).

Of Arianna Stassinopoulos, Greek-born writer and socialite:

2 So boring you fall asleep halfway through her name.

Alan Bennett, English playwright and actor (1934–). Quoted in *The Observer* (18 September 1983). (Heaven knows what he would have said when marriage led to the woman being known as 'Arianna Stassinopoulos Huffington'.)

A patrician lady in her country house invited an extremely boring and loquacious gentleman to come and pay her a visit. He ended up trapping her in a corner and talking and talking and talking to her. After a while, she said:

3 How very interesting, my dear. Why don't you go away and *write it all down*?

Anonymous. Quoted by Dr John Rae on BBC Radio *Quote ... Unquote* (30 July 1983).

4 Someone's boring me. I think it's me.

Dylan Thomas, Welsh poet (1914–53). Quoted in Rayner Heppenstall, *Four Absentees* (1960).

5 Society is now one polish'd horde, Form'd of two mighty tribes, the *Bores* and *Bored*.

Lord Byron, English poet (1788–1824). *Don Juan*, Canto 13, St. 95 (1819–24).

6 A bore is a man who, when you ask him how he is, tells you.

Bert Leston Taylor, American journalist (1866–1921). *The So-Called Human Race* (1922).

7 To be a bore is to have halitosis of the mind, as someone should probably have said before me.

Nigel Rees, English writer and journalist (1944–). *Best Behaviour* (1992).

8 I am one of those unhappy persons who inspires bores to the highest flights of art.

Dame Edith Sitwell, English poet (1887–1964). Quoted in *The Observer* (8 March 1998).

Boston (Massachusetts)

On Shakespeare:

9 A great man! Why, I doubt if there are six his equal in the whole of Boston.

Anonymous. Said to W. E. Gladstone by an unnamed Bostonian. Quoted in the book *Quote ... Unquote* (1978). H. L. Mencken's *Dictionary of Quotations* (1942) has it that Gladstone got it from Lionel A. Tollemache (23 December 1897) as, 'There are not ten men in Boston equal to Shakespeare.'

10 And this is good old Boston,
The home of the bean and the cod,
Where the Lowells talk only to Cabots,
And the Cabots talk only to God.

John Collins Bossidy, American oculist (1860–1928). Toast at a Harvard dinner (1910).

Bottoms

11 I do most of my work sitting down; that's where I shine.

Robert Benchley, American humorist (1889–1945). Quoted in R. E. Drennan, *Algonquin Wits* (1968). However, in Herbert V. Prochnow, Snr & Jnr, *A Treasury of Humorous Quotations* (1969), this is ascribed to Robert Bushby.

12 *Quand je regarde mon derrière, je vois qu'il est divisé en deux parties.*

Winston S. Churchill (later Sir Winston), British Conservative Prime Minister and writer (1874–1965). Quoted on BBC Radio *Quote ... Unquote* (29 January 1979). From an alleged speech in Paris just after the Second World War. He told his audience that, looking back, he saw his career divided into two distinct and separate periods. So what he meant by his '*derrière*' was not his backside but his past.

Bourne

13 Gone to that country from whose Bourne no Hollingsworth returns.

27

J. B. Morton (Beachcomber), English humorous writer (1893–1979). 'Another True Story', *Gallimaufry* (1936).

Boys

1 Little boys should be obscene and not heard.

Oscar Wilde, Irish playwright, poet and wit (1854–1900). Quoted in H. Montgomery Hyde, *Oscar Wilde* (1976).

Bracken, Brendan (1st Viscount Bracken)
Irish journalist and Conservative politician (1901–58)

Remark addressed to Bracken:

2 You're phoney. Everything about you is phoney. Even your hair – which looks false – is real.

Anonymous American diplomat. However, Charles Edward Lysaght, in *Brendan Bracken* (1979), attributes it to a 'journalist', in the form: 'I don't believe a word you say, Brendan. Everything about you is phoney. Even your hair, which looks like a wig, isn't.' Bracken was Churchill's Minister of Information during the Second World War.

3 A wartime Minister of Information is compelled, in the national interest, to such continuous acts of duplicity that even his natural hair must grow to resemble a wig.

Claud Cockburn, English journalist (1904–81). *Crossing the Line* (1958).

Brains

4 The brain is a wonderful organ. It starts working the moment you get up in the morning, and does not stop until you get into the office.

Robert Frost, American poet (1874–1963). Quoted in Herbert V. Prochnow, Snr & Jnr, *A Treasury of Humorous Quotations* (1969). Sometimes rendered as '… until you get up to make a speech.'

On F. E. Smith (1st Earl of Birkenhead):

5 He's very clever, but sometimes his brains go to his head.

Margot Asquith (later Countess of Oxford and Asquith) (1864–1945). Quoted by Lady Violet Bonham Carter in 'Margot Oxford', *The Listener* (11 June 1953).

Brassières

6 What the brassière said to the top hat: 'You go on ahead while I give these two a lift.'

Anonymous. Quoted in John G. Murray, *A Gentleman Publisher's Commonplace Book* (1996). Murray adds that when the travel writer Freya Stark told this to the ambassador in Cairo in 1942, it shocked him.

Brazil

7 I'm Charley's aunt from Brazil – where the nuts come from.

Brandon Thomas, English playwright (1856–1914). *Charley's Aunt*, Act 1 (1892).

Breakfast

8 To eat well in England, all you have to do is take breakfast three times a day.

W. Somerset Maugham, English writer (1874–1965). Quoted in Ted Morgan, *Somerset Maugham* (1980), as the response to a friend's statement that he 'hated the food in England': 'What rubbish. All you have to do is eat breakfast three times a day.'

9 He that looketh on a plate of ham and eggs to lust after it, hath already committed breakfast with it in his heart.

C. S. Lewis, English scholar, religious writer and novelist (1898–1963). Letter of 10 March 1954.

Breasts

As Governor William J. Le Petomane, Mel Brooks suddenly turns to his bikini-clad secretary and finds he is faced with her cleavage. He says:

10 Hello boys. Have a good night's rest? … I missed you.

Mel Brooks, American writer and actor (1926–). Film, *Blazing Saddles* (US, 1974).

Breeding

When told by the Mayor of Boston, 'Of course, up in Boston, we think breeding is everything!':

1 Well, down here in New York, we think it's quite fun, too, but we don't think it's everything.

Alfred E. Smith, American politician (1873–1944) – when Governor of New York. Told by Margaret R. Jackson, Chipping Campden (1994).

Broccoli

2 I do not like broccoli and I haven't liked it since I was a little kid. I am President of the United States and I am not going to eat it any more.

George Bush, American Republican President (1924–). Unverified statement (March 1990). Accordingly Bush banned broccoli from his plane, Air Force One. Outraged California farmers unloaded a 10-ton juggernaut of broccoli on the White House doorstep. Bush also said, 'I can't stand broccoli' and when this caused ructions among America's broccoli growers, he added: 'Wait till the country hears how I feel about cauliflower.' He also denounced carrots as 'orange broccoli'.

Bureaucracy

3 Guidelines for bureaucrats:
(1) When in charge, ponder.
(2) When in trouble, delegate.
(3) When in doubt, mumble.

James H. Boren, American business executive (1925–). In *The New York Times* (8 November 1970).

Buses

On his first trip by bus:

4 This omnibus business is not what it is reported to be. I hailed one at the bottom of Whitehall and told the man to take me to Carlton House Terrace. But the fellow flatly refused!

George Curzon (1st Marquess Curzon), English Conservative politician (1859–1925). Quoted in *The Oxford Book of Political Anecdotes* (1986), without source. However,

the origin of the tale could lie in *Punch* (10 April 1901), in which there was a cartoon by Everard Hopkins with this caption: 'A GIRLISH IGNORANCE. *Lady Hildegarde, who is studying the habits of the democracy, determines to travel by Omnibus. Lady Hildegarde.* "CONDUCTOR, TELL THE DRIVER TO GO TO NO. 104, BERKELEY SQUARE, AND THEN HOME!"'

Bush, George
American Republican President (1924–)

5 George Bush reminds every woman of her first husband.

Jane O'Reilly, American writer and editor (1936–). In *GQ* Magazine (1984).

6 Poor George, he can't help it – he was born with a silver foot in his mouth.

Ann Richards, American Democratic politician (1933–). Keynote speech at convention, quoted in *The Independent* (20 July 1988).

Business

On how to succeed in the jewellery business:

7 We even sell a pair of earrings for under £1, which is cheaper than a prawn sandwich from Marks & Spencers. But I have to say the earrings probably won't last as long.

Gerald Ratner, English businessman (1949–). Speech to the Institute of Directors, Albert Hall, London (23 April 1991). At the time he was Chairman of Ratners Group plc. The company's fortunes took a dive and Ratner resigned in 1992. In *The Independent* Saturday Magazine (14 February 1998), Ratner explained: 'It was a joke to make the speech more interesting. It was a dig at people who say "Our products are so cheap because we cut out the middleman" … It's all bollocks … we all buy our stuff the same way. So I said: "How can we sell this [decanter] at such a low price? Because it is total crap." It was just a joke that had nothing to do with what else I was saying.'

Bust

8 I must, I must, I must improve my bust.

Raquel Welch, American film actress (1940–). In her beauty book (1984), though a slogan not original to her.

On the films of Victor Mature:

1 I never go to movies where the hero's bust is bigger than the heroine's.

Groucho Marx, American comedian (1895–1977). Quoted in Leslie Halliwell, *The Filmgoer's Book of Quotes* (1978).

Probably regarding Mature's appearance in *Samson and Delilah* (1949).

Butlers

On the 17th Duke of Norfolk – among whose titles is 'Chief Butler of England':

2 And he's only just learned how to stack the dishwasher.

Anne, Duchess of Norfolk, in *c*.1984. Quoted in *A Year of Stings and Squelches* (1985).

C

Caesar's wife

1 A newly elected mayor said that he felt, during his year of office, he should lay aside all his political prepossessions and be, like Caesar's wife, 'all things to all men'.

Anonymous. Quoted by G. W. E. Russell in *Collections and Recollections* (1898).

Calamity

2 The calamity that comes is never the one we had prepared ourselves for.

Mark Twain, American writer (1835–1910). Quoted in *The Love Letters of Mark Twain*, ed. Dixon Wecter (1949).

California

3 California is a fine place to live – if you happen to be an orange.

Fred Allen, American comedian (1894–1956). In *American Magazine* (December 1945).

Callaghan, James (later Lord Callaghan)
British Labour Prime Minister (1912–)

4 Now, now, little lady, you don't want to believe all those things you read in the newspaper about crisis and upheavals, and the end of civilization as we know it. Dearie me, not at all.

John O'Sullivan, English journalist. In *The Daily Telegraph* (10 June 1976). This example of Callaghan's patronizing style when dealing, as Prime Minister, with the then Leader of the Opposition, Margaret Thatcher, was quoted in all seriousness by *Newsweek* Magazine. It was, in fact, a parody written by O'Sullivan.

Cambridge (England)

5 For Cambridge people rarely smile, Being urban, squat, and packed with guile.

Rupert Brooke, English poet (1887–1915). 'The Old Vicarage, Grantchester' (1912).

6 He glanced with disdain at the big centre table where the famous faces of the Cambridge theatre were eating a loud meal. 'So this is the city of dreaming spires,' Sheila said. 'Theoretically speaking that's Oxford,' Adam said. 'This is the city of perspiring dreams.'

Frederic Raphael, English novelist and screenwriter (1931–). *The Glittering Prizes* (1976).

Canada and the Canadians

7 You have to know a man awfully well in Canada to know his surname.

John Buchan (later Lord Tweedsmuir), Scottish politician and writer (1875–1940). Quoted in *The Observer*, 'Sayings of the Week' (21 May 1950).

8 Canada is a country so square that even the female impersonators are women.

Richard Benner, Canadian film director. From the film *Outrageous!* (1977). Quoted in *The Guardian* (21 September 1978).

9 I don't even know what street Canada is on.

Al Capone, American gangster (1899–1947). Remark (1931), quoted in Roy Greenaway, *The News Game* (1966).

10 'I'm world-famous,' Dr Parks said, 'all over Canada.'

Mordecai Richler, Canadian novelist (1931–). *The Incomparable Auk*, Chap. 4 (1963).

Canned goods

1 Carnation milk is the best in the land,
Here I sit with a can in my hand.
No tits to pull, no hay to pitch,
Just punch a hole in the son-of-a-bitch.

Anonymous. Quoted in David Ogilvy, *Confessions of an Advertising Man* (1963).

Cannibalism

When asked who the man was riding in a carriage with the portly Queen of Tonga at the 1953 Coronation:

2 Her lunch.

Noël Coward (later Sir Noël), English entertainer and writer (1899–1973). In fact, it was the Sultan of Kelantan. This famous story made an early appearance in Dick Richards, *The Wit of Noël Coward* (1968). It is often told differently and may well be apocryphal. About the only thing to be said for certain is that Coward *did* spend most of Coronation Day watching TV – he says so in his diaries. According to Ned Sherrin, *Theatrical Anecdotes* (1991), Coward always denied the story, 'not least because she [Queen Salote] was a personal friend and would have been very upset'. Sherrin suggests that Emlyn Williams was the perpetrator and, curiously, casts Emperor Haile Selassie in the role of 'the lunch' (he did not even attend the Coronation).

In his diary entry for Coronation Day, James Lees-Milne has the Coward story and wrongly identifies the man as Queen Salote's husband. The passage is included in the published diaries, *A Mingled Measure* (1994), but seems probably to have been inserted at a later date. In *The Sayings of Noël Coward* (1997), Philip Hoare reveals that 'Coward disowned the line, ceding credit to David Niven.'

Capital

3 Spending one's own capital is feeding a dog on his own tail.

Mark Twain, American writer (1835–1910). *Mark Twain's Notebook*, ed. A. B. Paine (1935).

Capitalism

4 Capitalism, it is said, is a system wherein man exploits man. And communism – is vice versa.

Daniel Bell, American sociologist (1919–). *The End of Ideology* (1960). Note the 'it is said'.

Laurence J. Peter in *Quotations for Our Time* (1977) describes it as a 'Polish proverb' and another source has it 'reported from Warsaw'.

Careers

5 His was the sort of career that made the Recording Angel think seriously about taking up shorthand.

Nicolas Bentley, English cartoonist and writer (1907–78). Quoted in *The Treasury of Humorous Quotations*, ed. Evan Esar & Nicolas Bentley (1951).

Caroline of Brunswick
Estranged wife and Queen of George IV (1768–1821)

6 Most Gracious Queen, we thee implore
To go away and sin no more,
But if that effort be too great,
To go away at any rate.

Anonymous. Quoted in *The Diary and Correspondence of Lord Colchester* (1861) – letter from Francis Burton (15 November 1820).

7 Fate wrote her a most tremendous tragedy, and she played it in tights.

Sir Max Beerbohm, English writer and caricaturist (1872–1956). In *The Yellow Book* (1894).

On her behaviour with the dey (governor) of Algiers:

8 She was happy as the dey was long.

Attributed to Lord Norbury (1820).

Cartland, Barbara (later Dame Barbara)
English romantic novelist (1901–)

9 The animated meringue.

Arthur Marshall, English writer and entertainer (1910–89). Recalled by him on BBC Radio *Quote … Unquote* (25 December 1979). Apparently, far from taking offence, Miss Cartland sent him a telegram of thanks.

Catch-22

Defining 'Catch-22':

10 DANEEKA: There's a rule saying I have to ground anyone who's crazy.

YOSSARIAN: Then why can't you ground me? I'm crazy.
DANEEKA: Anyone who wants to get out of combat duty isn't really crazy.

Joseph Heller, American novelist (1923–). *Catch-22* (1961).

Cats

1 Alfred de Musset
Used to call his cat Pusset.
His accent was affected.
That was only to be expected.

Maurice Evan Hare, English writer (1886–1967). 'Byway in Biography' (undated).

2 The thing that astonished him was that cats should have two holes cut in their coat, exactly at the place where their eyes are.

George Christoph Lichtenberg, German scientist and drama critic (1742–99). Unverified.

Cauliflower

3 Training is everything. The peach was once a bitter almond; cauliflower is nothing but cabbage with a college education.

Mark Twain, American writer (1835–1910). *Pudd'nhead Wilson* (1894).

Celebrities

4 A celebrity is one who works hard all his life to become well-known and then goes through back streets wearing dark glasses so he won't be recognized.

Fred Allen, American comedian (1894–1956). *Treadmill to Oblivion* (1956). Has also been attributed to Jane Powell, the American film actress (1929–).

Censorship

5 Assassination is the extreme form of censorship.

Bernard Shaw, Irish playwright and critic (1856–1950). *The Shewing-Up of Blanco Posnet* (1911).

6 A censor is a man who knows more than he thinks you ought to.

Laurence J. Peter, Canadian writer (1919–90). In *Quotations for Our Time* (1977).

Censure

7 Censure is the tax a man pays to the public for being eminent.

Jonathan Swift, Anglo-Irish writer and clergyman (1667–1745). *Thoughts on Various Subjects* (1706).

Centipedes

8 A centipede was happy quite,
Until a frog in fun
Said, 'Pray, which leg comes after which?'
This raised her mind to such a pitch,
She lay distracted in a ditch
Considering how to run.

Mrs Edmund Craster, English poet (d.1874). 'The Puzzled Centipede', quoted in *The Penguin Dictionary of Quotations* (1960).

Certainty

9 Our new Constitution is now established, and has an appearance that promises permanency; but in this world nothing can be said to be certain, except death and taxes.

Benjamin Franklin, American politician and scientist (1706–90). Quoted in *Writings of Benjamin Franklin*, ed. A. H. Smyth (1905) – for 13 November 1789.

Chamberlain, Neville

British Conservative Prime Minister (1869–1940)

10 Listening to a speech by [Neville] Chamberlain is like paying a visit to Woolworths; everything in its place and nothing over sixpence.

Aneurin Bevan, Welsh Labour politician (1897–1960). In *Tribune* (1937).

11 A good mayor of Birmingham in an off-year.

David Lloyd George (1st Earl Lloyd George of Dwyfor), British Liberal Prime Minister (1863–1945). Chamberlain came to national politics after long experience in local government. Quoted in A. J. P. Taylor, *English History 1914–1945* (1965). Also, in the form: 'He might make an adequate Lord Mayor of Birmingham in a lean year', quoted in Leon Harris, *The Fine Art of Political Wit* (1965). In *Future Indefinite* (1954), Noël Coward ascribes to Lord

Birkenhead (F. E. Smith), 'The most we can hope for from dear Neville is that he should be a good Lord Mayor of Birmingham in a lean year.' Also attributed (and possibly more correctly) to Lord Hugh Cecil in the form 'He is no better than a Mayor of Birmingham, and in a lean year at that. Furthermore he is too old. He thinks he understands the modern world. What should an old hunk like him know of the modern world?' Quoted in Lord David Cecil, *The Cecils of Hatfield House* (1973).

Champagne

1 Real pain for your sham friends, champagne from your real friends.

Anonymous. An Edwardian toast that the Irish-born painter Francis Bacon (1909–92) acquired from his father, according to Daniel Farson, *The Gilded Gutter Life of Francis Bacon* (1993).

2 In victory you deserve it: in defeat you need it.

Napoleon I, French Emperor (1769–1821). Unverified. On the other hand, 'Aid is ... like champagne: in success you deserve it, in failure you need it' is ascribed to Lord Bauer (b.1915), English economist, in Graham Hancock, *Lords of Poverty* (1989).

Changes

Refusing to accept any more changes when Irving Berlin was still fiddling with a song lyric just prior to the opening of a show:

3 Call me Miss Birds Eye, this show is frozen.

Ethel Merman, American actress and singer (1909–84). Quoted in *The Times* (13 July 1985). The song may have been from *Annie Get Your Gun* or *Call Me Madam*.

Charisma

Concerning a Texas gubernatorial primary:

4 When Loeffler started the campaign, his name recognition was well under 10% ... Part of the problem, according to one Republican consultant, is his rather plodding nature. 'The guy is in desperate need of a charisma bypass,'

said the consultant. 'But if he gets into the runoff against Clements, he might get some charisma in a hurry.'

Anonymous consultant. In *The Washington Post* (2 May 1986).

5 It is difficult to describe Norwegian charisma precisely but it is somewhere between a Presbyterian minister and a tree.

Johnny Carson, American entertainer (1925–). Unverified remark when Senator Walter Mondale (of Norwegian stock) challenged President Reagan in his bid for re-election (1984).

Charity

Encountering a group from the Salvation Army and dropping a $50 dollar bill into one of their tambourines:

6 Don't bother to thank me. I know what a perfectly ghastly season it's been for you Spanish dancers.

Tallulah Bankhead, American actress (1903–68). Recounted in Dorothy Herrmann, *With Malice Towards All* (1980).

Chastity

7 Chastity: the most unnatural of the sexual perversions.

Aldous Huxley, English novelist and writer (1894–1963). *Eyeless in Gaza* (1936).

Chatter

8 Every time a sheep bleats it misses a nibble.

Anonymous saying. Quoted on BBC Radio *Quote ... Unquote* (25 August 1984). Sometimes rendered as 'Every time a sheep ba's it loses a bite.' H. L. Mencken's *Dictionary of Quotations* (1942) has 'Every time the sheep bleats it loses a mouthful' as an English proverb 'apparently borrowed from the Italian and familiar since the 17th century'. In this form it certainly appears in Thomas Fuller's *Gnomologia* (1732).

9 When the eagles are silent, the parrots begin to jabber.

Winston S. Churchill (later Sir Winston), British Conservative Prime Minister and writer (1874–1965). A sort of proverb, possibly original to Churchill. Quoted in Sykes & Sproat, *The Wit of Sir Winston* (1965).

Chauvinism

To Adam Smith who was boasting about the charms of Glasgow:

1 Pray, Sir, have you ever seen Brentford?

Samuel Johnson, English writer and lexicographer (1709–84). In James Boswell, *Life of Johnson* (1791) – for 1783.

2 She said that all the sights in Rome were called after London cinemas.

Nancy Mitford, English author (1904–73). *Pigeon Pie* (1940). Compare the caption to a cartoon by Bert Thomas in *Punch* (12 January 1921): 'The Profiteer's Lady (in Rome): "Wot *was* the Coliseum, 'Enry? A cinema?"'

Cheerfulness

3 It's being so cheerful as keeps me going.

Joan Harben, English actress (1909–53) as the character Mona Lott, a gloomy laundrywoman with a dreary, flat voice, in *ITMA*, the BBC's immensely popular radio comedy show (1939–49). When told to 'keep her pecker up' by the star of the show, Tommy Handley, she would reply, 'I always do, sir, it's being so cheerful as keeps me going.' Her family was always running into bad luck, so she had plenty upon which to exercise her cheerfulness. Scripts for the show were by Ted Kavanagh and Handley himself. The catchphrase had earlier appeared in a *Punch* cartoon during the First World War (27 September 1916): 'Wot a life. No rest, no beer, no nuffin. It's only us keeping so cheerful as pulls us through.'

4 I have tried too in my time to be a philosopher; but I don't know, cheerfulness was always breaking in.

Oliver Edwards, English lawyer (1711–91). Quoted in James Boswell, *Life of Samuel Johnson* (1791) – for 17 April 1778.

5 I went out to Charing Cross, to see Major-General Harrison hanged, drawn and quartered; which was done there, he looking as cheerful as any man could do in that condition.

Samuel Pepys, English civil servant and diarist (1633–1703). Diary entry for 13 October 1660. Thomas Harrison was one of the regicides. Pepys reflects that not only had he seen King Charles I beheaded but now he had seen 'the first blood shed in revenge for the blood of the King'.

Cheese

6 Milk is rendered immortal in cheese.

Enoch Powell, English Conservative then Ulster Unionist politician (1912–98). In a broadcast talk in 1967, I quoted Powell as having said this but have no idea where I got it from. If, indeed, Powell did say it, he had been anticipated by Clifton Fadiman (1904–) in *Any Number Can Play* (1957), where he wrote of: 'Cheese, milk's leap toward immortality.'

Cheques

7 We have come to an arrangement with our bankers. They have agreed not to sell drink. We, on our part, have agreed not to cash cheques.

Anonymous. Quoted in Flann O'Brien's column for the *Irish Times* (early 1940s).

Cherubims and Seraphims

On the difference between a cherubim and a seraphim:

8 I have always believed that a cherubim was a seraphim beneath the age of consent.

Anonymous (professor). Quoted by Sir Huw Wheldon on BBC Radio *Quote ... Unquote* (1 December 1981).

Children

Approached by a woman who thought herself to be a fine physical specimen and who suggested that they combine to make a baby, saying: 'You have the greatest brain in the world and I have the most beautiful body; so we ought to produce the most perfect child.' His reply:

9 What if the child inherits my beauty and your brains?

Bernard Shaw, Irish playwright and critic (1856–1950). Alas, this was not said to Isadora Duncan or any of the other women who have been woven into the tale. Hesketh Pearson in *Bernard Shaw* (1942) said the request came from 'a woman in Zurich', though no trace of a letter containing it has ever been found.

10 I love children – especially when they cry, for then someone takes them away.

Nancy Mitford, English author (1904–73). Attributed on BBC Radio *Quote ... Unquote* (26 April 1978), but unverified.

Of W. C. Fields:

1 Any man who hates children and dogs can't be all bad.

Leo Rosten, American writer (1908–97). Or 'Anybody who hates dogs and babies can't be all bad.' Often ascribed to Fields himself (as, for example, by *Radio Times*, 12 August 1965), it was, in fact, said about Fields by Rosten at a Masquer's Club dinner (16 February 1939).

When asked whether he liked children:

2 Boiled or fried?

W. C. Fields, American comedian (1879–1946). Quoted on BBC Radio *Quote ... Unquote* (22 June 1977), but unverified. Perhaps based on *Fields for President* (ed. Michael M. Taylor, 1971), in which the answer to the question whether he liked children is, 'I do if they're properly cooked.' Compare Charles Lamb's response to a woman who asked, 'Mr Lamb, how do you like babies?' 'B-b-boiled, ma'am.' Quoted in Frank Muir, *The Oxford Book of Humorous Prose* (1992).

China

3 The Great Wall, I've been told, is the only man-made structure on earth that is visible from the moon. For the life of me I cannot see why anyone would go to the moon to look at it, when, with almost the same difficulty, it can be viewed in China.

John Kenneth Galbraith, Canadian-born economist (1908–). In *The Sunday Times Magazine* (23 October 1977) – a prime example of Galbraith's laconic style. At the time, China had not opened itself up to tourism. The idea of 'the Wall of China' being 'the only work of man visible from the moon' was current by August 1939 when it was mentioned in the *Fortnightly Review*.

Chivalry

4 Definition of chivalry: 'going about releasing beautiful maidens from other men's castles, and taking them to your own castle.'

Henry W. Nevinson, English journalist and essayist (1856–1941). Quoted in The *Treasury*

of Humorous Quotations, ed. Evan Esar & Nicolas Bentley (1951).

Choice

Pointing at stamp in middle of sheet, at Post Office:

5 I'll have that one, please.

Sir Herbert Beerbohm Tree, English actor-manager (1853–1917). Quoted in Hesketh Pearson, *Beerbohm Tree* (1956).

6 More than any other time in history, mankind faces a crossroads. One path leads to despair and utter hopelessness. The other to total extinction. Let us pray we have the wisdom to choose correctly.

Woody Allen, American film actor, writer and director (1937–). *Side Effects* (1980).

When asked by a waiter what she would like to order, another woman (Sally) having just faked an orgasm in the middle of a crowded restaurant:

7 I'll have what she's having.

Estelle Reiner as Woman in Restaurant. Film, *When Harry Met Sally* (US, 1989). Written by Nora Ephron.

Christianity

To Frank Harris who had claimed that Christianity and journalism were the two main curses of civilization:

8 Christianity, yes, but why journalism?

Arthur Balfour (later 1st Earl of Balfour), British Conservative Prime Minister (1848–1930). Quoted in Margot Asquith, *The Autobiography of Margot Asquith*, Chap. 10 (1920–22).

In a debate on the Middle East question, a US delegate to the United Nations exhorted warring Jews and Arabs to:

9 Sit down and settle their differences like Christians.

Warren Austin, American diplomat (1877–1962). Quoted in Fadiman & Van Doren, *The American Treasury* (1955).

10 Christianity has not been tried and found wanting; it has been found difficult and not tried.

G. K. Chesterton, English poet, novelist and critic (1874–1936). Quoted in *The Treasury of Humorous Quotations*, ed. Evan Esar & Nicolas Bentley (1951).

Christmas

1 I have often thought, says Sir Roger, it happens very well that Christmas should fall out in the Middle of Winter.

Joseph Addison, English essayist and politician (1672–1719). In *The Spectator*, No. 269 (8 January 1712).

2 The little Strangs say the 'good words,' as they call them, before going to bed, aloud and at their father's knee, or rather in the pit of his stomach. One of them was lately heard to say 'Forgive us our Christmasses, as we forgive them that Christmas against us.'

Samuel Butler, English author (1835–1902). *Notebooks* (*c*.1890).

Church

On the Church of England:

3 I see it as an elderly lady, who mutters away to herself in a corner, ignored most of the time.

George Carey, English Archbishop of Canterbury (1935–). Interview, *Readers Digest* (UK edn, March 1991).

4 The hippopotamus's day
Is passed in sleep; at night he hunts;
God works in a mysterious way –
The Church can feed and sleep at once.

T. S. Eliot, American-born English poet, playwright and critic (1888–1965). 'The Hippopotamus' (1920).

Church-going

5 I am not a pillar of the church but a buttress – I support it from the outside.

Winston S. Churchill (later Sir Winston), British Conservative Prime Minister and writer (1874–1965). Recalled by Montague Browne in a speech to the International Churchill Society, London (25 September 1985). Note, however, that it was said of John Scott, Lord Eldon (1751–1838): 'He may be one of its [the Church's] buttresses, but certainly not one of its pillars, for he is never found within it'

(H. Twiss, *Public and Private Life of Eldon*, 1844). *The Oxford Dictionary of Quotations* (1992) adds that this remark was later attributed to Lord Melbourne.

6 As for the British churchman, he goes to church as he goes to the bathroom, with the minimum of fuss and no explanation if he can help it.

Ronald Blythe, English writer (1922–). *The Age of Illusion* (1963).

7 It is my aim to get the violence off the streets and into the churches where it belongs.

Jonathan Miller, English entertainer, writer and director (1934–). Spoken as a trendy vicar in 'Man Bites God', *Beyond the Fringe* (1961) – script credited to whole cast. Compare 'Get Bingo out of the supermarkets and into the churches where it really belongs' – performed on CBS TV *Rowan and Martin's Laugh-In* and included on the record album *Laugh-In '69* (1969).

Churchill, Randolph
English journalist and politician (1911–68)

8 Dear Randolph, utterly unspoiled by failure.

Noël Coward (later Sir Noël), English entertainer and writer (1899–1973). Attributed by Leslie Thomas on BBC Radio *Quote ... Unquote* (31 May 1978). Dick Richards, *The Wit of Noël Coward* (1968), has the remark, rather, aimed at an unnamed playwright.

Churchill, Winston S. (later Sir Winston)
British Conservative Prime Minister and writer (1874–1965)

9 Winston has devoted the best years of his life to preparing his impromptu speeches.

F. E. Smith (1st Earl of Birkenhead), English politician and lawyer (1872–1930). Quoted in the book *Quote ... Unquote* (1978), but otherwise unverified.

10 He would make a drum out of the skin of his mother the louder to sing his own praises.

David Lloyd George (1st Earl Lloyd George of Dwyfor), British Liberal Prime Minister (1863–1945). Quoted by Peter Kellner on BBC Radio *Quote ... Unquote* (15 August 1987).

Chutzpah

1 The classic definition of chutzpa is what the man had who killed his parents and then threw himself on the mercy of the court on the grounds that he was an orphan.

Leo Rosten, *The Joys of Yiddish* (1968).

Defending his taste for alcohol:

2 I'm so holy that when I touch wine, it turns into water.

Aga Khan III, Muslim leader (1877–1957). Quoted in John Colville, *Footprints in Time* (1976).

Civil servants

A minister making a speech in the House of Lords inadvertently read out an annotation which a civil servant had scrawled on his brief:

3 This is a rotten argument but it should be enough for their Lordships on a hot summer afternoon.

Anonymous. Quoted in Lord Home, *The Way the Wind Blows* (1976).

Civilization

On being asked why he was not fighting to defend civilization in the First World War:

4 Madam, I am the civilization they are fighting to defend.

Heathcote William Garrod, English academic (1878–1960). Attributed by Dacre Balsdon, *Oxford Then and Now* (1970).

When asked what he thought of modern civilization:

5 That would be a good idea.

Mahatma Gandhi, Indian politician (1869–1948). Quoted in E. F. Schumacher, *Good Work* (1979), where Schumacher describes seeing a newsreel film of Gandhi's visit to England in 1930. Disembarking at Southampton, Gandhi was swamped by journalists, one of whom put this question to him (sometimes reported as 'what do you think of *Western* civilization?') and got this reply.

Clarity

In the revival of his play Hay Fever *which Coward directed at the National Theatre in 1964, Edith Evans always said one line wrong. 'On a clear day you can see Marlow' was invariably changed by her to: 'On a very clear day ...' Coward would not let her get away with it. Said he:*

6 Edith, dear, the line is 'On a clear day you can see Marlow.' On a *very* clear day you can see Marlowe and Beaumont and Fletcher as well ...

Noël Coward (later Sir Noël), English entertainer and writer (1899–1973). The earliest showing of this story would appear to be in Dick Richards, *The Wit of Noël Coward* (1968).

Class

When asked by a radio interviewer whether she thought British class barriers had come down:

7 Of course they have, or I wouldn't be sitting here talking to someone like you.

Barbara Cartland (later Dame Barbara), English romantic novelist (1902–). Attributed by Jilly Cooper in *Class* (1979). The interviewer was Sandra Harris of the BBC Radio *Today* programme.

8 Like many of the Upper Class
He liked the Sound of Broken Glass.

Hilaire Belloc, French-born English poet and writer (1870–1953). 'About John who Lost a Fortune Throwing Stones', *New Cautionary Tales* (1930).

9 The stately homes of England
How beautiful they stand
To prove the upper classes
Have still the upper hand.

Noël Coward (later Sir Noël), English entertainer and writer (1899–1973). Song, 'The Stately Homes of England', *Operette*, Act 1 (1937).

10 He [Sir Alec Douglas-Home] is used to dealing with estate workers. I cannot see how anyone can say he is out of touch.

Caroline Douglas-Home, daughter of the English Prime Minister (1937–). Quoted in *Daily Herald* (21 October 1963).

Classics

1 '*Classic.*' A book which people praise and don't read.

Mark Twain, American writer (1835–1910). Epigraph to *Following the Equator: A Journey Around the World* (1897).

Cleopatra

2 How different – how very different from the home life of our own dear Queen!

Anonymous. Quoted by Irvin S. Cobb in *A Laugh a Day Keeps the Doctor Away . . .* (1921). One night Sarah Bernhardt (1844–1923) essayed the role of Cleopatra in Shakespeare's *Antony and Cleopatra* during a London season some time in the reign of Queen Victoria. In the scene where Cleopatra receives the news of Mark Antony's defeat at the battle of Actium, she stabbed the messenger who brought her the news, 'stormed, raved, frothed at the mouth, wrecked some of the scenery in her frenzy and finally, as the curtain fell, dropped in a shuddering convulsive heap.' As the applause died down, an American visitor overheard a middle-aged British matron saying the above to her friend in the next seat.

Clergymen

3 Don't you know, as the French say, there are three sexes – men, women, and clergymen.

Revd Sydney Smith, English clergyman, essayist and wit (1771–1845). Quoted in Lady Holland, *A Memoir of Sydney Smith* (1855).

4 What bishops like best in their clergy is a dropping-down-deadness of manner.

Revd Sydney Smith. 'First Letter to Archdeacon Singleton' (1837), *Works*, Vol. 2 (1859).

5 Would you, my dear young friends, like to be inside with the five wise virgins or outside, alone, and in the dark, with the five foolish ones?

Henry Montagu Butler, English academic (1833–1918). Quoted in Edward

Marsh/Christopher Hassall, *Ambrosia and Small Beer* (1964). A favourite story, to be taken with a pinch of salt, but if true, coming in the category of Sermons One Would Like To Have Heard Preached. Dr Butler, who was Headmaster of Harrow then, from 1886, Master of Trinity College, Cambridge, was preaching a sermon in the college chapel when he is supposed to have put this misguided rhetorical question.

6 Of late years an abundant shower of curates has fallen upon the North of England.

Charlotte Brontë, English novelist (1816–55). *Shirley*, Chap. 2 (1849).

Cleverness

Of Dr Jonathan Miller, the English polymath, in the mid-1970s, it was said:

7 He's too clever by three-quarters.

Anonymous. Quoted on BBC Radio *Quote . . . Unquote* (13 July 1977). I find this phrase used in my diary about Keith Kyle, the writer and broadcaster on 12 November 1971, so perhaps this expression was fairly widely used in the 1970s.

Clichés

On a long-winded memorandum by Anthony Eden:

8 As far as I can see, you have used every cliché except 'God is love' and 'Please adjust your dress before leaving'.

Winston S. Churchill (later Sir Winston), British Conservative Prime Minister and writer (1874–1965). This is quoted in Maurice Edelman, *The Mirror: A Political History* (1966) together with Churchill's comment: 'This offensive story is wholly devoid of foundation.' In 1941, Churchill took the unusual course of writing to Cecil King of the *Daily Mirror* about the matter. The columnist 'Cassandra' had used the story, though labelling it apocryphal and saying he had taken it from *Life* Magazine. *Reader's Digest* in August 1943 certainly carried this version by Allan A. Michie: 'Asked once to look over a draft of one of Anthony Eden's vague speeches on the post-war world, he sent it back to the Foreign Minister with this curt note: "I have read your speech and find that you have used every cliché known to the English language except 'Please adjust your dress before leaving'."'

On the cliché-ridden content of a speech by another politician (possibly Anthony Eden):

1 It was clitch after clitch after clitch.

Ernest Bevin, English Labour politician (1881–1951). Quoted in *The Penguin Dictionary of Modern Quotations* (1980).

Climate

2 What men call gallantry, and gods adultery,
Is much more common where the climate's sultry.

Lord Byron, English poet (1788–1824). *Don Juan*, Canto 1, St. 63 (1819–24).

Clocks

3 When a clock strikes thirteen, not only do you know it is wrong now, but you have a suspicion it has never been right before.

A. P. Herbert (later Sir Alan), English writer and politician (1890–1971). Quoted on BBC Radio *Quote ... Unquote* (1 June 1977). Unverified.

Clubs

4 Please accept my resignation. I don't care to belong to any club that will have me as a member.

Groucho Marx, American comedian (1895–1977). Quoted in Arthur Sheekman's introduction to *The Groucho Letters* (1967). Zeppo Marx recalled that this was about The Friars Club, a theatrical organization, for which his brother did not have much use. Hector Ace added that Groucho had some misgivings about the quality of the members – 'doubts verified a few years later when an infamous card-cheating scandal erupted there'. The actual letter unfortunately does not survive. In *Groucho and Me* (1959), the man himself supplied the version: 'PLEASE ACCEPT MY RESIGNATION. I DON'T WANT TO BELONG TO ANY CLUB THAT WILL ACCEPT ME AS A MEMBER.' Woody Allen in *Annie Hall* (1977) appears to suggest that the joke first appeared in Freud.

Clues

Crossword clue:

5 Listen carefully, or a sexual perversion (5,2,4,4).

Anonymous. In *The Financial Times, c.*1974. (Answer: Prick up your ears).

Cocaine

6 Cocaine is God's way of telling you you've got too much money.

Robin Williams, American comedian and actor (1951–) . Quoted in Leslie Halliwell, *Halliwell's Filmgoer's Companion* (1995). Attributed by 1986.

Cold

7 Better the chill blast of winter than the hot breath of a pursuing elephant.

Anonymous 'Chinese saying'. Quoted in *Livres Sans Nom*, five anonymous pamphlets (1929–33) by Geoffrey Madan (though not in all versions). As with most such sayings, authenticity is in doubt. In any case, might not Madan have invented it himself? The matter is discussed in *The Lyttelton Hart-Davis Letters*, Vol. 4 (1982).

8 Eskimos are God's frozen people.

Anonymous. Included in *Graffiti 3* (1981).

9 Many are cold, but few are frozen.

Anonymous. On the service sheet at Frank Muir's funeral on a wintry day in January 1998 was inscribed, 'Many are cold but few are frozen: F Muir.' I am sure this attribution is correct – although it does not appear to be the concluding line to one of his published *My Word* stories, as might be expected, and I have no idea when he produced the pun. Just a footnote, though: the line occurs in (the American) Howard Engel's thriller *Death on Location* (1983); it was available on a T-shirt printed in the US (1982); and also, it was listed under 'whimsy' in Reisner & Wechsler's *The Encyclopedia of Graffiti* (1974). So, probably, Muir was not the first to come up with the line.

Colonialism

10 Originally, the Africans had the land and the English had the Bible. Then the missionaries came to Africa and got the Africans to close their eyes and fold their

hands and pray. And when they opened their eyes, the English had the land and the Africans had the Bible.

Jomo Kenyatta, Kenyan President (*c.*1889–1978). This saying was attributed to Kenyatta on BBC Radio *Quote ... Unquote* (13 October 1984), but later *The Observer*, 'Sayings of the Week' (16 December 1984), had Desmond Tutu, Bishop of Johannesburg, saying it. A version relating to the American Indians had earlier been said by Chief Dan George (d.1982): 'When the white man came we had the land and they had the Bibles; now they have the land and we have the Bibles' – *Bloomsbury Dictionary of Quotations* (1987).

Columnists

1 Give someone half a page in a newspaper and they think they own the world.

Jeffrey Bernard, English journalist (1932–97). Quoted in *The Observer*, 'Sayings of the Week' (1 June 1986).

Comedians

2 The test of a real comedian is whether you laugh at him before he opens his mouth.

George Jean Nathan, American drama critic (1882–1958). In *The American Mercury* (September 1929).

Comedy

3 Comedy, like sodomy, is an unnatural act.

Marty Feldman, English comedian and writer (1933–83). In *The Times* (9 June 1969).

4 Any fool can play tragedy, but comedy, sir, is a damned serious business.

David Garrick, English actor (1717–79). Attributed, also in the form 'Comedy is a very serious thing', in conversation with the actor Jack Bannister. The date 1778 was applied to this by Richard Briers. Hence, *A Damned Serious Business*, title of the later memoirs (1990) of Sir Rex Harrison – who does not, however, give a source for the observation. Probably a more accurate rendering of this tale occurs in *Garrick and His Circle* (1906) by Mrs Clement Parsons, in which it is related that when Charles Bannister tired of tragic parts and begged to be allowed to do comedy,

Garrick told him: 'No, no! You may humbug the town some time longer as a tragedian, but comedy is a serious thing.'

On Freud's theory that a good joke will lead to great relief and elation:

5 The trouble with Freud is that he never played the Glasgow Empire Saturday night.

Ken Dodd, English comedian and singer (1927–). In the ATV programme *The Laughter Makers* (and so quoted in *The Times*, 7 August 1965). Dodd's remark has appeared in several versions since that date. For example, with the addition of 'after Rangers and Celtic had both lost' in *The Guardian* (30 April 1991).

Comfortable

6 The duty of a newspaper is to comfort the afflicted and afflict the comfortable.

Anonymous. Quoted in *H. L. Mencken's Dictionary of Quotations* (1942). In the film *Inherit the Wind* (1960), Gene Kelly gets to say to Fredric March: 'Mr Brady, it's the duty of a newspaper to comfort the afflicted and to flick the comfortable.' To Michael Ramsey, the former Archbishop of Canterbury (1904–88), has been attributed the version: 'The duty of the church is to comfort the disturbed and to disturb the comfortable.' Clare Booth Luce introduced Eleanor Roosevelt at a 1950 dinner, saying: 'No woman has ever so comforted the distressed – or so distressed the comfortable.'

Commandments

7 The eleventh commandment: mind your own business.

Anonymous. Quoted in *H. L. Mencken's Dictionary of Quotations* (1942) where the remark is said to be 'borrowed from Cervantes, Don Quixote, 1605'. Indeed, it is to be found there (in Pt I, Bk 3, Chap. 8), although it is not described as the 'eleventh commandment'. But Mencken also records, 'The Eleventh Commandment: Thou shalt not be found out – George Whyte-Melville, *Holmby House*, 1860', and this is certainly the more usual meaning. The *OED2* adds from the *Pall Mall Gazette* (10 September 1884): 'The new and great commandment that nothing succeeds like success'; and from *Paston Carew* (1886) by Mrs Lynn Lynton that the eleventh commandment was 'do not tell tales out of school'.

Unverified is Charles Kingsley's 1850 observation that it is, 'Buy cheap, sell dear'. William Safire, *Safire's Political Dictionary* (1978), reports that 'Thou Shalt Not Speak Ill of Fellow Republicans' was the eleventh commandment advanced by Dr Gaylord E. Parkinson, California State Republican Chairman, in the run-up to the 1966 governorship elections. The 1981 re-make of the film *The Postman Always Rings Twice* was promoted with the slogan: 'If there was an 11th Commandment, they would have broken that too.'

Comment

1 I don't believe in all that 'no comment' business. I always have a comment.

Martha Mitchell, American wife of John Mitchell, President Nixon's Attorney-General (1918–76). Quoted in Barbara Rowes, *The Book of Quotes* (1979).

Committees

2 What is a committee? A group of the unwilling, picked from the unfit, to do the unnecessary.

Richard Harkness (untraced). Quoted in *The New York Herald Tribune* (15 June 1960). Or Carl C. Byers (untraced).

3 The number one book of the ages was written by a committee, and it was called the Bible.

Louis B. Mayer, American film producer (1885–1957). Quoted in *The Oxford Dictionary of Literary Quotations*, ed. Peter Kemp (1997).

4 A committee is a cul de sac down which ideas are lured and then quietly strangled.

Sir Barnett Cocks, English parliamentary official (1907–89). Quoted in the *New Scientist* (8 November 1973). Also attributed to John A. Lincoln in Herbert V. Prochnow, Snr & Jnr, *A Treasury of Humorous Quotations* (1969).

5 If Moses had been a committee, the Israelites would still be in Egypt.

J. B. Hughes (untraced). Quoted in Herbert V. Prochnow, Snr & Jnr, *A Treasury of Humorous Quotations* (1969). Or, '... never would have got across the Red Sea' in a remark attributed in 1965 to General Booth, founder of the Salvation Army.

6 A committee should consist of three men, two of whom are absent.

Sir Herbert Beerbohm Tree, English actor-manager (1853–1917). Quoted in Hesketh Pearson, *Beerbohm Tree* (1956). Also attributed to Lord Mancroft (1914–87) in some anthologies. *The Treasury of Humorous Quotations*, ed. Evan Esar & Nicolas Bentley (1951), has E.V. Lucas (1868–1938) saying, 'The best committee is a committee of two when one is absent.'

7 Nothing is ever accomplished by a committee unless it consists of three members, one of whom happens to be sick and the other absent.

Hendrik Van Loon, Dutch-born American writer (1882–1944). *America* (1927).

8 A camel is a horse designed by a committee.

Anonymous. Quoted in American *Vogue* (1958) – and bearing an interesting resemblance to 'A donkey is a horse translated into Dutch' – Georg Christoph Lichtenberg, German scientist and drama critic (1742–99), *Aphorisms*.

9 A committee is an animal with four back legs.

John Le Carré, English novelist (1931–). *Tinker, Tailor, Soldier, Spy* (1974).

10 A committee is a group of men who, individually, can do nothing, but collectively can meet and decide that nothing can be done.

Anonymous. Quoted in Herbert V. Prochnow, Snr & Jnr, *A Treasury of Humorous Quotations* (1969). Compare: 'A conference is a gathering of important people who singly can do nothing, but together can decide that nothing can be done' – Fred Allen, American comedian (1894–1956). Quoted in *The Treasury of Humorous Quotations*, ed. Evan Esar & Nicolas Bentley (1951).

Common people

11 The Lord prefers common-looking people. That is why he makes so many of them.

Abraham Lincoln, American Republican President (1809–65). There is no evidence that Lincoln said this. James Morgan in a book called *Our Presidents* (1928) was the first to put it in his mouth.

Company

1 He that lies down with dogs shall rise up with fleas.

Benjamin Franklin, American politician and scientist (1706–90). *Poor Richard's Almanack* (July 1733) – a work in which Franklin often revised already existing sayings.

Comparisons

Of Reykjavik:

2 About as exciting as Aberdeen on a Sunday night.

Anonymous. Quoted in *A Year of Stings and Squelches* (1985).

Of Liberal leader David Steel's rap record 'I Feel Liberal':

3 If he's going to take up pop singing, I'm going to take up belly dancing.

(Sir) Cyril Smith, Liberal politician (1928–). Quoted in *The Guardian* (24 September 1982).

On a highly idiosyncratic TV commentator:

4 Eddie Waring has done for Rugby League what Cyril Smith has done for hang-gliding.

Reggie Bowden (untraced). Quoted in *A Year of Stings and Squelches* (1985).

5 Then Petra flashed by in a wink.
It looked like Eaton Square – but pink.

Sir Charles Johnston, English diplomat, poet and translator (1912–86). 'Air Travel in Arabia', *Poems and Journeys* (1979).

Compensation

On dealing with adverse criticism:

6 I cried all the way to the bank.

Liberace, American entertainer (1919–87). *Autobiography* (1973): 'I think the people around me are more apt to become elated about good reviews (or depressed by bad ones) than I am. If they're good I just tell them, "Don't let success go to your head." When the reviews are bad I tell my staff that they can join me as I cry all the way to the bank.' Liberace was using the expression by 1954. In Alfred Hitchcock's film *North by Northwest* (US, 1959), Cary Grant gets to say: '... while we cry about it all the way to the bank'.

Compliments

7 Age shall not wither her, nor iron bars a cage.

Anonymous. Quoted in letter from Kenneth Williams to John Hussey (2 October 1971) in *The Kenneth Williams Letters* (1994). It has been ascribed to the BBC Radio show *Much Binding in the Marsh* (1947–53).

Spoken to a father by someone looking at his child:

8 What a very pretty woman your wife must be.

Anonymous. Caption to cartoon, *Punch*, Vol. 127 (3 August 1904).

Referring to his wife:

9 I am leaving tonight; Hannah and the rest of the heavy baggage will follow later.

Archibald Philip Primrose, 5th Earl of Rosebery, English Liberal Prime Minister (1847–1929). Quoted in Robert Rhodes James, *Rosebery* (1963) – where it is described as one of Rosebery's 'alleged mots'.

Composure

10 As someone pointed out recently, if you can keep your head when all about your are losing theirs, it's just possible you haven't grasped the situation.

Jean Kerr, American writer (1923–). *Please Don't Eat the Daisies*, Introduction (1958).

Computers

11 To err is human but to really foul things up requires a computer.

Anonymous. Quoted in *Farmers' Almanac* for 1978 and on Granada TV *Cabbages and Kings* (11 August 1979).

Concentration

12 Depend upon it, Sir, when a man knows he is to be hanged in a fortnight, it concentrates his mind wonderfully.

Samuel Johnson, English writer and lexicographer (1709–84). In James Boswell, *Life of Johnson* (1791) – for 19 September 1777.

Conscience

1 Conscience: the inner voice which warns us that somebody may be looking.

H. L. Mencken, American journalist and linguist (1880–1956). *A Little Book in C Major* (1916).

2 An uneasy conscience is a hair in the mouth.

Mark Twain, American writer (1835–1910). *Mark Twain's Notebook*, ed. A. B. Paine (1935).

Conservatives

3 A conservative is a man who will not look at the new moon, out of respect for that ancient institution, the old one.

Douglas Jerrold, English humorist and editor (1803–57). Quoted in *The Treasury of Humorous Quotations*, ed. Evan Esar & Nicolas Bentley (1951).

Consumers

4 The consumer isn't a moron; she is your wife.

David Ogilvy, English-born advertising executive (1911–). *Confessions of an Advertising Man* (1963).

Contraception

5 A fast word about oral contraception. I asked a girl to go to bed with me and she said 'no'.

Woody Allen, American film actor, writer and director (1937–). Monologue on record album *Woody Allen Volume Two* (1965).

6 Contraceptives should be used on every conceivable occasion.

Spike Milligan, Irish entertainer and writer (1918–). He spoke the line in BBC Radio's *The Last Goon Show of All* (1972), for which he wrote the script.

7 The best contraceptive is a glass of cold water: not before or after, but instead.

Anonymous Pakistani delegate at the International Planned Parenthood Federation Conference. Quoted in *The Penguin Dictionary of Modern Quotations* (1971).

Contracts

8 God is love – but get it in writing.

Gypsy Rose Lee, American striptease entertainer (1913–1970). Quoted in *The Guardian* (24 June 1975).

9 You can't fool me. There ain't no Sanity Clause!

Chico Marx, American comedian (1886–1961). Film, *A Night at the Opera* (US, 1935). As Fiorello, Chico says he is the manager of a tenor whom Groucho (Otis B. Driftwood) would like to sing with the New York Opera Company and they go through the contract in this fashion, Chico replying thus when Groucho says: 'If any of the parties participating in this contract is shown not to be in their right mind, the entire agreement is automatically nullified. That's what they call a sanity clause.'

Convenience

On his preference for flying Concorde:

10 I cannot get in and out of aircraft toilets but on three and a half hour flights I can hold out.

Luciano Pavarotti, Italian tenor (1935–). Quoted in *The Observer*, 'Sayings of the Week' (2 August 1987).

Conversation

11 'What ho!' I said.
'What ho!' said Motty.
'What ho! What ho!'
'What ho! What ho! What ho!'
    After that it seemed rather difficult to go on with the conversation.

P. G. Wodehouse (later Sir Pelham), English-born novelist and lyricist (1881–1975). 'Jeeves and the Unbidden Guest', *Carry On, Jeeves!* (1925).

12 MR BINKS: One of my ancestors fell at Waterloo.
LADY CLARE: Ah? Which platform?'

F. H. Townsend, English cartoonist. Caption to cartoon, *Punch*, Vol. 129 (1 November 1905). To this joke is often added the further response, 'Ha, ha! As if it mattered which platform!' Shamelessly misattributed over the years. *The Best of Myles* reprints as an overheard this from Flann O'Brien's Dublin newspaper column [early 1940s]: 'D'you know that my great-grandfather was killed at Waterloo ...

Which platform?' A. L. Rowse writes of Lord David Cecil in *Friends and Contemporaries* (1989): 'Anything for a laugh – simplest of jokes. I think of him now coming into my room [at Christ Church in the early 1920s], giggling and sputtering with fun. Someone had said, "My grandfather was killed at Waterloo" "I'm so sorry – which platform?"'

1 Although there exist many thousand subjects for elegant conversation, there are persons who cannot meet a cripple without talking about feet.

Ernest Bramah, English writer (1868–1942). *The Wallet of Kai Lung* (1900). Compare: 'I cried because I had no shoes, until I met a man who had no feet' – sometimes described as a Zen saying.

2 Yes, 'e come up to me an' I sez, 'Oh!' – an' 'e sez, 'Oh, it's "Oh," is it?' – an' I sez 'yes, it is "Oh"!'

Frank Reynolds, English cartoonist. Caption to cartoon, *Punch* (30 March 1921).

To a lady at dinner who wanted action against Russia and asked him what was he waiting for:

3 Potatoes at the moment, Madam.

Benjamin Disraeli (later 1st Earl of Beacons-field), British Conservative Prime Minister and writer (1804–81). Quoted in Wilfrid Meynell, *The Man Disraeli* (1927 edn).

A 'blocking phrase' to say when putting down experts while in conversation with them:

4 'Yes, but not in the South', with slight adjustments will do for any argu-ment about any place, if not about any person.

Stephen Potter, English humorist (1900–69). *Lifemanship* (1950). In a footnote, he remarks: 'I am required to state that World Copyright of this phrase is owned by its brilliant inventor, Mr Pound' – though which 'Pound' he does not reveal. Indeed, the blocking move was known before this. Richard Usborne wrote of it in a piece called 'Not in the South' included in *The Pick of 'Punch'* (1941). He introduced a character called Eustace who had found a formula 'for appearing to be a European, and world, pundit. It was a formula that let me off the boredom of finding out facts and retaining knowledge.' It was to remark, 'Not in the South.'

Conversational gambits

At the end of the First World War, General Nivelle, hero of Verdun, made a tour of the United States. When he reached Los Angeles, a big public reception was held so that he could meet members of the movie colony. Among those invited were Charles Chaplin and Will Rogers. Chaplin was oddly nervous about meeting this great war hero and confided in Rogers that he had absolutely no idea how he would start up a conversation. Advised Rogers:

5 Well, you might ask him if he was in the war, and which side he was on ...

Will Rogers, American humorist (1879–1935). Quoted in Irvin S. Cobb, *A Laugh a Day Keeps the Doctor Away* (1921). This turns up later in the caption to a *Punch* cartoon (4 July 1934): (Two bored people) 'My grandfather fought in the Zulu War.' 'On which side?'

During an audience with the Pope:

6 I expect you know my friend, Evelyn Waugh, who, like you, your holiness, is a Roman Catholic.

Randolph Churchill, English journalist and politician (1911–68). Quoted in *The Penguin Dictionary of Modern Quotations* (1971).

7 How's the old complaint?

Benjamin Disraeli (later 1st Earl of Beacons-field), British Conservative Prime Minister and writer (1804–81). Unverified.

On being told that the person sitting next to him at a dinner party was 'writing a book':

8 Neither am I.

Peter Cook, English humorist (1937–95). Quoted by Richard Ingrams on BBC Radio *Quote ... Unquote* (25 August 1984), though Cook declined to claim it as original.

Cooks

9 The cook was a good cook, as cooks go; and as cooks go she went.

'Saki' (H. H. Munro), English writer (1870–1916). 'Reginald on Besetting Sins', *Reginald* (1904).

Cooking

Of Ian Fleming's hospitality:

10 The food was so abominable that I used

to cross myself before taking a mouthful ... I used to say, 'Ian, it tastes like armpits.'

Noël Coward (later Sir Noël), English entertainer and writer (1899–1973). Quoted in John Pearson, *The Life of Ian Fleming* (1966).

Of a hostess:

1 She did not so much cook as assassinate food.

Storm Jameson, English novelist (1891–1986). Quoted in *The Penguin Dictionary of Modern Quotations* (1980 edn).

2 'Turbot, Sir,' said the waiter, placing before me two fishbones, two eyeballs, and a bit of black mackintosh.

Thomas Earle Welby, English writer (1881–1933). 'Birmingham or Crewe?', *The Dinner Knell* (1932).

3 Housewarming at Zola's. Very tasty dinner, including some grouse whose scented flesh Daudet compared to an old courtesan's flesh marinated in a bidet.

Edmond de Goncourt, French novelist (1822–96). *Journal*. Quoted in *The 'Quote ... Unquote' Book of Love, Death and the Universe* (1980).

4 I thought my mother was a bad cook but at least her gravy used to move about a bit.

Tony Hancock, English comedian (1924–68). 'A Sunday Afternoon at Home', BBC Radio *Hancock's Half-Hour* (22 April 1958). Script by Alan Simpson and Ray Galton.

Coolidge, Calvin
American Republican President (1872–1933)

5 Looked as if he had been weaned on a pickle.

Alice Roosevelt Longworth, American political hostess (1884–1980). She admitted hearing this 'at my dentist's office. The last patient had said it to him and I just seized on it. I didn't originate it – but didn't it describe him exactly?' (*The New York Times*, 25 February 1980). It first appeared as an 'anonymous remark' quoted in Longworth's *Crowded Hours* (1933).

6 He laughed until you could hear a pin drop.

Ring Lardner, American screenwriter (1915–). Quoted in *Wit's End*, ed. Robert E. Drennan (1973).

7 He opened his mouth and a moth flew out.

Anonymous. Quoted on BBC Radio *Quote ... Unquote* (10 August 1985).

8 Here, indeed, was his one really notable talent. He slept more than any other President, whether by day or by night ... Nero fiddled, but Coolidge only snored ... He had no ideas, and he was not a nuisance.

H. L. Mencken, American journalist and linguist (1880–1956). In *The American Mercury* (April 1933).

When told Coolidge had died:

9 How can they tell?

Dorothy Parker, American writer (1893–1967). Quoted in Bennett Cerf, *Try and Stop Me* (1944). As 'How do they know?', it appears in Malcolm Cowley, *Writers at Work*, Series 1 (1958). In that form it is also attributed to Wilson Mizner (Alva Johnston, *The Legendary Mizners*, 1953).

Cormorants

10 The common cormorant or shag
Lays eggs inside a paper bag
The reason you will see no doubt
It is to keep the lightning out.

Christopher Isherwood, English-born American writer (1904–86). 'The Common Cormorant' (*c.*1925).

Cosmetics

11 Most women are not so young as they are painted.

Sir Max Beerbohm, English writer and caricaturist (1872–1956). In *The Yellow Book* (1894).

Coughing

12 I tried to say more, but the Cough had come upon me, as it does these days. It starts as the smallest tickle in the throat and can build, though I say so

myself as shouldn't, into a not unimpressive display. Something between a vomiting donkey and an explosion at a custard factory.

Stephen Fry, English novelist and actor (1957–). *The Hippopotamus*, Chap. 1 (1995).

Brendel once stunned an expectorating concert audience at a pianissimo point by announcing:

1 I can hear you, but you can't hear me.

Alfred Brendel, Austrian pianist (1931–). Quoted in *The Observer* (20 May 1991). By saying this he ensured absolute silence for the remainder of his recital.

Countryside

2 I have no relish for the country; it is a kind of healthy grave.

Revd Sydney Smith, English clergyman, essayist and wit (1771–1845). Letter to Miss G. Harcourt (1838).

3 My living in Yorkshire was so far out of the way that it was actually twelve miles from a lemon.

Revd Sydney Smith. Quoted in Saba, Lady Holland, *Memoir* (1855).

4 Sylvia ... was accustomed to nothing much more sylvan than 'leafy Kensington'. She looked on the country as something excellent and wholesome in its way, which was apt to become troublesome if you encouraged it overmuch.

'Saki' (H. H. Munro), English writer (1870–1916). *The Chronicles of Clovis* (1911).

Courtesy

Replying to an actress, not noted for her good looks, who had said to him, 'Mr Wilde, you are looking at the ugliest woman in Paris':

5 In the world, madam.

Oscar Wilde, Irish playwright, poet and wit (1854–1900). Quoted on BBC Radio *Quote ... Unquote* (5 April 1978) and in Richard Ellman, *Oscar Wilde*, Chap. 13 (1987).

In reply to a man who said to him, 'Mr Wilde, I passed by your house earlier today':

6 Thank you so much.

Oscar Wilde. Quoted on BBC Radio *Quote ... Unquote* (1 January 1979).

When going through a swing-door together, Clare Booth Luce had used the customary phrase 'Age before beauty'. Came this response:

7 Pearls before swine.

Dorothy Parker, American writer (1893–1967). Quoted in John Keats, *You Might as Well Live* (1970). Mrs Luce described this account as completely apocryphal in answer to a question from Keats.

Courtship

8 Courtship to marriage, as a very witty prologue to a very dull play.

William Congreve, English playwright (1670–1729). *The Old Bachelor* (1693).

9 Have the florist send some roses to Mrs Upjohn and write 'Emily I love you' on the back of the bill.

Groucho Marx, American comedian (1895–1977). Film, *A Day At the Races* (US, 1937). Script by Robert Pirosh, George Seaton and George Oppenheimer.

Coward, Noël (later Sir Noël)
English entertainer and writer (1899–1973)

10 Forty years ago he was Slightly in Peter Pan, and you might say that he has been wholly in Peter Pan ever since.

Kenneth Tynan, English critic (1927–80). Article on Coward (1953), collected in *Curtains* (1961). He went on: 'Even the youngest of us will know, in fifty years' time, exactly what we mean by "a very Noël Coward sort of person".'

Cowardice

11 Coward: one who in a perilous emergency thinks with his legs.

Ambrose Bierce, American journalist (1842–?1914). Quoted in *The Treasury of Humorous Quotations*, ed. Evan Esar & Nicolas Bentley (1951).

Cremation

1 We hold these truths to be self-evident:
All men could be cremated equal.

Vern Partlow (untraced). Quoted in Laurence
J. Peter, *Quotations for Our Time* (1977).
Ascribed to Goodman Ace in *The New
Yorker* (1977).

Cricket

2 Personally, I have always looked on
cricket as organized loafing.

William Temple, English theologian and
Archbishop (1881–1944). Remark to
parents when headmaster of Repton School.
Quoted in *The Penguin Dictionary of Modern
Quotations* (1971).

3 Cricket – a game which the English, not
being a spiritual people, have invented
in order to give themselves a conception
of eternity.

Lord Mancroft, English writer (1914–87).
Bees in Some Bonnets (1979).

A cricket enthusiast on baseball:

4 I don't think I can be expected to
take seriously any game which takes
less than three days to reach its
conclusion.

(Sir) Tom Stoppard, English playwright
(1937–). In *The Guardian* (24 December
1984).

Cripps, Sir Stafford
**English Labour politician and economist
(1889–1952)**

5 He has a brilliant mind until he makes
it up.

Margot Asquith (later Countess of Oxford and
Asquith) (1864–1945). *The Autobiography of
Margot Asquith* (1936 edn).

6 There, but for the grace of God,
goes God.

Winston S. Churchill (later Sir Winston),
British Conservative Prime Minister and writer
(1874–1965). Quoted in Willans & Roetter,
The Wit of Winston Churchill (1954) but had
already been noted by Geoffrey Madan who
died in July 1947 (see his *Notebooks*, published
in 1981).

Of Cripps at a dinner:

7 Who will relieve me of this Wuthering
Height?

Winston Churchill. Quoted in Leslie Frewin,
Immortal Jester (1973).

Critics and Criticism

8 Critics are like eunuchs in a harem:
they know how it's done, they've seen it
done every day, but they're unable to
do it themselves.

Brendan Behan, Irish playwright (1923–64).
Quoted in Laurence J. Peter, *Quotations
for Our Time* (1977).

9 A critic is a man who knows the way
but can't drive the car.

Kenneth Tynan, English critic (1927–80).
In *The New York Times Magazine*
(9 January 1966).

*In a letter (1906) to the music critic
Rudolph Louis:*

10 I am sitting in the smallest room of
my house. I have your review before me.
In a moment it will be behind me.

Max Reger, German composer (1873–1916).
Quoted in N. Slonimsky, *Lexicon of Musical
Invective* (1953), having been translated
from the German.

11 Unless the bastards have the courage
to give you unqualified praise, I say
ignore them.

John Steinbeck, American writer (1902–68).
Quoted in J. K. Galbraith, *A Life in Our
Times* (1981).

12 I can take any amount of criticism, so
long as it is unqualified praise.

Noël Coward (later Sir Noël), English
entertainer and writer (1899–1973). Quoted
in *The Sayings of Noel Coward*, ed. Philip
Hoare (1997).

13 You know who the critics are? – the men
who have failed in literature and art.

Benjamin Disraeli (later 1st Earl of Beaconsfield), British Conservative Prime Minister and
writer (1804–81). *Lothair*, Chap. 35 (1870).

14 Pay no attention to what the critics
say. No statue has ever been put up to
a critic.

Jean Sibelius, Finnish composer (1865–1957). Quoted in Bengt de Törne, *Sibelius: A Close-Up* (1937).

1 When I am abroad I always make a rule never to criticize or attack the Government of my country. I make up for lost time when I come home.

Winston S. Churchill (later Sir Winston), British Conservative Prime Minister and writer (1874–1965). Speech, House of Commons (18 April 1947).

To a would-be dramatist:

2 Dear Sir, I have read your play. Oh, my dear Sir. Yours faithfully ...

Sir Herbert Beerbohm Tree, English actor-manager (1853–1917). Quoted in *A Year of Stings and Squelches* (1985).

3 My native habitat is the theatre. I toil not, neither do I spin. I am a critic and a commentator. I am essential to the theatre – as ants to a picnic, as the boll weevil to a cotton field.

Joseph L. Mankiewicz, American film producer and writer (1909–93). Film, *All About Eve* (US, 1950). Spoken by George Sanders as the critic 'Addison de Witt'.

Book review:

4 People who like this sort of thing will find this the sort of thing they like.

Abraham Lincoln, American Republican President (1809–65). Quoted in G. W. E. Russell, *Collections and Recollections* (1898).

5 One of the most characteristic sounds of the English Sunday is the sound of Harold Hobson barking up the wrong tree.

Penelope Gilliatt, English writer and critic (1933–93). In *Encore* (November–December 1959). Hobson was for many years drama critic of *The Sunday Times*.

6 Asking a working writer what he thinks about critics is like asking a lamp-post how it feels about dogs.

Christopher Hampton, English playwright (1946–). In *The Sunday Times* Magazine (16 October 1977).

On Clive Barnes when drama critic of The New York Times*:*

7 He was given the CBE for services to the theatre – which seemed to me at the time like Goering being given the DSO for services to the RAF.

Alan Bennett, English playwright and actor (1934–). On BBC Radio *Today* (3 March 1977).

8 It is a pity that critics should show so little sympathy with writers, and curious when we consider that most of them tried to be writers themselves, once.

Sir Max Beerbohm, English writer and caricaturist (1872–1956). In *The Yellow Book*, Vol. 2 (1894–97), answering serious abuse poured upon his essay in Vol. 1. Said to contain 'the second most effective comma I know in literature'.

9 So, naturalists, observe a flea
Hath smaller fleas that on him prey;
And these have smaller fleas to bite 'em,
And so proceed ad infinitum.
Thus every poet, in his kind,
Is bit by him that comes behind .

Jonathan Swift, Anglo-Irish writer and clergyman (1667–1745). 'On Poetry: A Rhapsody' (1733).

Crowds

10 Every crowd has a silver lining.

P. T. Barnum, American showman (1810–91). Quoted in *The Treasury of Humorous Quotations*, ed. Evan Esar & Nicolas Bentley (1951).

Cuckoos

11 First cuckoo I ever heard outside of a clock. Was surprised how closely it imitated the clock – and yet of course it could never have heard a clock. The hatefulest thing in the world is a cuckoo clock.

Mark Twain, American writer (1835–1910). *Mark Twain's Notebook*, ed. A .B. Paine (1935).

Cucumbers

12 It has been a common saying of physicians in England, that a cucumber should be well sliced, and dressed with

pepper and vinegar, and then thrown out, as good for nothing.

Samuel Johnson, English writer and lexicographer (1709–84). In James Boswell, *Life of Johnson* (1791) – for 5 October 1773.

Custody

1 I suppose they'll give you the custody of the Daimler?

Noël Coward (later Sir Noël), English entertainer and writer (1899–1973). Quoted in *The Treasury of Humorous Quotations*, ed. Evan Esar & Nicolas Bentley (1951).

Cynics

Lord Darlington's definition:

2 A man who knows the price of everything and the value of nothing.

Oscar Wilde, Irish playwright, poet and wit (1854–1900). *Lady Windermere's Fan*, Act 3 (1892).

3 A cynic is a man who looks at the world with a monocle in his mind's eye.

Carolyn Wells, American writer (187?–1942). Quoted in *The Treasury of Humorous Quotations*, ed. Evan Esar & Nicolas Bentley (1951).

4 Major Strasser has been shot. Round up the usual suspects.

'Louis Renault' (Claude Rains) in the film *Casablanca* (US, 1942). Script by Julius J. Epstein, Philip G. Epstein and Howard Koch, from an unproduced play *Everybody Comes To Rick's* by Murray Burnett and Joan Alison.

D

Dancing

1 I could dance with you till the cows come home. On second thoughts, I'd rather dance with the cows till you came home.

Groucho Marx, American comedian (1895–1977). Film, *Duck Soup* (US, 1933). Script by various.

2 Dancing is wonderful training for girls; it's the first way you learn to guess what a man is going to do before he does it.

Christopher Morley, American writer and editor (1890–1957). Quoted in *The Treasury of Humorous Quotations*, ed. Evan Esar & Nicolas Bentley (1951).

3 I am now going to the ball, to save my eyes from reading and my mind from thinking.

Philip Dormer Stanhope, 4th Earl of Chesterfield, English politician and writer (1694–1773). Quoted in *The 'Quote ... Unquote' Newsletter* (October 1992).

After the opening night of Oh, Calcutta!*:*

4 The trouble with nude dancing is that not everything stops when the music stops.

Sir Robert Helpmann, Australian dancer and choreographer (1909–86). Quoted in *The Frank Muir Book* (1976). Also in the form: 'No. You see there are portions of the human anatomy which would keep swinging after the music had finished', when asked if the fashion for nudity on stage would extend to dance (Elizabeth Salter, *Helpmann*, 1978).

5 A perpendicular expression of a horizontal desire.

Bernard Shaw, Irish playwright and critic (1856–1950). Quoted in the *New Statesman* (23 March 1962).

Day, Doris

American singer and film actress (1924–)

6 Doris Day is as wholesome as a bowl of cornflakes and at least as sexy.

Dwight MacDonald (untraced). Quoted in *A Year of Stings and Squelches* (1985).

Days of the month

7 Thirty days hath September,
All the rest I can't remember.
The calendar hangs on the wall;
Why bother me with this at all.

Anonymous. Quoted in *The 'Quote ... Unquote' Newsletter* (January 1998).

8 Dirty days hath September
April June and November.
February's days are quite alright
It only rains from morn to night.
All the rest have thirty-one
Without a blessed gleam of sun.
And if any of them had two and thirty
They'd be just as wet and just as dirty.

Ibid. (October 1997) .

9 Dirty days hath September
April June and November.
All the rest are dirty too
Except February –
and that's positively filthy.

Ibid. (July 1997).

10 Thirty days hath September,
April, June and no wonder.
All the rest have peanut butter
Except Pasadena
Which has the Rose Bowl .

Ibid. (April 1997).

1 Thirty days hath Septober
April, June, and no wonder,
All the rest have peanut butter,
Except my second cousin Henry,
Who married a chiffonier,
Which is a tall thing with drawers.

Ibid.

2 Thirty days hath September,
April, June and no wonder,
All the rest have porridge for breakfast,
Except my grandma
And she rides a bike.

Ibid. (October 1997). A bizarre disc with the title 'I'm In Love With My Little Red Tricycle' was recorded by one Napoleon XIV in 1966 and would seem to be based on a blend of this and the previous version, starting as it does: 'Thirty days hath Septober/April, June, and no wonder,/All the rest have peanut butter/All except my dear grandmother./She had a little red tricycle./I stole it. Ha ha ha!'

3 Thirty days hath September, and my Uncle Fred for speeding.

Morey Amsterdam, American comedian (*fl.* 1950s). Quoted in *ibid.*

4 My favourite poem is the one that starts 'Thirty days hath September' because it actually tells you something.

Groucho Marx, American comedian (1895–1977). Quoted in Ned Sherrin, *Cutting Edge* (1984).

De Gaulle, Charles
French soldier and politician
(1890–1970)

5 [He is] like a female llama surprised in her bath.

Winston S. Churchill (later Sir Winston), British Conservative Prime Minister and writer (1874–1965). Quoted in Lord Moran, *The Struggle for Survival* (1966), which also includes his denial that he ever said it.

Deafness

An MP observed Churchill as a very old man paying one of his infrequent visits to the House of Commons and remarked, 'After all, they say he's potty.' Came the muttered reply:

6 They say he can't hear either.

Winston S. Churchill (later Sir Winston), British Conservative Prime Minister and writer (1874–1965). Quoted in William Manchester, *The Last Lion* (1983).

Death

7 But this *long run* is a misleading guide to current affairs. *In the long run* we are all dead.

John Maynard Keynes (later Lord Keynes), English economist (1883–1946). *A Tract on Monetary Reform* (1923).

8 Waldo is one of those people who would be enormously improved by death.

'Saki' (H. H. Munro), English writer (1870–1916). Quoted in *The Treasury of Humorous Quotations*, ed. Evan Esar & Nicolas Bentley (1951).

9 It is tragic that Howard Hughes had to die to prove that he was alive.

Walter Kane (untraced). Quoted in Barbara Rowes, *The Book of Quotes* (1979).

10 Corpses always turned me up – even when I was doing Bereaved Households on the old Maida Vale *Intelligencer* . . . I remember once I was drinking tea in one of these front rooms with a middle-aged lady who'd just lost her husband, and she asked me if I'd like to have a look at him . . . Over we went to the coffin . . . Well, you don't really know what to say, do you, so I said, 'He looks well, doesn't he?' and she said, 'He ought to. We only came back from Brighton last week.'

Robert Robinson, English writer and broadcaster (1927–). *Landscape With Dead Dons*, Chap. 12 (1956). However, this is an old story. In Irvin S. Cobb's *A Laugh a Day Keeps the Doctor Away* (1921), story number 254 tells of 'two sympathic friends' calling at a house of mourning in the Bronx. The bereft husband of the late Mrs Levinsky sat alongside the casket. 'Doesn't she look wonderful?' said one of them. The widower replied, 'Why shouldn't she look wonderful? Didn't she spend the whole winter in Palm Beach?'

At the age of 92, on death:

11 Sometimes I think people see it as an indecent race between me, the Pope and Boris Yeltsin.

(Sir) John Gielgud, English actor (1904–).
Quoted in *The Independent on Sunday*
(10 November 1996).

1 Many people's tombstones should read,
'Died at 30. Buried at 60.'

Nicholas Murray Butler, American teacher
and writer (1862–1947). Quoted in *A Year of
Stings and Squelches* (1985).

*On hearing of Truman Capote's death
in 1984:*

2 Good career move.

Gore Vidal, American novelist, playwright and
critic (1925–). Confirmed by him in BBC
TV *Gore Vidal's Gore Vidal* (1995). According
to Time Magazine (8 April 1985), the graffito
'Good career move' had earlier appeared
following Elvis Presley's death in 1977.

Of a rock musician:

3 He died in a bizarre gardening accident.

Dialogue from film, *This Is Spinal Tap*,
(US, 1984). Written by Christopher Guest,
Michael McKean, Harry Shearer and the
director Rob Reiner.

4 Ain't It Grand To be Bloomin' Well
Dead?

Leslie Sarony, English entertainer and writer
(1897–1985). Title of song (1932).

5 LITTLE SIMPKINS: Nearly all our best
men are dead! Carlyle, Tennyson,
Browning, George Eliot! – I'm not
feeling very well myself.

Anonymous cartoonist. Caption to cartoon
entitled 'A lament'. *Punch*, Vol. 104
(6 May 1893).

*Man registering complaint with
pet shop owner:*

6 It's not pining, it's passed on. This parrot
is no more. It's ceased to be. It's expired.
It's gone to meet its maker. This is a late
parrot. It's a stiff. Bereft of life it rests in
peace. It would be pushing up the daisies
if you hadn't nailed it to the perch.
It's rung down the curtain and joined
the choir invisible. It's an ex-parrot.

'Parrot sketch', BBC TV *Monty Python's
Flying Circus* (first shown 7 December 1969).
Script by the team. The complainer ('Praline')
was played by John Cleese.

7 Once you're dead, you're made for life.

Jimi Hendrix, American rock musician
(1942–70). This attributed remark, dating
from *c*.1968, was certainly prescient in Hendrix's
own case. His success was enhanced following
his early death in September 1970. Within
six weeks he had a No. 1 hit in the UK with
'Voodoo Experience'.

8 As far as I'm concerned, there won't
be a Beatles reunion as long as John
Lennon remains dead.

George Harrison, English pop singer and
musician (1943–). Quoted in *The Independent*
Magazine (28 October 1995).

Taking a man's pulse:

9 Either this man is dead or my watch
has stopped.

Groucho Marx, American comedian
(1895–1977). Film, *A Day At the Races*
(US, 1937). Script by Robert Pirosh, George
Seaton and George Oppenheimer.

10 I have never wanted to see anybody
die, but there are a few obituary notices
I have read with pleasure.

Clarence Darrow, American lawyer (1857–
1938). Quoted in *The Treasury of Humorous
Quotations*, ed. Evan Esar & Nicolas
Bentley (1951).

11 It's not that I'm afraid to die. I just don't
want to be there when it happens.

Woody Allen, American film actor, writer
and director (1937–). *Death* (1975).

12 [Lord] Tyrawley and I have been dead
these two years; but we don't choose
to have it known.

Philip Dormer Stanhope, 4th Earl of Chester-
field, English politician and writer (1694–1773).
Quoted by Dr Samuel Johnson in James Boswell,
Life of Johnson (1791) – for 3 April 1773.

13 Death is nature's way of telling you to
slow down.

Anonymous. Quoted in *Newsweek* Magazine
(25 April 1960). It has been specifically attributed to Severn Darden (1937–), the American
film character actor. It is capable of infinite
variation: from Punch (3 January 1962):
'Some neo-Malthusians have been heard to
suggest that the bomb is Nature's way ... of
checking ... the over-spawning of our species.'

In 1978, the American cartoonist Garfield produced a bumper-sticker with the slogan: 'My car is God's way of telling you to slow down.'

Reason for her refusal to say prayers on one occasion:

1 God will be too busy unpacking King Edward.

The 'little daughter of Lord Kinnoull' who had been an 'awed witness' of the funeral of King Edward VII (1910). Quoted in Lord Riddell, *More Pages from My Diary 1908–14* (1934).

On hearing of the death of a corrupt politician:

2 I refused to attend his funeral. But I wrote a very nice letter explaining that I approved of it.

Mark Twain, American writer (1835–1910). Quoted in *Everybody's Mark Twain*, ed. C. T. Harnsberger (1972).

Death-wish

3 The minority parties have walked into a trap ... It is the first time in recorded history that turkeys have been known to vote for an early Christmas.

James Callaghan (later Lord Callaghan), British Labour Prime Minister (1912–). Speech, House of Commons (28 March 1979), deriding the Liberal Party and the Scottish National Party. He described the phrase as a 'joke going about the House'.

Decisions

4 If you can avoid a decision, do so. If you can get somebody else to avoid a decision, don't avoid it yourself. If you cannot get one person to avoid a decision, appoint a committee.

Anonymous. Attributed to Sharu S. Ragnekar in *The Art of Avoiding Decisions* in Winston Fletcher, *Meetings, Meetings* (1983).

Decomposition

In response to a woman who had asked, 'Do tell me: what is Baytch [Bach] doing just now? Is he still composing?':

5 Now Bach is decomposing.

(Sir) W. S. Gilbert, English writer and lyricist

(1836–1911). Quoted in Hesketh Pearson, *Gilbert and Sullivan* (1947).

Dedication

Dedication of his book The Heart of a Goof *(1926):*

6 To my daughter Leonora, without whose never-failing sympathy and encouragement this book would have been finished in half the time.

P. G. Wodehouse (later Sir Pelham), English-born novelist and lyricist (1881–1975). Not the first use by Wodehouse of this formula. In the first edition of *A Gentleman of Leisure* (1910) appears: 'To Herbert Westbrook, without whose never-failing sympathy and encouragement this book would have been finished in half the time.'

Deeds

7 When there is a great cry that something should be done, you can depend on it that something remarkably silly probably will be done.

Anonymous (nineteenth-century English statesman?). Quoted in *The 'Quote ... Unquote' Newsletter* (January 1997).

8 Step One: We must do something. Step Two: This is something. Step Three: Therefore we must do it.

Anonymous (civil servant?). 'The politicians' syllogism, quoted in Jonathan Lynn & Antony Jay, *Yes Prime Minister*, Vol.2 (1987).

Deflation

9 Collapse of stout party.

Anonymous. Supposed catchphrase of nineteenth-century *Punch* (used as the tagline to a story about the humbling of a pompous person). The phrase has not been found. The words 'Stout Party', however, appear in the caption to a cartoon in the edition of 25 August 1855.

Defrocking

On a clergyman who had been involved in a scandal:

10 [Having] ceased to be a pillar of the Church, [he was] now two columns of the *Evening Standard*.

William Inge, English clergyman and theologian (1860–1954). Quoted in Alfred Noyes, *Two Worlds for Memory* (1953). Sometimes rendered as 'a lot of pillars of society end up as columns in the *News of the World*'.

Democracy

1 Democracy substitutes election by the incompetent many for appointment by the corrupt few.

Bernard Shaw, Irish playwright and critic (1856–1950). 'Maxims for Revolutionaries', *Man and Superman* (1903).

2 Democracy is the theory that the common people know what they want, and deserve to get it good and hard.

H. L. Mencken, American journalist and linguist (1880–1956). *A Little Book in C major* (1916).

3 Democracy: in which you say what you like and do what you're told.

Gerald Barry, English editor and publicist (1898–1968). Quoted in *The Treasury of Humorous Quotations*, ed. Evan Esar & Nicolas Bentley (1951).

Democratic Party

4 The Democratic Party is like a mule – without pride of ancestry or hope of posterity.

Edmund Burke, Irish-born politician and philosopher (1729–97). Quoted in Laurence J. Peter, *Quotations for Our Time* (1977). *Bartlett's Familiar Quotations* (1992) ascribes it rather to Ignatius Donnelly (1831–1901).

Deodorants

A most ladylike American advertising slogan for a deodorant spray called Stopette:

5 Makes your armpit your charm pit!

Anonymous, *c*.1953. Quoted in Isobel Barnett, *My Life Line* (1956).

Deprivation

6 Deprivation is for me what daffodils were for Wordsworth.

Philip Larkin, English poet (1922–85). *Required Writing* (1983).

Descriptions of people

Of John Stuart Mill, the English philosopher and social reformer:

7 [He is] prominent because of the flatness of the surrounding countryside.

Karl Marx, German political theorist (1818–83). *Das Kapital*, Vol. 1, Chap. 16 (1867). After having demolished one of Mill's arguments, Marx says, rather, in these words: 'On a level plain, simple mounds look like hills; and the insipid flatness of our present bourgeoisie is to be measured by the altitude of its "great intellects".'

Of Andrew Neil, Scottish journalist, when editor of The Sunday Times:

8 If you can't plug it in the mains or fuck it, the editor's not interested.

Anonymous. Quoted in *The Independent* (31 January 1990).

Of Sir Ian McKellen, actor:

9 When he talks, he waves his arms and leaves long dramatic pauses – while he is Thinking – and his voice sounds a little as though he is eating biscuits.

Marianne Macdonald, English journalist. In *The Observer Magazine* (8 March 1998).

On being attacked in the House of Commons by Sir Geoffrey Howe:

10 That part of his speech was rather like being savaged by a dead sheep.

Denis Healey (later Lord Healey), English politician (1917–). Speech, House of Commons (14 June 1978).

On being attacked by Sir Geoffrey Howe:

11 Like being nibbled by a hearthrug.

Denis Healey. Quoted in Ned Sherrin, *Cutting Edge* (1984).

12 Tony Blair [leader of the British Labour Party] is a fresh face in British politics and the sort of chap the country needs, whereas John Prescott [the deputy leader] has the face of a man who clubs baby seals to death, but is, none the less, extremely pragmatic.

Denis Healey (later Lord Healey), English politician (1917–). Quoted in *The Sunday Telegraph* (17 July 1994).

Of a certain person:

1 A mouse studying to be a rat.

Chuck Jones, American cartoon animator (1912–). Quoted in *The 'Quote ... Unquote' Newsletter* (October 1996).

Of Jeanette Macdonald's face:

2 It reminds me of an Aardvaark's ass.

W. C. Fields, American comedian (1879–1946). Quoted in Ned Sherrin, *Cutting Edge* (1984).

On President Nasser and Sir Anthony Eden:

3 The camel that broke the straw's back.

Andrew Cavendish, 11th Duke of Devonshire, English politician (1920–). Quoted in *The Oxford Dictionary of Humorous Quotations*, ed. Ned Sherrin (1995).

Of V. M. Molotov, Russian politician:

4 A refrigerator when the light has gone out.

Anonymous British diplomat. Quoted in *Time* Magazine (24 November 1986). Winston Churchill said Molotov had 'a smile like the Siberian winter'.

Of his fellow conductor Sir Adrian Boult:

5 He came to see me this morning – positively reeking of Horlicks.

Sir Thomas Beecham, English conductor (1879–1961). Quoted in Ned Sherrin, *Cutting Edge* (1984).

Of Malcolm Fraser when he became Prime Minister of Australia in 1975:

6 He is the cutlery man of Australian politics. He was born with a silver spoon in his mouth, speaks with a forked tongue, and knifes his colleagues in the back.

Bob Hawke, Australian trade unionist and politician (1929–). Quoted in *The Observer*, 'Sayings of the Week' (14 December 1975). Hawke succeeded Fraser in 1983.

On Francis Wilson, TV weatherman:

7 Listen to him, and it's like sitting on wet seaweed on Land's End at the end of February.

Jean Rook, English journalist (1931–91). *Quoted in A Year of Stings and Squelches* (1985).

On Richard Ingrams, when editor of Private Eye*:*

8 He looks like the painting in Wedgwood Benn's attic.

William Rushton, English entertainer and cartoonist (1937–96). Quoted in *A Year of Stings and Squelches* (1985).

9 One of the finest women who ever walked the streets.

Mae West, American vaudeville and film actress (1893–1980). Of the character she plays called Lady Lou in the film *She Done Him Wrong* (US, 1933). Script adapted from her stage play *Diamond Lil* (first performed 9 April 1928).

Of Sir Richard Jebb, later Professor of Greek at Cambridge:

10 What time he can spare from the adornment of his person he devotes to the neglect of his duties.

William Hepworth Thompson, English scholar (1810–86). Quoted in M. R. Bobbit, *With Dearest Love to All* (1960).

11 Daniel Webster struck me much like a steam-engine in trousers.

Revd Sydney Smith, English clergyman, essayist and wit (1771–1845). Quoted in Lady Holland, *A Memoir of Sydney Smith* (1855).

12 In Pierre Elliott Trudeau, Canada has at last produced a political leader worthy of assassination.

Irving Layton, Romanian-born Canadian poet (1912–). 'Obo II', *The Whole Bloody Bird* (1969).

Of John Foster Dulles, US Secretary of State:

13 Dull, duller, Dulles.

Winston S. Churchill (later Sir Winston), British Conservative Prime Minister and writer (1874–1965). So ascribed in Piers Brendon, *Winston Churchill: a Brief Life* (1984).

Of Thomas Gray, the poet:

14 He walks as if he had fouled his small-clothes, and looks as if he smelt it.

Christopher Smart, English poet (1722–71). Quoted from *Facetiae Cantabrigienses*, some kind of nineteenth-century Cambridge University rag, in Christopher Devlin, *Poor Kit Smart* (1961).

1 Dr Polycarp was, as you all know, an unusually sallow bimetallist. 'There,' people of wide experience would say, 'There goes the sallowest bimetallist in Cheshire.'

G. K. Chesterton, English poet, novelist and critic (1874–1936). *The Napoleon of Notting Hill*, Chap. 3 (1904). A bimetallist was one who supported the unrestricted currency of both gold and silver at a fixed ratio to each other as coinage.

2 LADY RUMPERS: As I say there was a black-out. I saw his face only in the fitful light of a post-coital Craven A. He was small, but perfectly pro-portioned. In some respects more so.

Alan Bennett, English playwright and actor (1934–). *Habeas Corpus*, Act 2 (1973).

Of Fyfe Robertson, the gaunt Scots TV interviewer of yesteryear:

3 He looks as if someone has just poured cold porridge into his Wellingtons.

Anonymous. Quoted in *The 'Quote … Unquote' Newsletter* (April 1994).

Of Paul Johnson, journalist:

4 [He looks like] an explosion in a pubic hair factory.

Jonathan Miller, English entertainer, writer and director (1934–). Quoted in Alan Watkins, *Brief Lives* (1982).

Of Sir Hartley Shawcross (Attorney-General in the 1945 Labour Government who, wearying of the party, resigned his parlia-mentary seat in 1958):

5 Sir Shortly Floorcross.

Winston S. Churchill (later Sir Winston), British Conservative Prime Minister and writer (1874–1965). So ascribed in Piers Brendon, *Winston Churchill: a Brief Life* (1984).

Deserts

6 [The Dean of York] deserves to be preached to death by wild curates.

Revd Sydney Smith, English clergyman, essayist and wit (1771–1845). Quoted in Lady Holland, *A Memoir of Sydney Smith* (1855).

Desires

7 The other day we had a long discourse with [Lady Orkney] about love; and she told us a saying … which I thought excellent, that in men, desire begets love, and in women that love begets desire.

Jonathan Swift, Anglo-Irish writer and clergyman (1667–1745). *Journal to Stella* – for 30 October 1712.

8 In this world there are only two tragedies. One is not getting what one wants, and the other is getting it.

Oscar Wilde, Irish playwright, poet and wit (1854–1900). *Lady Windermere's Fan*, Act 3 (1892).

9 There are two tragedies in life. One is to lose your heart's desire. The other is to gain it.

Bernard Shaw, Irish playwright and critic (1856–1950). *Man and Superman*, Act 4 (1903).

Despair

10 Been Down So Long, It Looks Like Up to Me.

Richard Farina, American author (1936?–66). Title of book (1966; film US, 1971).

Diamonds

An ex-boyfriend of much-married actress Zsa Zsa Gabor commented:

11 She has proved beyond doubt that diamonds are the hardest thing in the world – to get back.

Anonymous. Quoted in *A Year of Stings and Squelches* (1985).

Diaries

12 I always say, keep a diary and some day it'll keep you.

Mae West, American vaudeville and film actress (1893–1980). Film, *Everyday's a Holiday* (US, 1937).

13 GWENDOLEN: I never travel without my diary. One should always have something sensational to read on the train.

Oscar Wilde, Irish playwright, poet and wit (1854–1900). *The Importance of Being Earnest*, Act 2 (1895).

1 Only good girls keep diaries. Bad girls don't have the time.

Tallulah Bankhead, American actress (1903–68). Attributed in *The Bloomsbury Dictionary of Quotations* (1987).

2 Things of so small concern or
    moment, who
Would stuff his Diary with, or care
    to know?
As what he wore, thought, laugh'd at,
    where he walked,
When farted, where he pissed, with
    whom he talked.

Robert Heath, English poet (seventeenth century). 'Satyr 1', *Clarastella* (1650).

3 To write a diary every day is like returning to one's own vomit.

Enoch Powell, English Conservative then Ulster Unionist politician (1912–98). In *The Sunday Times* (6 November 1977).

Dictators

4 I believe in benevolent dictatorships, provided I am the dictator.

Richard Branson, English entrepreneur (1950–). A much-repeated observation. Quoted in *The Observer* (25 November 1984).

Diets

Having taken it into his head not to eat vegetables, Brummell was asked by a lady if he had never eaten any at all in his life:

5 Yes, madam, I once ate a pea.

Beau Brummell, English dandy (1778–1840). Quoted in Charles Dickens, *Bleak House*, Chap. 12 (1852–53).

Dining

6 If the soup had been as warm as the wine, and the wine as old as the fish, and the fish as young as the maid, and the maid as willing as the hostess, it would have been a very good meal.

Anonymous (Austro-Hungarian). Quoted by Clement Freud on BBC Radio *Quote ... Unquote* (1979).

7 Dinner at the Huntercombes' possessed 'only two dramatic features – the wine was a farce and the food a tragedy'.

Anthony Powell, English novelist (1905–). *The Acceptance World* (1955).

8 At a dinner party one should eat wisely but not too well, and talk well but not too wisely.

W. Somerset Maugham, English writer (1874–1965). Written in 1896 but not reproduced until *A Writer's Notebook* (1949).

9 The best number for a dinner party is two: myself and a damn good head waiter.

Nubar Gulbenkian, English industrialist and philanthropist (1896–1972). Quoted in *The Daily Telegraph* (14 January 1965).

10 The number must neither be less than the graces, nor more than the muses.

Fanny Trollope, English novelist and travel-writer (1780–1863). *The Blue Belles of England* (1842).

11 If Jesus Christ were to come today, people would not even crucify Him. They would ask Him to dinner, and hear what He had to say, and make fun of it.

Thomas Carlyle, Scottish historian and philosopher (1795–1881). Quoted in *The Treasury of Humorous Quotations*, ed. Evan Esar & Nicolas Bentley (1951).

Diplomacy

12 A diplomat these days is nothing but a head-waiter who's allowed to sit down occasionally.

(Sir) Peter Ustinov, English actor and writer (1921–). *Romanoff and Juliet* (1956).

13 We exchanged many frank words in our respective languages.

Peter Cook, English humorist (1937–95). Impersonating Harold Macmillan in the sketch 'T.V.P.M.', *Beyond the Fringe* (1961).

14 Talking jaw to jaw is better than going to war.

Winston S. Churchill (later Sir Winston), British Conservative Prime Minister and writer (1874–1965). At a White House lunch (26 June 1954).

1 Diplomacy is the art of saying 'Nice Doggie!' till you can find a rock.

Wynn Catlin, unidentified (1930–). Quoted in Laurence J. Peter, *Quotations for Our Time* (1977).

2 Megaphone diplomacy leads to a dialogue of the deaf.

Sir Geoffrey Howe (later Lord Howe), English Conservative politician (1926–). Quoted in *The Observer*, 'Sayings of the Week' (29 September 1985).

3 Diplomacy – lying in state.

Oliver Herford, American humorist (1863–1935). Quoted in Laurence J. Peter, *Quotations for Our Time* (1977).

Dirt

Of Hannen Swaffer, journalist:

4 Whenever I see his fingernails, I thank God I don't have to look at his feet.

Athene Seyler (later Dame Athene), English actress (1889–1990). Remark, quoted in Bryan Forbes, *Ned's Girl* (1977).

Disbelief

5 Oh, life is a glorious cycle of song,
A medley of extemporanea;
And love is a thing that can never
   go wrong
And I am Marie of Roumania.

Dorothy Parker, American writer (1893–1967). 'Comment', *Not So Deep as a Well* (1937).

6 My god, my god, I shall die a happy man if I can make one person disbelieve in God.

A. J. Ayer (later Sir Alfred), English philosopher (1910–89). Quoted in *The Observer*, 'Sayings of the Week' (1 July 1989).

Disc jockeys

7 The wriggling ponces of the spoken word.

D. G. Bridson, English radio producer (1910–80). Attributed on BBC Radio *Quote . . . Unquote* (10 May 1978).

Disgruntlement

8 He spoke with a certain what-is-it in his voice, and I could see that, if not actually disgruntled, he was far from being gruntled.

P. G. Wodehouse (later Sir Pelham), English-born novelist and lyricist (1881–1975). *The Code of the Woosters* (1938).

Dishevelment

Of a close friend:

9 One cannot say that she was dressed. She was clothed. And so uncertainly that it was unsure she would remain even that.

Ivy Compton-Burnett (later Dame Ivy), English novelist (1884–1969). Quoted by Julian Mitchell on BBC Radio *Quote . . . Unquote* (5 January 1982).

Dismissal

10 Go, and never darken my towels again!

Groucho Marx, American comedian (1895–1977). Film, *Duck Soup* (US, 1933). Script by various.

Divorce

11 It was partially my fault that we got divorced . . . I tended to place my wife under a pedestal.

Woody Allen, American film actor, writer and director (1937–). 'I Had a Rough Marriage' (monologue, 1964).

12 Divorces are made in heaven.

Oscar Wilde, Irish playwright, poet and wit (1854–1900). Quoted in *The Treasury of Humorous Quotations*, ed. Evan Esar & Nicolas Bentley (1951).

Dobedobedo

13 To do is to be – Rousseau.
To be is to do – Sartre.
Dobedobedo – Sinatra.

Anonymous (graffito). A version is included in Reisner & Wechsler, *Encyclopedia of Graffiti* (1974).

Doctors

14 It's amazing the little harm they do

when one considers the opportunities they have.

Mark Twain, American writer (1835–1910). Attributed.

1 My dear old friend King George V told me he would never have died but for that vile doctor, Lord Dawson of Penn.

Margot Asquith (later Countess of Oxford and Asquith) (1864–1945). An observation that Lady Asquith made several times in her old age, but especially to Lord David Cecil (and recorded first by Mark Bonham Carter in his introduction to *The Autobiography of Margot Asquith*, 1962 edn).

To Christine Keeler, the 'good time girl' in the British political Profumo scandal of 1963:

2 A few days on your feet and we'll soon have you back in bed.

Anonymous (doctor). Quoted in H. Montgomery Hyde, *A Tangled Web*, Chap. 10 (1986).

3 The best doctors in the world are Doctor Diet, Doctor Quiet and Doctor Merryman.

Jonathan Swift, Anglo-Irish writer and clergyman (1667–1745). *Polite Conversation*, 2 (1738) – a work made up of well-established sayings and expressions.

Doing

4 The prime truth of woman, the universal mother ... that if a thing is worth doing, it is worth doing badly.

G. K. Chesterton, English poet, novelist and critic (1874–1936). 'Folly and Female Education', *What's Wrong with the World* (1910).

5 Go directly, and see what she's doing, and tell her she mustn't!

Anonymous cartoonist (possibly George Du Maurier). Caption to cartoon entitled 'EXPERIENTIA DOCET' in *Punch*, vol. 63 (16 November 1872). It shows a girl talking to her nanny. 'Where's baby, Madge?' Madge replies, 'In the other room, I think, Emily.' And then Emily comes up with this pronouncement.

6 Let's find out what everyone is doing, And then stop everyone from doing it.

A. P. Herbert (later Sir Alan), English writer and politician (1890–1971). 'Let's Stop Somebody from Doing Something' (1930).

7 All the things I really like to do are either illegal, immoral or fattening.

Alexander Woollcott, American writer and critic (1887–1943). *The Knock at the Stage Door* (1933).

8 Do not do unto others as you would that they should do unto you. Their tastes may not be the same.

Bernard Shaw, Irish playwright and critic (1856–1950). 'Maxims for Revolutionaries', *Man and Superman* (1903).

Domesticity

9 Sex and socks are not compatible.

Angela Carter, English writer (1940–92). Quoted in *The Observer*, 'Sayings of the Year' (27 December 1987).

Donne, John
English poet and priest (1572–1631)

10 As a youth, John Donne
Had a lot of fun.
After he hung up his balls
He became Dean of St Paul's.

Ivan Berger (untraced).

Double-entendres

To Howard Dietz on his musical
Beat the Devil:

11 I understand your play is full of single entendre.

George S. Kaufman, American playwright (1889–1961). Quoted in Ned Sherrin, *Cutting Edge* (1984).

Doubt

12 If you are ever in doubt as to whether or not you should kiss a pretty girl, always give her the benefit of the doubt.

Thomas Carlyle, Scottish historian and philosopher (1795–1881). Quoted in *The Treasury of Humorous Quotations*, ed. Evan Esar & Nicolas Bentley (1951).

Dreams

13 Last night I dreamt I ate a ten-pound marshmallow. When I woke up the pillow was gone.

Tommy Cooper, English comedian

(1921–84). Quoted in John Fisher, *Funny Way To Be a Hero* (1973).

Dress

Edward VII had an obsessive interest in correct attire. On one occasion when a courtier unwisely appeared in a loud check suit, the King said:

1 Goin' rattin', 'arris?

Edward VII, British King (1841–1910). Quoted on BBC Radio *Quote … Unquote* (1986). Another version is that the offending Harris appeared at Ascot in a brown bowler hat.

Drinking

2 Candy
Is dandy
But liquor
Is quicker.

Ogden Nash, American poet (1902–71). 'Reflection on Ice-Breaking', *Hard Lines* (1931).

3 An alcoholic is someone you don't like who drinks as much as you do.

Dylan Thomas, Welsh poet (1914–53). Quoted in Constantine Fitzgibbon, *Life of Dylan Thomas* (1965).

4 I have taken more out of alcohol than alcohol has taken out of me.

Winston S. Churchill (later Sir Winston), British Conservative Prime Minister and writer (1874–1965). Quoted in Willans & Roetter, *The Wit of Winston Churchill* (1954).

5 I've made it a rule never to drink by daylight and never to refuse a drink after dark.

H. L. Mencken, American journalist and linguist (1880–1956). Quoted in the *New York Post* (18 September 1945).

6 A man shouldn't fool with booze until he's fifty; then he's a damn fool if he doesn't.

William Faulkner, American novelist (1897–1962). Quoted in Webb & Green, *William Faulkner of Oxford* (1965).

7 I was in love with a beautiful blonde once, dear. She drove me to drink.

That's the one thing I'm indebted to her for.

W. C. Fields, American comedian (1879–1946). Film, *Never Give a Sucker an Even Break* (US, 1941).

When asked why he did not drink water:

8 Fish fuck in it.

W. C. Fields. Quoted in Leslie Halliwell, *The Filmgoer's Book of Quotes* (1973).

9 Some weasel took the cork out of my lunch.

W. C. Fields. Film, *You Can't Cheat an Honest Man* (US, 1939).

10 A soft drink turneth away company.

Oliver Herford, American humorist (1863–1935). Quoted in Herbert V. Prochnow, Snr & Jnr, *A Treasury of Humorous Quotations* (1969).

Drugs

On being asked to autograph a fan's school chemistry book:

11 Sure thing, man. I used to be a laboratory myself once.

Keith Richard, English rock musician and songwriter (1943–). Quoted in *The Independent on Sunday* (7 August 1994).

Drunks

12 I'm not so think as you drunk I am.

Sir John Squire, English poet, essayist and critic (1884–1958). 'Ballade of Soporific Absorption' in Maurice Baring, *One Hundred and One Ballades* (1931).

13 You're not drunk if you can lie on the floor without holding on.

Dean Martin, American entertainer (1917–95). Quoted in Paul Dickson, *The Official Rules* (1978).

14 Most British statesmen have either drunk too much or womanised too much. I never fell into the second category.

George Brown (later Lord George-Brown), English Labour politician (1914–85). Quoted in *The Observer* (11 November 1974).

1 I saw a notice which said 'Drink Canada Dry' and I've just started.

Brendan Behan, Irish playwright (1923–64). Quoted in *The 'Quote ... Unquote' Book of Love, Death and the Universe* (1980), but probably a line ascribed to any famous drinker. The following version was used in his act by the American comedian Pat Henning (*fl.*1950s): 'He was a drinkin' man, my fadder. One day he's standin' onna banks of the river, wonderin' what the hell folks can do with all that water, when suddenly he sees a great sign on the other side DRINK CANADA DRY. [Pause] So he went up there.'

2 Starkle, starkle, little twink,
Who the hell you are, you think?
I'm not under the alcofluence
   of incohol,
Though some thinkle peep I am.
I fool so feelish. I don't know who is me
For the drunker I sit here, the longer
   I get.

Anonymous. Said to have been published in the small magazine *Argosy* (*c.*1943). A musical version was recorded by the English comedian Charlie Drake in 1959. A drunken parody of 'Twinkle, twinkle, little star'.

Dying words

As he called for champagne when he was approaching death in 1900:

3 'Ah, well then,' said Oscar, 'I suppose that I shall have to die beyond my means.'

Oscar Wilde, Irish playwright, poet and wit (1854–1900). Quoted in R. H. Sherard, *Life of Oscar Wilde* (1906). Alternatively, 'I am dying, as I have lived, beyond my means' – quoted in Barnaby Conrad, *Famous Last Words* (1961). Richard Ellman, in *Oscar Wilde* (1987), has: 'I am dying beyond my means, I will never outlive the century' as said to Wilde's sister-in-law. Either way, they were not his 'dying words'. He lived for another month or so.

About the furnishings in his room:

4 This wallpaper'll be the death of me – one of us'll have to go.

Oscar Wilde. Quoted in Sherard, (*ibid.*). Not said in extremis. Another version is that Wilde said to Claire de Pratz: 'My wallpaper and I are fighting a duel to the death. One or the other of us has to go' – reported in Guillot de Saix, 'Souvenirs inédits', also in Frank Harris, *Oscar Wilde, His Life and Confessions* (1930).

Last words:

5 If this is dying, then I don't think much of it.

Lytton Strachey, English biographer (1880–1932). Quoted in Michael Holroyd, *Lytton Strachey*, Vol. 2 (1968).

Last words:

6 What is the answer? ... In that case, what is the question?

Gertrude Stein, American poet (1874–1946). Quoted in D. Sutherland, *G. S., a Biography of her Work* (1951).

Last words before being shot by a sniper at the Battle of Spotsylvania in the American Civil War:

7 They couldn't hit an elephant at this dist–.

John Sedgwick, American general (1813–64). Quoted in J. Green, *Famous Last Words* (1979). Sedgwick was with the Union Army.

Last words:

8 Die, my dear doctor? That's the last thing I shall do.

Lord Palmerston, British Prime Minister (1784–1865). Quoted in E. Latham, *Famous Sayings and their Authors* (1961).

Suggested dying words of a notable gourmand:

9 My exit is the result of too many *entrées*.

Richard Monckton Milnes (1st Baron Houghton), English politician and writer (1809–85). Quoted in Barnaby Conrad, *Famous Last Words* (1961).

10 I am dying with the help of too many physicians.

Alexander the Great, King of Macedonia (356–323 BC). Quoted in *The Treasury of Humorous Quotations,* ed. Evan Esar & Nicolas Bentley (1951). No other evidence has been found to support this attribution. The idea surfaces elsewhere, however, in the classical world. The dying Emperor Hadrian (AD76–138) apparently came out with 'the popular saying "many physicians have slain a king"' (according to Chap. 69 of the Roman history by the Greek historian Dion Cassius). Pliny the Elder quoted an epitaph in AD77 which goes *turba se medicorum periisse* or, in another version, *turba medicorum perii* (translated as, 'the brawling of the doctors killed me'). There is also said to be a more recent Czech proverb, 'Many doctors, death accomplished.' In addition, Molière, in the opening line of Act 2 of *L'Amour Médecin*, comes close to the sense: *'Que voulez-vous donc faire, Monsieur, de quatre médecins? N'est-ce pas assez d'un pour tuer une personne?* [What do you want with four doctors? Isn't one enough to kill someone?]'

During his final illness when it was suggested that he might like to receive a visit from Queen Victoria:

1 No, it is better not ... she would only ask me to take a message to Albert.

Benjamin Disraeli (later 1st Earl of Beaconsfield), British Conservative Prime Minister and writer (1804–81). Quoted by Robert Blake in his life, *Disraeli* (1966).

E

Eccentricity

One day Morton was walking down a crowded Fleet Street with Rupert Hart-Davis, the publisher. He suddenly went up to a pillar box and shouted into the slot:

1 You can come out now!

J. B. Morton (Beachcomber), English humorous writer (1893–1979). Quoted in *The Lyttelton Hart-Davis Letters* (for 5 February 1956) where it is said to have happened '20 years ago'.

Economics and Economists

2 Did y'ever think, Ken, that making a speech on economics is a lot like pissing down your leg? It seems hot to you, but it never does to anyone else.

Lyndon B. Johnson, American Democratic President (1908–73). Quoted in J. K. Galbraith, *A Life in Our Times* (1981).

3 An economist is a man who couldn't tell the difference between chicken salad and chicken shit.

Lyndon B. Johnson. Attributed. In Ned Sherrin, *Cutting Edge* (1984), this is given as a comment on a speech by Richard Nixon: 'Boys, I may not know much, but I know chicken shit from chicken salad!'

4 If all economists were laid end to end, they would not reach a conclusion.

Bernard Shaw, Irish playwright and critic (1856–1950). Attributed in *The Sayings of Bernard Shaw*, ed. Joseph Spence (1993).

To Franco Zeffirelli who explained that the high cost of the TV film Jesus of Nazareth *(1977) was partly because there had to be twelve apostles:*

5 Twelve! So who needs twelve? Couldn't we make do with six?

Lew Grade (later Lord Grade), Russian-born English media tycoon (1906–). Quoted in *Radio Times* (October 1983).

On producing the famously expensive and unsuccessful film Raise the Titanic *(1980):*

6 It would have been cheaper to lower the Atlantic.

Lew Grade. Attributed. Alas, on TV-am's *Frost on Sunday* (23 November 1987), Grade denied having said it. All he had actually managed was, 'I didn't raise the Titanic high enough.'

7 I am a great friend of Israel. Any country that can stand Milton Friedman as an adviser has nothing to fear from a few million Arabs.

John Kenneth Galbraith, Canadian-born American economist (1908–). Quoted in *A Year of Stings and Squelches* (1985).

8 Due to the present financial situation, the light at the end of the tunnel will be turned off at the week-ends.

Anonymous (graffito) from Dublin. Reported by Darren Hickey, Leixlip, Co. Kildare, in 1987.

Eden, Sir Anthony (later 1st Earl of Avon)
British Conservative Prime Minister (1897–1977)

When Eden had been described as the offspring of a mad baronet and a beautiful woman:

9 That's Anthony for you – half mad baronet, half beautiful woman.

R. A. Butler (later Lord Butler), English Conservative politician (1902–82). Untraced quotation in David Carlton, *Anthony Eden* (1981).

Edinburgh

1 McFee ... whose chief delusion is
that Edinburgh is the Athens of the
North ... McFee's dead ... He took
offence at my description of Edinburgh
as the Reykjavik of the South.

(Sir) Tom Stoppard, English playwright
(1937–). *Jumpers* (1972).

Editors

2 Editor: a person employed by a newspaper whose business it is to separate
the wheat from the chaff and to see that
the chaff is printed.

Elbert Hubbard, American writer and editor
(1856–1915). *The Roycroft Dictionary* (1914).

3 An editor is one who separates the
wheat from the chaff and prints
the chaff.

Adlai Stevenson, American Democratic
politician (1900–65). Attributed in Bill Adler,
The Stevenson Wit (1966).

Education

4 LADY BRACKNELL: Ignorance is like
a delicate exotic fruit; touch it and the
bloom is gone. The whole theory of
modern education is radically unsound.
Fortunately, in England, at any rate,
education produces no effect whatsoever. If it did, it would prove a serious
danger to the upper classes, and
probably lead to acts of violence in
Grosvenor Square.

Oscar Wilde, Irish playwright, poet and wit
(1854–1900). *The Importance of Being
Earnest*, Act 1 (1895).

5 Soap and education are not as sudden
as a massacre, but they are more deadly
in the long run.

Mark Twain, American writer (1835–1910).
'Facts Concerning the Recent Resignation',
A Curious Dream (1872).

6 Educated: in the holidays from Eton.

Sir Osbert Sitwell, English writer
(1892–1969). Entry in *Who's Who* (1929).

7 Nothing that you will learn in the
course of your studies will be of
the slightest possible use to you in after
life – save only this – that if you work
hard and intelligently you should be
able to detect when a man is talking rot,
and that, in my view, is the main, if
not the sole, purpose of education.

J. A. Smith, Professor of Moral Philosophy at
Oxford (1863–1939). Quoted in John Julius
Norwich, *A Christmas Cracker* (1980).
Opening a lecture course (1914).

8 Gentlemen: I have not had your
advantages. What poor education
I have received has been gained
in the University of Life.

Horatio Bottomley, English journalist,
financier and politician (1860–1933). Speech
at the Oxford Union (2 December 1920),
quoted in Beverley Nichols, *25* (1926).

Edward the Confessor
King of England (*c.*1003–66)

9 Edward the Confessor
Slept under the dresser.
When that began to pall
He slept in the hall.

E. C. Bentley, English novelist, journalist
and poet (1875–1956). *Biography for
Beginners* (1905).

Eggheads

10 Eggheads of the world, arise – I was
even going to add that you have nothing
to lose but your yolks.

Adlai Stevenson, American Democratic
politician (1900–65). Speech at Oakland,
California (1 February 1956).

Elections

11 'Vote early and vote often' is the
Politishun's golden rule.

Henry Wheeler Shaw, American humorist
(1818–85). *Josh Billings' Wit and Humour*
(1874). Earlier, William Porcher Miles had said
in a speech to the House of Representatives
(31 March 1858) : '"Vote early and vote often",
the advice openly displayed on the election
banners in one of our northern cities.' William
Safire, *Safire's Political Dictionary* (1978),
ignores both these sources but mentions that
historian James Morgan found 'in his 1926
book of biographies' that the original jokester

was John Van Buren (d.1866), a New York lawyer and son of President Martin Van Buren.

1 If voting changed anything they would make it illegal.

Anonymous. Has been dubiously ascribed to Tony Benn, English Labour politician (1925–). Fred Metcalf in *The Penguin Dictionary of Modern Humorous Quotations* (1987) merely places the slogan as on a 'badge, London, 1983'. In Rennie Ellis's *Australian Graffiti Revisited* (1979), there is a photograph of a wall slogan in Carlton, Victoria: 'IF VOTING COULD CHANGE THINGS, IT WOULD BE ILLEGAL.' This may predate the original publication of the book in 1975.

2 The trouble with free elections is, you never know who is going to win.

Leonid Brezhnev, Soviet politician (1906–82). Attributed. It is, however, just the kind of thing Joseph Stalin might have said at the Potsdam Conference in 1945 when Winston Churchill's fate in the British General Election hung in the balance. V. M. Molotov has also been suggested.

3 You won the elections, but I won the count.

Anastasio Somoza, Nicaraguan dictator (1925–80). Quoted in *The Guardian* (17 June 1977). Ironically, this remark had been anticipated by Tom Stoppard in his play *Jumpers* (1972): 'It's not the voting that's democracy, it's the counting.'

On the British General Election fight between Harold Wilson and Edward Heath, 1970:

4 A choice between a man with a pipe and a man with a boat.

Enoch Powell, English Conservative then Ulster Unionist politician (1912–98). Quoted in *The Independent* (9 February 1998).

5 There is no city in the United States in which I get a warmer welcome and fewer votes than Columbus, Ohio.

John F. Kennedy, American Democratic President (1917–63). Quoted in Herbert V. Prochnow, Snr & Jnr, *A Treasury of Humorous Quotations* (1969).

Elephants

6 SHERIFF: Where are you going with that elephant?
DURANTE: What elephant?

Jimmy Durante, American comedian (1893–1980). Film, *Jumbo* (US, 1962). The film was based on the 1935 Rodgers-Hart-Hecht-MacArthur stage show *Jumbo* in which Durante delivered the same joke. It is specifically credited to Charles Lederer.

Embarrassment

On arriving at a Tomorrow Club meeting in full evening dress and finding himself the only person so dressed:

7 Now, I don't want anybody to feel embarrassed.

Noël Coward (later Sir Noël), English entertainer and writer (1899–1973). Quoted in Cole Lesley, *The Life of Noël Coward* (1976).

Encouragement

8 In this country [England] it is thought well to kill an admiral from time to time to encourage the others.

Voltaire, French writer and philosopher (1694–1778). *Candide*, Chap. 23 (1759). This was a reference to the case of Admiral Byng who, in 1756, was sent to relieve Minorca which was blockaded by a French fleet. He failed and, when found guilty of neglect of duty, he was condemned to death and shot on board the *Momarque* at Portsmouth.

Enemies

9 A man cannot be too careful in the choice of his enemies.

Oscar Wilde, Irish playwright, poet and wit (1854–1900). *The Picture of Dorian Gray*, Chap. 1 (1891).

On being told that another Labourite was 'his own worst enemy', Bevin replied:

10 Not while I'm alive, he ain't.

Ernest Bevin, English Labour politician (1881–1951). Reputedly levelled at Aneurin Bevan, Herbert Morrison, Emanuel Shinwell and others, and quoted by Michael Foot in *Aneurin Bevan* (Vol. 2, 1973). Foot footnoted: 'Perhaps once [Bevin] had made it he recited it about all of them. Impossible to determine who was the original victim.' Douglas Jay in *Change and Fortune* (1980) adds that it was 'Made, I have little doubt, though there is no conclusive proof, about Bevan [being the victim] ... I could never discover direct evidence for this oft-told story.'

1 Beware of meat twice boil'd, and an old foe reconciled.

Benjamin Franklin, American politician and scientist (1706–90). *Poor Richard's Almanack* (April 1733) – a work in which Franklin often revised already existing sayings.

Engagements

2 An engagement should come on a young girl as a surprise, pleasant or unpleasant, as the case may be.

Oscar Wilde, Irish playwright, poet and wit (1854–1900). *The Importance of Being Earnest*, Act 1 (1895).

England

3 The cold of the polar regions was nothing to the chill of an English bedroom.

Fridtjof Nansen, Norwegian explorer (1861–1930). Quoted in *The Laughing Diplomat* (1939) by Daniele Varè. Nansen made several voyages in the Arctic regions. He was also the first Norwegian ambassador to London (1906–8), which is when he presumably acquired his knowledge of the bedrooms.

4 I remember remarking bitterly at the time [1933] that if I wrote a book about England I should call it 'What about Wednesday Week?' which is what English people say when they are making what they believe to be an urgent appointment.

Claud Cockburn, English journalist (1904–81). *In Time of Trouble* (1956).

English language

5 English is the great vacuum cleaner of languages: it sucks in anything it can get.

David Crystal, English lexicographer (1941–). Quoted in 'They Said It In 1995', *The Daily Telegraph* (30 December 1995).

Englishness and Englishmen

6 In Bangkok at twelve o'clock
They foam at the mouth and run.
But mad dogs and Englishmen
Go out in the mid-day sun.

Noël Coward (later Sir Noël), English entertainer and writer (1899–1973). Song, 'Mad Dogs and Englishmen', *Words and Music* (1932).

7 Continental people have sex lives; the English have hot-water bottles.

George Mikes, Hungarian-born writer in Britain (1912–87). *How To Be An Alien* (1946). Later, in *How To Be Decadent* (1977), Mikes commented: 'Things *have* progressed. Not on the continent, where people still have sex lives; but they have progressed here because the English now have electric blankets. It's a pity that electricity so often fails in this country.'

8 An Englishman, even if he is alone, forms an orderly queue of one.

George Mikes, in *ibid*.

9 The English may not like music – but they absolutely love the noise it makes.

Sir Thomas Beecham, English conductor (1879–1961). Quoted in L. Ayre, *The Wit of Music* (1966).

10 I know why the sun never sets on the British Empire: God wouldn't trust an Englishman in the dark.

Anonymous. In Nancy McPhee, *The Book of Insults* (1978), this is ascribed to 'Duncan Spaeth' (is this John Duncan Spaeth, the US educator?). An Irish Republican placard held up during Prince Charles's visit to New York in June 1981 had the slogan: 'The sun never sets on the British Empire because God doesn't trust the Brits in the dark.'

11 They tell me that the English are a people who travel all over the world to laugh at other people.

Anonymous (Spaniard). Quoted by Gerald Brenan, *The Face of Spain*, 1950.

12 If an Englishman gets run down by a truck, he apologises to the truck.

Jackie Mason, American comedian (1931–). Quoted in *The Observer*, 'Sayings of the Week' (23 September 1990).

1 Let us pause to consider the English,
   Who when they pause to consider
      themselves they get all
      reticently thrilled and tinglish,
   Because every Englishman is convinced
      of one thing, viz.:
   That to be an Englishman is to belong
      to the most exclusive club there is.

Ogden Nash, American poet (1902–71).
'England Expects', *I'm a Stranger
Here Myself* (1938).

Enmity

2 Nobody ever forgets where he buried
   a hatchet.

Frank McKinney ('Kin') Hubbard, American
humorist (1868–1930). *Abe Martin's Broadcast* (1930).

Enough

*Said by Mr Bennet to his daughter Mary
who has been singing:*

3 You have delighted us long enough.

Jane Austen, English novelist (1775–1817).
Pride and Prejudice, Chap. 18 (1813).

Epigrams

4 The day of the jewelled epigram is past
   and, whether one likes it or not, one
   is moving into the stern puritanical era
   of the four-letter word.

Noël Annan (later Lord Annan), English
academic and writer (1916–). Quoted in
The Observer (20 February 1966) as having
being spoken in the House of Lords. Compare
Curzon on Disraeli: 'Men were on the look out
for the jewelled phrase, the exquisite epigram,
the stinging sneer' – quoted in Kenneth
Rose, *Superior Person* (1969).

5 An epigram is only a wisecrack that's
   played Carnegie Hall.

Oscar Levant, American pianist and actor
(1906–72). Quoted in *The Treasury of
Humorous Quotations*, ed. Evan Esar &
Nicolas Bentley (1951).

Epitaphs

6 Man is a noble animal, splendid in
   ashes, and pompous in the grave.

Sir Thomas Browne, English author and

physician (1605–82). *Hydriotaphia (Urn-
Burial)*, Chap. 5 (1658).

*On the memorial to Sir Christopher Wren,
architect, in St Paul's Cathedral:*

7 LECTOR, SI MONUMENTUM
   REQUIRIS, CIRCUMSPICE ...
   [Reader, if you seek his monument,
   look around ...]

Anonymous, though reputedly composed
by his son. Horace Smith (1779–1849)
commented drily that it would 'be equally
applicable to a physician buried in a
churchyard'.

*Epitaph on a hypochondriac – from
the southern USA:*

8 I told you I was sick.

Anonymous. Quoted on BBC Radio
Quote ... Unquote (22 December 1981).
In January 1994, it was reported that the
dying wish of Keith Woodward of Shrivenham,
Wiltshire, had been to ha͟e a tombstone
bearing the joke 'I told them I was ill'. However, parish councillors ordered the message
to be removed.

On a mule, in the USA:

9 Here lies Bill. He done his damnedest.

Anonymous. Quoted by Naomi Lewis on
BBC Radio *Quote ... Unquote* (1 December
1981). Compare what President Harry S
Truman said in Winslow, Arizona on 15 June
1948: 'You know, the greatest epitaph in the
country is here in Arizona. It's in Tombstone
and says, "Here lies Jack Williams. He done his
damnedest." I think that is the greatest epitaph
a man could have. Whenever a man does the
best he can, then that is all he can do; and
that is what your President has been trying to
do for the last three years for this country.' In
1964, Truman more precisely located the
epitaph in Boot Hill Cemetery, Tombstone,
and said that it went on, 'What more could
a person do?' He added, of himself, 'Well,
that's all I could do. I did my damnedest and
that's all there is to it.'

10 Here lies
   Captain Ernest Bloomfield
   Accidentally shot by his Orderly
   March 2nd 1789
   'Well done, thou good and faithful
      servant'.

Anonymous. Quoted in W. H. Beable, *Epitaphs: Graveyard Humour & Eulogy* (1925), which has not only this, but also a version involving 'Major James Brush . . . 1831 (Woolwich Churchyard)'. Beable also finds the similar, 'Erected to the Memory of/John Phillips/Accidentally Shot/As a mark of affection by his brother'. Earlier, David Mackae, *A Pennyworth of Queer Epitaphs* (?1910) had found the same epitaph in India. *Pass the Port Again* (1980) ascribed it confidently to the grave of David Warnock in Simla. The *Faber Book of Anecdotes* has it that James Whitcomb Riley (1849–1916), the American poet, said of a cook who had worked for a family many years, and who fell asleep over her stove and was burned to death, 'Well done, good and faithful servant.'

On a dentist:

1 Stranger! Approach this spot with gravity!
John Brown is filling his last cavity.

Anonymous. Quoted in *A Dictionary of Famous Quotations*, ed. Robin Hyman (1967). Peter Haining, *Graveyard Wit* (1973), has a similar rhyme more precisely from 'St George's Church, Edinburgh'.

2 Here lies John Bunn
Who was killed by a gun.
His name wasn't Bunn, but his real name was Wood,
But Wood wouldn't rhyme with gun,
So I thought Bunn should.

Anonymous. *W. Fairley, Epitaphiana: or the Curiosities of Churchyard Literature* (1875) and W. H. Beable, *Epitaphs: Graveyard Humour & Eulogy* (1925) both have this, the latter noting 'a distinctly American flavour'. William Tegg, *Epitaphs, Witty, Grotesque, Elegant & c.* (1876), has the similar: 'Underneath this ancient pew/Lie the remains of Jonathan Blue;/His name was Black, but that wouldn't do.'

3 Here lies the body of Joan Carthew,
Born at St. Columb, buried at St. Kew.
Children she had five,
Three are dead, and two alive.
Those that are dead chusing rather
To die with their Mother
Than live with their Father.

Anonymous. Quoted in Anon., *A Collection of Epitaphs and Monumental Inscriptions* (1806). 'Unfortunately cannot now be found,

but was inscribed on an 18th Century headstone' – according to the guidebook (1982) of the church at St Ewe, near St Austell, Cornwall. Joan Bakewell and John Drummond, *A Fine and Private Place* (1977), give the version as above as though from St Agnes, which is on the north coast of Cornwall, near Redruth. However, St Agnes *is* nearer to St Columb, if that is relevant.

4 Dorothy Cecil Unmarried
As Yet.

Anonymous. Quoted in an undated newspaper cutting (possibly from the early 1900s): "'C W.' writes: "While lately strolling through an old Surrey church containing altar-tombs, escutcheons and memorials of the House of Exeter, [this] epitaph on a large marble slab, suspended high in the mortuary chapel, arrested my attention. It is printed in uncials, and I reproduce the arrangement in facsimile."'

5 Here lies the bones of Copperstone Charlotte
Born a virgin, died a harlot.
For sixteen years she kep' her virginity
A damn'd long time in this vicinity.

Anonymous. Quoted in Raymond Lamont Brown, *A New Book of Epitaphs* (1973), which has this 'from the US'. Compare: 'Here lie the bones of Elizabeth Charlotte,/That was born a virgin and died a harlot./She was aye a virgin till seventeen – /An extraordinary thing for Aberdeen' – quoted in Donald and Catherine Carswell, *The Scots Week-End* (1936).

6 Deep in this grave lies lazy Dai
Waiting the last great trump on high.
If he's as fond of his grave as he's fond of his bed
He'll be the last man up when that roll call's said.

Anonymous. 'From Nevern – translated from the Welsh'. Quoted by Wynford Vaughan-Thomas on BBC Radio *Quote . . . Unquote* (26 January 1982).

7 Here lies the body of *Martha Dias*,
Who was always uneasy, and not over pious.
She liv'd to the age of threescore and ten,
And gave that to the worms she refus'd to the men.

Anonymous. Quoted in Anon., *A Collection of*

Epitaphs and Monumental Inscriptions (1806), from 'Shrewsbury church-yard'.

1 John Edwards who perished in
a fire 1904.
None could hold a candle to him.

Anonymous. An epitaph from the burial ground near the present Anglican Cathedral in Liverpool. Quoted by Beryl Bainbridge on BBC Radio *Quote . . . Unquote* (29 June 1988). She said that another in the same place, on a certain 'G. Wild', bore the words, 'Not worth remembering'.

2 Jonathan Grober
Died dead sober.
Lord thy wonders never cease.

Anonymous. Quoted on BBC Radio *Quote . . . Unquote* (22 December 1981), but untraced.

3 Here lies the body of Mary Gwynne,
Who was so very pure within,
She cracked the shell of her earthly skin,
And hatched herself a cherubim.

Anonymous. Said to be in Cambridge –
W. Fairley, *Epitaphiana: or the Curiosities of Churchyard Literature* (1875); in St Alban's, Hertfordshire – J. Potter Briscoe, *Gleanings from God's Acre Being a Collection of Epitaphs* (1901).

4 Here lies John Higley whose father and mother were drowned in the passage from America. Had they both lived, they would have been buried here.

Anonymous. W. Fairley, *Epitaphiana: or the Curiosities of Churchyard Literature* (1875). In 'Belturbet Churchyard, Ireland'.

5 In joyous memory of
George Jones
who was president of
the Newport Rifle Club
for twenty years.
'Always missed'.

Anonymous. 'From America, I think' –
A. Bune, Cambridge (1982).

6 Here lies the body of Mary,
wife of John Jones of this parish.
Here lies the body of Martha,
wife of John Jones of this parish.
Here lies the body of Jane,
wife of John Jones of this parish.
John Jones. At rest.

Anonymous. Adjacent epitaphs which used to be quoted by Lt Commander D. Gill Jones in his talk 'A quiet hour among the dead' (mid-twentieth century).

7 Here lies the body of Mary Ann Lowder,
She burst while drinking a seidlitz powder.
Called from the world to her heavenly rest,
She should have waited till it effervesced.

Anonymous. Quoted in W. H. Beable, *Epitaphs: Graveyard Humour & Eulogy* (1925) – 'in Burlington Churchyard'. John Diprose, *Diprose's Book of Epitaphs: Humorous, Eccentric, Ancient & Remarkable* (1879), had earlier put it in 'Burlington, Mass.'

8 Erected to the memory of
John MacFarlane
Drowned in the Water of Leith
By a few affectionate friends.

Anonymous. Quoted in W. H. Beable, *Epitaphs: Graveyard Humour & Eulogy* (1925).

9 In memory of
MAGGIE
Who in her time kicked
Two colonels,
Four majors,
Ten captains,
Twenty-four lieutenants,
Forty-two sergeants,
Four hundred and thirty-two
other ranks
AND
One Mills Bomb.

Anonymous. 'On the last resting place of an Army mule somewhere in France' –
J. H. A. Dick, Currie, Midlothian (1981).

10 Born a dog. Died a gentleman.

Anonymous. Quoted by Naomi Lewis on BBC Radio *Quote . . . Unquote* (1 December 1981). It seems to have been a Victorian epitaph from an unidentified pets' cemetery.

11 Here lies the body of Mary Anne
Safe in the arms of Abraham.
All very well for Mary Anne
But how about poor Abraham?

Anonymous. 'In a North Devon churchyard' –

D. Whitmore, Liphook, Hants. (1982);
'Mary Ann has gone to rest,/Safe at last on
Abraham's breast,/Which may be nuts for
Mary Ann,/But is certainly rough on
Abraham' – quoted in *A Dictionary of Famous
Quotations*, ed. Robin Hyman (1967).

1 Here lies the body of
LADY O'LOONEY
Great niece of BURKE
Commonly called the Sublime
She was Bland, Passionate
and deeply Religious, also
she painted in water colours
and sent several pictures
to the Exhibition
She was first Cousin to
LADY JONES
and of such is the
Kingdom of Heaven.

Anonymous. This most delightful of epitaphs
can no longer be found. W. Fairley, *Epitaphiana: or the Curiosities of Churchyard Literature*
(1875), placed it in 'Pewsey churchyard';
William Tegg, *Epitaphs, Witty, Grotesque,
Elegant & c.* (1876), in 'Pewsey, Bedfordshire'
(which does not exist); Aubrey Stewart, *English
Epigrams and Epitaphs* (1897), in 'Pewsey,
Wiltshire'; J. Potter Briscoe, *Gleanings from
God's Acre Being a Collection of Epitaphs* (1901),
in 'Dorsetshire'; David Mackae, *A Pennyworth
of Queer Epitaphs* (?1910), placed it in 'Devon';
Peter Haining, *Graveyard Wit* (1973), in
'Bridgewater Cemetery, Somerset'. Compare
from Philip Reder, *Epitaphs* (1969), in
Bandon, Ireland: 'Sacred to the memory of
Mrs Maria Boyle/Who was a good wife, a
devoted Mother/And a kind and charitable
neighbour./She painted in water colours,/And
was the first cousin to the Earl of Cork,/And
of such is the Kingdom of Heaven.' At which
point one wonders whether what G. W. E.
Russell, *Collections and Recollections* (1898),
calls 'the best-known of all epitaphs' ever
existed anywhere at all.

2 Here lies, in horizontal position,
the outside case of
GEORGE ROUTLEIGH, Watchmaker;
Whose abilities in that line
Were an honour to his profession.
Integrity was the Mainspring, and
prudence the Regulator
Humane, generous and liberal,

his Hand never stopped
till he had relieved Distress.
So nicely regulated were all his motions,
that he never went wrong,
except when set a-going
by people
who did not know his Key;
Even then he was easily
set right again.
He had the art of disposing his time
  so well,
that his hours glided away
in one continual round
of pleasure and delight,
until an unlucky minute put a period
to his existence.
He departed this life,
Nov. 14, 1802,
aged 57:
wound up,
in hopes of being taken in hand
by his Maker;
and of being thoroughly cleaned,
repaired,
and set a-going
in the world to come.

Anonymous. Quoted in full in Geoffrey
N. Wright, *Discovering Epitaphs* (1972).
In Lydford church, Devon. *Benham's Book of
Quotations* (1948) has only an extract and
puts the name as 'George Roughfield'.

3 In memory of Jane Emily Smith
Died 10 Apr. 1804, aged 74
'Believing, we rejoice to see the curse
removed'.

Anonymous. 'In South Ealing cemetery',
according to a correspondent, but untraced.

4 Her Time Was Short.

Anonymous. Quoted in Michael Holroyd,
Bernard Shaw Vol. II: The Pursuit of Power
(1989). On the tombstone of Mary Ann
South in Ayot St Lawrence churchyard, Hertfordshire. She had lived in the village for
seventy years, from 1825–95. Bernard Shaw,
when asked why he had chosen to live in the
same village, would explain that if the biblical
span of three score years and ten was considered short there, it had to be a good
place to live. He himself managed to live to
the age of 94.

1 IN LOVING MEMORY
OF
FRANK STAINER
OF
STAFFORDSHIRE
WHO LEFT US IN PEACE
FEB. 2ND. 1910

Anonymous. In the English cemetery on
the island of San Michele, Venice.
Quoted by a correspondent, Margaret
R. Jackson of Chipping Camden (1982),
though it had already been transcribed
(differently) in James Morris, *Venice*
(1960/1974).

2 Here lies a poor woman who always
        was tired,
For she lived in a place where help
        wasn't hired,
Her last words on earth were, 'Dear
        friends, I am going,
Where washing ain't done nor cooking
        nor sewing
And everything there is exact to
        my wishes,
For there they don't eat, there's no
        washing of dishes,
I'll be where loud anthems will always
        be ringing
(But having no voice, I'll be out of
        the singing).
Don't mourn for me now, don't grieve
        for me never,
For I'm going to do nothing for ever
        and ever'.

Anonymous. Quoted in E. Jameson, *1000
Curiosities of Britain* (1937). Sometimes
referred to as 'The Maid-of-all-Works' Epitaph'
or 'The Tired Woman's Epitaph', this has two
possible sources. As 'an epitaph for Catherine
Alsopp, a Sheffield washerwoman, who hanged
herself, 7 August 1905', it was composed by
herself and included in Jameson. But a letter in
the *Spectator* (2 December 1922) from a correspondent at the British Museum states that the
inscription was once to be found in Bushey
churchyard. A copy of the text was made
before 1860, but the actual stone had been
destroyed by 1916. Stewart (1897) has it as
'quoted by James Payn in the *Cornhill Magazine*'. It was also discussed in Notes and
Queries for March 1889 and *Longman's
Magazine* for January 1884. W. Gurney

Benham, *Cassell's Book of Quotations* (1907),
states that it had been quoted 'before 1850'.

3 Lord she is thin.

Anonymous. It is said that this epitaph
appears at the bottom of a Tasmanian tombstone. The 'e' is on the back, the stonemason
not having left himself enough room to carve
it on the front. Is there a source for this?

4 Wherever you be
Let your wind go free.
For it was keeping it in
That was the death of me.

Anonymous. 'Traditional, from Ireland',
quoted on BBC Radio *Quote . . . Unquote*
(2 March 1982).

5 Beneath this Marble is Buried
Tho. Welsted
Who was Struck Down by the
        Throwing of a Stone.
He was First in this School
And we Hope is not Last in Heaven
Whither he went
Instead of to Oxford.
January 13, 1676
Aged 18.

Anonymous. Quoted in *The Oxford Book of
Oxford*, ed. Jan Morris (1978). Translation
of a Latin inscription to be found in
the Old Cloisters at Winchester College.

Epitaphs, literary

*On Sir John, later Viscount, Simon
(1873–1954), lawyer and Liberal
politician:*

6 This stone with not unpardonable
        pride,
Proves by its record what the world
        denied :
Simon could do a natural thing –
        he died.

John Sparrow, English scholar (1906–92).
Grave Epigrams and Other Verses (1981) –
where 'Simon' is replaced with '*Nemo*'.
'Lord Simon has died . . . John Sparrow
wrote this epitaph many years ago . . . But
then John Simon helped John Sparrow
to become Warden of All Souls, and the latter
came to regret his epigram' – *Harold Nicolson's Diaries and Letters 1945–1962* (entry for
11 January 1954).

Mock epitaph on G. K. Chesterton:

1 Poor G.K.C., his day is past –
Now God will know the truth at last.

E. V. Lucas, English writer (1868–1938).
Quoted in Dudley Barker, *G. K. Chesterton*
(1973).

2 Here lies an honest lawyer, –
That is Strange.

Anonymous. On the 'eminent barrister, Sir
John Strange' – quoted in W. Fairley, *Epitaphiana: or the Curiosities of Churchyard Literature*
(1875); 'on Mr Strange, a lawyer' – William
Tegg, *Epitaphs, Witty, Grotesque, Elegant & c.*
(1876). The only notable lawyer of this name
mentioned in the *Dictionary of National Biography* is Sir John Strange (1696–1754), who
was Master of the Rolls. Compare what John
Aubrey earlier recorded: 'Ben J o (h) n s o n,
riding through Surrey, found the Women
weeping and wailing, lamenting the Death of a
Lawyer, who lived there: He enquired why so
great Grief for the Losse of a Lawyer? Oh, said
they, we have the greatest Loss imaginable; he
kept us all in Peace and Quietness, and was a
most charitable good Man: Whereupon Ben
made this Distich: "God works Wonders
now and then,/Behold a Miracle, deny't who
can,/Here lies a Lawyer and an honest man."
'Tis Pity that good Man's Name should
not be remember'd.'

Epitaph on an unknown man:

3 Under this sod lies another one.

Anonymous. Quoted in the book
Quote ... Unquote (1978).

4 Below the high Cathedral stairs,
Lie the remains of Agnes Pears.
Her name was Wiggs; it was not Pears.
But Pears was put to rhyme with stairs.

Anonymous. Quoted in Edward Lear's diary
(entry for 20 April 1887). With 'Susan Pares'
replacing 'Agnes Pears', the rhyme was first
published without date in *Queery Leary
Nonsense* (1911), edited from manuscripts
by Lady Constance Strachey.

5 This is the grave of Mike O'Day
Who died maintaining his right of way.
His right was clear, his will was strong.
But he's just as dead as if he'd been
   wrong.

Anonymous. Quoted in *Bartlett's Familiar*

Quotations (1968). Another version: 'Here lies
the body of Edmund Gray/Who died maintaining his right of way./He was right – dead
right – as he drove along./But he's just as dead
as if he'd been wrong' – quoted by Sir Huw
Wheldon on BBC Radio *Quote ... Unquote*
(1 December 1981). There is also one to
'Timothy Jay', as in 'jay-walking'.

*Of Sir Henry Campbell-Bannerman
(1836–1908), British Liberal Prime
Minister from 1905–8:*

6 He is remembered chiefly as the man
about whom all is forgotten.

Nicolas Bentley, English cartoonist
and writer (1907–78). *An Edwardian
Album* (1974).

7 Miss Emily Stamp, postmistress.
Returned opened.

Anonymous. 'On a comic post card [of a
gravestone] at Blackpool' – quoted by Bryan
Glover on BBC Radio *Quote ... Unquote*
(9 February 1982).

8 Down the lanes of memory
The lights are never dim
Until the stars forget to shine
We shall remember her.

Anonymous. Quoted by Alan Bennett
from 'a Lancashire newspaper' on *Quote ...
Unquote*, BBC Radio (26 January 1982).
He had earlier included the lines in
'The English Way of Death' in *Beyond the
Fringe* (Broadway version, 1964).

9 The angel's trumpet sounded,
St Peter called out 'Come',
The pearly gates swung open,
And in walked Mum.

Anonymous. 'This must have appeared at
least 30 years ago ... I remember a correspondence about it in the Live Letters column
of the *Daily Mirror*, where some readers
condemned its tastelessness, and others praised
its simple sentiment' – letter from Margaret
Holt, Manchester (1981). In *Ego 7* (for
6 March 1944), James Agate stakes an earlier
claim: 'The members [of the Column Club]
were delighted with something I bagged
out of the obituary notices in an august
paper a few days ago: "The silver trumpets
sounded loud,/The angels shouted 'Come!'/
Opened wide the Golden Gate,/And in
walked Mum!"'

1 Posterity will ne'er survey
   A nobler grave than this.
   Here lie the bones of Castlereagh.
   Stop, Traveller –

Lord Byron, English poet (1788–1824).
'Epitaph' (1821). Byron wrote this epitaph on
Viscount Castlereagh (1769–1822) apparently
the year *before* the Foreign Secretary's death
by suicide. Castlereagh is actually buried in
Westminster Abbey and attracted the poet's
enmity either because Byron supported Napoleon or on account of Castlereagh's presumed
role in the Peterloo massacre of 1819.

*Epitaph on Frederick Louis, Prince of
Wales (1707–1751), eldest son of George II
and father of George III:*

2 Here lies Fred,
   Who was alive and is dead:
   Had it been his father,
   I had much rather;
   Had it been his brother,
   Still better than another;
   Had it been his sister
   No one would have missed her;
   Had it been the whole generation,
   Still better for the nation:
   But since 'tis only Fred,
   Who was alive and is dead, –
   There's no more to be said.

Anonymous. Quoted by Horace Walpole in an
appendix to his *Memoirs of George II* (1847).
Compare from *Frobisher's New Select Collection
of Epitaphs* ... (?1790), 'On a tombstone in
Cornwall: Here lies honest Ned,/Because he is
dead./Had it been his father ...' *A Collection
of Epitaphs* ... (1806) has from 'a headstone in
the church-yard of Storrington in the County
of Sussex: "Here lies the body of Edward
Hide;/We laid him here because he died./
We had rather it had been his father./If it had
been his sister,/We should not have miss'd
her./But since 'tis honest Ned/No more shall
be said ..."' Peter Haining, *Graveyard Wit*
(1973), has a version beginning 'Here lies
HONEST NED ...' from 'Kirkby Stephen
parish church, Westmorland'.

3 When I am dead, I hope it may be said:
   'His sins were scarlet, but his books
      were read'.

Hilaire Belloc, French-born English poet and
writer (1870–1953). 'On his Books', *Sonnets
and Verse* (1923).

*On Sir John Vanbrugh (1664–1726),
the dramatist and architect:*

4 Under this stone, Reader, survey
   Dead Sir John Vanbrugh's house of clay.
   Lie heavy on him, Earth! for he
   Laid many heavy loads on thee!

Dr Abel Evans (1679–1737), though it has
also been ascribed to the architect, Nicholas
Hawksmoor. Thinking of Blenheim Palace,
Castle Howard, and so on. This version
is the one in Revd John Booth, *Metrical
Epitaphs, Ancient and Modern* (1868).
Anon., *A Collection of Epitaphs and Monumental Inscriptions* (1806), has: 'Lie light
upon him earth! tho' he/Laid many a heavy
load on thee.' (Compare, on Pelham:
'Lie heavy on him, land, for he/Laid many
a heavy tax on thee'.)

Epitaph for his cat Bathsheba:

5 To whom none ever said scat,
   No worthier cat
   Ever sat on a mat
   Or caught a rat:
   Requies – cat.

John Greenleaf Whittier, American poet
(1807–92). Quoted in Janice Anderson,
The Cat-a-Logue (1987).

6 Here lies the grave of Keelin,
   And on it his wife is kneeling;
   If he were alive, she would be lying,
   And he would be kneeling.

Anonymous (graffito). Quoted in Oliver
St John Gogarty, *As I Was Going Down
Sackville Street* (1937).

Epitaphs, suggested

7 This is where the real fun starts.

Ben Travers, English playwright
(1886–1980). In *The Listener*
(31 December 1981).

Epitaph for himself:

8 Here lies Fuller's Earth.

Thomas Fuller, English preacher and historian
(1608–61). Quoted in T. Webb, *A New Select
Collection of Epitaphs* (1775). Fuller was buried
in the church of which he had been rector, at
Cranford, west London, but the grave no
longer survives. His actual epitaph was a sober
Latin text.

*Suggested epitaph for one Thomas
Longbottom who died young:*

1 *Ars longa, vita brevis.*

Anonymous. Contributed to BBC Radio
Quote . . . Unquote (17 May 1978). In the
same edition, Richard Stilgoe suggested rather
that *Punch* in its early days had reproduced the
death announcement of a man called 'Longbottom' and put over it the headline 'Vita
brevis'. Hence, also, 'Ars Longa, Vita Sackville-
West', which was used as a chapter heading
in the book *Quote . . . Unquote* (1978).

2 This is on me.

Dorothy Parker, American writer (1893–1967).
Quoted in Alexander Woollcott, *While Rome
Burns* (1934). Other epitaphs she suggested
for herself *c.*1925 were 'Excuse my dust' and
'If you can read this you are standing too close'.

Suggested epitaph for an actress:

3 She sleeps alone at last.

Robert Benchley, American humorist (1889–
1945). Quoted in *The Book of Hollywood
Quotes* (*c.*1980).

4 On the whole I'd rather be in
Philadelphia.

W. C. Fields, American comedian (1879–
1946). What the comedian actually submitted
as a suggested epitaph to *Vanity Fair* Magazine
in 1925 was: 'Here lies W. C. Fields. I would
rather be living in Philadelphia.'

Epitaph for himself:

5 He never used a sentence if a paragraph
would do.

Sir Huw Wheldon, Welsh broadcaster and
TV executive (1916–86). Quoted in the *Daily
Mail* (9 June 1976). The actual headstone
of his grave in Nant Peris, Snowdonia, calls him
'Soldier, Broadcaster, Administrator'.

6 Been there, done that.

Michael Caine, English actor (1933–). 'Caine
was once asked if he had a motto: "Yeah – Been
There, Done That. It'll certainly be on my
tombstone. It'll just say, "Been There, Done
That"' – quoted in Elaine Gallagher *et al*,
Candidly Caine (1990).

7 Here lies one Foote, whose death may
   thousands save,
For death has now one foot within
   the grave.

Anonymous. Quoted in Anon., *A Collection of
Epitaphs and Monumental Inscriptions* (1806).
A punning epitaph on Samuel Foote (1720–77),
actor and dramatist, famous for his mimicry
and for making Samuel Johnson laugh against
his will. He was, however, buried in Westminster Abbey cloister by torchlight and in
an unmarked grave.

8 At last I get top billing.

Wallace Ford, English film actor (1897–1966).
Quoted by Terence Frisby on BBC Radio *Quote
. . . Unquote* (16 February 1979). Ford went to
Hollywood in the early 1930s. After a number of
'semi-leads', he was condemned to a succession
of supporting roles in Hollywood films and
decided that his gravestone epitaph should read,
'At last – I get top billing.' This inscription was
duly put on his grave. Then along came a graffiti
artist and chalked above it, 'Clark Gable and
Myrna Loy supported by . . . ' I have no idea
what is actually written on his grave.

9 The body
   of Benjamin Franklin, printer,
   (Like the cover of an old book,
   Its contents worn out,
   And stript of its lettering and gilding)
   Lies here, food for worms!
   Yet the work itself shall not be lost,
   For it will, as he believed, appear
      once more
   In a new
   And more beautiful edition,
   Corrected and amended
   By its Author!

Benjamin Franklin, American politician and
scientist (1706–90). Written *c.*1728. William
Andrews, *Curious Epitaphs* (1899), compares it
to other similarly punning printers' epitaphs.
W. Gurney Benham, *Cassell's Book of Quotations*
(1907), quotes the Revd Joseph Capen (19th
century), 'Lines on Mr John Foster': 'Yet at the
resurrection we shall see/A fair edition, and
of matchless worth,/Free from erratas, new in
heaven set forth.' Benham also suggests that the
idea was borrowed from the Revd Benjamin
Woodbridge, chaplain to Charles II, who wrote
these 'Lines of John Cotton' (1652): 'O what a
monument of glorious worth,/When in a new
edition he comes forth,/Without erratas, may we
think he'll be/In leaves and covers of eternity!'
In fact, Franklin lies with his wife under a simple
inscription in Christ Church, Philadelphia:
'Benjamin and Deborah Franklin 1790'.

1 Believing that his hate for queers
Proclaimed his love for God,
He now (of all queer things, my dears)
Lies under his first sod.

Paul Dehn, English writer (1912–76). He
won a *New Statesman* competition in 1962
with this epitaph on John Gordon (1890–
1974), editor-in-chief of the *Sunday
Express*, and a columnist famous for his
outspoken views.

2 Here lies the body of Charlotte Greer,
Whose mouth would stretch from
   ear to ear.
Be careful as you tread this sod
For if she gapes, you're gone, by God!

Anonymous. 'My father maintained that
in the Vale of Aylesbury about 1900 he
encountered this epitaph ... I'm afraid it
was apocryphal' – E. J. Burdon, Preston,
Lancs. (1982).

3 Pardon me for not getting up.

Ernest Hemingway, American novelist
(1899–1961). One of the playful epitaphs
that celebrities were invited to suggest for
themselves, usually by American magazines
in the 1920s/30s. He is buried at Ketchum,
Idaho, where he shot himself.

4 Over my dead body.

George S. Kaufman, American playwright
(1889–1961). Quoted in *The Book of
Hollywood Quotes* (*c.*1980).

5 Here lies Groucho Marx
and Lies and Lies and Lies.
PS He never kissed an ugly girl.

Groucho Marx, American comedian
(1895–1977). *The Secret Word is
Groucho* (1976).

Equality

6 His lordship may compel us to be
equal upstairs, but there will never be
equality in the servants' hall.

J. M. Barrie, Scottish playwright (1860–1937).
The Admirable Crichton, Act 1, Sc. 1 (1902).
Crichton speaking.

7 All animals are equal, but some are more
equal than others.

George Orwell, English novelist and journalist
(1903–50). *Animal Farm* (1945).

Eroticism

8 Erotic is when you do something
sensitive and imaginative with
a feather. Kinky is when you use
the whole chicken.

Elmore Leonard, American novelist (1925–).
Attributed to Leonard by William Rushton
in 1987, but otherwise untraced. However,
in a BBC TV *Moving Pictures* profile of
Roman Polanski (reviewed in *The Guardian*,
25 November 1991), Peter Coyote ascribed
the remark to Polanski in the form: 'Eroticism
is using a feather, while pornography is using
the whole chicken.' Another version uses
'perverted' instead of 'kinky'.

Errata

9 Erratum. In my article on the Price
of Milk, 'Horses' should have read
'Cows' throughout.

J. B. Morton (Beachcomber), English
humorous writer (1893–1979). *The Best of
Beachcomber* (1963).

Etiquette

The Red Queen to Alice:

10 It isn't etiquette to cut any one you've
been introduced to. Remove the joint!

Lewis Carroll, *Through the Looking-Glass and
What Alice Found There*, Chap. 9 (1872).

*Having left the table to be sick, at a
formal dinner in the home of the producer
Arthur Hornblow Jr:*

11 It's all right, Arthur. The white wine
came up with the fish.

Herman J. Mankiewicz, American screen-
writer (1897–1953). Attributed in Max Wilk,
The Wit and Wisdom of Hollywood (1972).
Also attributed to Howard Dietz.

12 Etiquette is knowing how to yawn
with your mouth closed.

Herbert V. Prochnow, American writer
(1897–). Quoted in Herbert V. Prochnow,
Snr & Jnr, *A Treasury of Humorous
Quotations* (1969).

Euphemisms

13 The answer is in the plural and they
bounce.

Sir Edwin Lutyens, English architect (1869–1944). Said to have been the euphemistic response given by Lutyens to a Royal Commission (quoted without source in *The Penguin Dictionary of Modern Quotations*, 1971). However, according to Robert Jackson, *The Chief* (1959), when Gordon (later Lord) Hewart was in the House of Commons, he was answering questions on behalf of David Lloyd George. For some time, one afternoon, he had given answers in the customary brief parliamentary manner – 'The answer is in the affirmative' or 'the answer is in the negative'. After one such non-committal reply, several members arose to bait Hewart with a series of rapid supplementary questions. He waited until they had all finished and then replied: 'The answer is in the plural!'

1 HONEY: I wonder if you could show me where the … I want to … put some powder on my nose.
   GEORGE: Martha, won't you show her where we keep the … euphemism?
   Edward Albee, American playwright (1928–). *Who's Afraid of Virginia Woolf?*, Act 1 (1962).

Europe

2 Baldwin thought Europe was a bore, and Chamberlain thought it was only a greater Birmingham.
   Winston S. Churchill (later Sir Winston), British Conservative Prime Minister and writer (1874–1965). In 1953.

3 The only cultural heritage that the 321 peoples of Europe share is that of America. That is why the organisers of Euro-Disneyland are on safe ground.
   Kenneth Hudson, English museums expert. Quoted in *The Independent* 'Quote Unquote' (30 June 1990).

Everest

When asked why he wanted to climb Mount Everest:

4 Because it's there.
   George Leigh Mallory, English mountaineer (1886–1924). Reported observation during a US lecture tour in 1923.

Evidence

5 Some circumstantial evidence is very strong, as when you find a trout in the milk.
   Henry David Thoreau, American writer (1817–62). Diary note (11 November 1850).

At the conclusion of the trial of the 'Luncheon Voucher' Madam, Cynthia Payne:

6 M'lud, we find the defendant not guilty – but we would love to hear all the evidence again.
   Anonymous (jury foreman). Quoted in *Sunday Today*, 'Quotes of the Week' (15 February 1987). In fact, this was not actually said in court (as a member of the jury pointed out to the author) but may have appeared as the caption to a cartoon.

Examinations

7 Expostulate (chiefly) on
   (a) The Curfew
   (b) Gray's Energy in the Country Churchyard.
   W. C. Sellar & R. J. Yeatman, English humorists (1898–1951; 1897–1968). *1066 and All That*, Chap. 21 (1930). 'Test Paper II, Up to the End of Henry III.'

8 Do not on any account attempt to write on both sides of the paper at once.
   Sellar & Yeatman in *ibid.* Chap. 62. 'Test Paper V, Up to the End of History.'

9 I would have liked to have been examined in history, poetry and writing essays … I should have liked to be asked what I knew. They always tried to ask me what I did not know.
   Winston S. Churchill (later Sir Winston), British Conservative Prime Minister and writer (1874–1965). *My Early Life* (1930).

Excess

10 Nothing succeeds like excess.
   Oscar Wilde, Irish playwright, poet and wit (1854–1900). Quoted in *The Treasury of Humorous Quotations*, ed. Evan Esar & Nicolas Bentley (1951).

Exclamation marks

Editing a radio script by Sheilah Graham:

1 Cut out all the exclamation points.
An exclamation point is like laughing
at your own joke.

F. Scott Fitzgerald, American novelist (1896–
1940). Quoted in Sheilah Graham and
Gerald Frank, *Beloved Infidel* (1959).

Excuses

*On why snow had disrupted rail services,
even though a big chill had been correctly
forecast:*

2 It was the wrong kind of snow.

Terry Worrall, British Rail's director of opera-
tions. Quoted in *The Independent* (16 February
1991). This remark became part of British
folklore as the archetypal limp excuse.

*When a man asked to be excused to go to
the men's room:*

3 He really needs to telephone, but he's
too embarrassed to say so.

Dorothy Parker, American writer (1893–
1967). Quoted in John Keats, *You Might as
Well Live* (1970).

4 One more drink and I'd be under
the host.

Dorothy Parker. Quoted in *ibid.*

On hearing that Harold Ross, editor of
The New Yorker, *had called while she was
on her honeymoon, demanding late copy:*

5 Tell him I've been too fucking busy –
or vice versa.

Dorothy Parker. Quoted in *ibid.*

Asked by Harold Ross, editor of The
New Yorker, *why she hadn't been
in to the office during the week to write
her piece:*

6 Someone was using the pencil.

Dorothy Parker. Quoted in *The Sayings
of Dorothy Parker*, ed. S. T. Brownlow
(1992).

*When asked about an unmarried
mother's baby:*

7 If you please, ma'am, it was a very
little one.

Frederick Marryat, English novelist

(1792–1848). *Mr Midshipman Easy*, Chap. 3
(1836). A line dating from before 1638,
however.

Exercise

8 Whenever I feel like exercise, I lie
down until the feeling passes.

Robert M. Hutchins, American educator
(1899–1977). Untraced, but apparently
said by the former University of Chicago
President rather than all the other candidates
(Wilde, Twain, W. C. Fields, and so on).
Ascribed by J. P. McEvoy in *Young Man
Looking Backwards* (1938). However,
Hutchins's biographer, Harry S. Ashmore,
ascribes it to McEvoy and says that it was
merely one of many sayings Hutchins
collected to use when appropriate. In the film
Mr Smith Goes to Washington (US, 1939),
Thomas Mitchell speaks the line: 'Every time
I think of exercise, I have to lie down till
the feeling leaves me.'

9 I take my only exercise acting as
pallbearer at the funerals of
my friends who exercise regularly.

Mark Twain, American writer (1835–1910).
Attributed but not verified. Quoted in
The Sayings of Mark Twain, ed. James
Munson (1992).

10 I am pushing sixty. That is enough
exercise for me.

Mark Twain. Quoted in *ibid.*

Exits

11 He flung himself from the room,
flung himself upon his horse and rode
madly off in all directions.

Stephen Leacock, English-born Canadian
writer and economist (1869–1944).
'Gertrude the Governess', *Nonsense
Novels* (1911).

Expenditure

*When the future King Edward VII said
to his mistress, 'I've spent enough on you to
buy a battleship', she replied:*

12 And you've spent enough in me to
float one.

Lily Langtry, English actress (1852–1929).
Source untraced.

Experience

1 You should make a point of trying every experience once, excepting incest and folk-dancing.

Anonymous ('sympathetic Scotsman'). Quoted by Sir Arnold Bax, English composer (1883–1953), in *Farewell, My Youth* (1943).

2 Experience is the comb that Nature gives us when we are bald.

Anonymous (Belgian proverb). Quoted in Herbert V. Prochnow, Snr & Jnr, *A Treasury of Humorous Quotations* (1969).

Experts

3 An expert is one who knows more and more about less and less.

Nicholas Murray Butler, American teacher and writer (1862–1947). Remark in a Commencement address at Columbia University (of which he was President 1901–45). Quoted in *The Treasury of Humorous Quotations*, ed. Evan Esar & Nicolas Bentley (1951).

Explanations

4 Never Explain – your friends do not need it and your enemies will not believe you anyway.

Elbert Hubbard, American writer and editor (1856–1915). *The Motto Book* (1907).

When his wife caught him kissing a chorus girl, he explained, creatively:

5 But, you see, I wasn't kissing her. I was whispering in her mouth.

Chico Marx, American comedian (1886–1961). Quoted in Groucho Marx & Richard Anobile, *The Marx Brothers Scrapbook* (1974).

6 Are you lost daddy I arsked tenderly. 'Shut up,' he explained.

Ring Lardner, American humorist (1885–1933). *The Young Immigrunts* (1920).

An actor was appearing in a long-running melodrama during which he had to stab another in the last act with a stiletto-type letter opener. One day, the props man forgot to put the knife on the table and there was no other murder implement to hand. Instead of throttling his victim, the actor apparently kicked him up the backside. The man fell down dead. The actor turned to the audience and said:

7 Fortunately, the toe of my boot was poisoned!

Osgood Perkins, American character actor (1892–1937). Quoted by Stanley Donen to Richard Burton who recorded it in his diary for 16 October 1968 (printed in Melvyn Bragg, *Rich: The Life of Richard Burton*, 1988).

Eyesight

8 Sir Thomas Robinson was always complaining that he kept seeing double and asked what he should do about it. Samuel Johnson said: Count your money.

Samuel Johnson, English writer and lexicographer (1709–84). Quoted in *A Year of Stings and Squelches* (1985).

F

Faces

1 [He has] one of those characteristic
British faces that, once seen, are never
remembered.

Oscar Wilde, Irish playwright, poet and
wit (1854–1900). Quoted in *The Treasury
of Humorous Quotations*, ed. Evan Esar &
Nicolas Bentley (1951).

2 I never forget a face, but in your case
I'll be glad to make an exception.

Groucho Marx, American comedian (1895–
1977). Quoted by Leo Rosten in 'Groucho',
People I Have Loved, Known or Admired (1970).

Facts

3 Comment is free but facts are on
expenses.

(Sir) Tom Stoppard, English playwright
(1937–). *Night and Day* (1978).

Failure

4 I have done my best to die before this
book is published.

Robert Runcie (Lord Runcie), English Archbishop of Canterbury (1921–). Letter to
Humphrey Carpenter quoted in the biographer's *Robert Runcie, The Reluctant Archbishop*
(1996). Runcie had co-operated with Carpenter (indeed, had invited him to write the
biography), believing that the book would
not be published until after his death.

5 Anybody seen in a bus after the age
of thirty has been a failure in life.

Loelia Westminster, English duchess
(1902–93). Quoted in *The Daily Telegraph*
(*c*.1980).

6 I haven't had a hit film since Joan
Collins was a virgin.

Burt Reynolds, American film actor (1936–).
Quoted in *The Observer*, 'Sayings of the Week'
(27 March 1988).

Faith

7 There are those who scoff at the schoolboy, calling him frivolous and shallow.
Yet it was the schoolboy who said, 'Faith
is believing what you know ain't so.'

Mark Twain, American writer (1835–1910).
Following the Equator (1897).

Fame

8 You're famous when they can spell
your name in Karachi.

Anonymous American showbiz observation.
Quoted by Steve Aronson in *Hype* (1983).
In David Brown, *Star Billing* (1985), 'You're
not a star until they can spell your name
in Karachi' is ascribed to Humphrey Bogart.

9 Fame is failure disguised as money.

Brendan Behan, Irish playwright (1923–64).
Quoted in *The Irish Digest* (1963).

Familiarity

10 Familiarity breeds contempt – and
children.

Mark Twain, American writer (1835–1910).
Notebooks (published 1935).

11 Dear 338171 (May I call you 338?)

Noël Coward (later Sir Noël), English entertainer and writer (1899–1973). Writing to
T. E. Lawrence in the R A F, when Lawrence
was hiding under the name 'Shaw'. Included
in *Letters to T. E. Lawrence*, ed. D. Garnett
(1938) – letter dated 25 August 1930.

12 The first Rotarian was the first man to
call John the Baptist Jack.

H. L. Mencken, American journalist and

linguist (1880–1956). Quoted in *The Treasury of Humorous Quotations*, ed. Evan Esar & Nicolas Bentley (1951).

Family life

1 LADY BRACKNELL: To be born, or at any rate bred, in a hand-bag, whether it had handles or not, seems to me to display a contempt for the ordinary decencies of family life that reminds one of the worst excesses of the French Revolution.

Oscar Wilde, Irish playwright, poet and wit (1854–1900). *The Importance of Being Earnest*, Act 1 (1895).

Farce

When someone said to Gwenn, on his deathbed, 'It must be hard, very hard, Ed?', he replied:

2 It is. But not as hard as farce.

Edmund Gwenn, Welsh-born character actor (1875–1959). Quoted in *Time* Magazine (30 January 1984). One version has it that the visitor was Jack Lemmon.

3 Sergeant, arrest several of these vicars!

Philip King, English playwright (1904–79). Tom Stoppard once claimed this as the funniest line anywhere in English farce. Alas, King's *See How They Run* (first performed in 1944) does not have quite this line in it. For reasons it would be exhausting to go into, the stage gets filled with various people who are, or are dressed up as, vicars, and the order is given: 'Sergeant, arrest most of these people.'

Farewells

4 BURNS: Say goodnight, Gracie.
ALLEN: Goodnight, Gracie.

George Burns, American comedian (1896–1996). Exchange with his wife, Gracie Allen – the customary ending of their TV series, *The George Burns and Gracie Allen Show* (1950–58). Subsequently, in NBCTV *Rowan and Martin's Laugh-In* (1967–73), Dan Rowan would say, 'Say goodnight, Dick' and Dick Martin would reply, 'Goodnight, Dick.'

Farts

The Earl of Oxford, Edward de Vere, 'making of his low obeisance to Queen Elizabeth,

happened to let a fart, at which he was so abashed and ashamed that he went to travel, seven years.' On his return, the Queen welcomed him home with:

5 My lord, we have forgot the fart.

Elizabeth I, English Queen (1533–1603). Quoted in John Aubrey, *Brief Lives* (c.1693). It is said that a similar story occurs in the *Arabian Nights' Entertainments*.

6 Every man likes the smell of his own farts.

Anonymous. Quoted in the *Viking Book of Aphorisms*, ed. Auden & Kronenberger (1962), and described as of Icelandic origin. Might it have been the editors' invention?

Fascination

7 Mrs Skinner told Jones that Mrs N. was a very fascinating woman, and that Mr W. was very fond of fascinating with her.

Samuel Butler, English author (1835–1902). *Notebooks* (c.1890).

Fashion

8 Fashion is what one wears oneself. What is unfashionable is what other people wear.

Oscar Wilde, Irish playwright, poet and wit (1854–1900). *An Ideal Husband*, Act 3 (1895).

Fast-talking

9 Hubert Humphrey talks so fast that listening to him is like trying to read *Playboy* magazine with your wife turning the pages.

Barry Goldwater, American Republican politician (1909–98). Quoted in Ned Sherrin, *Cutting Edge* (1984).

Fate

10 I'm not absolutely certain of my facts, but I rather fancy it's Shakespeare – or, if not, it's some equally brainy bird – who says that it's always just when a fellow is feeling particularly braced with things in general that Fate sneaks up behind him with the bit of lead piping. And what I'm driving at is that the man is perfectly right.

P. G. Wodehouse (later Sir Pelham), English-born novelist and lyricist (1881–1975). 'Jeeves and the Unbidden Guest', in *Carry On, Jeeves!* (1925).

Fathers

1 When I was a boy of fourteen, my father was so ignorant I could hardly stand to have the old man around. But when I got to be twenty-one, I was astonished at how much he had learned in seven years.

Mark Twain, American writer (1835–1910). Attributed in *Reader's Digest* (September 1939). But if Twain ever said this, there was more than a hint of poetic licence about it. His own father died when Twain was eleven.

Fatness

2 If the fence is strong enough I'll sit on it.

(Sir) Cyril Smith, English Liberal politician (1928–). Quoted in *The Observer* (15 September 1974). Member of Parliament for Rochdale (1972–92), 'Big Cyril' weighed something like twenty-five stones.

3 Elizabeth Taylor is wearing Orson Welles designer jeans.

Joan Rivers, American entertainer (1937–). Quoted in Ned Sherrin, *Cutting Edge* (1984).

4 Elizabeth Taylor's so fat, she puts mayonnaise on an aspirin.

Joan Rivers. Quoted in *A Year of Stings and Squelches* (1985).

To a young Scot who was about to marry an Irish widow twice his age and twice his size:

5 Going to marry her! Impossible! You mean a part of her; he could not marry her all himself ... There is enough of her to furnish wives for a whole parish ... You might people a colony with her; or give an assembly with her; or perhaps take your morning's walk round her, always provided there were frequent resting-places, and you were in rude health.

Revd Sydney Smith, English clergyman, essayist and wit (1771–1845). Quoted in Hesketh Pearson, *The Smith of Smiths*, Chap. 11 (1934).

6 The Right Hon was a tubby little chap who looked as if he had been poured into his clothes and had forgotten to say 'When!'

P. G. Wodehouse (later Sir Pelham), English-born novelist and lyricist (1881–1975). 'Jeeves and the Impending Doom', *Very Good, Jeeves* (1930).

7 ALFRED HITCHCOCK: One look at you, Mr Shaw, and I know there's famine in the land.
   BERNARD SHAW: One look at you, Mr Hitchcock, and I know who caused it.

Bernard Shaw, Irish playwright and critic (1856–1950). Quoted in Blanche Patch, *Thirty Years With G BS* (1951).

8 I'm fat, but I'm thin inside. Has it ever struck you that there's a thin man inside every fat man, just as they say there's a statue inside every block of stone?

George Orwell, English novelist and journalist (1903–50). *Coming Up for Air* (1939).

9 Imprisoned in every fat man a thin one is wildly signalling to be let out.

Cyril Connolly, English writer and critic (1903–74). *The Unquiet Grave* (1944).

10 Outside every fat man there was an even fatter man trying to close in.

Kingsley Amis, English novelist, poet and critic (1922–95). *One Fat Englishman* (1963).

11 Inside every fat Englishman is a thin Hindu trying to get out.

Timothy Leary, American hippie guru (1920–96).

12 A fat man should not play the concertina.

Mao Zedong, Chinese revolutionary and Communist leader (1893–1976). Attributed on BBC Radio *Quote ... Unquote* (10 May 1978). Perhaps attributed to Mao simply as a change from Confucius?

Fecundity

The children of a famous diplomat, Lord Lytton, organized a charade. The scene displayed a Crusader knight returning from the wars to his ancestral castle. At the castle-gate he was welcomed by his beautiful and rejoicing wife, to whom, after tender salutations, he recounted his triumphs on the tented fields and the number of paynim whom he had slain. Replied his wife, pointing with conscious pride to a long row of dolls of various sizes:

1 And I, too, my lord, have not been idle.

Anonymous. Quoted in G. W. E. Russell, *Collections and Recollections* (1898).

Feeling

Retiring from the US Supreme Court in 1992, he was asked at a press conference the cliché question, 'How do you feel?' He replied:

2 With my hands.

Thurgood Marshall, American judge (1908–93). Quoted in the *Texas Lawyer* (6 January 1992).

Feminism

3 We are becoming the men we wanted to marry.

Gloria Steinem, American feminist writer (1934–). In *Ms* Magazine (July/August 1982).

4 I was the first woman to burn my bra – it took the fire department four days to put it out.

Dolly Parton, American singer (1946–). Quoted in Barbara Rowes, *The Book of Quotes* (1979).

Fiction

5 MISS PRISM: The good ended happily, and the bad unhappily. That is what fiction means.

Oscar Wilde, Irish playwright, poet and wit (1854–1900). *The Importance of Being Earnest*, Act 2 (1895).

6 The author of this novel and all the characters mentioned in it are completely fictitious. There is no such city as Manchester.

Howard Spring, Welsh novelist (1889–1965). *Shabby Tiger* (1934).

7 If this were played upon a stage now, I could condemn it as an improbable fiction.

William Shakespeare, English playwright and poet (1564–1616). *Twelfth Night*, Act III, Sc.iv (1600).

8 'Very strange!' he said to himself, vacantly. 'It's like a scene in a novel – it's like nothing in real life.'

Wilkie Collins, English novelist (1824–89). *No Name* (1862–63).

9 I'm really very sorry for you all, but it's an unjust world, and virtue is triumphant only in theatrical performances.

(Sir) W. S. Gilbert, English writer and lyricist (1836–1911). *The Mikado*, Act II (1885).

Fidelity

10 ROBERT (to Diana): Your idea of fidelity is not having more than one man in the bed at the same time ... You're a whore, baby, that's all, just a whore, and I don't take whores in taxis.

Frederic Raphael, English novelist and screenwriter (1931–). Film, *Darling* (UK, 1965), with Dirk Bogarde as Robert Gold and Julie Christie as Diana Scott.

Film criticism

During a viewing of the lengthy film Exodus:

11 Let my people go!

Mort Sahl, American satirist (1926–). As told on his record album 'The New Frontier' (1961). Another version is that Sahl, invited by the director, Otto Preminger, to a preview, stood up after three hours and said, 'Otto – let my people go!'

Of the film Love Story:

12 Happiness is a warm bed pan.

Christopher Hudson (untraced). Quoted in *A Year of Stings and Squelches* (1985).

Of the film I Am a Camera *(US, 1955):*

13 Me no Leica.

C(aroline) A. Lejeune, English film critic (1897–1973). Quoted in *The Penguin Dictionary of Modern Quotations* (1980 edn). Also attributed to George Jean Nathan, Walter Kerr and Kenneth Tynan.

Of the film My Son My Son *(US, 1940):*

1 My Son My Son, my sainted aunt!
C. A. Lejeune. Attributed.

Of the film No Leave No Love *(US, 1946):*

2 No comment.
C. A. Lejeune. Attributed.

Of the film I Was Framed *(untraced):*

3 Yes, but was you hung?
C. A. Lejeune. In the *News Chronicle*.
Quoted in *The Observer* (21 December 1997).

Of the film Anything Goes *(US, 1956):*

4 Obviously.
C. A. Lejeune. Quoted in *The Observer*
(4 January 1998).

On the film Her Primitive Man
(US, 1944):

5 Cave.
C. A. Lejeune. Quoted in *The Observer*
(11 January 1998).

Of the film Gilda *(US, 1946) and its slogan,
'There never was a woman like Gilda!':*

6 There never was.
C. A. Lejeune. Quoted in *The Observer*
(18 January 1998).

*On Charlton Heston's performance
as a doctor:*

7 It makes me want to call out, Is there
an apple in the house?
C. A. Lejeune. Quoted in *The 'Quote . . .
Unquote' Book of Love, Death and the
Universe* (1980).

Films

8 JOE: You're Norma Desmond – used
to be in silent pictures – used to
be big.
NORMA: I am big. It's the pictures
that got small.
Gloria Swanson as Norma Desmond
and William Holden as Joe Gillis. Film,
Sunset Boulevard (US, 1950). Script
by Charles Brackett, Billy Wilder and
D. M. Marshman Jr.

9 Every film should have a beginning, a
middle and an end – but not necessarily
in that order.

Jean-Luc Godard, French film director
(1930– . Quoted in Len Deighton,
Close Up (1972). Has also been ascribed to
the French film director Georges Franju
(1912–87) – as in *Time* Magazine
(14 September 1981).

Financiers

10 A financier is a pawnbroker with
imagination.
Sir Arthur Wing Pinero, English playwright
(1855–1934). Quoted in *The Treasury of
Humorous Quotations*, ed. Evan Esar &
Nicolas Bentley (1951).

Flattery

11 I suppose flattery hurts no one – that
is, if he doesn't inhale.
Adlai Stevenson, American Democratic
politician (1900–65). On *Meet the Press*,
TV broadcast (29 March 1952).

*A schoolboy applicant for a naval college
is being interviewed. An examining
admiral asks him, 'Now mention three
great admirals.' The candidate replies:*

12 Drake, Nelson and – I beg your pardon,
Sir, I didn't quite catch your name.
Anonymous (cartoonist). Caption to cartoon
in *Punch* (24 June 1914).

To a young lady:

13 Won't you come into the garden?
I would like my roses to see you.
Richard Brinsley Sheridan, English dramatist
and politician (1751–1816). Attributed in
The Oxford Dictionary of Humorous Quotations,
ed. Ned Sherrin (1995).

Flirting

Man flirting with a woman:

14 Tell me about yourself – your struggles,
your dreams, your telephone number.
Peter Arno, American cartoonist (1904–68).
Quoted in A. Andrews, *Quotations for Speakers
and Writers* (1969).

*To Bernard Shaw after an empty
flirtation (1887):*

15 You had no right to write the Preface if
you were not going to write the book.
E(dith) Nesbit, English writer (1858–1924).

Quoted in Michael Holroyd, *Bernard Shaw*, Vol. 1 (1988).

1 ALGERNON: The amount of women in London who flirt with their husbands is perfectly scandalous. It looks so bad. It is simply washing one's clean linen in public.

Oscar Wilde, Irish playwright, poet and wit (1854–1900). *The Importance of Being Earnest*, Act 1 (1895).

2 Flirt: a woman who thinks it's every man for herself.

Anonymous. Quoted in *The Penguin Dictionary of Modern Humorous Quotations*, ed. Fred Metcalf (1987).

Food and Food criticism

3 Eating cottage cheese is like kissing your sister.

Anonymous. Overheard remark quoted by Isabelle Lucas on BBC Radio *Quote ... Unquote* (19 January 1982).

To a waiter:

4 When I ask for a watercress sandwich, I do not mean a loaf with a field in the middle of it.

Oscar Wilde, Irish playwright, poet and wit (1854–1900). Recounted in a letter from Max Beerbohm to Reggie Turner (15 April 1893).

5 Eat to live, and not live to eat.

Benjamin Franklin, American politician and scientist (1706–90). *Poor Richard's Almanack* (May 1733) – a work in which Franklin often revised already existing sayings.

6 The piece of cod passeth all understanding.

Sir Edwin Lutyens, English architect (1869–1944). Quoted in Robert Lutyens, *Sir Edwin Lutyens* (1942).

Of champagne arriving with the pudding after a series of poorly-heated courses at a public dinner:

7 Thank God for something warm at last.

Benjamin Disraeli (later 1st Earl of Beaconsfield), English politician and writer (1804–81). Quoted in *The Sayings of Disraeli*, ed. Robert Blake (1992).

Fools

To a tiresome escort who exclaimed, 'I can't bear fools':

8 That's queer. Your mother could.

Dorothy Parker, American writer (1893–1967). Quoted in Ned Sherrin, *Cutting Edge* (1984).

9 When he said we were trying to make a fool of him, I could only murmur that the Creator had beat us to it.

Ilka Chase, American actress and author (1900–78). Quoted in *The Treasury of Humorous Quotations*, ed. Evan Esar & Nicolas Bentley (1951).

10 I have always heard it said, that to do a kindness to clowns, is like throwing water into the sea.

Cervantes, Spanish novelist (1547–1616). *Don Quixote*, Pt 1 Chap. 23, translated by Peter Motteux (1700–3).

Foot in mouth

11 Every time he opens his mouth at the Town Hall, he puts his foot in it, so they call him 'the foot and mouth disease'. Ha. Ha.

J. B. Priestley, English novelist and playwright (1894–1984). *When We Are Married* (1938).

12 'Dentopedology' is the science of opening your mouth and putting your foot in it. I've been practising it for years.

Prince Philip (Duke of Edinburgh), Greek-born consort of Queen Elizabeth II (1921–). Quoted in Herbert V. Prochnow, Snr & Jnr, *A Treasury of Humorous Quotations* (1969).

Football

13 Some people think football is a matter of life and death. I don't like that attitude. I can assure them it is much more serious than that.

Bill Shankly, Scottish football manager (1914–81). Quoted in *The Guardian*, 'Sports Quotes of the Year' (24 December 1973).

Forbidding Cornell's first intercollegiate football game with the University of Michigan at Cleveland, Ohio, in 1873:

1 I will not permit thirty men to travel four hundred miles to agitate a bag of wind.

Andrew D. White, American academic (1832–1918). White was the first President of Cornell University (1867–85). Quoted in Stuart Berg Flexner, *Listening to America* (1982).

Ford, Gerald R.
American Republican President (1913–)

2 A year ago Gerald Ford was unknown throughout America, now he's unknown throughout the world.

Anonymous. Quoted in *The Guardian* (August 1974) and then in *The Penguin Dictionary of Modern Quotations* (1980). When he replaced Spiro Agnew as US Vice-President.

3 He looks like the guy in a science fiction movie who is the first to see the Creature.

David Frye, American impressionist and comedian (1934–). Attributed in 1975. Quoted in the book *Quote ... Unquote* (1978).

4 That Gerald Ford. He can't fart and chew gum at the same time.

Lyndon B. Johnson, American Democratic President (1908–73). Quoted in Richard Reeves, *A Ford Not a Lincoln* (1975) and J. K. Galbraith, *A Life in Our Times* (1981).

5 He played too much football without a helmet.

Anonymous. Quoted in the book *Quote ... Unquote* (1978). Other criticisms: 'He'd fuck up a two-car funeral'; 'He couldn't find the seat of his pants with both hands.'

Foreign affairs

6 I'd never heard of this place Guatemala until I was in my seventy-ninth year.

Winston S. Churchill (later Sir Winston), British Conservative Prime Minister and writer (1874–1965). During his visit to the US (June 1954), recorded by Lord Moran in *The Struggle for Survival* (1966). Earlier,

Moran recorded Churchill saying on 28 April 1953: 'I have lived seventy-eight years without hearing of bloody places like Cambodia.'

Foreign policy
On his foreign policy:

7 My policy is to be able to take a ticket at Victoria Station and go anywhere I damn well please.

Ernest Bevin, English Labour politician (1881–1951). Quoted in *The Spectator* (20 April 1951). When Labour Foreign Secretary.

Foreigners

8 'Frogs,' he would say, 'are slightly better than Huns or Wops, but abroad is unutterably bloody and foreigners are fiends.'

Nancy Mitford, English novelist (1904–73). *The Pursuit of Love* (1945).

9 Everybody has the right to pronounce foreign names as he chooses.

Winston S. Churchill (later Sir Winston), British Conservative Prime Minister and writer (1874–1965). Quoted in *The Observer* (5 August 1951).

Foreplay

10 He twisted my nipples as though tuning a radio.

Lisa Alther, American writer (1944–). *Kinflick* (1976). Quoted in *The Penguin Dictionary of Modern Humorous Quotations*, ed. Fred Metcalf (1987).

Forgetfulness

11 There are three things I always forget. Names, faces, and – the third I can't remember.

Italo Svevo, Italian novelist (1861–1928). Quoted in *The Penguin Dictionary of Modern Quotations* (1971).

12 Only three men in Europe had ever understood [the Schleswig-Holstein question], and of these the Prince Consort is dead, a Danish statesman is in an asylum, and I myself have forgotten it.

Lord Palmerston, British Prime Minister (1784–1865). Quoted in R. W. Seton-Watson, *Britain in Europe 1789–1914* (1937).

Forster, E. M.
English novelist (1879–1970)

1 E. M. Forster never gets any further than warming the teapot. He's a rare fine hand at that. Feel this teapot. Is it not beautifully warm? Yes, but there ain't going to be no tea.

Katherine Mansfield, New Zealand-born writer (1888–1923). *Journal* (1927) – entry for May 1917.

Forty

One actress about another:

2 Pushing forty? She's clinging on to it for dear life!

Anonymous. Quoted by Julian Mitchell on BBC Radio *Quote … Unquote* (5 January 1982).

Fragility

3 He was in the sort of overwrought state when a fly treading a little too heavily on the carpet is enough to make a man think he's one of the extras in *All Quiet On the Western Front.*

P. G. Wodehouse (later Sir Pelham), English-born novelist and lyricist (1881–1975). 'The Luck of the Stiffhams', *Young Men in Spats* (1936).

4 He says his memory is blurred. All he can recall is waking next morning on the floor of his bedroom and shooting up to the ceiling when a sparrow on the window-sill chirped unexpectedly.

P. G. Wodehouse. 'The Right Approach', *A Few Quick Ones* (1936).

5 'Have you an aspirin about you?'
   'Certainly, m'lord. I have just been taking one myself.'
   He produced a small tin box, and held it out.
   'Thank you, Jeeves. Don't slam the lid.'

P. G. Wodehouse, *Ring for Jeeves*, Chap. 18 (1953).

Having had too little to smoke:

6 Yes, he felt, analysing his emotions, he was distinctly nervous. The noise of the cat stamping about in the passage outside caused him exquisite discomfort.

P. G. Wodehouse. 'The Man Who Gave Up Smoking', *Mr Mulliner Speaking* (1929).

France and the French

7 France is the only place where you can make love in the afternoon without people hammering on your door.

Barbara Cartland (later Dame Barbara), English romantic novelist (1901–). Quoted in *The Observer*, 'Sayings of the Week' (28 October 1984).

8 France is a country where the money falls apart in your hands and you can't tear the toilet paper.

Billy Wilder, American film director and writer (1906–). Quoted in Leslie Halliwell, *The Filmgoer's Book of Quotes* (1973).

Friends

9 God protect me from my friends.

Anonymous saying. Used as the title of a book (1956) by Gavin Maxwell about Salvatore Giuliano, the Sicilian bandit. From the proverbial expression: 'I can look after my enemies, but God protect me from my friends.'

10 With friends like that, who needs enemies? With a Hungarian for a friend, who needs an enemy?

Anonymous sayings. Quoted in Eric Partridge, *A Dictionary of Catch Phrases* (1977).

11 Give me the avowed, the erect,
     the manly foe,
   Bold I can meet – perhaps may turn
     his blow!
   But of all plagues, Good Heaven,
     thy wrath can send,
   Save, save, Oh, save me from the
     candid friend!

George Canning, English Prime Minister (1770–1827). 'New Morality' (1821).

12 GEKKO: If you want a friend, get a dog.

Dialogue from film *Wall Street* (US, 1987).
Written by Stanley Weiser and Oliver Stone.
With Michael Douglas as Gordon Gekko.

1 Whenever a friend succeeds, a little
something in me dies.

Gore Vidal, American novelist, playwright
and critic (1925–). Interviewed on TV by
David Frost and quoted in *The Sunday Times*
Magazine (16 September 1973).

*On the 'Night of the Long Knives', when
Prime Minister Harold Macmillan sacked
half his Cabinet (13 July 1962):*

2 Greater love hath no man than this,
that he lay down his friends for
his life.

Jeremy Thorpe, English liberal politician
(1929–). Quoted in D. E. Butler & A. King,
The General Election of 1964 (1965).

3 Making and preserving friends. Select
some sound hearts. Be careful not to
bruise them with unfeeling words.
Take of milk of human kindness one
heartful. Add to this plenty of tact.
Warm the mixture with plenty of
sympathy. Do not let it get *too* hot at
first, lest it only ferment mischief.
Knead with plenty of oil of unselfish-
ness to make all smooth. Beware of jars
(lovely wording). The mixture should
be kept in a warm corner of the heart.
Years only serve to improve the flavour
of friends thus preserved.

'Dame Edna Everage' (Barry Humphries,
Australian entertainer, 1934–). 'A Recipe for
Happiness', *A Nice Night's Entertainment*
(1981). Humphries has admitted that this
recipe was taken in its entirety from a
women's magazine.

4 There is no spectacle more agreeable
than to observe an old friend fall
from a roof-top.

Confucius, Chinese philosopher (551–
479 BC). Attributed. Sometimes it is a 'neighbour': 'Even a virtuous and high-minded
man may experience a little pleasure when he
sees his neighbour falling from a roof.'

5 In the misfortune of our best friends, we
find something that is not displeasing
to us [*Dans l'adversité de nos meilleurs*

*amis, nous trouvons toujours quelque
chose qui ne nous deplaît pas*].

Duc de La Rochefoucauld, French moralist
(1613–80). *Réflexions ou Maximes Morales*,
Maxim 99 (1665).

Frogs

6 What a wonderful bird the frog are!
When he walk, he fly almost;
When he sing, he cry almost.
He ain't got no tail hardly, either.
He sit on what he ain't got almost.

Anonymous. A leading article in *The Times*
(20 May 1948) ascribed these lines to the pen
of an African schoolgirl, causing one reader to
write in and say he had always believed they
had come from the mouth of a French Canadian. He also said he had an idea that he had
first seen them in the *Manchester Guardian*
'about twenty years ago'. The version that
appears in Arnold Silcock's *Verse and Worse*
(1952) is also ascribed to 'Anon (French
Canadian)' and is fractionally different.

Frost, David (later Sir David)
English broadcaster (1939–)

*When asked by a nun if her future
husband was religious:*

7 Oh, yes, he thinks he's God Almighty.

Lady Carina Frost (1952–). Quoted in
The Sunday Times (28 July 1985).

On rescuing David Frost from drowning:

8 I had to pull him out, otherwise
nobody would have believed I didn't
push him in.

Peter Cook, English humorist (1937–
95). *Quoted in A Year of Stings and
Squelches* (1985).

Funerals

*When asked if he would attend his ex-wife
Marilyn Monroe's funeral (1962):*

9 Why should I go? She won't be there.

Arthur Miller, American playwright
(1915–). Attributed.

10 There is nothing like a morning
funeral for sharpening the appetite
for lunch.

Arthur Marshall, English writer and

entertainer (1910–89). *Life's Rich Pageant* (1984). It was quoted at his own (pre-lunch) memorial service in 1989.

On the large number of mourners at film producer Harry Cohn's funeral (in 1958):

1 Same old story: you give 'em what they want and they'll fill the theatre.

George Jessel, American entertainer (1898–1981). Quoted by Lillian Hellman in *Scoundrel Time* (1976). Earlier quoted, as said on TV by Red Skelton (1910–97), in Philip French, *The Movie Moguls* (1969). An unattributed version appears in Oscar Levant, *The Unimportance of Being Oscar* (1968).

Attending a funeral towards the end of his life:

2 There's not much point going home really, is there?

Robb Wilton, English comedian (1881–1957). Quoted on BBC Radio *Quote ... Unquote* (1991). Ned Sherrin, in *Theatrical Anecdotes* (1991), has Lorenz Hart saying something similar about his Uncle Willie at his (Hart's) mother's funeral in 1943. As it happens, Hart himself died first.

3 'If you don't go to other men's funerals,' he told Father stiffly, 'they won't go to yours.'

Clarence Day, American humorist (1874–1935). *Life with Father* (1935).

On Louis B. Mayer's funeral:

4 The reason so many people showed up at his funeral was because they wanted to make sure he was dead.

Sam Goldwyn, Polish-born American film producer (1882–1974). Quoted in Bosley Crowther, *Hollywood Rajah* (1960). Probably apocryphal, if only because the funeral was in fact sparsely attended.

Funny

5 What do you mean, funny? Funny peculiar, or funny ha-ha?

Ian Hay, Scottish novelist and playwright (1876–1952). Play, *Housemaster*, Act 3 (1936).

6 'I liked that song, myself,' he said, 'even if it isn't classical. It's funny, anyhow.'
Genevieve Gertrude raised her hand.
   'Do you mean funny peculiar, or funny ha-ha?' she inquired politely.
   ... ''Cause,' explained his mentor gravely, 'our teacher don't allow us to say funny when we mean peculiar. It's bad English, you know.'

Meriel Brady, American novelist. *Genevieve Gertrude*, Chap. 7 (1928).

Futile gestures

7 The attempt of the Lords to stop the progress of Reform reminds me very forcibly of the great storm of Sidmouth, and of the conduct of the excellent Mrs Partington on that occasion. In the winter of 1824 there set in a great flood upon that town – the tide rose to an incredible height, the waves rushed in upon the houses, and everything was threatened with destruction! In the midst of this sublime and terrible storm, Dame Partington, who lived upon the beach, was seen at the door of her house with mop and pattens, trundling her mop, squeezing out the sea-water, and vigorously pushing away the Atlantic Ocean. The Atlantic was roused. Mrs Partington's spirit was up; but I need not tell you that the contest was unequal. The Atlantic Ocean beat Mrs Partington. She was excellent at a slop, or a puddle, but she should not have meddled with a tempest. Gentlemen, be at your ease – be quiet and steady. You will beat Mrs Partington.

Revd Sydney Smith, English clergyman, essayist and wit (1771–1845). Speech at Taunton on Parliamentary Reform (1831).

Future

8 He did not seem to mind having a future behind him.

C. P. Snow (later Lord Snow), English novelist and scientist (1905–80). *The Affair,*

Chap. 2 (1960). An early appearance of this line. Compare:

Of Marilyn Monroe:

1 There's a broad with her future behind her.

Constance Bennett, American film actress (1904–65). Quoted in Leslie Halliwell, *Halliwell's Filmgoer's Companion* (1984, and subsequently).

2 He was a man with a great future behind him.

Angela Carter, English novelist (1940–92). *Wise Children*, Chap. 3 (1991).

Of Bill Clinton, when the youngest defeated state governor in US history:

3 At 34, he fit the ironic description of the quintessential Rhodes Scholar: someone with a great future behind him.

David Maraniss, American journalist and author (1949–). *First in His Class* (1995).

G

Gable, Clark
American film actor (1901–60)

1 That man's ears make him look like a taxi-cab with both doors open.

Howard Hughes, American industrialist and film producer (1905–76). Quoted in Charles Higham and Joel Greenberg, *Celluloid Muse* (1969).

2 Clark Gable has the best ears of our lives.

Milton Berle, American comedian (1908–). Quoted in Leslie Halliwell, *The Filmgoer's Book of Quotes* (1973).

Gabor, Zsa Zsa
American film actress (1919–)

3 She not only worships the Golden Calf, she barbecues it for lunch.

Oscar Levant, American pianist and actor (1906–72). Quoted in *The Penguin Dictionary of Modern Quotations* (1985 edn).

Gambling

4 Horse sense is a good judgement which keeps horses from betting on people.

W. C. Fields, American comedian (1879–1946). Quoted by Sam Ervin on record album *Senator Sam at Home* (1974).

When a gambler asks 'Cuthbert J. Twillie', 'Is this a game of chance?':

5 Not the way I play it.

W. C. Fields. Film, *My Little Chickadee* (US, 1939).

6 The race is not always to the swift nor the battle to the strong, but that's the way to bet.

Damon Runyon, American writer (1884–1946). Quoted in *The Treasury of Humorous Quotations*, ed. Evan Esar & Nicolas Bentley (1951).

Games-playing

When a poor bridge partner asked how he should have played a hand:

7 Under an assumed name.

George S. Kaufman, American playwright (1889–1961). Quoted in Scott Meredith, *George S. Kaufman and the Algonquin Round Table* (1974).

Gardening

8 A garden is a lovesome thing? What rot!

J. A. Lindon (untraced). 'My Garden with a stern look at T. E. Brown'. In *Yet More Comic and Curious Verse*, ed. J. M. Cohen (1959).

9 A garden is a loathsome thing, God wot!
  ... That geezer should be shot
What wrote that lot
Of Palgrave's Golden Tommy-rot ...
I'd rather sun myself on Uncle's yacht.

Gerard Benson (untraced). Included in *Imitations of Immortality*, ed. E. O. Parrott (1986).

On finding that a grand Italian house had a garden that was a bit of shambles:

10 This garden rather looks as if it was laid out by Incapability Bruno.

Leonard Miall, English broadcaster and executive, latterly historian and obituarist (1914–). Quoted by Sir Huw Wheldon on BBC Radio *Quote ... Unquote* (10 August 1985).

Generalization

11 He who generalizes generally lies.

Anonymous. Quoted in *The 'Quote ... Unquote' Newsletter* (January 1997).

1 A generalizer is a man who learns less and less about more and more until he knows nothing about everything.

Anonymous. Quoted in *ibid.*

2 All generalizations are dangerous, even this one.

Alexandre Dumas fils, French writer (1824–95). Quoted on BBC Radio *Quote ... Unquote* (8 September 1984).

Genetics

3 If a queen bee were crossed with a Friesian bull, would not the land flow with milk and honey?

Oliver St John Gogarty, Irish writer (1878–1957). Quoted on BBC Radio *Quote ... Unquote* (8 September 1984).

Genius

4 Genius does what it must, and Talent does what it can.

Owen Meredith (1st Earl of Lytton), English poet (1831–91). 'Last Words of a Sensitive Second-Rate Poet' (1868). Compare:

Contrasting Mozart and Salieri in Pushkin's play Mozart and Salieri:

5 We see the contrast between the genius which does what it must and the talent which does what it can.

Maurice Baring, English writer (1874–1945). *An Outline of Russian Literature*, Chap. 3 (1914).

Discussing H. G. Wells:

6 If a man is going to behave like a bastard, he'd better be a genius.

Jill Craigie, English writer and film-maker (1914–). On BBC2 TV *Bookmark* (24 August 1996), in conversation with her husband, Michael Foot.

At the New York Custom House, on arriving in the United States (1882) and asked by the customs officer if he had anything to declare:

7 I have nothing to declare except my genius.

Oscar Wilde, Irish playwright, poet and wit (1854–1900). Quoted in Frank Harris, *Oscar Wilde* (1918).

8 I'm going to live forever. Geniuses don't die.

Salvador Dali, Spanish artist (1904–89). Quoted in *The Observer*, 'Sayings of the Week' (27 July 1986).

9 When a true genius appears in the world, you may know him by this sign, that the dunces are all in confederacy against him.

Jonathan Swift, Anglo-Irish writer and clergyman (1667–1745). *Thoughts on Various Subjects* (1706).

10 Genius is an infinite capacity for giving pains.

Don Herold, American humorist and artist (1889–1966). Quoted in *The Treasury of Humorous Quotations*, ed. Evan Esar & Nicolas Bentley (1951).

Gentility

11 Phone for the fish knives, Norman, As Cook is a little unnerved.

(Sir) John Betjeman, English poet (1906–84). 'How to Get on in Society' (1954). The poem concerns 'Non-U' language and behaviour – that is to say genteel rather than 'U' language and behaviour of the upper-classes. In that milieu, special knives for eating are frowned upon, the full word 'telephone' is preferred, and so on.

Gentlemen

12 A gentleman should be able to play the flute, but not too expertly.

Aristotle, Greek philosopher (384–322 BC). Attributed – possibly an encapsulation of the point he makes in Bk 8 of his *Politics* where he says that children of free men should learn and practise music only until they are able to feel delight in it and should not become professional musicians because this would make them vulgar.

To a certain person:

13 Had your father spent more of your mother's immoral earnings on your education you would not even then have been a gentleman.

Sir Seymour Hicks, English actor-manager (1871–1949). *Vintage Years* (1943).

1 A gentleman is any man who wouldn't hit a woman with his hat on.

Fred Allen, American comedian (1894–1956). Quoted in Laurence J. Peter, *Quotations for Our Time* (1977).

Definition of an English gentleman:

2 Useful at a hunt ball. Invaluable in a shipwreck.

Anonymous. Quoted on BBC Radio *Quote ... Unquote* (18 June 1986).

Of Michael Arlen:

3 For all his reputation [he] is not a bounder. He is every other inch a gentleman.

Alexander Woollcott, American writer and critic (1887–1943). Quoted in R. E. Drennan, *Wit's End* (1973). The same remark has also been attributed to Rebecca West (by Ted Morgan in *Somerset Maugham*, 1980) on the same person.

4 No gentleman ever has any money.

Oscar Wilde, Irish playwright, poet and wit (1854–1900). *The Importance of Being Earnest*, Act 2 (1895).

5 DUMBY: Awful manners young Hopper has!

CECIL GRAHAM: Ah! Hopper is one of Nature's gentlemen, the worst type of gentleman I know.

Oscar Wilde. *Lady Windermere's Fan*, Act 2 (1892).

6 I do hope I shall enjoy myself with you ... I am parshial to ladies if they are nice I suppose it is my nature. I am not quite a gentleman but you would hardly notice it.

Daisy Ashford, English child author (1881–1972). *The Young Visiters*, Chap. 1 (1919).

7 No gentleman writes about his private life.

Hilaire Belloc, French-born English poet and writer (1870–1953). Quoted in Hugh Kingsmill and Hesketh Pearson, *Talking About Dick Whittington* (1947).

8 Gentlemen do not take soup at luncheon.

George Curzon (1st Marquess Curzon), English Conservative politician (1859–1925). Quoted in E. L. Woodward, *Short Journey* (1912). Curzon also said: 'Gentlemen never wear brown in London.'

9 Gentlemen prefer blondes, but take what they can get.

Don Herold, American humorist and artist (1889–1966). Quoted in *The Treasury of Humorous Quotations*, ed. Evan Esar & Nicolas Bentley (1951).

George III
British King (1738–1820)

10 George the Third
Ought never to have occurred.
One can only wonder
At so grotesque a blunder.

E. Clerihew Bentley, English novelist, journalist and poet (1875–1956). *Biography for Beginners* (1905).

George, David Lloyd
(1st Earl Lloyd George of Dwyfor)
British Prime Minister (1863–1945)

11 When he's alone in a room, there's nobody there.

John Maynard Keynes, English economist (1883–1946). Quoted by Baroness Asquith in BBC TV *As I Remember* (30 April 1967). However, James Agate in *Ego 5* (for 30 September 1941): 'Sat next to Lady Oxford, who was in great form ... "Lloyd George? There is no Lloyd George. There is a marvellous brain; but if you were to shut him in a room and look through the keyhole there would be nobody there."'

12 *Ah, si je pouvais pisser comme il parle!* [If I could piss the way he speaks!]

George Clemenceau, French Prime Minister (1841–1929). Quoted in A. Andrews, *Quotations for Speakers and Writers* (1969).

13 He couldn't see a belt without hitting below it.

Margot Asquith (later Countess of Oxford and Asquith) (1864–1945). Quoted in Mark Bonham Carter's Introduction to *The Autobiography of Margot Asquith* (1962 edn).

14 Mr Lloyd George spoke for a hundred and seventeen minutes, in which period

he was detected only once in the use of an argument.

Arnold Bennett, English novelist (1867–1931). 'After the March Offensive', *Things That Have Interested Me* (1921–5).

1 He did not care which direction the car was travelling, so long as he was in the driver's seat.

Maxwell Aitken (1st Baron Beaverbrook), Canadian-born English politician and newspaper proprietor (1879–1964). *The Decline and Fall of Lloyd George* (1963).

2 Lloyd George knew my father, My father knew Lloyd George.

Anonymous, sung to the tune of 'Onward Christian Soldiers'. Known before Lloyd George's death in 1945. In Welsh legal and Liberal circles the credit for the coinage has been given to Tommy Rhys Roberts QC (1910–75), whose father did indeed know Lloyd George.

German language

3 I once heard a Californian student in Heidelberg say, in one of his calmest moods, that he would rather decline two drinks than one German adjective.

Mark Twain, American writer (1835–1910). *A Tramp Abroad*, Appendix D (1880).

Gifts

His idea of the gift he would give his worst enemy for Christmas:

4 Dinner with Princess Michael of Kent.

Viscount Linley, English designer (1961–). Quoted in the *Daily Mail* (16 April 1985). Allegedly spoken in November 1983.

On her ex-husband, pop singer Rod Stewart:

5 What do you give the man who's had everyone?

Alana Stewart. Quoted in *Sunday Today*, 'Quotes of the Week' (4 January 1987).

Gin

6 The wages of gin is breath.

Oliver Herford, American humorist (1863–1935), and Addison Mizner, American architect (1872–1933). *The Cynic's Calendar* (1902).

Girls

7 I am fond of children (except boys).

Lewis Carroll (C. L. Dodgson), English writer (1832–98). Letter to Kathleen Eschwege (1879), quoted in Stuart Dodgson Collingwood, *The Life and Letters of Lewis Carroll* (1898).

8 Good girls go to heaven, bad girls go everywhere.

Helen Gurley Brown, American journalist (1922–). Promotional line for *Cosmopolitan* Magazine when she relaunched it in 1965.

Gladstone, W. E.
British Prime Minister (1809–98)

9 He has not a single redeeming defect.

Benjamin Disraeli (later 1st Earl of Beaconsfield), English politician and writer (1804–81). Quoted in A. K. Adams, *The Home Book of Humorous Quotations* (undated).

10 For the purposes of recreation he has selected the felling of trees, and we may usefully remark that his amusements, like his politics, are essentially destructive ... The forest laments that Mr Gladstone may perspire.

Lord Randolph Churchill, English politician (1849–94). Speech on financial reform, Blackpool (24 January 1884). Gladstone's 'arboreal assaults' (in Roy Jenkins's phrase) became one of his central occupations, almost akin – though publicly better known – to his picking up of fallen women.

11 An old man in a hurry.

Lord Randolph Churchill. Speech to the electors of South Paddington (19 June 1886).

12 Mr Gladstone read Homer for fun, which I thought served him right.

Winston S. Churchill (later Sir Winston), British Conservative Prime Minister and writer (1874–1965). *My Early Life*, Chap. 2 (1930).

Glyn, Elinor
English novelist (1864–1943)

13 Would you like to sin
With Elinor Glyn
On a tiger-skin?
Or would you prefer
To err with her
On some other fur?

Anonymous. Quoted in A. Glyn, *Elinor Glyn* (1955). Written *c.*1907.

God

1 To the lexicographer, God is simply the word that comes next to go-cart.

Samuel Butler, English writer (1835–1902). Quoted in *The Treasury of Humorous Quotations*, ed. Evan Esar & Nicolas Bentley (1951).

2 God don't make mistakes. That's how he got to be God.

'Archie Bunker' in American TV series *All in the Family* (1971–80). Script by various. Attributed.

3 When God made man she was only testing.

Anonymous (graffito), North Kensington, London. Contributed to BBC Radio s*Quote ... Unquote* (26 April 1978).

4 God can stand being told by Professor Ayer and Marghanita Laski that he doesn't exist.

J. B. Priestley, English playwright, novelist and author (1894–1984). Quoted in *The Listener* (1 July 1965).

5 I am ready to meet my Maker. Whether my Maker is ready for the ordeal of meeting me is another matter.

Winston S. Churchill (later Sir Winston), British Conservative Prime Minister and writer (1874–1965). Speech (30 November 1949). On his 75th birthday.

While reading the Bible from cover to cover in response to a bet:

6 Isn't God a shit!

Randolph Churchill, English journalist and politician (1911–68). Quoted in Evelyn Waugh, *The Diaries of Evelyn Waugh* (1976) – entry for 11 November 1944.

7 Forgive, O Lord, my little jokes on Thee And I'll forgive Thy great big one on me.

Robert Frost, American poet (1874–1963). 'Cluster of Faith' (1962).

8 God, whatever else He is, and of course He is everything else, – is not a fool.

Alan Bennett, English playwright and actor (1934–). *Forty Years On*, Act 2 (1969).

9 Not only is there no God, but try getting a plumber on weekends.

Woody Allen, American film actor, writer and director (1937–). 'My Philosophy', *Getting Even* (1975).

14th Earl of Gurney:

10 I know I am God because when I pray to him I find I'm talking to myself.

Peter Barnes, English playwright (1931–). *The Ruling Class* (1968).

11 The ordinary Britisher imagines that God is an Englishman.

Bernard Shaw, Irish playwright and critic (1856–1950). Quoted in Herbert V. Prochnow, Snr & Jnr, *A Treasury of Humorous Quotations* (1969).

12 Never mind, God isn't an Albanian ...

Anonymous (Greek) saying.

When H. M. Butler, Master of Trinity College, Cambridge, drew attention to the fact that 'both the Sovereign and the Prime Minister are Trinity men':

13 The Master should have added that he can go further, for it is obvious that the affairs of the world are built upon the momentous fact that God also is a Trinity man.

Augustine Birrell, English Liberal politician and writer (1850–1933). Quoted by Harold Laski in a letter to Oliver Wendell Holmes (4 December 1926).

14 God is not dead but alive and working on a much less ambitious project.

Anonymous (graffito). Quoted in *The Guardian* (26 November 1975).

15 An honest God is the noblest work of man.

Robert Green Ingersoll, American lawyer and writer (1833–99). Quoted in *The Treasury of Humorous Quotations*, ed. Evan Esar & Nicolas Bentley (1951).

Godfathers

On being invited to be a godparent by Kenneth Tynan (1967):

16 Always a godfather, never a God.

Gore Vidal, American novelist, playwright and critic (1925–). Quoted in Kathleen Tynan, *The Life of Kenneth Tynan* (1987). Has also been ascribed to Alexander Woollcott.

Goldwynisms

The mostly apocryphal sayings of Samuel Goldwyn, Polish-born American film producer (1882–1974)

1 Let's have some new clichés.

Quoted in *The Observer* (24 October 1948).

2 An oral [or verbal] contract isn't worth the paper it's written on.

Quoted in Alva Johnston, *The Great Goldwyn* (1937).

3 That's the way with these directors, they're always biting the hand that lays the golden egg.

Ibid.

4 In two words – impossible!

Quoted in *ibid.* along with the information that the joke appeared in a humour magazine late in 1925, and was subsequently imposed upon Goldwyn. *H. L. Mencken's Dictionary of Quotations* (1942) has: 'I can answer in two words – im possible' and ascribes it to 'an American movie magnate, 1930.' Curiously, however, the following is to be found in *Punch* (10 June 1931) – caption to cartoon by George Belcher: 'Harassed Film-Producer. "This business can be summed up in two words: IM-POSSIBLE."'

When his secretary suggested weeding out files:

5 A good idea, only be sure to make a copy of everything before getting rid of it.

Quoted in Michael Freedland, *The Goldwyn Touch* (1986).

6 What we want is a story that starts with an earthquake and works its way up to a climax ...

Quoted in Leslie Halliwell, *The Filmgoer's Book of Quotes* (1973).

7 Tell me, how did you love the picture?

Ibid.

8 Let's bring it up to date with some snappy nineteenth century dialogue.

Ibid.

9 I had a great idea this morning but I didn't like it.

Ibid.

10 Next time I want to send an idiot on some errand, I'll go myself.

Attributed.

11 If you can't give me your word of honour, will you give me your promise?

Quoted in the book *Quote ... Unquote* (1978).

12 First you have a good story, then a good treatment, and next a first-rate director. After that you hire a competent cast and even then you have only the mucus of a good picture.

Attributed by Terry Wogan on BBC Radio *Quote ... Unquote* (29 May 1980), but probably another invention. In P. G. Wodehouse's Mr Mulliner story 'The Castaways' (1933), set in Hollywood, Mr Schnellenhamer, the film mogul, says of a script he has bought, 'It has the mucus of a good story. See what you can do with it.'

13 Why should people go out and pay to see bad movies when they can stay at home and see bad television for nothing?

Quoted in *The Observer* (9 September 1956). As 'Who wants to go out and see a bad movie when they can stay at home and see a bad one free on television' – quoted in Philip French, *The Movie Moguls* (1969).

14 We have all passed a lot of water since then.

Quoted in Ezra Goodman, *The Fifty Year Decline of Hollywood* (1961).

15 Anyone who goes to a psychiatrist needs to have his head examined.

Attributed in Norman Zierold, *Moguls* (1969).

On films with a 'message':

16 Pictures are for entertainment, messages should be delivered by Western Union.

Attributed in Arthur Marx, *Goldwyn* (1976), and earlier in Leslie Halliwell, *The Filmgoer's Book of Quotes* (1973). However, in his 1978 edition, Halliwell also attributes to Jack Warner: 'We'll make the pictures: let Western Union deliver the messages.'

When Busby Berkeley, who had made his first musical for Goldwyn, was discovered moonlighting for Warner Brothers, Goldwyn said to Warner:

1 How can we sit together and deal with this industry if you're going to do things like this to me? If this is the way you do it, gentlemen, include me out!

Attributed. Goldwyn himself appeared to acknowledge this when speaking at Balliol College, Oxford, on 1 March 1945: 'For years I have been known for saying "Include me out" but today I am giving it up for ever.' On the other hand, Boller & George, in *They Never Said It* (1989), report Goldwyn as having denied saying it, claiming rather to have said to members of the Motion Picture Producers and Distributors of America: 'Gentlemen, I'm withdrawing from the association.'

Waving from an ocean-going liner to friends on the quayside:

2 Bon Voyage!

Quoted in Lillian Hellman, *Pentimento* (1974).

3 I took it all with a dose of salts.

Ibid.

Proposing toast at banquet to Field Marshal Montgomery:

4 A long life to Marshall Field Montgomery Ward.

Ibid.

When James Thurber was arguing with Goldwyn over the amount of violence that had crept in to a film treatment of his story The Secret Life of Walter Mitty, *eventually released in 1947, Goldwyn said:*

5 I'm sorry you felt it was too bloody and thirsty.

Quoted in Arthur Marx, *Goldwyn: A Biography of the Man Behind the Myth* (1976). Thurber, with commendable presence of mind, replied, 'Not only did I think so, I was horror and struck.'

6 Goldwynisms! Don't talk to me about Goldwynisms. Talk to Jesse Lasky!

Attributed.

7 Going to call him William? What kind of a name is that? Every Tom, Dick and Harry's called William. Why don't you call him Bill?

Quoted by Benny Green on BBC Radio *Quote ... Unquote* (22 June 1977).

8 I would be sticking my head in a moose.

Quoted in book *Quote ... Unquote* (1978).

9 I read part of the book all the way through.

Quoted in Philip French, *The Movie Moguls* (1969).

10 The trouble with this business is the dearth of bad pictures.

Ibid.

11 It rolls off my back like a duck.

Invented for him by George Oppenheimer and quoted in *ibid.*

12 I'll give you a definite maybe.

Attributed in *The Penguin Dictionary of Modern Quotations*, ed. J. M. & M. J. Cohen (1971).

13 It's more than magnificent – it's mediocre.

Ibid.

During filming of The Last Supper:

14 'Why only twelve [disciples]?' 'That's the original number.' 'Well, go out and get thousands!'

Ibid.

To a man who said, 'What beautiful hands your wife has':

15 Yes, I'm going to have a bust made of them.

Ibid.

16 You ought to take the bull between the teeth.

Ibid.

17 Chaplin is no business man – all he knows is that he can't take anything less.

Quoted in Charles Chaplin, *My Autobiography*, Chap. 19 (1964).

1 This makes me so sore, it gets my dandruff up.

Attributed in Herbert V. Prochnow, Snr & Jnr, *A Treasury of Humorous Quotations* (1969).

2 That's my *Toujours* Lautrec.

Quoted in Lillian Ross, 'Throw the Little Old Lady Down the Stairs', *Picture* (1952).

3 I want you to be sure and see my *Hans Christian Andersen*. It's full of charmth and warmth.

Attributed in book *Foot in Mouth* (1982).

4 We can get all the Indians we need at the reservoir.

Attributed in *ibid.*

5 Too caustic? To hell with the cost, we'll make the picture anyway.

Attributed in *ibid.*

6 It's spreading like wildflowers!

Attributed in *ibid.*

7 The A-bomb – that's dynamite!

Attributed in *ibid.*

8 I don't remember where I got this new Picasso. In Paris, I think. Somewhere over there on the Left Wing.

Attributed in *ibid.*

9 You just don't realise what life is all about until you have found yourself lying on the brink of a great abscess.

Attributed in *ibid.*

10 This is written in blank werse.

Attributed in *ibid.*

11 If Roosevelt were alive today, he'd turn over in his grave.

Quoted in *The Penguin Dictionary of Modern Quotations* (1971).

In answer to Samuel Goldwyn's inquiry, 'Do you really say all those things which the papers report that you say?':

12 Do you?

Dorothy Parker, American writer (1893–1967). Quoted in *The Sayings of Dorothy Parker*, ed. S. T. Brownlow (1992).

Golf

13 Golf is a good walk spoiled.

Mark Twain, American writer (1835–1910). Quoted by Laurence J. Peter in *Quotations for Our Time* (1977). The German author Kurt Tucholsky (1890–1935) wrote: '*Golf, sagte einmal jemand, ist ein verdorbener Spaziergang* [Golf, someone once said, is a walk spoiled]'.

Good news

14 Good news rarely comes in a brown envelope.

Sir Henry D'Avigdor Goldsmid, English politician and bullion broker (1909–76). Quoted by John Betjeman in a letter to Tom Driberg (21 July 1976).

Goodness

15 When I'm good, I'm very, very good. But when I'm bad, I'm better.

Mae West, American vaudeville and film actress (1893–1980). Film, *I'm No Angel* (US, 1933).

Replying to exclamation, 'Goodness, what beautiful diamonds!':

16 Goodness had nothing to do with it, dearie.

Mae West. Film, *Night After Night* (US, 1932). Script by Vincent Laurence, from novel by Louis Bromfield, 'with additional dialogue' by West.

17 No good deed goes unpunished.

Oscar Wilde, Irish playwright, poet and wit (1854–1900). Unverified. Joe Orton recorded it in his diary for 13 June 1967: 'Very good line George [Greeves] came out with at dinner: "No good deed ever goes unpunished."' James Agate in *Ego 3* (for 25 January 1938) states: '[Isidore Leo] Pavia was in great form today: "Every good deed brings its own punishment."' Note that neither of these sources mentions Wilde.

Government

18 Too bad that all the people who know how to run the country are busy driving taxicabs and cutting hair.

George Burns, American comedian (1896–1996). Remark attributed to him, by 1977. Also quoted in *Life* Magazine (December 1979).

1 All governments of any period provide comedy for the discerning mind.

Anonymous. Quoted by John Mortimer in *The Times* (7 March 1998).

Grace

2 For rabbits young and rabbits old,
For rabbits hot and rabbits cold,
For rabbits tender, rabbits tough,
We thank thee, Lord, we've had enough.

Anonymous. Quoted in *The 'Quote ... Unquote' Book of Love, Death and the Universe* (1980).

Graffiti

3 If God had not meant us to write on walls, he would never have given us the example.

Anonymous. Quoted in book *Graffiti 2* (1980).

4 Graffiti should be obscene and not heard.

Anonymous. Quoted in *ibid.*

5 When a society has to resort to the lavatory for its humour, the writing is on the wall.

Alan Bennett, English playwright and actor (1934–). *Forty Years On*, Act 2 (1969).

6 Popular education was bringing the graffito lower on the walls.

Oliver St John Gogarty, Irish writer (1878–1957). *As I Was Going Down Sackville Street* (1937).

Greatness

7 All my shows are great. Some of them are bad. But they are all great.

Lew Grade (later Lord Grade), Russian-born English media tycoon (1906–). Quoted in *The Observer* (14 September 1975).

Greetings

8 I met Curzon in Downing Street, from whom I got the sort of greeting a corpse would give to an undertaker.

Stanley Baldwin (later 1st Earl Baldwin of Bewdley), English Prime Minister (1867–1947). Quoted in A. & V. Palmer, *Quotations from History* (1976). On becoming Prime Minister – a job Curzon had always wanted – in 1933.

Growing Up

To Nina Hamnett:

9 We have become, Nina, the sort of people our parents warned us about.

Augustus John, Welsh artist (1878–1961). Attributed about the time Michael Holroyd's two-volume biography of John appeared (1974–5), but it is not in that book. It was quoted, in this precise form, on BBC Radio *Quote ... Unquote* in January 1977.

Growth

Little slave girl, Topsy, asserts that she has no mother or father, and replies on being asked who made her:

10 I s'pect I growed. Don't think nobody ever made me.

Harriet Beecher Stowe, American novelist (1811–96). *Uncle Tom's Cabin* (1852).

Grumbling

11 There are two powers at which men should never grumble – the weather and their wives.

Benjamin Disraeli (later 1st Earl of Beaconsfield), English politician and writer (1804–81). Quoted in Wilfrid Meynell, *The Man Disraeli* (1927 edn).

Guests

When he felt his Rothschild relatives had kept him up long enough:

12 To your tents, O Israel!

Archibald Philip Primrose, 5th Earl of Rosebery, British Liberal Prime Minister (1847–1929). Attributed.

On visiting royalty who overstayed their welcome:

13 Don't these people have palaces to go to?

Anonymous (old duke). Quoted by Patrick Garland on BBC Radio *Quote ... Unquote* (11 September 1979).

1 Frank Harris is invited to all the great houses of England – once.

Oscar Wilde, Irish playwright, poet and wit (1854–1900). Quoted in William Rothenstein, *Men and Memories* (1931).

2 I'm a particularly loathsome guest and I eat like a vulture. Unfortunately, the resemblance doesn't end there.

Groucho Marx, American comedian (1895–1977). *The Groucho Letters* (1967) – letter of 15 August 1956.

In her hostess's elaborate visitor's book:

3 'Quoth the raven ...'

Mrs Patrick Campbell, English actress (1865–1940). Quoted in Bennett Cerf, *Shake Well Before Using* (1948). Also ascribed to John Barrymore.

H

Habit

1 Habit with him was all the test of truth,
It must be right: I've done it from
  my youth.

George Crabbe, English poet (1754–1832).
Quoted in Walter Redfern, *Clichés and
Coinages* (1989).

Hairdressers

*When asked by a barber how he would
like his hair cut:*

2 In silence.

Archelaus, Macedonian King (reigned
413–399 BC). Quoted by W. & A. Durant
in *The Story of Civilization* (1935–64).
Possibly said, rather, by a successor,
Philip II. Plutarch, however, in his *Moralia*,
attributes it to Archelaus.

Halitosis

On Professor Tancred Borenius:

3 Oh! that halitosis. It's so thick – a
greyhound couldn't jump it.

(Sir) Cecil Beaton, English designer and
photographer (1904–80). Quoted in Hugo
Vickers, *Cecil Beaton* (1985).

Hamlet

4 A ghost and a prince meet
And everyone ends in mincemeat.

Howard Dietz, American writer and
film executive (1896–1983). Song,
'That's Entertainment', from the film
The Band Wagon (US, 1953).

*To Sir Henry Beerbohm Tree about
his Hamlet:*

5 Funny without being vulgar.

(Sir) W. S. Gilbert, English writer and lyricist
(1836–1911). Quoted in David Bispham,

Recollections (1920). He claimed to have heard
Gilbert say something like this to Tree on
the stage of the Haymarket Theatre, London,
after the first performance: 'My dear fellow,
I never saw anything so funny in my life,
and yet it was not in the least vulgar.'

6 Hamlet is the tragedy of tackling a
family problem too soon after college.

Tom Masson, American humorist (1866–
1934). Quoted in *The Treasury of Humorous
Quotations*, ed. Evan Esar & Nicolas
Bentley (1951).

*In answer to the question much puzzled
over by Shakespearean scholars, 'Did
Hamlet actually sleep with Ophelia?', an
old actor-manager is said to have replied:*

7 In our company – always!

Anonymous. Quoted by Sir Cedric
Hardwicke in *A Victorian in Orbit* (1961).
Peter Hay in *Broadway Anecdotes* (1989)
identifies the actor specifically as
John Barrymore.

Hampstead

8 In fact when somebody from
Hampstead is drowning, all their
previous furniture passes in
front of them.

Alexei Sayle, English comedian (1952–).
In BBC TV, *Comic Roots*, quoted in
The Listener (1 September 1983).

Handicaps

*In answer to the question, 'What's your
golf handicap?':*

9 I'm a coloured, one-eyed Jew – do I
need anything else?

Sammy Davis Jnr, American entertainer
(1925–90). *Yes I Can* (1966).

Handshakes

When a young man accosted him in Zurich and asked, 'May I kiss the hand that wrote Ulysses*?':*

1 No, it did a lot of other things, too.

James Joyce, Irish novelist (1882–1941). Quoted in Richard Ellman, *James Joyce* (1959).

Handwriting

2 Most people enjoy the sight of their own handwriting as they enjoy the smell of their own farts.

W. H. Auden, Anglo-American poet (1907–73). 'Writing', *The Dyer's Hand* (1962).

Of a child's handwriting:

3 With the dawn of legibility comes the horrendous revelation that he cannot spell.

Ian Hay, Scottish novelist and playwright (1876–1952). Unverified. Not from his book *The Lighter Side of School Life* (1914), nor from the play or book *Housemaster* (both 1936). Arthur Marshall quoted a school report (possibly as coming from *The Daily Telegraph*), 'Now that her handwriting has improved we can tell how very little she knows ...' on BBC Radio *Quote ... Unquote* (14 August 1980).

4 I never saw Monty James's writing but doubt whether he can have been more illegible than Lady Colefax: the only hope of deciphering *her* invitations, someone said, was to pin them up against the wall and *run* past them!

Rupert Hart-Davis, English publisher (1907–). Letter to George Lyttelton (13 November 1955).

Happiness

5 [He] is as happy as a martyr when the fire won't burn.

Mark Twain, American writer (1835–1910). Quoted in Mark Webster, *Mark Twain, Business Man* (1946).

6 Leavin' me as happy as a dog with two tails.

Mark Twain. Quoted in *The Adventures of Thomas Jefferson Snodgrass* (1928).

Lunching with friends at the time of her husband's retirement, Madame de Gaulle was asked what she was looking forward to in the years ahead. 'A penis', she replied without hesitation. The embarrassed silence that followed was broken by the former President:

7 My dear, I don't think the English pronounce the word like that. It is 'appiness'.

Charles de Gaulle, French general and President (1890–1970). Quoted in Robert Morley, *Book of Bricks* (1978) – but probably applied to de Gaulle and 'Tante Yvonne' simply because they were a famous French couple. The same pronunciation is delivered as a joke in the film version of Terence Frisby's *There's A Girl in My Soup* (1970) – by a French hotel manager welcoming a honeymoon couple. In *The Diaries of Kenneth Williams* (1993), the entry for 10 April 1966 has it as told by Michael Codron and involving Lady Dorothy Macmillan who asks Mme de Gaulle if there is any desire she has for the future and the reply is, 'Yes – a penis'.

Harpsichords

8 Sounds like two skeletons copulating on a corrugated tin roof.

Sir Thomas Beecham, English conductor (1879–1961). Quoted in Harold Atkins and Archie Newman, *Beecham Stories* (1978). Sometimes quoted as 'resembles a bird-cage played with toasting-forks'.

Headlines

On the Wall Street crash (30 October 1929):

9 WALL ST. LAYS AN EGG.

Variety, American show business newspaper, founded 1905.

Meaning that cinema-goers in rural areas were not attracted to films with bucolic themes:

10 STICKS NIX HICK PICS.

Ibid. (17 July 1935).

On the marriage of playwright Arthur Miller to Marilyn Monroe (1956):

11 EGGHEAD WEDS HOURGLASS.

Ibid. Quoted in Leslie Halliwell, *The Filmgoer's Book of Quotes* (1973).

1 SMALL EARTHQUAKE IN CHILE. NOT MANY DEAD.

Claud Cockburn, English journalist (1904–81). *In Time of Trouble* (1956) (incorporated in *I Claud...*, 1967). Cockburn claimed to have won a competition for dullness among sub-editors on *The Times* with this headline in the late 1920s: 'It had to be a genuine headline, that is to say one which was actually in the next morning's newspaper. I won it only once.' At Cockburn's death it was said, however, that an exhaustive search had failed to find this particular headline in the paper.

Healey, Denis (Lord Healey)
English Labour politician (1917–)

2 I plan to be the Gromyko of the Labour Party for the next thirty years.

Denis Healey. Quoted in *The Observer*, 'Sayings of the Week' (5 February 1984).

Health

3 Early to rise and early to bed makes a male healthy and wealthy and dead.

James Thurber, American cartoonist and writer (1894–1961). Quoted in *The Treasury of Humorous Quotations*, ed. Evan Esar & Nicolas Bentley (1951).

Heartbreak

4 When people say, 'You're breaking my heart,' they do in fact usually mean that you're breaking their genitals.

Jeffrey Bernard, English journalist (1932–97). In *The Spectator* (31 May 1986). However, this saying had appeared earlier, quoted in *The Observer*, 'Sayings of the Week' (19 May 1985), suggesting he used it more than once.

Heaven

5 —'s idea of heaven is eating *pâté de foie gras* to the sound of trumpets.

Revd Sydney Smith, English clergyman, essayist and wit (1771–1845). Quoted in *Recollections of the Table-Talk of Samuel Rogers* (1887). He did not mean that this was his own view of heaven. It seems probable that he was referring to his friend Henry Luttrell.

6 At any rate there will be no wedding presents in heaven.

Samuel Butler, English author (1835–1902). Quoted in *The Treasury of Humorous Quotations*, ed. Evan Esar & Nicolas Bentley (1951).

On the existence of heaven and hell:

7 I don't want to express an opinion. You see, I have friends in both places.

Mark Twain, American writer (1835–1910). Quoted in Archibald Henderson, *Mark Twain* (1911).

Heckling

When Harold Wilson asked rhetorically, 'Why do I emphasize the importance of the Royal Navy?':

8 Because you're in Chatham.

Anonymous heckler (1964). Quoted in A. Andrews, *Quotations for Speakers and Writers* (1969).

Heels

9 High heels were invented by a woman who had been kissed on the forehead.

Christopher Morley, American writer and editor (1890–1957). Quoted in *The Treasury of Humorous Quotations*, ed. Evan Esar & Nicolas Bentley (1951).

Hell

10 *L'Enfer, c'est les Autres* [Hell is other people].

Jean-Paul Sartre, French philosopher and writer (1905–80). *Huis Clos* (1944).

11 There have been many definitions of hell, but for the English the best definition is that it is a place where the Germans are the police, the Swedish are the comedians, and the Italians are the defence force, Frenchmen dig the roads, the Belgians are the pop singers, the Spanish run the railways, the Turks cook the food, the Irish are the waiters, the Greeks run the government and the common language is Dutch.

David Frost and Antony Jay, *To England with Love* (1967).

Hemingway, Ernest
American novelist (1899–1961)

1 Always willing to lend a helping hand to the one above him.

F. Scott Fitzgerald, American novelist (1896–1940). Quoted in *A Year of Stings and Squelches* (1985).

Henry VIII
English King (1491–1547)

2 Have you ever noticed ... that all hot-water bottles look like Henry the Eighth?

Sir Max Beerbohm, English writer and caricaturist (1872–1956). Quoted in S. N. Behrman, *Conversations with Max* (1960).

Heroines

3 Heroine: girl who is perfectly charming to live with in a book.

Mark Twain, American writer (1835–1910). In *More Maxims of Mark Twain*, ed. Merle Johnson (1927).

Highbrow

4 What is a highbrow? He is a man who has found something more interesting than women.

Edgar Wallace, English writer (1875–1932). In *The New York Times* (24 January 1932).

Hippies

5 A hippie is someone who looks like Tarzan, walks like Jane, and smells like Cheeta.

Ronald Reagan, American film actor and President (1911–). Quoted in Nancy McPhee, *The Second Book of Insults* (1981).

Hippopotamus

6 I shoot the Hippopotamus with bullets made of platinum, Because if I use leaden ones his hide is sure to flatten 'em.

Hilaire Belloc, French-born English poet and writer (1870–1953). 'The Hippopotamus', *The Bad Child's Book of Beasts* (1896).

7 The broad-backed hippopotamus Rests on his belly in the mud; Although he seems so firm to us He is merely flesh and blood.

T. S. Eliot, American-born English poet, playwright and critic (1888–1965). 'The Hippopotamus' (1920).

History and Historians

8 History is too serious to be left to historians.

Iain Macleod, English Conservative politician (1913–70).

9 God cannot alter the past; that is why he is obliged to connive at the existence of historians.

Samuel Butler, English author (1835–1902). Quoted in *The Treasury of Humorous Quotations*, ed. Evan Esar & Nicolas Bentley (1951).

10 History repeats itself. Historians repeat each other.

Philip Guedalla, English biographer and historian (1889–1944). 'Some Historians', *Supers and Supermen* (1920). Also ascribed to A. J. Balfour.

During the Second World War, Winston Churchill had to announce to the House of Commons that the British had, rather illicitly, taken bases in the Azores. He apparently thought he could gloss it over with a splendid speech, so he rose and said 'I must ask the House now to come with me back over four hundred years of our eventful history ...' Bevan interrupted:

11 Good God, he's looked into his in-tray at last!

Aneurin Bevan, Welsh Labour politician (1897–1960). Quoted by Wynford Vaughan-Thomas on BBC Radio *Quote ... Unquote* (1980).

Hitler, Adolf
German Nazi leader (1889–1945)

Famous for never having a bad word to say about anybody, he said of Hitler:

12 Well, he was the best in the field.

Bobby Hackett, jazz musician (1915–76). Quoted in *Jazz Anecdotes*, ed. Bill Crow (1991).

1 **And looking very relaxed – Adolf Hitler on vibes.**

Vivian Stanshall, English entertainer and eccentric (1942–95). Written and spoken by Stanshall in a number called 'The Intro and the Outro' (1967), performed by the Bonzo Dog Band.

2 **I wouldn't believe Hitler was dead, even if he told me so himself.**

Hjalmar Schacht, German banker (1877–1970). Attributed remark on 8 May 1945. Quoted on BBC Radio *Quote ... Unquote* (15 June 1977). Schacht was Hitler's Central Bank Governor.

Hits

3 **You write a hit the same way you write a flop.**

Alan Jay Lerner, American songwriter and playwright (1918–86). Attributed.

Holes

On US politicians having got themselves into a hole over the arms race:

4 **When you are in a hole, stop digging.**

Denis Healey (later Lord Healey), English politician (1917–). Remark, September 1983. However, on 7 January 1983, the *Financial Times* had quoted Kenneth Mayland, an economist with the First Pennsylvania Bank, as saying: 'The first rule of holes; when you're in one, stop digging.'

Hollywood

5 **Hollywood is a sewer with service from the Ritz Carlton.**

Wilson Mizner, American playwright (1876–1933). Quoted in Leslie Halliwell, *The Filmgoer's Book of Quotes* (1973).

6 **A trip through a sewer in a glass-bottomed boat.**

Wilson Mizner. Quoted in Alva Johnston, *The Legendary Mizners* (1953).

7 **Hollywood – a place where the inmates are in charge of the asylum.**

Laurence Stallings, American writer (1894–1968). Quoted in Laurence J. Peter, *Quotations for Our Time* (1977).

8 **A big hard-boiled city with no more personality than a paper cup.**

Raymond Chandler, American novelist (1888–1959). *The Little Sister* (1949).

9 **You can seduce a man's wife there, attack his daughter and wipe your hands on his canary, but if you don't like his movie, you're dead.**

Joseph von Sternberg, Austrian-born film director (1894–1969). Quoted in the book *Quote ... Unquote* (1978).

10 **Hollywood is a place where people from Iowa mistake themselves for movie stars.**

Fred Allen, American comedian (1894–1956). Quoted in Maurice Zolotow, *No People Like Show People* (1951). Said in about 1941.

11 **Strip the phoney tinsel off Hollywood and you'll find the real tinsel underneath.**

Oscar Levant, American pianist and actor (1906–72). Quoted in Leslie Halliwell, *The Filmgoer's Book of Quotes* (1973). In the early 1940s.

12 **Hollywood is no place for a professional comedian; the amateur competition is too great.**

Fred Allen, American comedian (1894–1956). Quoted in *The Treasury of Humorous Quotations*, ed. Evan Esar & Nicolas Bentley (1951).

Collecting an Oscar:

13 **If New York is the Big Apple, tonight Hollywood is the Big Nipple.**

Bernardo Bertolucci, Italian film director (1940–). Speech at the Academy Awards ceremony, Los Angeles (1988). Quoted in *The Observer*, 'Sayings of the Week' (17 April 1988). In an attempt at clarification, the film director explained: 'It is a big suck for me.'

Holy Grail

14 **What were they going to do with the Grail when they found it, Mr Rossetti?**

Sir Max Beerbohm, English writer and caricaturist (1872–1956). Caption to cartoon (*c.*1916), based on a remark allegedly made by Benjamin Jowett, Master of Balliol, about the murals in the Oxford Union.

Home

1 Home is where the television is.

Anonymous, from Covent Garden, London.
In book *Graffiti 4* (1982).

2 Be it ever so humbug, there's no place
like home.

Noël Coward (later Sir Noël), English enter-
tainer and writer (1899–1973). Quoted in
The Treasury of Humorous Quotations, ed.
Evan Esar & Nicolas Bentley (1951).

3 Home is where you go to when
you've nowhere to go.

Bette Davis, American film actress (1908–
89). Quoted by Katharine Whitehorn in
The Observer (20 September 1987).

*Parodying official jargon which had become
all the rage under the then Labour government and which had redesignated 'homes' as
'accommodation units':*

4 Accommodation Unit Sweet Accommodation Unit.

Winston S. Churchill (later Sir Winston),
British Conservative Prime Minister
and writer (1874–1965). In speech at
Cardiff in 1950. Quoted in Leslie Frewin,
Immortal Jester (1973).

Home Counties

5 Our Farnham which art in Hendon,
Harrow be thy Name. Thy Kingston
come. Thy Wimbledon, in Erith as it is
in Heston. Give us this day our Leather-
head. And forgive us our Westminsters.
As we forgive them that Westminster
against us. And lead us not into Thames
Ditton; But deliver us from Ealing: For
thine is the Kingston, The Purley, and the
Crawley, For Iver and Iver. Crouch End.

Anonymous 'Home Counties' version of the
Lord's Prayer. Quoted in book *Say No More!*
(1987). Correspondence in the magazine
Oxford Today (Hilary/Trinity terms 1990)
produced a number of variations and a date
of composition somewhere in the 1930s,
but no author.

Homosexuality

6 I became one of the stately homos
of England.

Quentin Crisp, English professional personality (1908–). *The Naked Civil Servant* (1968).

*Written by another hand under the graffito,
'My mother made me a homosexual':*

7 If I got her the wool, would she make
me one?

Anonymous. Quoted in *Graffiti Lives OK*
(1979).

*Telegram said to have been sent to
Tom Driberg MP on the occasion of his
marriage (to a woman) (1951):*

8 I pray that the church is not struck
by lightning.

Evelyn Waugh, English novelist (1903–66).
Attributed. According to Alan Watkins, *Brief
Lives* (1982), Waugh in fact wrote – rather
than telegraphed – to the effect: 'I will think
of you intently on the day and pray that the
church is not struck by lightning.' The letter
is not, alas, included in Waugh's published
correspondence. Watkins adds: 'This sentence
in this same connection is, oddly enough,
attributed to Aneurin Bevan and Winston
Churchill also.' Driberg was a notorious and
active homosexual.

9 WINSTON CHURCHILL: I once went to
bed with a man to see what it was like.
SOMERSET MAUGHAM: Who was the
man?
WINSTON CHURCHILL: Ivor Novello.
SOMERSET MAUGHAM: And what was
it like?
WINSTON CHURCHILL: Musical.

Winston S. Churchill (later Sir Winston),
British Conservative Prime Minister and
writer (1874–1965). Quoted in Ted Morgan,
Somerset Maugham (1980). The source
for this story was Alan Searle, one of
Maugham's acolytes. Churchill's daughter,
Mary Soames, questioned it when it was
included in my *Dictionary of Twentieth
Century Quotations* (1987), and it is surely
of dubious veracity.

*When Sheridan Morley was keen to discuss
Coward's sexuality in his biography and
pointed out that theatre critic T. C. Worsley
had recently 'come out':*

10 There is one essential difference
between me and Cuthbert Worsley.
The British public at large would not

care if Cuthbert Worsley had slept with mice.

Noël Coward (later Sir Noël), English entertainer and writer (1899–1973). Quoted in *The Times* (1994).

About his affection for a rather plain young lady:

1 Buggers can't be choosers.

Sir Maurice Bowra, English academic (1898–1971). Quoted in Jan Morris, *The Oxford Book of Oxford* (1978).

2 If God had meant to have homosexuals, he would have created Adam and Bruce.

Anita Bryant, American anti-gay campaigner. Quoted in Barbara Rowes, *The Book of Quotes* (1979).

Honey

3 When Rabbit said, 'Honey or condensed milk with your bread?' [Pooh] was so excited he said, 'Both,' and then, so as not to seem greedy, he added, 'But don't bother about the bread, please.'

A. A. Milne, English writer (1882–1956). *Winnie-The-Pooh* (1926).

Honour

4 The louder he talked of his honour, the faster we counted our spoons.

Ralph Waldo Emerson, American poet and essayist (1803–82). 'Worship', *The Conduct of Life* (1860). This had been anticipated by Samuel Johnson, as reported in Boswell's *Life* (1791 – for 14 July 1763): 'But if he [Macpherson] does really think that there is no distinction between virtue and vice, why, Sir, when he leaves our houses, let us count our spoons.'

Hope

5 When I am sad and weary
When I think all hope has gone
When I walk along High Holborn
I think of you with nothing on.

Adrian Mitchell, English poet and playwright (1932–). 'Celia Celia' (1968).

Hopelessness

6 Since I gave up hope, I feel so much better.

John Osborne, English playwright (1929–94). Quoted in *The Independent* (26 April 1994). This was a badge displayed in his bathroom – 'it always made him smile'.

Refusing any last-ditch attempts to rescue President Ford's re-election campaign in 1976:

7 I'm not going to do anything to rearrange the furniture on the deck of the *Titanic*.

Rogers Morton, American government official (1914–79). Quoted in *The Times* (13 May 1976). He was Ford's campaign manager.

8 If we see light at the end of the tunnel, It's the light of the oncoming train.

Robert Lowell, American poet (1917–77). 'Since 1939' (1977). Probably not original. Paul Dickson cited 'Rowe's Rule: the odds are five to six that the light at the end of the tunnel is the headlight of an oncoming train' in *Washingtonian* (November 1978). On BBC Radio *Quote ... Unquote* (1980), John Lahr said it had been a favourite remark of his father – the actor, Bert Lahr (d.1967).

Horses

9 I know two things about the horse
And one of them is rather coarse.

Anonymous. However, in *The Weekend Book* (1928), it is attributed to Naomi Royde-Smith (c.1875–1964).

10 Dangerous at both ends and uncomfortable in the middle.

Ian Fleming, English novelist and journalist (1908–64). Quoted in *The Sunday Times* (9 October 1966).

Hosts

To a visitor, Denton Welch:

11 Come again when you can't stay so long.

Walter Sickert, German-born English painter (1860–1942). Quoted by Welch in 'Sickert at St Peter's' in *Horizon*, Vol. 6, No. 32 (1942). In *Taken Care of* (1965), Edith Sitwell comments on the article but gives the tag as 'Come again – when you have a little less time'. Either way, this farewell was not originated by Sickert. Indeed, Welch ends his article by saying, 'And at these words a strange pang went through me, for it was what my father had always said as he closed the book, when I had finished my bread and butter and milk, and it was time for bed.'

1 I am a man more dined against than dining.

Sir Maurice Bowra, English academic (1898–1971). Attributed in John Betjeman, *Summoned by Bells* (1960).

2 I maintain that though you would often in the fifteenth century have heard the snobbish Roman say, 'I am dining with the Borgias to-night,' no Roman ever was able to say, 'I dined last night with the Borgias.'

Sir Max Beerbohm, English writer and caricaturist (1872–1956). *Hosts and Guests* (1920).

Hot dogs

3 The noblest of all dogs is the hot-dog; it feeds the hand that bites it.

Laurence J. Peter, Canadian writer (1919–90). *Quotations for Our Time* (1977). Although compiling a book of quotations, Peter inserted several observations of his own.

Hot pants

4 Those hot pants of hers were so damned tight, I could hardly breathe.

Benny Hill, English television comedian (1924–92). Quoted in *The Penguin Dictionary of Modern Humorous Quotations*, ed. Fred Metcalf (1987).

House of Lords

5 A severe though not unfriendly critic of our institutions said that 'the *cure* for admiring the House of Lords was to go and look at it'.

Walter Bagehot, English constitutional historian (1826–77). 'The House of Lords', *The English Constitution* (1867).

6 The House of Peers, throughout the war,
Did nothing in particular,
And did it very well.

(Sir) W. S. Gilbert, English writer and lyricist (1836–1911). *Iolanthe*, Act 2 (1882).

On learning that Pitt had accepted an earldom:

7 Pitt has had a bad fall upstairs to that Hospital for Incurables, the House of Lords.

Philip Dormer Stanhope, 4th Earl of Chesterfield, English politician and writer (1694–1773).

8 The House of Lords, an illusion to which I have never been able to subscribe – responsibility without power, the prerogative of the eunuch throughout the ages.

(Sir) Tom Stoppard, English playwright (1937–). *Lord Malquist and Mr Moon* (1966).

On becoming a peer:

9 I am dead, dead but in the Elysian Fields.

Benjamin Disraeli (later 1st Earl of Beaconsfield), English politician and writer (1804–81). Quoted in Moneypenny & Buckle, *Life of Disraeli* (1910–20).

Housework

10 There was no need to do any housework at all. After the first four years the dirt doesn't get any worse.

Quentin Crisp, English professional personality (1908–). *The Naked Civil Servant* (1968).

Hughes, Ted
English Poet Laureate (1930–)

11 We had the old crow over at Hull recently, looking like a Christmas present from Easter Island.

Philip Larkin, English poet (1922–85). *Required Writing* (1983).

Human race

12 The human race, to which so many of my readers belong, has been playing at children's games from the beginning, and will probably do it till the end, which is a nuisance for the few people who grow up.

G. K. Chesterton, English poet, novelist and critic (1874–1936). *The Napoleon of Notting Hill*, Chap. 1 (1904).

Humiliation

On the climate of Washington DC when McCarthyism was at its height:

1 It's not so much the heat, it's the humiliation.

Anonymous. Quoted by Leonard Miall in *The 'Quote ... Unquote' Newsletter* (October 1992).

Humility

2 In 1969 I published a small book on Humility. It was a pioneering work which has not, to my knowledge, been superseded.

Francis Pakenham, 7th Earl of Longford, English writer and politician (1905–). In *The Tablet*, quoted in *The Observer*, 'Sayings of the Week' (30 January 1994).

Humour

3 Every good joke has a philosophical idea somewhere inside it.

G. K. Chesterton, English poet, novelist and critic (1874–1936). Untraced. Possibly a rendering of the view put forward in his essay 'Cockneys and Their Jokes': 'When once you have got hold of a vulgar joke, you may be certain that you have got hold of a subtle and spiritual idea.'

4 Everything human is pathetic. The secret source of Humor itself is not joy but sorrow. There is no humor in heaven.

Mark Twain, American writer (1835– 1910). *Following the Equator* (1897).

5 I think there's a terrific merit in having no sense of humour, no sense of irony, practically no sense of anything at all. If you're born with these so-called defects you have a very good chance of getting to the top. That's what's enabled her [Mrs Thatcher] to turn Britain into a cross between Singapore and Telford.

Peter Cook, English humorist (1937– 95). In *The Guardian* (23 July 1988).

Hunting

6 'Unting is all that's worth living for – all time is lost wot is not spent in 'unting – it is like the hair we breathe – if we have it not we die – it's the sport of kings, the image of war without its guilt, and only five-and-twenty per cent of its danger.

R. S. Surtees, English novelist and journalist (1805–64). *Handley Cross*, Chap. 7 (1843).

7 The English country gentleman galloping after a fox – the unspeakable in full pursuit of the uneatable.

Oscar Wilde, Irish playwright, poet and wit (1854–1900). *A Woman of No Importance*, Act 1 (1893).

Husbands

In answer to the question 'How many husbands have you had?':

8 You mean apart from my own?

Zsa Zsa Gabor, Hungarian-born film actress (1919–). Quoted in Kenneth Edwards, *I Wish I'd Said That!* (1976).

On her second husband:

9 I only saw him twice and we have two children.

Sheilah Graham, British-born Hollywood gossip columnist (1904–88). Quoted in *The Observer*, 'Sayings of the Week' (25 March 1984).

10 Do married men make the best husbands?

James Gibbons Huneker, American writer (1860–1921). Quoted in *The Treasury of Humorous Quotations*, ed. Evan Esar & Nicolas Bentley (1951).

Hymns

11 Our Lady sings Magnificat
With tune surpassing sweet;
And all the Virgins bear their parts,
Sitting about her feet.

Anonymous? Verse 23 (of 26), No. 638 in *The English Hymnal*. Drawn to my attention by D. J. Strawbridge of Bridport, Dorset.

Hypochondria

1 Hypochondria is the one disease I haven't got.

David Renwick, English writer (1951–), with Andrew Marshall. In BBC Radio *The Burkiss Way* (14 February 1978).

Hypotheses

On being asked what would have happened if Khruschev rather than Kennedy had been assassinated in 1963:

2 With history one can never be certain, but I think I can safely say that Aristotle Onassis would not have married Mrs Khruschev.

Gore Vidal, American novelist, playwright and critic (1925–). Quoted in *The Sunday Times* (4 June 1989).

I

Ibsen, Henrik
Norwegian playwright (1828–1906)

1 In every play a stranger comes into the room, opens a window to let in fresh air and everyone dies of pneumonia.

W. Somerset Maugham, English novelist and short-story writer (1874–1965). Quoted by Robin Bailey on BBC Radio *Quote ... Unquote* (27 July 1985). Unverified.

Ideas

In answer to the journalists' clichéd question 'Where do you get your ideas from?':

2 If I knew, I'd go there.

(Sir) Tom Stoppard, English playwright (1937–). Attributed. Compare what Joyce Grenfell wrote in *Joyce Grenfell Requests the Pleasure* (1976). She stated that this was her reply to the question, 'Where do you get the ideas for your monologues?'

In answer to boy's question, 'Where do you get your incredible ideas from?':

3 There's this warehouse called Ideas Are Us.

Terry Pratchett, English novelist (1948–). Quoted in *The Observer* (8 November 1992).

4 All I know is, if someone says, 'Hey, what a great idea for a musical', it usually isn't.

(Sir) Tim Rice, English lyricist (1944–). Quoted in *The Independent* (19 August 1989).

Identification

5 A nobleman (as he was riding) met with a yeoman of the country, to whom he said, 'My friend, I should know thee. I do remember I have often seen thee.'

'My good lord,' said the countryman, 'I am one of your honour's poor tenants, and my name is T. I.' 'I remember thee better now' (saith my lord) 'There were two brothers but one is dead. I pray thee, which of you doth remain alive?'

John Taylor, English poet and writer (?1578–1653). *Wit and Mirth* (1630).

Identifying marks

Until quite recently a small spot was reserved by the River Cherwell in Oxford for dons to swim in the nude. Some young wags decided to go up the river in a punt in order to be able to see their tutors so disporting themselves. They braved the rapids and came into the quiet patch of the river where these rather corpulent dons were sitting naked on the sward. As the old gentlemen saw their pupils going past, they all – except Bowra – covered their loins with their hands. Bowra put his hands over his eyes – and explained to his colleagues:

6 In Oxford I'm known by my face ...

Sir Maurice Bowra, English academic (1898–1971). Quoted by A. N. Wilson on BBC Radio *Quote ... Unquote* (1990). In his published diary for 4 February 1992, Anthony Powell notes how he had written to *The Daily Telegraph* about this story, adding: 'It was a chestnut when Maurice was born, as usual journalists missing the point, especially as they were all Balliol dons. As it was, just as the punt was disappearing, a lady was heard to say: "I think that must have been Mr Paravicini. He is the only *red-haired* don in Balliol."'

Identity

When he was President, George Bush paid a visit to an old people's home. After chatting to patients for a little while, he asked one of them, 'And do you know who I am?' Came the reply from one old biddie:

1 No, but if you ask in reception I'm sure they will be able to tell you.

Anonymous. Quoted by Derek Parker in *The Author* (Summer 1993). Also told variously about other celebrities.

If God …

2 If God had intended us to fly, he'd never have given us the railways.

Michael Flanders, English writer and entertainer (1922–75). 'By Air', *At the Drop of Another Hat* (1963).

3 If God had intended us to fly, would have sent us tickets.

Mel Brooks, American writer and actor (1926–). Attributed by Frederic Raphael in 1994. Frank Muir, *A Kentish Lad* (1997), mentions that the line, 'If God had meant us to fly he would have given us the money' was spoken in a TV show called *Thingummybob* (*c.*1969).

4 If God had meant us to travel tourist class He would have made us narrower.

Martha Zimmerman, American air hostess (untraced). Quoted in *The Wall Street Journal* (1977).

5 RUBY: Me mother says if God had intended men to smoke He'd have put chimneys in their heads.
ORMONROYD: Tell your mother from me that if God had intended men to wear clothes He'd have put collar studs at back of their necks.

J. B. Priestley, English novelist and playwright (1894–1984). *When We Are Married* (1938).

6 If God had not meant everyone to be in bed by ten-thirty, He would never have provided the ten o'clock newscast.

Garrison Keillor, American writer (1942–). *Lake Wobegon Days* (1985).

Immaturity

7 Basically my wife was immature. I'd be at home in the bath and she'd come in and sink my boats.

Woody Allen, American film actor,

writer and director (1937–). Quoted in *Nudge Nudge, Wink Wink* (1986).

Impropriety

8 An improper mind is a perpetual feast.

Logan Pearsall Smith, American writer (1865–1946). As 'a filthy mind is a continual feast' this has also been ascribed to Edward Heron-Allen and Vyvyan Holland, acquaintance of and son of Oscar Wilde, respectively. In John G. Murray's *A Gentleman Publisher's Commonplace Book*, 1996, there is a version 'from [note rather than by] Osbert Lancaster' with 'perpetual feast'. There is little reason to doubt that Smith was the originator, however.

Incest

9 Incest – a game the whole family can play.

Anonymous. Included in the book *Graffiti 3* (1981). But on 14 November 1959, Rupert Hart-Davis was already writing: 'I'm also told that the latest popular game is called Incest – all the family can join in!' (*The Lyttelton Hart-Davis Letters*, 1982).

Incompatibility

10 I believe a little incompatibility is the spice of life, particularly if he has income and she is pattable.

Ogden Nash, American poet (1902–71). 'I Do, I Will, I have', *Versus* (1949).

Indecision

11 PHILIP (bewildered): I'm sorry. (Pause.) I suppose I am indecisive. (Pause.) My trouble is, I'm a man of no convictions. (Longish pause.) At least, I think I am.

Christopher Hampton, English playwright (1946–). *The Philanthropist* (1970).

12 I used to be indecisive, but now I'm not so sure.

Boscoe Pertwee (untraced). M. M. Harvey of Andover sent this quotation to BBC Radio *Quote … Unquote* in 1977, but it has proved impossible to trace a source or, indeed, the existence of its author. A little later it was said to be a graffito and was quoted as such by Brian Johnston on BBC Radio *Quote … Unquote* (21 August 1979).

Indexers and Indexes

1 Should not the Society of Indexers be known as Indexers, Society of, The?

Keith Waterhouse, English journalist, novelist and playwright (1929–). *Bookends* (1990).

Index entry for one of Samuel Pepys's mistresses, slightly abbreviated:

2 BAGWELL, Mrs, wife of William: her good looks, 4/222; P plans to seduce, 4/222, 266; visits, 4/233–4; finds her virtuous, 4/234; and modest, 5/163; asks P for place for husband, 5/65–6, 163; P kisses, 5/287; she grows affectionate, 5/301–2; he caresses, 5/313; she visits him, 5/316, 339; her resistance collapses in alehouse, 5/322; amorous encounters with: at her house, 5/350–1; 6/40, 162, 189, 201, 253, 294; 7/166 ... asks for promotion for husband, 6/39–40; P strains a finger, 6/40; has sore face, 7/191; servant dies of plague, 7/166.

Anonymous. *The Diary of Samuel Pepys*, ed. Latham & Matthews, Vol. 11 (1983).

Index entry for one of James Boswell's mistresses, slightly edited:

3 LEWIS, Mrs (Louisa), actress. JB anticipates delight with, page 96. JB lends two guineas to, 97. Consummation with JB interrupted, 117. Spends night with JB at Hayward's, 137–40. JB enraged at perfidy of, 158. JB asks his two guineas back, 174.

Anonymous. *James Boswell's London Journal*, ed. Frederick A. Pottle (1950).

Indiscretion

4 Indiscretion is the better part of valour.

Oscar Wilde, Irish playwright, poet and wit (1854–1900). *The Critic As Artist* (1890).

Indispensability

5 Graveyards are full of indispensable men.

Charles de Gaulle, French general and President (1890–1970). Attributed in *The Penguin Dictionary of Modern Quotations* (1980 edn) but a proverbial view in any language.

Individuals

6 I have ever hated all nations, professions and communities, and all my love is towards individuals ... I hate and detest that animal called man; although I heartily love John, Peter, Thomas and so forth. This is the system upon which I have governed myself many years.

Jonathan Swift, Anglo-Irish writer and clergyman (1667–1745). Letter to Alexander Pope (29 September 1725).

Inevitability

7 I had never had a piece of toast
Particularly long and wide,
But fell upon the sanded floor,
And always on the buttered side.

James Payn, English novelist and poet (1830–98). In *Chamber's Journal* (2 February 1884).

Infamy

Julius Caesar fending off the knives in an assassination attempt:

8 Infamy, infamy – they've all got it in for me!

Talbot Rothwell, English writer (1916–74). Film, *Carry on Cleo* (UK, 1964). However, Frank Muir wrote to *The Guardian* (22 July 1995), asserting that this line was the product of his and Denis Norden's joint pen. It was spoken by Dick Bentley as Caesar in a sketch for the BBC Radio show *Take It From Here* (1948–59). Moreover, he added, Talbot Rothwell had very properly asked their permission to use the line. So it was a bit much always hearing Rothwell praised for writing it. The letter concluded, 'Please may we have our line back.'

Inflation

9 Having a little inflation is like being a little pregnant.

Leon Henderson, American economist (1895–1986). Quoted by John Kenneth Galbraith in *A Life in Our Times* (1981). Henderson was appointed by President Roosevelt to the National Defense Advisory Commission in 1940.

Information

1 Sure, the next train has gone ten
   minutes ago.

   Anonymous (cartoonist). Caption to cartoon
   in *Punch*, Vol. 60 (1871). This reappeared
   in the Will Hay film *Oh Mr Porter* (UK, 1937)
   in which a ticket seller slings up his shutter,
   shouts 'Next train gone!' and slams it
   down again.

Inhumanity

*At Lord's, a South African googly bowler
named 'Tufty' Mann was tying a Middlesex
tail-end batsman named George Mann
into such knots that the crowd was reduced
to laughter. When it occurred for the fourth
time in a single over, the BBC Radio commentator, apparently without a moment's
thought, reported:*

2 So what we are watching here is a clear
   case of Mann's inhumanity to Mann.

   John Arlott, English journalist and radio
   cricket commentator (1914–91). Quoted in
   the *Daily Mail* (3 September 1980).

Innocence

Of the actress Maureen O'Hara:

3 She looked as though butter wouldn't
   melt in her mouth. Or anywhere else.

   Elsa Lanchester, English film actress
   (1902–86). Quoted in *News Summaries*
   (30 January 1950).

Inspiration

4 Inspiration is the act of drawing up
   a chair to the writing desk.

   Anonymous. Quoted in *Chambers Dictionary
   of Modern Quotations* (1993).

Insults

5 Do not insult the mother alligator
   until after you have crossed
   the river.

   Anonymous (Haitian proverb). Quoted
   in Herbert V. Prochnow, Snr & Jnr,
   Treasury of Humorous Quotations (1969).
   Compare the reputed Chinese proverb: 'One
   does not insult the River God while crossing
   the river.'

Intellect

Of his son, later Edward VII:

6 His intellect is no more use than a
   pistol packed in the bottom of a trunk
   if one were attacked in the robber-
   infested Apennines.

   Prince Albert, German-born British Prince
   (1819–61). Quoted in Nancy McPhee,
   The Second Book of Insults (1981).

On Huey Long:

7 The trouble with Senator Long is
   that he is suffering from halitosis of
   the intellect. That's presuming
   Emperor Long has an intellect.

   Harold L. Ickes, American politician (1874–
   1952). Quoted in Arthur M. Schlesinger,
   The Politics of Upheaval (1960).

Intellectuals

8 To the man-in-the-street, who,
      I'm sorry to say
   Is a keen observer of life,
   The word Intellectual suggests
      straight away
   A man who's untrue to his wife.

   W. H. Auden, Anglo-American poet (1907–
   73). *New Year Letter* (1941), also published
   as 'Note on Intellectuals' (1947).

9 An intellectual is someone who has
   found something more interesting to
   think about than sex.

   Aldous Huxley, English novelist and writer
   (1894–1963). Quoted in Robert Irwin,
   Exquisite Corpse (1996).

Intervention

Objecting to government meddling:

10 Don't just do something, stand there.

   George Shultz, American Republican
   politician (1920–). As Labor Secretary, in
   a speech (1970). Quoted in William Safire,
   Safire's Political Dictionary (1978).

Intolerance

11 If Woody Allen were a Muslim, he'd
   be dead by now.

   Salman Rushdie, Indian-born author
   (1947–). Quoted in *The Observer*, 'Sayings
   of the Week' (18 February 1989).

Invitations

1 I must decline your invitation owing to a subsequent engagement.

Oscar Wilde, Irish playwright, poet and wit (1854–1900). Quoted in *The Treasury of Humorous Quotations*, ed. Evan Esar & Nicolas Bentley (1951).

To Somerset Maugham, who had said he was leaving a function early 'to keep his youth':

2 Then why didn't you bring him with you? I should be delighted to meet him.

Lady ('Emerald') Cunard, American-born society figure in Britain (1872–1948). Quoted in Daphne Fielding, *Emerald and Nancy* (1968).

Irish Question

3 [Gladstone] spent his declining years trying to guess the answer to the Irish Question; unfortunately, whenever he was getting warm, the Irish secretly changed the question.

W. C. Sellar & R. J. Yeatman, English humorists (1898–1951) and (1897–1968). *1066 and All That*, Chap. 57 (1930).

On how to resolve the Irish Question:

4 You've got to exchange the populations of Holland and Ireland. Then the Dutch will turn Ireland into a beautiful garden and the Irish will forget to mend the dikes and will all be drowned.

Otto von Bismarck, Prusso-German statesman (1815–98). Quoted by Lord Healey on BBC Radio *Quote ... Unquote* (23 May 1995).

Irishness and the Irish

On the situation in Ulster, 1970s:

5 Ah, well, they say it's not as bad as they say it is.

Anonymous Irish woman. Quoted in book *Quote ... Unquote* (1978).

6 Anyone who isn't confused here doesn't really understand what's going on.

Anonymous Belfast citizen (1970). Quoted in the book *Quote ... Unquote* (1978). However, Walter Bryan, *The Improbable Irish* (1969) has: 'As Ed Murrow once said about Vietnam, anyone who isn't confused doesn't really understand the situation.'

7 The Irish are a fair people; – they never speak well of one another.

Samuel Johnson, English writer and lexicographer (1709–84). Remark to Dr Barnard, Bishop of Killaloe. In James Boswell, *Life of Johnson* (1791) – for 1775.

8 The Irish do not want anyone to wish them well; they want everyone to wish their enemies ill.

(Sir) Harold Nicolson, English politician and writer (1886–1968). Quoted in *The Treasury of Humorous Quotations*, ed. Evan Esar & Nicolas Bentley (1951).

9 The Irish don't know what they want and won't be happy till they get it.

Anonymous (graffito). Quoted in *Graffiti 5* (1986).

10 I said, 'It is most extraordinary weather for this time of year.' He replied, 'Ah, it isn't this time of year at all.'

Oliver St John Gogarty, Irish writer (1878–1957). *It Isn't This Time of Year at All* (1954).

11 There are three things I don't like about New York: the water, the buses and the professional Irishmen. A professional Irishman is one who is terribly anxious to pass as a middle-class Englishman.

Brendan Behan, Irish playwright (1923–64). Quoted in the *Daily News* (1961) and included in *The Sayings of Brendan Behan*, ed. Aubrey Dillon-Malone (1997).

12 Ireland is a country in which the probable never happens and the impossible always does.

John Pentland Mahaffy, Irish scholar (1839–1919). Quoted in *The Treasury of Humorous Quotations*, ed. Evan Esar & Nicolas Bentley (1951).

Irony

1 I have been assured by a very knowing American of my acquaintance in London, that a young healthy child well nursed is at a year old a most delicious, nourishing, and wholesome food, whether stewed, roasted, baked, or boiled, and I make no doubt that it will equally serve in a fricassee, or a ragout.

Jonathan Swift, Anglo-Irish writer and clergyman (1667–1745). *A Modest Proposal for Preventing the Children of Ireland from being a Burden to their parents or country* (1729).

James, Henry
American novelist (1843–1916)

1 The nicest old lady I ever met.

William Faulkner, American novelist (1897–1962). Quoted in Edward Stone, *The Battle and the Books* (1964).

2 The work of Henry James has always seemed divisible by a simple dynastic arrangement into three reigns: James I, James II, and the Old Pretender.

Philip Guedalla, English writer (1889–1944). 'Men of Letters: Mr Henry James', *Collected Essays* (1920). Guedalla also used this device in his introduction to *The Queen and Mr Gladstone* (1933). There were really three Queen Victorias, he wrote: 'The youngest of the three was Queen Victoria I ... distinguished by a romping sort of innocence ... She was succeeded shortly after marriage by Victoria II ... [bearing] the unmistakable impress of her married life ... [Then] the Queen became Queen-Empress ... her third and final manner.'

Jazz

When asked what jazz was:

3 If you still have to ask ... shame on you.

Louis Armstrong, American jazzman (1901–71). Quoted in Max Jones *et al., Salute to Satchmo* (1970). Often rendered as, 'Man, if you gotta ask you'll never know.'

Jefferson, Thomas
American polymath and President (1743–1826)

4 I think it's the most extraordinary collection of talent, of human knowledge, that has ever been gathered together at the White House –

with the possible exception of when Thomas Jefferson dined alone.

John F. Kennedy, American Democratic President (1917–63). Speech at dinner for Nobel prizewinners (29 April 1962).

Jesus Christ
Founder of Christianity
(*c.*6 BC – *c.*AD 30)

5 Jesus! with all thy faults I love thee still.

Samuel Butler, English author (1835–1902). *Further Extracts from Notebooks* (1934).

Jewishness

6 I'm not really a Jew; just Jew-ish, not the whole hog, you know.

Jonathan Miller, English entertainer, writer and director (1934–). 'Real Class', *Beyond the Fringe* (1961).

7 Q. Are you Jewish?
A. No, a tree fell on me.

Spike Milligan, English entertainer and writer (1918–). Quoted in *Private Eye* (1973).

When excluded from a beach club on racial grounds:

8 Since my daughter is only half-jewish, could she go in the water up to her knees?

Groucho Marx, American comedian (1895–1977). Quoted in *The Observer* (21 August 1977).

Reply to small child who asked, 'What does two and two make?':

9 Are you buying or selling?

Lew Grade (later Lord Grade), Russian-born English media tycoon (1906–). Quoted in *The Observer* during 1962. Apocryphal, according to Grade, but an essential piece of Gradiana.

1 If God had intended Jewish women to exercise, he'd have put diamonds on the floor.

Joan Rivers, American entertainer (1937–). Quoted in *The 'Quote ... Unquote' Newsletter* (April 1995).

2 When they circumcised Herbert Samuel they threw away the wrong bit.

David Lloyd George (1st Earl Lloyd George of Dwyfor), British Liberal Prime Minister (1863–1945). Attributed by John Grigg in *The Listener* (7 September 1978). Samuel was a prominent Jewish Liberal politician around the time of the First World War.

Jews

3 How odd
Of God
To choose
The Jews.

W. N. Ewer, English journalist (1885–1976). Quoted in *The Week-End Book* (1924).

4 But not so odd
As those who choose
A Jewish God
Yet spurn the Jews.

Cecil Browne (untraced). Rejoinder apparently published in 1924.

5 Who said he did?
Moses. But he's a yid.

Anonymous. Current in the 1960s.

Leaping out of a second-floor window:

6 I'm Super-jew!

Lenny Bruce, American satirist (1923–66). Quoted in *The Observer* (21 August 1966). He sustained only a broken leg.

Jobs

Answering criticism from Senator Daniel Inouye that he interrupted too much and that his client, Oliver North, should be the one to speak up:

7 I'm not a potted plant ... I'm here as the lawyer. That's my job.

Brendan V. Sullivan, American lawyer

(1942–). Quoted in *The New York Times* (10 July 1987). During the 1987 hearings into the 'Iran-contra' affair (after which North was found guilty of taking part in illegal military and security actions).

Johnson, Samuel
English writer and lexicographer (1709–84)

8 There is no arguing with Johnson; for when his pistol misses fire, he knocks you down with the butt end of it.

Oliver Goldsmith, Irish-born playwright and writer (1730–74). Quoted in James Boswell, *The Life of Samuel Johnson* (1791) – for 26 October 1769.

9 When I called upon Dr. Johnson next morning, I found him highly satisfied with his colloquial prowess the preceding evening. 'Well, (said he) we had a good talk.' BOSWELL 'Yes, Sir; you tossed and gored several persons.'

James Boswell in *ibid.* – relating to the summer of 1768.

Jokes

10 When is a door not a door? When it's ajar.

Anonymous. *Punch* in its 'comic chronology' (17 December 1872, i.e. its Almanack for 1873) has 'A D 1001 invention of the riddle "When is a door not a door?"'

11 'By the way, Mrs Jocelyn, I hear you've taken a rippin' little place on the river this year.' 'Yes. I hope, when you're passing, that you'll – er – drop in!'

Anonymous. Caption to cartoon in *Punch* (15 August 1900).

Defining a joke:

12 An idea going in one direction meets an idea going in the opposite direction.

Mack Sennett, Canadian-born comedy filmmaker (1880–1960). Quoted in *The 'Quote ... Unquote' Newsletter* (July 1994).

13 A joke goes a great way in the country. I have known one last pretty well for seven years.

Revd Sydney Smith, English clergyman, essayist and wit (1771–1845). Quoted in Saba, Lady Holland, *Memoir* (1855).

1 Anyone like myself who thinks making jokes is a serious matter must regret the eclipse of the Book of Common Prayer because it has diminished the common stock of shared reference on which jokes – and of course it's not only jokes – depend.

Alan Bennett, English playwright and actor (1934–). *Writing Home* (1994).

2 The marvellous thing about a joke with a double meaning is that it can only mean one thing.

Ronnie Barker, English comedian and actor (1929–). 'Daddie's Sauce', *Sauce* (1977).

Jolson, Al
American entertainer (1888–1950)

Of his voice:

3 Like playing a trombone underwater.

Anonymous. Quoted by Humphrey Lyttelton on BBC Radio *Quote ... Unquote* (13 July 1988).

Journalism

4 Rock journalism is people who can't write interviewing people who can't talk for people who can't read.

Frank Zappa, American rock musician (1940–93). Quoted in L. Botts, *Loose Talk* (1980). Originally in *Rolling Stone* Magazine (1970).

5 That awful power, the public opinion of a nation, is created in America by a horde of ignorant, self-complacent simpletons who failed at ditching and shoemaking and fetched up in journalism on their way to the poorhouse.

Mark Twain, American writer (1835–1910). In *Mark Twain's Speeches*, ed. A. B. Paine (1923).

6 If you don't know what's going on in Portugal, you must have been reading the papers.

Paul Foot, English journalist (1937–). Attributed in 1975. This was at the time

when Portugal was undergoing political upheaval following a revolution against a dictatorship.

7 Journalism largely consists in saying 'Lord Jones Dead' to people who never knew Lord Jones was alive.

G. K. Chesterton, English poet, novelist and critic (1874–1936). 'The Purple Wig', *The Wisdom of Father Brown* (1914).

8 Journalism could be described as turning one's enemies into money.

Craig Brown, English journalist (1957–). In *The Daily Telegraph* (28 September 1990).

9 Journalism is to politician as dog is to lamppost.

H. L. Mencken, American journalist and linguist (1880–1956). Attributed in *The Oxford Dictionary of Literary Quotations*, ed. Peter Kemp (1997).

Journalists

Definition of a journalist:

10 Someone who stays sober right up to lunch-time.

Anonymous. Quoted by Godfrey Smith on BBC Radio *Quote ... Unquote* (27 July 1985).

11 All journalists are spies – I know, I have been one.

Sese Seko Mobutu, Zaïrean President (1930–). Quoted in *The Sunday Times* (28 May 1978).

12 You cannot hope
to bribe or twist,
thank God! the
British journalist.
But, seeing what
the man will do
unbribed, there's
no occasion to.

Humbert Wolfe, English poet and critic (1885–1940). 'Over the Fire', *The Uncelestial City* (1930).

On the sports journalist Clifford Makins (1924–90):

13 A legend in his own lunchtime.

Christopher Wordsworth, English journalist and critic (1914–). Attributed remark made in book review by 1976. However, according to

Ned Sherrin, in *Theatrical Anecdotes* (1991), 'David Climie, the witty revue and comedy writer ... claims to have invented the phrase "A legend in his own lunchtime" and to have lavished it on the mercurial BBC comedy innovator, Dennis Main Wilson.'

1 No news is good news; no journalists is even better.

Nicolas Bentley, English cartoonist and writer (1907–78). Quoted in *The Treasury of Humorous Quotations*, ed. Evan Esar & Nicolas Bentley (1951).

2 Journalists say a thing that they know isn't true, in the hope that if they keep on saying it long enough it *will* be true.

Arnold Bennett, English novelist (1867–1931). *The Title*, Act 1 (1918).

Of a foreign correspondent:

3 He's someone who flies around from hotel to hotel and thinks the most interesting thing about any story is the fact that he has arrived to cover it.

(Sir) Tom Stoppard, English playwright (1937–). *Night and Day*, Act 1 (1978).

Judges

To a convicted criminal who had exclaimed, 'As God is my judge – I am innocent':

4 He isn't; I am, and you're not!

Norman (later Lord) Birkett, English barrister and judge (1883–1962). Attributed in Matthew Parris, *Scorn* (1994).

5 F. E. SMITH: He was drunk as a judge.
   JUDGE: The expression as I have always understood it is 'sober as a judge'. Perhaps you mean 'as drunk as a lord'?
   F. E. SMITH: Yes, my lord.

F. E. Smith (1st Earl of Birkenhead), English politician and lawyer (1872–1930). Smith was placed in this famous exchange by Bryan Magee in BBC Radio *Quote ... Unquote* (26 April 1994).

6 And what's more, being a miner, as soon as you're too old and tired and ill and sick and stupid to do the job

properly, you have to go. Well, the very opposite applies with the judges.

Peter Cook, English humorist (1937–95). 'Sitting on the Bench', *Beyond the Fringe* (1961).

July 4

7 JULY 4. Statistics show that we lose more fools on this day than in all the other days of the year put together. This proves, by the number left in stock, that one Fourth of July per year is now inadequate, the country has grown so.

Mark Twain, American writer (1835–1910). *Puddn'head Wilson* (1894).

Juries

8 We have a criminal system which is superior to any in the world; and its efficiency is only marred by the difficulty of finding twelve men every day who don't know anything and can't read.

Mark Twain, American writer (1835–1910). *Sketches New and Old* (1875).

Justice

9 In England, Justice is open to all, like the Ritz hotel.

Sir James Mathew, Irish judge (1830–1908). Attributed by R. E. Megarry in *Miscellany-at-Law* (1955).

10 Justice must not only be seen to be done but has to be seen to be believed.

J. B. Morton (Beachcomber), English humorous writer (1893–1979). Attributed by Peter Cook on BBC Radio *Quote ... Unquote* (5 June 1980).

On being defeated in a libel action, when editor of Private Eye:

11 If this is justice, I'm a banana.

Ian Hislop, English journalist (1960–). Quoted in *The Observer*, 'Sayings of the Week' (28 May 1989). *Private Eye* had been sued by Sonia Sutcliffe, wife of the 'Yorkshire Ripper'.

K

Kings

1 The whole world is in revolt. Soon there will be only five kings left – the King of England, the King of Spades, the King of Clubs, the King of Hearts and the King of Diamonds.

Farouk I, Egyptian King (1920–65). Remark to Lord Boyd-Orr (1948). Quoted in *Life* Magazine (10 April 1950).

Jesting epitaph on Charles II:

2 Here lies a great and mighty king
Whose promise none relies on;
He never said a foolish thing
Nor ever did a wise one.

John Wilmot, 2nd Earl of Rochester, English poet (1647–80). Quoted in Thomas Traherne: Remarks and Collections (1885–1921). Other versions include, 'Here lies our sovereign Lord the King ...' and 'Here lies our mutton-eating king' (where 'mutton' = prostitute). Charles II's reply is said to have been: 'This is very true: for my words are my own, and my actions are my ministers'' (also in Traherne ...).

Remark on declining a formal coronation (1740):

3 *Une couronne n'est qu'un chapeau qui laisse passer la pluie* [A crown is no more than a hat that lets in the rain].

Frederick the Great, Prussian King (1712–86). Quoted in Alan and Veronica Palmer, *Quotations in History* (1976).

4 My people and I have come to an agreement which satisfies us both. They are to say what they please, and I am to do what I please.

Frederick the Great. Attributed definition of 'benevolent despotism' in *The Oxford Dictionary of Quotations* (1953).

Kipling, Rudyard
**English poet and novelist
(1865–1936)**

5 Do you like Kipling?
I don't know, you naughty boy, I've never kippled.

Donald McGill, English comic postcard artist (1875–1962). Caption to one of McGill's postcards – undated, but possibly from the 1930s.

6 Will there ever come a season
Which shall rid us from the curse
Of a prose which knows no reason
And an unmelodious verse ...
When there stands a muzzled stripling,
Mute, beside a muzzled bore:
When the Rudyards cease from kipling
And the Haggards ride no more.

J. K. Stephen, English journalist and light versifier (1859–92). 'To R. K.' (1891).

7 From the point of view of literature Mr Kipling is a genius who drops his aspirates.

Oscar Wilde, Irish playwright, poet and wit (1854–1900). *The Critic As Artist* (1890).

Kissing

8 Kissing don't last: cookery do!

George Meredith, English novelist and poet (1828–1909). *The Ordeal of Richard Feverel* (1859).

On kissing Margaret Thatcher (when they were both candidates for the Conservative leadership, 1975):

9 I have over a period of time, when I have met her – as indeed one does –

I have kissed her often before. We have not done it on a pavement outside a hotel in Eastbourne before. But we have done it in various rooms in one way and another at various functions – it is perfectly genuine and normal – and normal and right – so to do.

William Whitelaw (later Viscount Whitelaw), English politician (1918–). Reported in *The Observer* (9 February 1975).

Knickers

Of Jilly Cooper as romantic novelist:

1 Barbara Cartland without the iron knickers.

Anonymous. Quoted in *A Year of Stings and Squelches* (1985).

2 Why can't a woman with a wooden leg give change for a pound note?
   Because she's only got half a knicker!

Anonymous. Revived by Spike Milligan in his script for BBC Radio *The Last Goon Show Of All* (5 October 1972) – though it had been used in the original *Goon Show* in the 1950s.

Knowledge

3 First come I; my name is Jowett.
   There's no knowledge but I know it.
   I am the Master of this College:
   What I don't know isn't knowledge.

H. C. Beeching, English clergyman and writer (1859–1919). In 'The Masque of Balliol' (1870s). Benjamin Jowett was Master of Balliol College, Oxford, from 1870.

L

Labour Party

1 I do not often attack the Labour Party. They do it so well themselves.

(Sir) Edward Heath, English Prime Minister (1916–). Quoted in *A Year of Stings and Squelches* (1985).

2 A divorced woman on the throne of the house of Windsor would be a pretty big feather in the cap of that bunch of rootless intellectuals, alien Jews and international pederasts who call themselves the Labour Party.

Alan Bennett, English playwright and actor (1934–). *Forty Years On*, Act 2 (1969). In Bulldog Drummond parody.

Landslides

3 I just received the following wire from my generous Daddy – 'Dear Jack. Don't buy a single vote more than is necessary. I'll be damned if I'm going to pay for a landslide.'

John F. Kennedy, American Democratic President (1917–63). Speech, Washington D.C. (1958). Quoted in Bill Adler, *The Wit of President Kennedy* (1964).

Language

4 England and America are two countries separated by the same language.

Bernard Shaw, Irish playwright and critic (1856–1950). Quoted in *Reader's Digest* (November 1942) and *The Treasury of Humorous Quotations*, ed. Evan Esar & Nicolas Bentley (1951).

5 We have really everything in common with America nowadays except, of course, language.

Oscar Wilde, Irish playwright, poet and wit (1854–1900). *The Canterville Ghost* (1887).

6 It is a misfortune for Anglo-American friendship that the two countries are supposed to have a common language

Bertrand Russell (3rd Earl Russell), English mathematician and philosopher (1872–1970). In *Saturday Evening Post* (3 June 1944).

7 [European writers and scholars in America are] up against the barrier of a common language.

Dylan Thomas, Welsh poet (1914–53). Radio talk published in *The Listener* (April 1954).

To a young man who had bemoaned that he had lost all his Greek:

8 I believe it happened at the same time, Sir, that I lost all my large estates in Scotland.

Samuel Johnson, English writer and lexicographer (1709–84). Quoted in Nancy McPhee, *The Second Book of Insults* (1981). Frank Muir, *A Kentish Lad* (1997) has it rather as 'lost all my large estate in Yorkshire' and seems to suggest it was reported in a letter by a friend and not by Boswell.

9 MIKE: There's no word in the Irish language for what you were doing.

WILSON: In Lapland they have no word for snow.

Joe Orton, English playwright (1933–67). *The Ruffian on the Stair* (rev. edn 1967). What they were doing was, naturally, of a homosexual and possibly even incestuous nature.

10 You English ... think we know damn nothing but I tell you we know damn all.

Nicholas Monsarrat, English novelist (1910–79). *The Cruel Sea* (1951). Compare this: in the second volume of David Niven's autobiography to which he gave the title

Bring On the Empty Horses (1975), he talked of Michael Curtiz, the Hungarian-born American film director (1888–1962). During the filming of *The Charge of the Light Brigade* (1936), Curtiz ordered the release of a hundred riderless steeds by shouting: 'Bring on the empty horses!' David Niven and Errol Flynn fell about with laughter at this. Curtiz rounded on them and said, 'You and your stinking language! You think I know f-- nothing. Well, let me tell you, I know f-- all!'

1 I speak Spanish to God, Italian to women, French to men – and German to my horse.

Charles V, Holy Roman Emperor (1500–58). Attributed remark. Alluded to in Lord Chesterfield, *Letters to His Son* (1832 edn).

Marginal comment on document:

2 This is the sort of English up with which I will not put.

Winston S. Churchill (later Sir Winston), British Conservative Prime Minister and writer (1874–1965). Quoted in Sir Ernest Gowers, 'Troubles with Prepositions', *Plain Words* (1948).

Presenting the Thomas Cranmer Schools Prize, organized by the Prayer Book Society, in 1989, Prince Charles delivered an attack on the 'dismal wasteland of banality, cliché and casual obscenity' of everyday language. 'Is it entirely an accident,' he wondered, 'that the defacing of Cranmer's Prayer Book has coincided with a calamitous decline in literacy and the quality of English?' He went on to deliver a rendering of Hamlet's 'To be or not to be' speech in modern English:

3 Well, frankly, the problem as I see it
At this moment in time is whether I
Should just lie down under all this
  hassle
And let them walk all over me.
Or, whether I should just say: 'OK,
I get the message', and do myself in.
I mean, let's face it, I'm in a no-win
  situation,
And quite honestly, I'm so stuffed up
  to here with the
Whole stupid mess that, I can tell you,
  I've just
Got a good mind to take the quick
  way out.

That's the bottom line. The only
  problem is:
What happens if I find that when
  I've bumped
Myself off, there's some kind of
  a, you know,
All that mystical stuff about when
  you die,
You might find you're still – know
  what I mean?

Charles, Prince of Wales (1948–). Quoted in *The Independent* (20 December 1989). Full marks to the speechwriter.

4 Tim was so learned that he could name a Horse in nine languages, but bought a cow to ride on.

Benjamin Franklin, American politician and scientist (1706–90). *Poor Richard's Almanack* (November 1750) – a work in which Franklin often revised already existing sayings.

Laps

5 She's been on more laps than a napkin.

Walter Winchell, American journalist and broadcaster (1897–1972). Quoted in *The Penguin Dictionary of Modern Humorous Quotations*, ed. Fred Metcalf (1987).

Last person

6 Would the last person to leave the country please switch off the lights.

Anonymous. Quoted in the book *Graffiti 2* (1980). On 9 April 1992, this line suffered a revival when on the day of the British General Election, the Sun newspaper's front page headline was: 'IF KINNOCK WINS TODAY WILL THE LAST PERSON IN BRITAIN PLEASE TURN OUT THE LIGHTS'. In Maxime Rodinson, *Israel and the Arabs* (1969), it is reported that in *c*.1966, when due to the political situation many people decided to leave Israel, a notice was put up at Lydda Airport near Tel Aviv: 'Will the last to leave kindly turn out the light.'

Laughter

7 I remember a methodist preacher who on perceiving a profane grin on the faces of part of his congregation – exclaimed 'no *hopes* for *them* as *laughs*'.

Lord Byron, English poet (1788–1824). Letter

to Augusta Leigh (19 December 1816). In a note to *Hints from Horace*, Byron gave the name of the preacher as John Stickles.

1 One must have a heart of stone to read the death of Little Nell without laughing.

Oscar Wilde, Irish playwright, poet and wit (1854–1900). Quoted in Ada Leverson, *Letters to the Sphinx from Oscar Wilde and Reminiscences of the Author* (1930).

Lavatories

On being approached by the Secretary of the Athenaeum whose lavatory he was in the habit of using on his way to the office:

2 Good God, do you mean to say this place is a club?

F. E. Smith (1st Earl of Birkenhead), English politician and lawyer (1872–1930). Quoted in John Campbell, *F. E. Smith, First Earl of Birkenhead* (1983). Campbell claims to have established that it must have been, rather, the National Liberal Club.

Law

3 The Law is the true embodiment
Of everything that's excellent.
It has no kind of fault or flaw,
And I, my Lord, embody the Law.

(Sir) W. S. Gilbert, English writer and lyricist (1836–1911). *Iolanthe*, Act 1 (1882).

4 No brilliance is needed in the law. Nothing but common sense, and relatively clean finger nails.

(Sir) John Mortimer, English author, playwright and lawyer (1923–). *A Voyage Round My Father* (1970).

When a Yorkshire miner put in a very late claim for compensation, the judge told his counsel: 'Your client is no doubt aware of vigilantibus, et non dormientibus, jura subveniunt?' *The counsel replied:*

5 Why, in Barnsley, m'lud, they speak of little else.

Anonymous. In *Pass the Port Again* (1980), there is quoted a version involving Serjeant Sullivan – 'the last serjeant of the Irish Bar to practise in the English courts' (Alexander Martin Sullivan, 1871–1959). Here, the legal tag is *'Assignatus utitur jure auctoris'* and the

place where they speak of little else is Ballynattery. The legal maxims in each case are genuine. The first means, 'The laws assist the watchful, not the sleepers' and the second, 'An assignee is clothed with the right of his principal.'

6 The penalty for laughing in the courtroom is six months in jail: if it were not for this penalty, the jury would never hear the evidence.

H. L. Mencken, American journalist and linguist (1880–1956). Quoted in Andrew & Jonathan Roth, *Devil's Advocates* (1989).

Law-making

7 If you like laws and sausages, you should never watch either one being made.

Otto von Bismarck, Prusso-German statesman (1815–98). Unverified. A slightly different version, 'Laws are like sausages; you should never watch them being made', has been credited to the French revolutionary statesman Honoré Gabriel de Riqueti, Comte de Mirabeau (1749–91).

Laws, informal

8 If anything can go wrong, it will.

Anonymous 'Murphy's Law'. Quoted in *Scientific American* (April 1956), but said to date from the late 1940s.

9 No matter how you have searched, there will always be one teaspoon left at the bottom of the washing-up water.

Irene Thomas, English broadcaster (1920–). *The Bandsman's Daughter* (1979).

10 When your cat has fallen asleep on your lap and looks utterly content and adorable you will suddenly have to go to the bathroom.

Anonymous 'Rule of Feline Frustration'. Quoted in Arthur Bloch, *Murphy's Law and Other Reasons Why Things Go Wrong* (1977).

11 The amount of flak received on any subject is inversely proportional to the subject's true value.

Anonymous 'Potter's Law' in *ibid*.

12 When all else fails, read the instructions.

Anonymous 'Cahn's Axiom'. Quoted by Paul Dickson in *Playboy* (April 1978).

1 A falling body always rolls to the most inaccessible place.

Theodore M. Bernstein (untraced). *The Careful Writer* (1967).

2 Gnomes always draw curtains where there are views.

Ada Louise Huxtable (untraced). In *The New York Times* (16 November 1975).

3 The possibility of a young man meeting a desirable and receptive young female increases by pyramidal progression when he is already in the company of (1) a date (2) his wife (3) a better-looking and richer male friend.

Ronald Beifield (untraced). Quoted by Allan L. Otten, in *The Wall Street Journal* (2 February 1975).

4 A shortcut is the longest distance between two points.

Charles Issawi (untraced). In *Columbia Forum* (Summer, 1970).

5 Did you ever notice how much faster wood burns when you personally cut and chop it yourself?

Anonymous. Quoted on CBS TV *Apple's Way* (12 January 1975).

6 As soon as you replace a lost object, you will find it.

David Brinkley, American broadcaster (1920–). Quoted by Ann Landers, in the *Poughkeepsie Journal* (26 March 1978).

7 At bank, post office or supermarket, there is one universal law which you ignore at your own peril: the shortest line moves the slowest.

Bill Vaughan (untraced). Quoted in *Reader's Digest* (July 1977).

8 The longer one saves something before throwing it away, the sooner it will be needed after it is thrown away.

James J. Caulfield (untraced). Quoted in Harold Faber, *The Book of Laws* (1979). Promulgated in March 1968.

9 If it works well, they'll stop making it.

Jane Otten and Russell Baker. Quoted by Alan L. Otten in *The Wall Street Journal* (26 February 1976).

10 Whatever happens in government could have happened differently, and it usually would have been better if it had.

Charles Frankel (untraced). *High on Foggy Bottom* (1970).

11 The more underdeveloped the country, the more overdeveloped the women.

John Kenneth Galbraith, Canadian-born American economist (1908–). Quoted in *Time* Magazine (17 October 1969).

12 Anyone who says he isn't going to resign four times, definitely will.

John Kenneth Galbraith. Quoted in *Time* Magazine (7 November 1973).

13 News expands to fill the time and space allocated to its coverage.

William Safire, American journalist (1929–). In *The New York Times* (6 September 1973).

14 When the weight of the paperwork equals the weight of the plane, the plane will fly.

Donald Douglas, American aircraft designer and manufacturer (1892–1981). Quoted by Alan L. Otten in *The Wall Street Journal* (26 February 1976).

15 Seven-eighths of everything can't be seen.

Anonymous 'Iceberg Theorem'. Quoted in the *Daily Mail* (10 March 1979).

16 The easiest way to find something lost around the house is to buy a replacement.

Anonymous 'Rosenbaum's Law'. Quoted in *ibid.*

17 It is impossible to make anything foolproof because fools are so ingenious.

H. W. Robinson of Co. Down (unidentified). Quoted in the *Daily Mail* (29 November 1980).

18 The place you are trying to get to is always on the extreme edge of the page on the street-map.

Violet Rutter of London W6 (unidentified). Contributed to BBC Radio *Quote ... Unquote* and quoted in book *Say No More* (1987).

1 When ripping an article from a news-paper, the tear is always into and never away from the required article.

Alan Fraser of Stockport (unidentified). Contributed as above.

2 When all else fails – and the instructions are missing – kick it.

Anonymous (in the Department of Anaesthetics at Harrow hospital). Contributed as above.

3 Acceptable invitations only arrive when you can't accept them.

Anonymous. Contributed as above.

4 If you buy a record for the A side, in time you will find that you are only able to tolerate the B side.

Anonymous. Contributed as above.

5 When your car or central heating is due for servicing – and nothing is positively wrong with it – the servicing will result in the machine having to be serviced again within the month.

Anonymous. Contributed as above.

Lawrence of Arabia (T. E. Lawrence)
English soldier and writer (1888–1935)

6 He's always backing into the limelight.

Lord Berners, English writer and composer (1883–1950). Quoted in *The Oxford Dictionary of Quotations* (1979), citing 'oral tradition'. Winston Churchill said the same thing, according to his secretary, Montague Brown (speech to the International Churchill Society, 25 September 1985): 'He had the art of backing uneasily into the limelight. He was a very remarkable character and very careful of that fact.'

Lawyers

7 A lawyer with his briefcase can steal more than a thousand men with guns.

Mario Puzo, American novelist (1920–). *The Godfather* (1969).

8 ... as scarce as lawyers in heaven.

Mark Twain, American writer (1835–1910). 'Information for the Millions', *The Celebrated Jumping Frog of Calaveras County* (1867).

9 A man who is his own lawyer has a fool for a client.

Anonymous proverb first recorded in Philadelphia (1809).

Lays

10 And there was that wholesale libel on a Yale prom. If all the girls attending it were laid end to end, Mrs Parker said, she wouldn't be at all surprised.

Dorothy Parker, American writer (1893–1967). Quoted in Alexander Woollcott, *While Rome Burns* (1934).

On her requirements for an apartment:

11 [Enough space] to lay a hat – and a few friends.

Dorothy Parker. Quoted in John Keats, *You Might as Well Live* (1970).

Leadership

12 I must follow them for I am their leader.

Alexandre Auguste Ledru-Rollin, French politician (1807–74). Ledru-Rollin became Minister of the Interior in the provisional government during the 1848 Paris revolution. He was looking from his window one day as a mob passed by and he said: *'Eh, je suis leur chef, il fallait bien les suivre* [Ah well, I'm their leader, I really ought to follow them].' It is said that 'he gave offence by his arbitrary conduct' (of which this would seem to be a prime example) and had to resign.

13 Leadership, like swimming, cannot be learned by reading about it.

Henry Mintzberg, American business expert (1939–). At McGill University School of Management.

Leaks

How Noah plugged a leak in the Ark using various parts of the anatomy, including a bloodhound's:

14 And that is how Noah got 'em all
   safe ashore,
But ever since then, strange to tell,
Them as helped save the Ark has all
   carried a mark,
Aye, and all their descendants as well.

That's why dog has a cold nose, and
  ladies cold elbows
– You'll also find if you enquire
That that's why a man takes his
  coat-tails in hand
And stands with his back to
  the fire.

Marriott Edgar, English writer
(1880–1951). 'The 'Ole in the Ark'
(1937). Famously recited by Stanley
Holloway.

Legs

1 There are two reasons why I'm in
show business, and I'm standing on
both of them.

Betty Grable, American actress (1916–73).
Quoted in Barbara Rowes, *The Book
of Quotes* (1979).

Leisure

2 Leisure tends to corrupt, and
absolute leisure corrupts absolutely.

Edgar A. Shoaff (unidentified). Quoted
in Laurence J. Peter, *Quotations for
Our Time* (1977).

Lending

3 Never lend books, for no one ever
returns them; the only books I have
in my library are books that other
people have lent me.

Anatole France, French novelist and critic
(1844–1924). Quoted in *The Treasury of
Humorous Quotations*, ed. Evan Esar &
Nicolas Bentley (1951).

4 Please return this book; I find that
though many of my friends are poor
arithmeticians, they are nearly all
good bookkeepers.

Sir Walter Scott, Scottish novelist (1771–
1832). Quoted in *The Treasury of Humorous
Quotations*, ed. Evan Esar & Nicolas Bentley
(1951).

5 I don't trust a bank that would lend
money to such a poor risk.

Robert Benchley, American humorist
(1889–1945). Attributed in *The Bloomsbury Dictionary of Quotations* (1987).

Length

*Of an article (said by Frank Muir to
be 'full of declamation and invective')
sub-mitted by Lord Brougham to
Smith's* Edinburgh Review:

6 Brougham's review is not in good taste;
he should have put on an air of serious
concern, not raillery and ridicule;
things are too serious for that. It is
long yet vigorous, like the penis of
a jackass.

Revd Sydney Smith, English clergyman,
essayist and wit (1771–1845). Letter
(1809), quoted in *The Oxford Book of
Humorous Prose* (1990).

Lesbianism

7 Many years ago I chased a woman
for almost two years, only to discover
her tastes were exactly like mine: we
were both crazy about girls.

Groucho Marx, American comedian (1895–
1977). In *The Groucho Letters* (1967) –
letter of 28 March 1955.

Lesser

*On the first wife (with whom he was having
a feud) of the composer Frank Loesser:*

8 Lynn is the evil of two Loessers.

Harry Kurnitz, American screenwriter
(*c.*1907–68). Quoted in *The Observer*
(31 March 1968).

Letters

9 I would have answered your letter
sooner, but you didn't send one.

Goodman Ace, American writer (1899–
1982). Letter (1950) to Groucho Marx,
quoted in *The Groucho Letters* (1967).

10 An odd thought strikes me: we shall
receive no letters in the grave.

Samuel Johnson, English writer and lexicographer (1709– 84). Quoted in James
Boswell, *Life of Johnson* (1791) – a remark
from the last few weeks of his life in December 1784.

11 Correspondences are like small-clothes
before the invention of suspenders; it is
impossible to keep them up.

Revd Sydney Smith, English clergyman, essayist and wit (1771–1845). Letter to Catherine Crowe (31 January 1841).

1 Beware of writing to me. I always answer ... My father spent the last 20 years of his life writing letters. If someone thanked him for a wedding present, he thanked them for thanking him and there was no end to the exchange but death.

Evelyn Waugh, English novelist (1903–66). Letter to Lady Mosley (30 March 1966). In *Life* Magazine (8 April 1946), he made the same point: 'His courtesy was somewhat extravagant. He would write and thank people who wrote to thank him for wedding presents and when he encountered anyone as punctilious as himself the correspondence ended only with death.'

2 Never burn an uninteresting letter is the first rule of British aristocracy.

Frank Moore Colby, American editor and writer (1865–1925). Quoted in *The Treasury of Humorous Quotations*, ed. Evan Esar & Nicolas Bentley (1951).

Levity

3 Nothing like a little judicious levity.

Robert Louis Stevenson, Scottish writer (1850–94) and Lloyd Osbourne, American writer (1868–1947). *The Wrong Box*, Chap. 7 (1889).

Liberals

4 A liberal is a conservative who has been arrested.

Anonymous. Quoted (twice) in Tom Wolfe, *The Bonfire of the Vanities* (1987).

5 There aren't any liberals left in New York. They've all been mugged.

James Q. Wilson (untraced). Quoted in *Policy Review* (Fall 1993).

Lies

Of Harold Wilson:

6 How can you tell when he's lying? When his lips are moving.

Anonymous. Quoted in *A Year of Stings and Squelches* (1985).

7 I have been thinking that I would make a proposition to my Republican friends ... That if they will stop telling lies about the Democrats, we will stop telling the truth about them.

Adlai Stevenson, American Democratic politician (1900–65). Remark during election campaign (10 September 1952). However, it was originated by Republican Senator Chauncey Depew about the Democrats earlier in the century. Depew was a senator in 1899–1911.

Of a friend:

8 She tells enough white lies to ice a wedding cake.

Margot Asquith (later Countess of Oxford and Asquith) (1864–1945). Quoted by Baroness Asquith in BBC TV *As I Remember* (30 April 1967).

Life

9 Life is just a bowl of toenails.

Anonymous graffito on the wall of an Oxford college. Contributed to BBC Radio *Quote ... Unquote* (31 May 1978) by John Colman of Chesham, Buckinghamshire.

10 This is not a dress rehearsal, this is real life.

Anonymous. Quoted in book *Graffiti 3* (1981). Collected at the Eight-O Club, Dallas, Texas.

11 Laugh it off, laugh it off; it's all part of life's rich pageant.

Arthur Marshall, English writer and entertainer (1910–89). 'The Games Mistress', recorded monologue (1937).

12 Oh, isn't life a terrible thing, thank God?

Dylan Thomas, Welsh poet (1914–53). *Under Milk Wood* (1954), opening words.

13 Life is like playing a violin solo in public and learning the instrument as one goes on.

Edward Bulwer-Lytton (1st Baron Lytton), English novelist and politician (1803–73). Quoted in *The Treasury of Humorous Quotations*, ed. Evan Esar & Nicolas Bentley (1951). Later quoted by Samuel Butler, English author (1835–1902), during a speech at the Somerville Club (27 February 1895).

1 Life ... is like a cup of tea; the more heartily we drink, the sooner we reach the dregs.

J. M. Barrie, Scottish playwright (1860–1937). *The Admirable Crichton*, Act 1, Sc. 1 (1902).

2 Life is like a sewer. What you get out of it depends on what you put in.

Tom Lehrer, US songwriter and entertainer (1928–). On record album, *An Evening Wasted with Tom Lehrer* (1953).

3 Take me or leave me. Or as most people do: both.

Dorothy Parker, American writer (1893–1967). Quoted in book *Nudge Nudge, Wink Wink* (1986).

When someone said, 'They're ducking for apples' at a Hallowe'en party:

4 There, but for a typographical error is the story of my life.

Dorothy Parker. Quoted in John Keats, *You Might as Well Live* (1970).

5 No good worry worry anything. By'm by, we all asame – Nothing!

Anonymous Australian aborigine. Quoted in *The 'Quote ... Unquote' Newsletter* (April 1994).

6 Is there a life before death? That's chalked up
In Ballymurphy. Competence with pain, Coherent miseries, a bite and sup, We hug our little destiny again.

Seamus Heaney, Irish poet (1939–). 'Whatever You Say Say Nothing', *North* (1975). Earlier, 'Is there life before death?' was the epigraph to Chap. 9 of Stephen Vizinczey's novel *In Praise of Older Women* (1966). There, it is credited to 'Anon. Hungarian'.

7 Life is just one damned thing after another.

Elbert Hubbard, American writer and editor (1856–1915). In *The Philistine* (December 1909). Also attributed to Frank Ward O'Malley (1875–1932).

8 People say that life is the thing, but I prefer reading.

Logan Pearsall Smith, American writer (1865–1946). 'Myself', *Afterthoughts* (1931).

9 To the recent query, 'If you could ask one question about life, what would the answer be?' Eugène Ionesco responded, 'No'.

Eugène Ionesco, Romanian-born playwright (1912–94). Quoted in *Esquire* (December 1974).

In parody of an Anglican church sermon:

10 Life, you know, is rather like opening a tin of sardines. We're all of us looking for the key.

Alan Bennett, English playwright and actor (1934–). 'Take a Pew', *Beyond the Fringe* (1961).

11 If I had to live my life all over again, I would change one thing: I wouldn't read *Moby Dick*.

Woody Allen, American film actor, writer and director (1937–). Quoted in *The Daily Telegraph* (24 February 1994).

Liking

12 Will Rogers never met Marvin Hamlisch.

Anonymous car sticker in New York. Quoted in *The Independent*, (15 May 1987). Will Rogers, the folksy American comedian, had been famous for saying, 'When I die, my epitaph is going to read, "I never met a man I didn't like."'

Limericks

13 There once was a young man called Stencil
Whose prick was as sharp as a pencil.
He punctured an actress,
Two sheets and a mattress,
And dented the bedroom utensil.

Anonymous, current in the early 1980s. Does not appear in G. Legman's magisterial survey *The Limerick* (two vols, 1964, 1969).

14 A tired old fairy from Rome
Took a leprechaun back to his home.
As he entered the elf
He said to himself
I'd be much better off in a gnome.

Anonymous, ditto.

1 Nymphomaniacal Alice
Used a dynamite stick for a phallus.
They found her vagina
In North Carolina
And her ass-hole in Buckingham Palace.

Anonymous. Legman dates this '1942–1951'.

2 On the chest of a barmaid in Sale
Were tattooed the prices of ale,
And on her behind,
For the sake of the blind,
Was the same information in Braille.

Anonymous. Legman has a version
of this about a 'harlot from Yale',
dated 1941.

3 There was a young man from Calcutta
Who had the most terrible stutta.
He said, 'Pass the h-ham
And the j-j-j-jam,
And the b-b-b-b-b-b-butta.'

Anonymous. Source forgotten, not in Legman.

4 There was a young lady of Tottenham,
Who'd no manners or else she'd
    forgotten 'em.
At tea at the vicar's
She tore off her knickers,
Because, she explained, she felt
    'ot in 'em.

Anonymous. Legman finds a source for this
in 1903.

5 There was a young girl of Madras
Who had the most beautiful ass.
But not as you'd think
Firm, round and pink,
But grey, with long ears, and eats grass.

Anonymous. Legman finds a source for this
in 1940.

6 There was a young lady of Exeter
So pretty that men craned their nexetter.
One was even so brave
As to take out and wave
The distinguishing mark of his sexetter.

Anonymous. Legman finds this '1927–1941'.

7 There was a young man in Florence
To whom all art was abhorrence.
So he got slightly tipsy
Went to the Uffizi
And peed on the paintings in torrents.

Anonymous. Quoted in the book *Graffiti 2*
(1980). Legman finds two limericks from
1941–42 which both make use of the
Florence/abhorrence/torrents rhyme but
on different themes.

8 There was a young gaucho named
    Bruno
Who said, 'Screwing is one thing I
    do know.
A woman is divine,
And a sheep is divine,
But a llama is Numero Uno.

Anonymous. Legman has this from 1942.

9 I wish that my room had a floor.
I don't so much care for a door
But this crawling around
Without touching the ground
Is beginning to be quite a bore.

Gelett Burgess, American writer and illustrator
(1866–1951). Attributed.

10 An incontinent man from Stoke Poges
In the theatre would often soak loges.
To take care of that
He'd pee in his hat
Or a chamber-pot made of Limoges.

Ken Thomson, English writer. As also:

11 An incontinent man from
    Stoke Poges
At the opera would often soak loges.
La Fenice included
Where he quietly exuded
In a loge which was meant for
    the Doges.

Lingerie

12 Brevity is the soul of lingerie – as the
Petticoat said to the Chemise.

Dorothy Parker, American writer (1893–
1967). Quoted in Alexander Woollcott,
While Rome Burns (1934). Said to have been
written as a caption for *Vogue* in 1916.

Lips

13 With Mick Jagger's lips, he could
French kiss a moose.

Joan Rivers, American entertainer (1937–).
Quoted in *A Year of Stings and Squelches*
(1985).

Lisps

1 Lisp: to call a spade a thpade.

Oliver Herford, American humorist (1863–1935). Quoted in *The Treasury of Humorous Quotations*, ed. Evan Esar & Nicolas Bentley (1951).

Literary criticism

An early book-reviewer writes:

2 And it shall be, when thou hast made an end of reading this book, that thou shalt bind a stone to it, and cast it into the midst of Euphrates.

Bible, Jeremiah 51:63.

3 [The Mormon Bible] is chloroform in print. If Joseph Smith composed this book, the act was a miracle – keeping awake while he did it was, at any rate.

Mark Twain, American writer (1835–1910). *Roughing It* (1872).

Of an early work by Congreve:

4 It is praised by the biographers ... I would rather praise it than read it.

Samuel Johnson, English writer and lexicographer (1709–84). 'Congreve', *The Lives of the English Poets* (1779–81).

5 To say Agatha [Christie]'s characters are cardboard cut-outs is an insult to cardboard.

Ruth Rendell (later Baroness Rendell), English crime novelist (1930–). Quoted in *The Independent* 'Quote Unquote' (3 April 1993).

6 This is not a novel to be tossed aside lightly. It should be thrown with great force.

Dorothy Parker, American writer (1893–1967). Quoted in R. E. Drennan, *Wit's End* (1973). In Matthew Parris, *Scorn* (1994), this is said to refer to Benito Mussolini's novel *Claudia Particella, L'Amante del Cardinale: Grande Romanzo dei Tempi del Cardinal Emanuel Madruzzo*. When this was published in the US as *The Cardinal's Mistress*, Parker reviewed it devastatingly (15 September 1928), but did not actually include this put-down.

Reviewing D. H. Lawrence's novel Lady Chatterley's Lover *when it was reissued in the United States by Grove Press (c.1928). Rather oddly, this was in the pages of* Field and Stream, *a journal aimed at followers of outdoor pursuits:*

7 This fictional account of the day-by-day life of an English gamekeeper is still of interest to outdoor-minded readers, as it contains many passages on pheasant-raising, the apprehending of poachers, ways to control vermin, and other chores and duties of professional gamekeepers. Unfortunately, one is obliged to wade through many pages of extraneous material in order to discover and savour these sidelights on the management of a Midland estate, and in this reviewer's opinion, the book cannot take the place of J. R. Miller's *Practical Gamekeeper*.

Anonymous. Quoted in the seventh volume of Rupert Furneaux's *Famous Criminal Cases* (1962) in its account of the Penguin Books/*Lady Chatterley* trial.

8 The want of human interest is always felt. *Paradise Lost* is one of the books which the reader admires and lays down, and forgets to take up again. Its perusal is a duty rather than a pleasure. None ever wished it longer than it is.

Samuel Johnson, English writer and lexicographer (1709–84). in 'Milton', *Lives of the English Poets* (1779–81).

On a book by John O'Hara:

9 Hard to lay down and easy not to pick up.

Malcolm Cowley, American critic (1898–1989). Quoted in Ned Sherrin, *Cutting Edge* (1984).

Of Monckton Milnes's Life of Keats:

10 A fricassee of dead dog.

Thomas Carlyle, Scottish historian and philosopher (1795–1881). Quoted in *A Year of Stings and Squelches* (1985).

Reviewing Cyril Connolly's The Rock Pool:

11 Even to want to write about so-called artists who spend on sodomy what they

have gained by sponging betrays a kind of spiritual inadequacy.

George Orwell, (1903–50). In the *New English Weekly* (23 July 1936).

On hearing that Watership Down *was a novel about rabbits written by a civil servant:*

1 I would rather read a novel about civil servants written by a rabbit.

Craig Brown, English journalist (1957–). Attributed in *The Oxford Dictionary of Literary Quotations*, ed. Peter Kemp (1997).

Of Abraham Cowley:

2 He more had pleased us, had he pleased us less.

Joseph Addison, English essayist and politician (1672–1719). *An Account of the Greatest English Poets* (1694).

3 I never read a book before reviewing it; it prejudices a man so.

Revd Sydney Smith, English clergyman, essayist and wit (1771–1845). Quoted in Hesketh Pearson, *The Smith of Smiths* (1934).

As 'Constant reader', reviewing A. A. Milne:

4 And it is that word 'hummy', my darlings, that marks the first place in 'The House at Pooh Corner' at which Tonstant Weader fwowed up.

Dorothy Parker, American writer (1893–1967). In *The New Yorker* (20 October 1928).

5 From the moment I picked up your book until I laid it down I was convulsed with laughter. Someday I intend reading it.

Groucho Marx, American comedian (1895–1977). Quoted in Hector Arce, *Groucho* (1979). Concerning *Dawn Ginsbergh's Revenge* (1928) by S. J. Perelman.

Reviewing a TV adaptation of M. M. Kaye's The Far Pavilions*:*

6 One of those big, fat paperbacks, intended to while away a monsoon or two, which, if thrown with a good overarm action, will bring a water buffalo to its knees.

Nancy Banks-Smith, English journalist (1929–). In *The Guardian* (4 January 1984).

Of James Laver's memoirs Museum Piece *(1963):*

7 Like someone coming for tea and staying a month.

Anonymous (critic in *The Times*). Quoted in Roy Strong, *The Roy Strong Diaries 1967–1987* (1997).

Literature

8 There was a time when I thought my only connection with the literary world would be that I had once delivered meat to T. S. Eliot's mother-in-law.

Alan Bennett, English playwright and actor (1934–). Quoted in *The Observer* (26 April 1992). Bennett's father was indeed a butcher and T. S. Eliot's second wife, Valerie Fletcher, came from the same town in Yorkshire. Bennett recounted this once more in the Introduction to his *Writing Home* (1994).

9 Literature is mostly about having sex and not much about having children. Life is the other way round.

David Lodge, English academic and novelist (1935–). *The British Museum is Falling Down* (1965).

Living

10 Earned a precarious living by taking in one another's washing.

Mark Twain, American writer (1835–1910). Loosely attributed. In *The Commonweal* (6 August 1887) an article entitled 'Bourgeois Versus Socialist' signed by William Morris ends: 'A bourgeois paradise will supervene, in which everyone will be free to exploit – but there will be no one to exploit ... On the whole, one must suppose that the type of it would be that town (surely in America and in the neighbourhood of Mark Twain) that I have heard of, whose inhabitants lived by taking in each other's washing.'

11 The living are just the dead on holiday.

Maurice Maeterlinck, Belgian poet and playwright (1862–1949). Quoted in *The Treasury of Humorous Quotations*, ed. Evan Esar & Nicolas Bentley (1951).

Lobotomies

1 I'd rather have a full bottle in front of me than a full frontal lobotomy.

Anonymous graffito from Leicester University. Contributed to BBC Radio *Quote ... Unquote* (19 February 1979) by Bob Baker.

Longevity

Asked, at the age of eighty, the secret of longevity:

2 Keep breathing.

Sophie Tucker, Russian-born American entertainer (1884– 1966). Quoted in *The Quotable Woman* (1978).

Looks

Of a certain actress not noted for her looks:

3 If she played Lady Godiva, the horse would have stolen the show.

Anonymous. Quoted in *The Penguin Dictionary of Modern Quotations* (1971).

When a proud mother said her baby looked like him:

4 Madam, all babies look like me.

Winston S. Churchill (later Sir Winston), British Conservative Prime Minister and writer (1874–1965). Quoted in Sykes & Sproat, *The Wit of Sir Winston* (1965).

On Ian Mikardo MP:

5 He's not as nice as he looks.

Winston S. Churchill. Quoted by Richard Boston on BBC Radio *Quote ... Unquote* (4 January 1976). Said to have been spoken to Christopher Soames, Churchill's PPS. According to Matthew Parris, *Scorn* (1994): 'Sir Edward Heath told us that this remark was made after a debate in the House of Commons in which Mr Mikardo "pressed the Prime Minister about anti-Semitic practices at the Mid-Ocean Club, Bermuda, somewhat to the irritation of the Prime Minister".'

Lord Privy Seal

6 It has been said that this minister is neither a Lord, nor a privy, nor a seal.

Sydney D. Bailey, English writer (1916–). *British Parliamentary Democracy* (3rd edn, 1971). However, this was not an original observation and had already been made on BBC TV's *The Frost Report* (1966–7). It was possibly inspired by Voltaire's joke that the Holy Roman Empire was neither holy, nor Roman, nor an empire (*Essai sur l'histoire générale et sur les moeurs et l'esprit des nations*, 1756). By the late 1960s there was also an observation current that the YMCA was joined by those who were neither young, male nor Christian.

Los Angeles

7 The difference between Los Angeles and yogurt is that yogurt has real culture.

Tom Taussik, American writer. *Legless in Gaza*. Quoted in *Contradictory Quotations*, ed. M. Rogers.

Loss

8 Losing one glove is sorrow enough
But nothing compared with the pain
Of losing one glove
Discarding the other
Then finding the first one again.

Piet Hein, Danish poet, designer and inventor (1905–96). Translation of one of his aphoristic *Grooks*, though as Hein lived from 1969–76 in Britain, it may have been written in English originally.

Love

9 Love is not the dying moan of a distant violin – it is the triumphant twang of a bedspring.

S. J. Perelman, American writer (1904–79). Quoted in Fred Metcalf, *The Penguin Dictionary of Modern Humorous Quotations* (1987).

10 Love – the delightful interval between meeting a beautiful girl and discovering that she looks like a haddock.

John Barrymore, American actor (1882–1942). Quoted in *The Treasury of Humorous Quotations*, ed. Evan Esar & Nicolas Bentley (1951).

11 If love is the answer could you rephrase the question?

Lily Tomlin, American actress (1939–). Quoted in Barbara Rowes, *The Book of Quotes* (1979).

Promotional slogan for the film The Abominable Dr Phibes *(UK, 1971):*

12 Love means never having to say you're ugly.

Anonymous. Quoted in J. R. Colombo, *The Wit and Wisdom of the Movie Makers* (1979).

1 Love is like the measles; we all have to go through it.

Jerome K. Jerome, English writer (1859–1927). *Idle Thoughts of an Idle Fellow* (1886).

2 Love's like the measles – all the worse when it comes late in life.

Douglas Jerrold, English writer (1803–57). 'Love', *The Wit and Opinions of Douglas Jerrold* (1859).

3 'Tis better to have loved and lost than never to have lost at all.

Samuel Butler, English author (1835–1902). *The Way of All Flesh*, Chap. 77 (1903).

4 It is difficult to love mankind unless one has a reasonable private income and when one has a reasonable private income one has better things to do than loving mankind.

Hugh Kingsmill, English writer (1889–1949). Quoted in Richard Ingrams, *God's Apology* (1977).

Love-making

5 Mrs Laye ... told a good thing of a very old man on his dying bed giving advice to a youngster: 'I've had a long life, and it's been a merry one. Take my advice. Make love to every pretty woman you meet. And remember, if you get 5 per cent on your outlay it's a good return.'

Arnold Bennett, English novelist (1867–1931). Diary entry for 24 May 1904, published in *The Journals* (1971). *The Treasury of Humorous Quotations*, ed. Evan Esar & Nicolas Bentley (1951), has this as though said by Bennett himself, in the form: 'Make love to every woman you meet; if you get five per cent on your outlay, it's a good investment.'

6 The only way to behave to a woman is to make love to her, if she is pretty, and to someone else, if she is plain.

Oscar Wilde, Irish playwright, poet and wit (1854–1900). *The Importance of Being Earnest*, Act 1 (1895).

Lower orders

7 ALGERNON: Really, if the lower orders don't set us a good example, what on earth is the use of them?

Oscar Wilde, Irish playwright, poet and wit (1854–1900). *The Importance of Being Earnest*, Act 1 (1895).

M

Macaulay, Thomas Babington, (1st Baron Macaulay)

English historian, poet and politician
(1800–59)

1 Macaulay is well for a while, but one wouldn't live under Niagara.

Thomas Carlyle, Scottish historian and philosopher (1795–1881). Quoted in Richard Monckton Milnes, *Notebook* (1838).

2 [Macaulay's] enemies might perhaps have said before (though I never did so) that he talked rather too much; but now he has occasional flashes of silence, that make his conversation perfectly delightful.

Revd Sydney Smith, English clergyman, essayist and wit (1771–1845). Quoted in Saba, Lady Holland, *A Memoir of Sydney Smith* (1855).

MacDonald, Ramsay

British Labour Prime Minister
(1866–1937)

3 [At Barnum's Circus] the exhibit on the programme I most desired to see was the one described as the Boneless Wonder. My parents judged that the spectacle would be too revolting and demoralizing for my youthful eyes, and I have waited fifty years to see the boneless wonder sitting on the Treasury bench.

Winston S. Churchill (later Sir Winston), British Conservative Prime Minister and writer (1874–1965). Speech, House of Commons (28 January 1931).

4 He has, more than any other man, the gift of compressing the largest amount of words into the smallest amount of thought.

Winston S. Churchill. Speech, House of Commons (23 March 1933).

5 He died as he lived – at sea.

Anonymous. Quoted in Atyeo & Green, *Don't Quote Me* (1981). He died during a cruise.

Maiden speeches

To A. P. Herbert (1935):

6 Call that a maiden speech? It was a brazen hussy of a speech. Never did such a painted lady of a speech parade itself before a modest parliament.

Winston S. Churchill (later Sir Winston), British Conservative Prime Minister and writer (1874–1965). Quoted in A. P. Herbert, *Independent Member* (1950).

Mail

7 Hate mail is the only kind of letter that never gets lost by the Post Office.

Philip Kerr, English novelist (1956–). *Dead Meat* (1993).

Malapropisms

8 He is the very pineapple of politeness!

Richard Brinsley Sheridan, English dramatist and politician (1751–1816). *The Rivals*, Act 3, Sc. 3 (1775). Mrs Malaprop speaking – after whom 'malapropisms' are called.

9 If I reprehend any thing in this world, it is the use of my oracular tongue, and a nice derangement of epitaphs!

Ibid.

10 It is no further from the north coast of Spitsbergen to the North Pole than it is from Land's End to John of Gaunt.

Revd William Spooner, English clergyman and academic (1844–1930). A malapropism spoken to Julian Huxley and recalled by him in *SEAC* (Calcutta) (27 February 1944). Also quoted in William Hayter, *Spooner* (1977).

1 Poor soul – very sad; her late husband, you know, a very sad death – eaten by missionaries – poor soul!

Ibid. A further malapropism, demonstrating that Spooner's talent did not just lie with Spoonerisms.

2 My son, the world is your lobster.

Leon Griffiths, English TV playwright (1928–92). In TV series *Minder*, quoted in *The Guardian* (16 June 1992).

3 He's so poor – he hasn't got a rag to stand on.

Linley Sambourne, English cartoonist and illustrator, principally for *Punch* (1844–1910). Quoted in literature on display at the 'Linley Sambourne House' in Kensington which is preserved by the Victorian Society and open to visitors.

4 There was such a silence afterwards that you could have picked up a pin in it.

Linley Sambourne. *Ibid.*

5 You're digging nails in your coffin with every stroke of your tongue.

Linley Sambourne. *Ibid.*

6 I don't care for Lady Macbeth in the street-walking scene.

Linley Sambourne. Quoted in R. G. C. Price, *A History of Punch* (1957).

Malignancy

When Randolph Churchill went into hospital to have a lung removed and the trouble was found to be non-malignant:

7 A typical triumph of modern science to find the only part of Randolph that was not malignant and remove it.

Evelyn Waugh, English novelist (1903–66). *The Diaries of Evelyn Waugh* (entry for March 1964).

Man

8 Man is the Only Animal that blushes. Or needs to.

Mark Twain, American writer (1835–1910). *Following the Equator* (1897).

9 Man was made at the end of a week's work when God was tired.

Mark Twain. Quoted in A. B. Paine, *Mark Twain: A Biography* (1912).

10 If they can put a man on the moon, why don't they put them all there.

Anonymous (graffito), reported by Ann Osborne, London (March 1998).

Manchester (England)

11 The shortest way out of Manchester is notoriously a bottle of Gordon's gin.

William Bolitho, English writer (1890–1930). 'Caliogstro and Seraphina', *Twelve Against the Gods* (1930). However, *The Times* (21 June 1921) was writing: 'Certainly if drink, in the proverbial saying, has proved on occasion "the shortest way out of Manchester ..."' – evidence of a much earlier source.

On living in Manchester, to the husband in a divorce case:

12 A totally incomprehensible choice for any free human being to make.

Sir Melford Stevenson, English judge (1902–87). Quoted in *The Daily Telegraph* (11 April 1979).

Manners

13 I am his Highness' dog at Kew;
Pray tell me, sir, whose dog are you?

Alexander Pope, English poet (1688–1744). 'Epigram Engraved on the Collar of a Dog which I gave to his Royal Highness' – Frederick, Prince of Wales – 1738.

One of Berners's acquaintances had the impertinent habit of saying to him, 'I've been sticking up for you.' He repeated this once too often and Berners replied:

14 Yes, and I have been sticking up for you. Someone said you aren't fit to live with pigs and I said you were.

Lord (Gerald) Berners, English writer, composer, painter and eccentric (1883–1950). Quoted in Edith Sitwell, *Taken Care Of* (1965). Compare the caption to a cartoon by A. Wallis Mills in *Punch* (28 June 1905): 'LADY A. Here comes that dreadful man who sat next to me at dinner. He hasn't the manners of a pig!" MRS B. "How funny! I thought he *had*!"'

On going into a bathroom and finding his hostess in the bath:

1 **I beg your pardon, *sir*!**

Anonymous – traditionally given as the correct thing to say in this situation. Compare 'John Michaelhouse' (a pen name of the Reverend Joseph McCulloch), in *Charming Manners* (1932): in the story, a group of Oxford undergraduates happen upon half-a-dozen naked nymphs dancing in the sunlight on the banks of the River Cherwell. 'We all collapsed in the punt at once, there being no chance of saying, "Sorry, gentlemen" in the approved style.'

In François Truffaut's film *Baisers Volés* (1968), the character played by Delphine Seyrig says that she was taught the difference between tact and politeness – if a man surprises a naked lady in the bathrooom, politeness is to say 'Sorry', tact is to say, 'Sorry, *sir*.'

The boot is on the other foot, so to speak, in a glancing comment in E. M. Forster's *A Room with a View* (1908): 'Mr Beebe [the clergyman] was not able to tell the ladies of his adventure at Modena, where the chambermaid burst in upon him in his bath, exclaiming cheerfully, "*Fa niente, sono vecchia*" [It doesn't matter, I'm an old woman].'

2 **A gentleman always gives up his seat to a lady in a public convenience.**

Anonymous platoon sergeant. Quoted in Gerald Kersh, *They Die With Their Boots Clean* (1941) – a record of his experiences in the Guards. Some young soldiers were being given a homily by their platoon sergeant on the subject of 'public duties' – that is, how they should behave when they were out of the barracks and moving about among civilians. He volunteered what would otherwise seem to be a music-hall joke.

Marginal comments

In a routine letter to the Foreign Office, the British Minister in Athens reported that the monks in some of the monasteries in northern Greece had allegedly violated their monastic vows. Unfortunately, due to a typing error, 'cows' appeared in the letter instead of 'vows'. On receiving this report, the Foreign Secretary pencilled a note in the margin:

3 **Appears to be a case for a Papal Bull.**

Arthur Balfour (later 1st Earl Balfour), British Conservative Prime Minister (1848–1930). Quoted on BBC Radio *Quote ... Unquote* (5 June 1979). In Lewis Broad, *Sir Anthony Eden* (1955), the marginal comment is said to have been written by Lord Curzon.

Marriage

4 **My Lord told me that among his father's many old sayings that he had writ in a book of his, this is one: that he that doth get a wench with child and marries her afterward it is as if a man should shit in his hat and then clap it upon his head.**

Samuel Pepys, English civil servant and diarist (1633–1703). Diary (7 October 1660). Pepys's patron (also his first cousin once removed) was the politician, naval commander and diplomat, Edward Mountagu, created 1st Earl of Sandwich in 1660. His father had been a royalist, whereas Mountagu espoused the parliamentarian cause. The book in question remains untraced.

5 **Strange to say what delight we married people have to see these poor fools decoyed into our condition.**

Samuel Pepys in *ibid.* (25 December 1665). On Christmas Day, Pepys saw 'a wedding in the church, which I have not seen many a day', and was particularly struck by how merry the young couple was with each other.

6 **Love seems the swiftest but it is the slowest of all growths. No man or woman really knows what perfect love is until they have been married for a quarter of a century.**

Mark Twain, American writer (1835–1910). *Notebooks* (published 1935).

7 **Even if we take matrimony at its lowest, even if we regard it as a sort of friendship recognised by the police.**

Robert Louis Stevenson, Scottish writer (1850–94). Title essay, *Travels With a Donkey* (1879).

8 **All men are born free, but some get married.**

Anonymous. Quoted in Herbert V. Prochnow, Snr & Jnr, *A Treasury of Humorous Quotations* (1969).

1 Keep your eyes wide open before marriage, half shut afterwards.

Benjamin Franklin, American politician and scientist (1706–90). *Poor Richard's Almanack* (June 1738) – a work in which Franklin often revised already existing sayings.

2 What they do in heaven we are ignorant of; what they do not we are told expressly, that they neither marry, nor are given in marriage.

Jonathan Swift, Anglo-Irish writer and clergyman (1667–1745). *Thoughts on Various Subjects* (1706).

3 Marriage: the state of condition of a community consisting of a master, a mistress, and two slaves, making, in all, two.

Ambrose Bierce, American journalist (1842–?1914). Quoted in *The Treasury of Humorous Quotations*, ed. Evan Esar & Nicolas Bentley (1951).

On being faithful in marriage (in his case to the actress Joanne Woodward):

4 Why have hamburger out when you've got steak at home?

Paul Newman, American film actor (1925–). Quoted in *The Observer* (11 March 1984). He also added: 'That doesn't mean it's always tender.'

5 Still I can't contradict, what so oft has been said,
'Though women are angels, yet wedlock's the devil.'

Lord Byron, English poet (1788–1824). 'To Eliza' (1806).

6 All tragedies are finished by death; all comedies are ended by a marriage.

Lord Byron. Quoted in *The Treasury of Humorous Quotations*, ed. Evan Esar & Nicolas Bentley (1951).

7 A man and woman marry because both of them don't know what to do with themselves.

Anton Chekhov, Russian playwright (1860–1904). Quoted in *The Treasury of Humorous Quotations*, ed. Evan Esar & Nicolas Bentley (1951).

8 Twenty years of romance make a woman look like a ruin, but twenty years of marriage make her something like a public building.

Oscar Wilde, Irish playwright, poet and wit (1854–1900). *A Woman of No Importance*, Act 1 (1893).

When asked if she had ever considered divorce during her long marriage to Sir Lewis Casson:

9 Divorce? Never. But murder often!

Sybil Thorndike (later Dame Sybil), English actress (1882–1976). The Scottish Liberal politician David Steel apparently said of his ally Dr David Owen on one occasion: 'I am reminded of Dame Sybil Thorndike's comment on her long marriage. She considered divorce never, murder frequently. With Dr Owen it is murder, occasionally.' Also attributed to Elizabeth Longford, historian wife of the 7th Earl of Longford, in John G. Murray, *A Gentleman Publisher's Commonplace Book* (1996).

10 Marriage is a great institution, but I'm not ready for an institution yet.

Mae West, American vaudeville and film actress (1893–1980). Quoted in Laurence J. Peter, *Quotations for Our Time* (1977).

11 Will you take this woman Matti Richards ... to be your awful wedded wife?

Dylan Thomas, Welsh poet (1914–53). Radio play, *Under Milk Wood* (1954). Opening words.

12 A woman with fair opportunities and without a positive hump, may marry whom she likes.

William Makepeace Thackeray, English novelist (1811–63). *Vanity Fair*, Chap. 4 (1847–8).

13 'Are you married, Mr Willoughby?' asked the wife of the Vice-Chancellor ...' I don't suppose he believes in it,' said the Vice-Chancellor in disgruntled tones. 'Well, why buy the cow,' asked Willoughby reasonably, 'when you can steal milk through the fence?'

Malcolm Bradbury, English academic and novelist (1932–). *Eating People Is Wrong*, Chap. 8 (1959). Using an established phrase.

1 Marriage is a wonderful invention; but, then again, so is a bicycle repair kit.

Billy Connolly, Scottish comedian (1942–). Quoted in Duncan Campbell, *Billy Connolly, the Authorised Version* (1976).

2 Advice to persons about to marry, – Don't.

Anonymous. *Punch*, Vol. 8 (1845). What is probably the most famous of all *Punch* jokes appeared on the January page of the 1845 Almanack. R. G. G. Price, in his history of the magazine, wonders whether it is perhaps 'the most famous joke ever made' and remarks that 'it needs an effort to realise how neat, ingenious and profound it must have seemed at the time'. It was based on an advertisement put out by a house furnisher of the day and was probably contributed by Henry Mayhew, better known for his serious surveys of *London Labour and the London Poor*, though others also claimed to have thought of it.

3 The only really happy people are married women and single men.

H. L. Mencken, American journalist and linguist (1880–1956). Quoted in *The 'Quote ... Unquote' Book of Love, Death and the Universe* (1980).

4 One fool at least in every married couple.

Henry Fielding, English novelist and judge (1707–54). *Amelia*, Bk 9, Chap. 4 (1751).

5 I have always thought that every woman should marry, and no man.

Benjamin Disraeli (later 1st Earl of Beaconsfield), British Conservative Prime Minister and writer (1804–81). *Lothair*, Chap. 30 (1830).

6 It was very good of God to let Carlyle and Mrs Carlyle marry one another and so make only two people miserable instead of four, besides being very amusing.

Samuel Butler, English author (1835–1902). Letter to Miss E. M. A. Savage (21 November 1884).

7 Greater luck hath no man than this, that he lay down his wife at the right moment.

Samuel Butler. *Notebooks* (c.1890).

8 The deep, deep peace of the double-bed after the hurly-burly of the chaise longue.

Mrs Patrick Campbell, English actress (1865–1940). Quoted in Alexander Woollcott, 'The First Mrs Tanqueray', *While Rome Burns* (1934).

9 He was reputed one of the wise men that made answer to the question when a man should marry? 'A young man not yet, an elder man not at all.'

Francis Bacon (1st Baron Verulam and Viscount St Albans), English philosopher and politician (1561–1626). 'Of Marriage and Single Life', *Essays* (1625).

Law student (in viva voce examination) when asked what was necessary to render a marriage valid in Scotland:

10 For a marriage to be valid in Scotland it is absolutely necessary that it should be consummated in the presence of two policemen.

Anonymous. Quoted in *Samuel Butler's Notebooks* (towards the end of the period 1874–1902).

11 I married him for better or worse, but not for lunch.

Duchess of Windsor (formerly Mrs Wallis Simpson), American-born wife of the Duke of Windsor (1896–1986). Quoted in J. Bryan III & Charles J. V. Murphy, *The Windsor Story* (1979). '[The Duke of Windsor] usually lunched alone on a salad while the duchess went out ("I married the Duke for better or worse but not for lunch").'

Conversation heard at a Hollywood wedding reception:

12 'What are you giving the bride and groom?' Reply: 'Oh, about three months.'

Anonymous. Quoted by Rula Lenska on BBC Radio *Quote ... Unquote* (16 February 1982).

13 Marriage is popular because it combines the maximum of temptation with the maximum of opportunity.

Bernard Shaw, Irish playwright and critic (1856–1950). 'Maxims for Revolutionists', *Man and Superman* (1903).

1 I'm not going to make the same mistake once.

Warren Beatty, US film actor (1937–). Quoted in Bob Chieger, *Was It Good For You Too?* (1983).

2 Marriage isn't a word ... it's a sentence!

King Vidor, American film director and writer (1895–1982). Film, *The Crowd* (1928).

To Lord Snowdon on the break-up of his marriage to Princess Margaret:

3 Your experience will be a lesson to all of us men to be careful not to marry ladies in very high positions.

Idi Amin, Ugandan soldier and President (1925–). Quoted in Barbara Rowes, *The Book of Quotes* (1979).

4 What God hath joined together no man shall ever put asunder; God will take care of that.

Bernard Shaw, Irish playwright and critic (1856–1950). Quoted in *The Treasury of Humorous Quotations*, ed. Evan Esar & Nicolas Bentley (1951).

Marx, Chico
American film comedian (1886–1961)

5 There are three things that my brother Chico is always on: a phone, a horse or a broad.

Groucho Marx, American comedian (1895–1977). Quoted in book *Nudge Nudge, Wink Wink* (1986).

Masturbation

6 A woman occasionally is quite a serviceable substitute for masturbation. It takes an abundance of imagination to be sure.

Karl Kraus, Austrian satirist (1874–1936). Quoted in Bob Chieger, *Was It Good For You Too?* (1983). Possibly from *Aphorism* (1909).

7 You know what I like about masturbation? You don't have to talk afterwards.

Milos Forman, Czech film director (1932–). Quoted in Bob Chieger, *Was It Good For You Too?* (1983). In 1980.

8 The good thing about masturbation is that you don't have to dress up for it.

Truman Capote, American writer (1924–84). Quoted in Bob Chieger, *Was It Good For You Too?* (1983).

On why she named her canary 'Onan':

9 Because he spills his seed on the ground.

Dorothy Parker, American writer (1893–1967). In John Keats, *You Might as Well Live* (1970).

10 Masturbation is the thinking man's television.

Christopher Hampton, English playwright (1946–). *The Philanthropist* (1970).

11 WOMAN: You are the greatest lover I have ever known.
ALLEN: Well, I practise a lot when I'm on my own.

Woody Allen, American film actor, writer and director (1937–). Film, *Love and Death* (US, 1975).

12 Hey! Don't knock masturbation. It's sex with someone I love.

Woody Allen. Film, *Annie Hall* (US, 1977).

Matzoh balls

On being served matzoh balls for supper at Arthur Miller's parents' house:

13 Isn't there another part of the matzoh you can eat?

Marilyn Monroe, American film actress (1926–62). Oral tradition, no doubt apocryphal. Gore Vidal merely cited 'the dumb starlet [who] would ask, What do they do with the rest of the matzoh?' in *The New York Review of Books* (17/31 May 1973).

Mayors

14 After you've met one hundred and fifty Lord Mayors, they all begin to look the same.

George V, British King (1865–1936). Quoted in Nigel Rees, *A Dictionary of Twentieth Century Quotations* (1987).

Meanness

In reply to robber demanding 'Your money or your life!':

15 I'm thinking it over.

Jack Benny, American comedian (1894–1974). Quoted in Silver & Haiblum, *Faster Than a Speeding Bullet* (1980). His basic joke, from the 1930s onwards.

Medals

To a soldier who had exclaimed 'No more bloody wars for me' as she presented medals during the First World War:

1 No more bloody wars, no more bloody medals.

Mary, British Queen of King George V (1867–1953). Attributed by Robert Lacey on BBC Radio *Quote ... Unquote* (19 February 1979).

Media

2 The media. It sounds like a convention of spiritualists.

(Sir) Tom Stoppard, English playwright (1937–). *Night and Day* (1978).

Medicine

3 The art of medicine consists of amusing the patient while nature cures the disease.

Voltaire, French writer and philosopher (1694–1778). Quoted in *The Treasury of Humorous Quotations*, ed. Evan Esar & Nicolas Bentley (1951).

4 I don't know much about medicine, but I know what I like.

S. J. Perelman, American humorist (1904–79). Quoted in Herbert V. Prochnow, Snr & Jnr, *A Treasury of Humorous Quotations* (1969).

Mediocrity

Of the British music-hall comic Dan Leno:

5 Often, even in his heyday, his acting and his waggishness did not carry him very far. Only mediocrity can be trusted to be always at its best. Genius must always have lapses proportionate to its triumphs.

Sir Max Beerbohm, English writer and caricaturist (1872–1956). In the *Saturday Review* (5 November 1904).

6 Only a very mediocre writer is always at his best, and Dorothy Parker is not a mediocre writer.

W. Somerset Maugham, English writer (1874–1965). In introduction to *The Portable Dorothy Parker* (1944).

7 I sometimes make pictures which are not up to my standard, but then it can only be said of a mediocrity that all his work is up to his standard.

Ernst Lubitsch, German film director (1892–1947). Quoted in Leslie Halliwell, *The Filmgoer's Book of Quotes* (1973).

8 Some men are born mediocre, some men achieve mediocrity, and some men have mediocrity thrust upon them. With Major Major it was all three.

Joseph Heller, American novelist (1923–). *Catch-22*, Chap. 9 (1961).

9 Modesty is the fig-leaf of mediocrity.

Charles Osborne, Australian-born writer and arts administrator (1927–). *Giving It Away: Memoirs of an Uncivil Servant* (1986). Compare: 'The man who is ostentatious of his modesty is twin to the statue that wears a fig-leaf' – Mark Twain, *Following the Equator*, II.xiv (1897).

Meekness

10 The meek shall inherit the earth, but not the mineral rights.

Anonymous. Quoted in the book *Graffiti 3* (1981). Had also been attributed to J. Paul Getty, the American oil tycoon (1892–1976) by that date.

11 We have the highest authority for believing that the meek shall inherit the earth; though I have never found any particular corroboration of this aphorism in the records of Somerset House [once the depository for British wills and testaments].

F. E. Smith (1st Earl of Birkenhead) English politician and lawyer (1872–1930). 'Marquess Curzon', *Contemporary Personalities* (1924).

Meetings

12 If you have enough meetings over a long enough period of time, the meetings

themselves become more important than the problem they were intended to solve.

Dr E. R. Hendrickson (untraced) in 1971. Quoted in Winston Fletcher in *Meetings, Meetings* (1983) – 'Hendrickson's Law'.

Melons

1 It is a good fruit: you eat, you drink, you wash your face.

Enrico Caruso, Italian singer (1873–1921). Quoted in Herbert V. Prochnow, Snr & Jnr, *A Treasury of Humorous Quotations* (1969).

Memoirs

2 If I were to say all the unpleasant things that occur to me about posthumous memoirs, I should have nothing left for my posthumous memoirs.

Samuel Butler, English author (1835–1902). Quoted in *The Treasury of Humorous Quotations*, ed. Evan Esar & Nicolas Bentley (1951).

Memorandums

3 A memorandum is written not to inform the reader but to protect the writer.

Dean Acheson, American Democratic politician (1893–1971). Quoted in *The Wall Street Journal* (8 September 1977).

To the economist Leon Henderson:

4 Are you labouring under the impression that I read these memoranda of yours? I can't even lift them.

Franklin D. Roosevelt, American Democratic President (1882–1945). Quoted in J. K. Galbraith, *Ambassador's Journal* (1969).

Memorial services

5 Memorial services are the cocktail parties of the geriatric set.

Sir Ralph Richardson, English actor (1902–83). Sometimes misattributed to Harold Macmillan, as in Alastair Horne, *Macmillan 1957–1986* (1989). In Ruth Dudley Edwards, *Harold Macmillan: a life in pictures* (1983), Macmillan (who is purported to have written the picture captions) states: 'I rather agree with Ralph Richardson [the actor] that

Memorial Services are the "cocktail parties of the geriatric set".'

Memory

6 My own wife, as some people know, had a lot of children – eight if I remember rightly.

Francis Pakenham, 7th Earl of Longford, English writer and politician (1905–). Quoted in *The Observer*, 'Sayings of the Week' (5 May 1985).

Celebrating his 75th birthday:

7 When I look back, the fondest memory I have is not really of the Goons. It is of a girl called Julia with enormous breasts.

Spike Milligan, English entertainer and writer (1918–). Quoted in *The Independent* 'Quote Unquote' (24 April 1993).

Men

8 Women's faults are many
Men have only two:
Everything they say
And everything they do.

Anonymous, 1970s, reproduced on T-shirts, badges, and so on. Compare, however, from H. L. Mencken's *Dictionary of Quotations* (1942), this well-documented rhyme from the eighteenth century – and note the change of gender: 'We men have many faults:/Poor women have but two – / There's nothing good they say,/There's nothing good they do.'

9 Men are those creatures with two legs and eight hands.

Jayne Mansfield, US film actress (1932–67). Quoted in book *Nudge Nudge, Wink Wink* (1986).

10 It's not the men in my life, but the life in my men.

Mae West, American film actress (1893–1980). In the film *I'm No Angel* (US, 1933).

11 A hard man is good to find.

Mae West. Quoted in book *Nudge Nudge, Wink Wink* (1986).

12 Give a man a free hand and he'll try to put it all over you.

Mae West. In the film *Klondike Annie* (US, 1936).

1 **The more I see of men, the more I like dogs.**

Madame Roland, French revolutionary (1756–93). Attributed remark in *The Oxford Dictionary of Quotations* (1979). However, later, A. Toussenel wrote in *L'Esprit des bêtes* (1847): 'The more one gets to know of men, the more one values dogs.'

2 **The more I see of men, the less I like them. If I could but say so of women too, all would be well.**

Lord Byron, English poet (1788–1824). *Journal* (1814).

3 **The trouble with Ian [Fleming] is that he gets off with women because he can't get on with them.**

Rosamond Lehmann, English novelist (1901–90). Quoted in John Pearson, *The Life of Ian Fleming* (1966). Apparently, Lehmann was borrowing a line from Elizabeth Bowen, though this is unverified.

4 **I married beneath me. All women do.**

Nancy Astor, Viscountess, American-born English politician (1879–1964). Speech, Oldham (1951). Quoted in the *Dictionary of National Biography 1961–70* (1981). She was the first British woman MP to take her seat in the House of Commons and, in fact, was wealthy in her own right.

Mental patients

5 **A visitor inquired as to what was the problem with a certain patient in a mental institution. 'Ah,' came the reply, 'he thinks he is a poached egg and spends his days seeking a suitable piece of toast upon which to sit.'**

Anonymous (cartoonist). Caption to cartoon in *Punch*, Vol. 122 (1902).

Meretricious

When Richard Adams chose to describe Vidal's novel about Abraham Lincoln as 'meretricious':

6 **Really? Well, meretricious and a happy New Year!**

Gore Vidal, American novelist, playwright and

critic (1925–). Quoted in Alan Bennett, *Writing Home* (1995) – entry for 25 September 1984. On the BBC Radio show *Start the Week*, Bennett comments: 'That's the way to do it.' But, unusually for Vidal, it now appears he was quoting another's line (a 'meretricious and a happy New Year'), ascribed to Franklin Pierce Adams in Scott Meredith, *George S. Kaufman and the Algonquin Round Table* (1977). It was also delivered by Chico Marx on the NBC Radio Series, *Flywheel, Shyster and Flywheel* (13 March 1933).

Merman, Ethel
American entertainer (1908–84)

Of her voice:

7 **A chorus of taxi horns.**

Anonymous. Quoted in *Time* Magazine (27 February 1984).

8 **A brass band going by.**

Cole Porter, American songwriter (1891–1964). Quoted in *The Guardian* (16 February 1984).

Metaphors

9 **The cure for mixed metaphors, I have always found, is for the patient to be obliged to draw a picture of the result.**

Bernard Levin, English journalist and critic (1928–). *In These Times* (1986).

10 **Ice formed on the butler's upper slopes.**

P. G. Wodehouse (later Sir Pelham), English-born novelist and lyricist (1881–1975). *Pigs Have Wings* (1952).

11 **Mr Speaker, I smell a rat; I see him forming in the air and darkening the sky; but I'll nip him in the bud.**

Sir Boyle Roche, Irish politician (1743–1807). Attributed remark in the Irish Parliament. In an untraced book – Wills, *The Irish Nation* – it is conceded that the chamberlain to the vice-regal court (in Dublin), as Roche later became, had a 'graceful address and ready wit', but, additionally, 'it was usual for members of the cabinet to write speeches for him, which he committed to memory, and, while mastering the substance, generally contrived to travesty the language and ornament with peculiar graces of his own'. Could this be the reason for Roche's peculiar sayings? *The Dictionary of National Biography* adds that 'he gained his lasting reputation as an inveterate perpetrator of "bulls" [i.e., ludicrous, self-contradictory propositions, often associated with the Irish]'.

1 How could the sergeant-at-arms stop him in the rear, while he was catching him at the front? Could he like a bird be in two places at once?

Sir Boyle Roche. Quoted in *A Book of Irish Quotations* (1984). Supposedly said in the Irish Parliament. *Brewer's Dictionary of Phrase and Fable* (1989) suggests that he was quoting from 'Jevon's play *The Devil of a Wife*' (untraced) and that what he said was, 'Mr Speaker, it is impossible I could have been in two places at once, unless I were a bird' – adding that the phrase was probably of even earlier origin.

Methods

Supposedly Chinese proverb:

2 Do not remove a fly from your friend's forehead with a hatchet.

Anonymous. Quoted in A. Andrews, *Quotations for Speakers and Writers* (1969).

Mexico

3 Poor Mexico! So far from God, so close to the United States.

Porfirio Diaz, Mexican President (1830–1915). Attributed in *Bartlett's Familiar Quotations* (1980).

Middle age

4 You know you are getting old when the policemen start looking younger.

Arnold Bennett, English novelist (1867–1931). Quoted in Arnold Bax, *Farewell My Youth* (1943). What Bax said of Bennett was: '[He] once remarked that his earliest recognition of his own middle age came at a certain appalling moment when he realized for the first time that the policeman at the corner was a mere youth.' This realization has also been attributed to Sir Seymour Hicks (1871–1949), the actor, in connection with *old* age (in C. R. D. Pulling, *They Were Singing*, 1952, for example). The source for this may be Hicks's own *Between Ourselves* (1930).

5 Middle age is when, wherever you go on holiday, you pack a sweater.

Denis Norden, English humorist (1922–). On Thames TV, *Looks Familiar* (1976).

Middle of the road

6 We know what happens to people who stay in the middle of the road. They get run over.

Aneurin Bevan, Welsh Labour politician (1897–1960). Quoted in *The Observer* (9 December 1953). According to Kenneth Harris, *Thatcher* (1988), Margaret Thatcher later said to James Prior: 'Standing in the middle of the road is very dangerous, you get knocked down by traffic from both sides.' And a TV play called *A Very British Coup* (1988) had a fictional Prime Minister saying, 'I once tried the middle of the road ... but I was knocked down by traffic in both directions.'

Military intelligence

7 Military Intelligence is a contradiction in terms.

Anonymous. Quoted in the book *Graffiti Lives OK* (1979). Said to come from a Ministry of Defence building in London (where it remained briefly). Attributed to Groucho Marx by A. Spiegelman and B. Schneider, *Whole Grains*.

Mind

On trying to engage in debate with Nancy Astor in the House of Commons:

8 It was like playing squash with a dish of scrambled eggs.

(Sir) Harold Nicolson, English writer and politician (1886–1968). Letter to his sons (18 March 1943). Nancy Astor was famous for not being able to stick to the point.

9 Minds are like parachutes: they only function when they are open.

Lord (Thomas Robert) Dewar, Scottish distiller (1864–1930). Quoted in *The Treasury of Humorous Quotations*, ed. Evan Esar & Nicolas Bentley (1951).

To a solicitor:

10 You will turn it over in what you are pleased to call your mind.

Richard Bethell, Baron Westbury, English judge (1800–73). Quoted in Nash, *Life of Westbury*. 'Noted for his sarcastic wit, he was an unpopular judge', notes *Chambers Biographical Dictionary* (1990).

1 A woman's mind is cleaner than a man's; she changes it more often.

Oliver Herford, American humorist (1863–1935). Quoted in *The Treasury of Humorous Quotations*, ed. Evan Esar & Nicolas Bentley (1951).

2 I shall be like that tree, I shall die at the top.

Jonathan Swift, Anglo-Irish writer and clergyman (1667–1745). Attributed in *The Sayings of Jonathan Swift*, ed. Joseph Spence (1994).

3 As to those who can find it in them to employ the doubtlessly useful word 'brunch', do they, I wonder, ever upgrade it to 'bruncheon'? This is the kind of question I ponder on while waiting for the kettle to boil. The active mind is never at rest.

Arthur Marshall, English writer and entertainer (1910–89). *Life's Rich Pageant* (1984).

Mini-skirts

4 We Bishops, in our proper dress, originated the mini-skirt. But we allowed Mary Quant to steal the thunder and make three million quid out of it last year.

Dr Victor J. Pike, English bishop (1907–). When Bishop Suffragan of Sherborne. Quoted in 1967 and re-quoted in *The Observer*, 'Sayings of the Decade' (1970).

Miracles

5 There is absolutely nothing wrong with Oscar Levant that a miracle cannot fix.

Alexander Woollcott, American writer and critic (1887–1943). Quoted in M. C. Harriman, *The Vicious Circle* (1951).

Misfortunes

Asked to define the difference between a calamity and a misfortune:

6 If, for instance, Mr Gladstone were to fall into the river, that would be a misfortune. But if anyone were to pull him out, that would be a calamity.

Benjamin Disraeli (later 1st Earl of Beaconsfield), British Conservative Prime Minister and writer (1804–81). Quoted in Hesketh Pearson, *Lives of the Wits* (1962). Almost certainly apocryphal. A similar story is told concerning Napoleon III and Plon-Plon, once designated as his heir, concerning the difference between an accident and a misfortune (related in Felix Markham, *The Bonapartes*, 1975).

7 I never knew a man in my life who could not bear another's misfortune perfectly like a Christian.

Jonathan Swift, Anglo-Irish writer and clergyman (1667–1745). Quoted in *The Treasury of Humorous Quotations*, ed. Evan Esar & Nicolas Bentley (1951).

Misprints

8 Printers indeed should be very careful how they omit a Figure or a Letter; For by such Means sometimes a terrible Alteration is made in the Sense. I have heard, that once, in a new edition of the *Common Prayer*, the following Sentence, *We shall all be changed in a Moment, in the Twinkling of an Eye*; by the omission of a single Letter, became, *We shall all be hanged in a Moment, &c.* to the no small Surprize of the first Congregation it was read to.

Benjamin Franklin, American politician and scientist (1706–90). *Poor Richard's Almanack* (Preface 1750) – a work in which Franklin often revised already existing sayings.

9 What do you think of this for a misprint: 'idle vistas and melancholy nooks' – '*idle sisters and melancholy monks*'!!

Henry James, American novelist (1843–1916). Letter (13 June 1874).

1 I am told that printer's readers no longer exist because clergymen are no longer unfrocked for sodomy.

Evelyn Waugh, English novelist (1903–66). Letter to Tom Driberg (11 June 1960).

Mistakes

2 Archduke Franz Ferdinand found alive. First World War a mistake.

Anonymous graffito contributed to BBC Radio *Quote ... Unquote* (29 January 1979) by John Butcher who said he saw it in the British Museum. Compare what Alan Clark, the English politician, wrote in his published *Diaries* (entry for 28 June 1983): 'I often think of that prize-winning spoof headline in the *New York Daily News* in 1920: "Archduke found alive, World War a Mistake".'

Mistresses

3 Next to the pleasure of taking a new mistress is that of being rid of an old one.

William Wycherley, English playwright and poet (*c*.1640–1716). *The Country Wife*, Act 1 (1675).

4 A mistress should be like a little country retreat near the town, not to dwell in constantly, but only for a night and away.

Ibid.

Moderates

5 An Iranian moderate is one who has run out of ammunition.

Henry Kissinger, American Republican politician (1923–). Quoted in *Today* (23 July 1987).

Modesty

Of her husband, H. H. Asquith:

6 His modesty amounts to deformity.

Margot Asquith (later Countess of Oxford and Asquith) (1864–1945). Quoted by her stepdaughter Baroness Asquith in BBC TV programme *As I Remember* (30 April 1967).

7 I was born modest, but it didn't last.

Mark Twain, American writer (1835–1910). In *Mark Twain's Speeches*, ed. A. B. Paine (1910).

Of Melvyn Bragg, TV presenter and novelist:

8 Modest? He's as modest as Larry Adler.

Jonathan Miller, English entertainer, writer and director (1934–). Quoted on BBC Radio *Quote ... Unquote* (13 July 1977).

Mona Lisa

9 [She has] the smile of a woman who has just dined off her husband.

Lawrence Durrell, English novelist (1912–90). *Justine*, Pt 2 (1957).

Money

10 Money can't buy friends, but you can get a better class of enemy.

Spike Milligan, English entertainer and writer (1918–). *Puckoon*, Chap. 6 (1963).

11 The money that men make lives after them.

Samuel Butler, English author (1835–1902). Quoted in *The Treasury of Humorous Quotations*, ed. Evan Esar & Nicolas Bentley (1951).

12 The lack of money is the root of all evil.

Mark Twain, American writer (1835–1910). In *More Maxims of Mark Twain*, ed. Merle Johnson (1927).

13 If you would know the value of Money, go and borrow some.

Benjamin Franklin, American politician and scientist (1706–90). *Poor Richard's Almanack* (April 1754) – a work in which Franklin often revised already existing sayings.

14 It has always been said that money talks, but I rather think that it is beginning to talk too loudly.

James Agate, English dramatic critic (1877–1947). Quoted in *The Treasury of Humorous Quotations*, ed. Evan Esar & Nicolas Bentley (1951).

Montgomery, Bernard
(1st Viscount Montgomery
of Alamein)
English field marshal (1887–1976)

1 In defeat unbeatable; in victory unbearable.

Winston S. Churchill (later Sir Winston), British Conservative Prime Minister and writer (1874–1965). Quoted in Edward Marsh, *Ambrosia and Small Beer* (1964).

Morals and Moralizing

2 PICKERING: Have you no morals, man?
DOOLITTLE: Can't afford them, Governor.

Bernard Shaw, Irish playwright and critic (1856–1950). *Pygmalion*, Act 2 (1913).

On George Orwell whose copious essays and journalism were later to fill three sizeable volumes:

3 He would not blow his nose without moralizing on conditions in the hand-kerchief industry.

Cyril Connolly, English writer and critic (1903–74). *The Evening Colonnade* (1973).

Morons

4 See the happy moron,
He doesn't give a damn,
I wish I were a moron,
My god! perhaps I am!

Anonymous. In *The Eugenics Review* (July 1929). In Herbert V. Prochnow, Snr & Jnr, *A Treasury of Humorous Quotations* (1969), Henry Pratt Fairchild is credited with this version: 'I don't know what a moron is,/And I don't give a damn./I'm thankful that I am not one – /My God, perhaps I am.'

Moses

5 Q.: Where was Moses when the light went out?
A.: In the dark.

Anonymous. Quoted in I. & P. Opie, *The Lore and Language of Schoolchildren* (1959), as an 'almost proverbial' riddle having been found in *The Riddler's Oracle* (*c.*1821). It is retold in Mark Twain, *The Adventures of Huckleberry Finn*, Chap. 17 (1884). Out of this may have grown the rhyme:

6 Where was Moses when the light went out?
Down in the cellar eating sauerkraut.

Anonymous.

Motherhood

7 Sometimes when I look at my children I say to myself, 'Lillian, you should have stayed a virgin.'

Lillian Carter, American mother of President Jimmy Carter (1898–1983). Quoted in *Woman* Magazine (9 April 1977), also recorded in the form, 'Wherever there's trouble – that's where Billy is! Sometimes ... I say to myself, "Lillian, you should have stayed a virgin"' – Bob Chieger, *Was It Good For You Too?* (1983).

Mothers

8 We're all good kids. We're all the kids our mothers warned us against.

Brendan Behan, Irish playwright (1923–64). *Borstal Boy* (1958).

9 ALGERNON: All women become like their mothers. That is their tragedy. No man does. That's his.

Oscar Wilde, Irish playwright, poet and wit (1854–1900). *The Importance of Being Earnest*, Act 1 (1895). The same words occurred before this (in dialogue form) in *A Woman of No Importance* (1893).

10 All women dress like their mothers, that is their tragedy. No man ever does. That is his.

Alan Bennett, English playwright and actor (1934–). *Forty Years On*, Act 1 (1969).

11 See the mothers in the park,
They are ugly chiefly.
Someone must have loved them once
But in the dark, and briefly.

Anonymous. Quoted in *The 'Quote ... Unquote' Newsletter* (October 1997).

Mothers-in-law

On the Grand Canyon:

12 What a marvellous place to drop one's mother-in-law.

Ferdinand Foch, French soldier (1851–1929). Quoted in Edmund Fuller, *2500 Anecdotes for All Occasions* (1943).

1 Peter remained on friendly terms with Christ notwithstanding Christ's having healed his mother-in-law.

Samuel Butler, English writer (1835–1902). Quoted in *The Treasury of Humorous Quotations*, ed. Evan Esar & Nicolas Bentley (1951).

2 My mother-in-law broke up my marriage. One day my wife came home early and found us in bed together.

Lenny Bruce, American satirist (1923–66). Quoted in *The Penguin Dictionary of Modern Humorous Quotations*, ed. Fred Metcalf (1987).

3 But there, everything has its drawbacks, as the man said when his mother-in-law died, and they came down upon him for the funeral expenses.

Jerome K. Jerome, English writer (1859–1927). *Three Men In a Boat*, Chap. 3 (1889).

Of his ex-wife Elaine:

4 She is the kind of girl who will not go anywhere without her mother. And her mother will go anywhere.

John Barrymore, American actor (1882–1942). Quoted in *The Treasury of Humorous Quotations*, ed. Evan Esar & Nicolas Bentley (1951).

5 I just came from a pleasure trip: I took my mother-in-law to the airport.

Henny Youngman, British-born American comedian (1906–98). Quoted in *The Times* (26 February 1998).

6 The awe and dread with which the untutored savage contemplates his mother-in-law are amongst the most familiar facts of anthropology.

(Sir) James George Fraser, Scottish anthropologist and folklorist (1854–1941). *The Golden Bough* (2nd edn, 1900).

7 My mother-in-law has come round to our house at Christmas seven years running. This year we're having a change. We're going to let her in.

Les Dawson, English comedian (1934–93). BBC TV *Pebble Mill* (27 December 1979).

Motivation

Author's notice:

8 Persons attempting to find a motive in this narrative will be prosecuted; persons attempting to find a moral in it will be banished; persons attempting to find a plot in it will be shot.

Mark Twain, American writer (1835–1910). *The Adventures of Huckleberry Finn* (1884).

On the death of the Turkish ambassador to France:

9 What does he mean by that?

Charles Maurice de Talleyrand, French statesman (1754–1838). Alluded to in Ben Pimlott, *Harold Wilson*, Chap. 29 (1992). However, another version is that it was said in the form 'Died, has he? Now I wonder what he meant by that?', *about* Talleyrand and *by* King Louis Philippe.

Telegraphed version of the outcome of a conversation with the film producer Sam Goldwyn:

10 The trouble, Mr Goldwyn, is that you are only interested in art and I am only interested in money.

Bernard Shaw, Irish playwright and critic (1856–1950). Quoted in Alva Johnson, *The Great Goldwyn* (1937). It has been said that this witticism was, in fact, the creation of Howard Dietz but that Shaw approved it.

When an actor, no doubt under the influence of The Method, was agonizing over his 'motivation' and asked his director, 'Just why do I cross the stage? Why, why?', Abbott told him:

11 To pick up your pay check.

George Abbott, American playwright, producer and director (1887–1995). Quoted by Mark Steyn on BBC Radio *Quote ... Unquote* (1990). *The Faber Book of Anecdotes* (1985) ascribes the remark to Noël Coward, without offering a source.

Motoring and Motorists

12 It is the overtakers who keep the undertakers busy.

William Pitts (untraced) (1900–80). Quoted in *The Observer*, 'Sayings of the Week' (22 December 1963).

1 There are a number of mechanical devices which increase sexual arousal, particularly in women. Chief among these is the Mercedes 380SL convertible.

P. J. O'Rourke, American humorist (1947–). *Modern Manners* (1983).

2 God would not have invented the automobile if he had intended me to walk.

J. E. Morpurgo, English publisher and academic (1918–). *The Road to Athens* (1963).

'Toad' on the joys of motoring:

3 The poetry of motion! The real way to travel! The only way to travel! Here today – in next week tomorrow! Villages skipped, towns and cities jumped – always somebody else's horizon! O bliss! O poop-poop! O my! O my!

Kenneth Grahame, Scottish-born writer (1859–1932). *The Wind in the Willows*, Chap. 2 (1908).

Mottoes

4 Our motto: Life is too short to stuff a mushroom.

Shirley Conran, English novelist and journalist (1932–). Epigraph, *Superwoman* (1975).

Mozart

His opinion of Mozart; walking out of a Glyndebourne performance:

5 Like piddling on flannel.

Noël Coward (later Sir Noël), English entertainer and writer (1899–1973). Quoted in Cole Lesley, *The Life of Noël Coward* (1976).

Mugwumps

6 A mugwump is a sort of bird that sits on a fence with his mug on one side and his wump on the other.

Anonymous. In *Blue Earth Post* (Minnesota), early 1930s.

Murder

7 Television has brought murder back into the home – where it belongs.

Alfred Hitchcock, British-born film director (1899–1980). Quoted in *The Observer*, 'Sayings of the Week' (19 December 1965).

Museums

Towards the end of his life, the English music-hall comedian Wee Georgie Wood (1895–1979) hailed a taxi and said to the driver, 'Take me to the British Museum.' The driver looked alarmed at this and said:

8 You're taking a bloody chance, aren't you?

Anonymous. Quoted by Peter Jones on BBC Radio *Quote ... Unquote* (1981). Joe Ging, who was curator of the National Museum Hall in Sunderland, wrote (8 May 1984) that Wood performed his museum's opening ceremony in July 1975. During his speech, Wood said, 'I was picked up at the Post House Hotel, Washington, by a taxi-driver from Sunderland. "Where are you going to, Mr Wood?" asked the taxi-driver. "I'm going to open a museum," I replied, proudly. To which he replied, "You're taking a bloody chance, aren't you?"' Joe Ging concedes that this was too good a story for Wood only to have used on one occasion.

Music

9 I hate music – especially when it is played.

Jimmy Durante, American comedian (1893–1980). Quoted in *An Encyclopedia of Quotations About Music*, ed. Nat Shapiro (1978).

When told his violin concerto needed a soloist with six fingers:

10 Very well, I can wait.

Arnold Schoenberg, German composer (1874–1951). Quoted in *The Penguin Dictionary of Modern Quotations* (1971).

When, as President and tone-deaf, he had to attend a concert:

11 I know only two tunes. One of them is 'Yankee Doodle' and the other isn't.

Ulysses S. Grant, American soldier and

President (1822–85). Quoted in Louis Unter-
meyer, *A Treasury of Laughter* (1946).

1 Live music is an anachronism, and now
is the winter of our discothèque.

Benny Green, English writer and broadcaster
(1927–98). Recalled on BBC Radio *Quote ...
Unquote* (1 June 1977).

Music-making

To a female cellist:

2 Madam, you have between your legs
an instrument capable of giving
pleasure to thousands – and all you
can do is scratch it.

Sir Thomas Beecham, English conductor
(1879–1961). Quoted in Ned Sherrin,
Cutting Edge (1984). Also attributed to
Arturo Toscanini.

3 There are two golden rules for an orchestra: start together and finish together.
The public doesn't give a damn what
goes on in between.

Sir Thomas Beecham. Quoted in H. Atkins
& A. Newman, *Beecham Stories* (1978).
See also 155:4,

Musical criticism

*Having listened to a performance of
an opera by a somewhat lesser composer:*

4 I like your opera – I think I will set it
to music.

Ludwig van Beethoven, German composer
(1770–1827). Contributed to BBC Radio
Quote ... Unquote (6 July 1977). Also attributed to Richard Wagner.

On Herbert von Karajan:

5 [He's a kind] of musical Malcolm
Sargent.

Sir Thomas Beecham, English conductor
(1879–1961). Quoted in Harold Atkins
& Archie Newman, *Beecham Stories* (1978).

6 If white bread could sing, it would
sound like Olivia Newton-John.

Anonymous. Quoted in *The Sunday Telegraph*
Magazine (September 1980).

Of Madonna:

7 [Sings] like Mickey Mouse on helium ...
Like a sheep in pain.

Anonymous. Quoted in *Time* Magazine
(1985).

Of Dame Ethel Smythe:

8 She would be like Richard Wagner, if
only she looked a bit more feminine.

Sir Osbert Sitwell, English writer (1892–
1969). Quoted in Elizabeth Lutyens, *A Gold-
fish Bowl* (1972).

Of Richard Clayderman, a popular pianist:

9 He is to piano playing as David Soul
is to acting; he makes Jacques Loussier
sound like Bach; he reminds us how
cheap potent music can be.

Richard Williams, English music critic.
Writing in *The Times*. Quoted in Ned Sherrin,
Cutting Edge (1984).

10 [Andrew] Lloyd Webber's music is
everywhere, but so is AIDS.

Malcolm Williamson, Australian-born
Master of the Queen's Musick (1931–).
Quoted in *The Daily Telegraph* (27 January
1992).

On the song, 'The Red Flag':

11 The funeral march of a fried eel.

Bernard Shaw, Irish playwright and critic
(1856–1950). Quoted in W. S. Churchill,
Great Contemporaries (1937).

To a fellow musician:

12 Oh, well, you play Bach *your* way. I'll
play him *his*.

Wanda Landowska, Polish-born harpsi-
chordist (1877–1959). Quoted in Harold C.
Schonberg, *The Great Pianists* (1963).

On hearing a violin solo:

13 Difficult do you call it, Sir? I wish it
were impossible.

Samuel Johnson, English writer and lexicographer (1709–84). Quoted in *Johnsonian
Miscellanies*, ed. Hill (1897).

Musicians

14 Please don't shoot the pianist; he is
doing his best.

Anonymous. Quoted in Oscar Wilde, 'Lead-
ville', *Impressions of America* (1906). Wilde
reports having seen this notice in a bar or
dancing saloon in the Rocky Mountains.

1 It's organ organ all the time with him ... Up every night until midnight playing the organ ... I'm a martyr to music.

Dylan Thomas, Welsh poet (1914–53). Radio play, *Under Milk Wood* (1954).

2 Every member of the orchestra carries a conductor's baton in his knapsack.

(Sir) Tom Stoppard, English playwright (1937–). *Every Good Boy Deserves Favour* (1978).

To a player in his orchestra:

3 We can't expect you to be with us all the time, but perhaps you would be good enough to keep in touch now and again.

Sir Thomas Beecham, English conductor (1879–1961). Quoted in Ned Sherrin, *Cutting Edge* (1984).

4 I have always laid it down as a golden rule that there are only two things requisite so far as the public is concerned for a good performance. That is, for the orchestra to begin together and end together. In between it doesn't matter much.

Sir Thomas Beecham. Recorded on an LP: *Sir Thomas Beecham in Rehearsal* (WRC SH 147). *See also* 154:3.

N

Nakedness

1 I have seen three emperors in their nakedness, and the sight was not inspiring.

Otto von Bismarck, Prusso-German statesman (1815–98). Quoted in *The Treasury of Humorous Quotations*, ed. Evan Esar and Nicolas Bentley (1951), but otherwise unverified.

On being asked what she wore in bed:

2 Chanel No. 5.

Marilyn Monroe, American film actress (1926–62). Quoted in Pete Martin, *Marilyn Monroe* (1956).

Name-calling

When Eva Perón complained to him that she had been called a 'whore' on a visit to northern Italy:

3 Quite so. But I have not been on a ship for fifteen years and they still call me 'Admiral'.

Anonymous Italian admiral. Quoted in 'The Power Behind the Glory', *Penthouse* Magazine (UK, August 1977). Said first to have appeared in an anecdotal notebook kept by Adlai Stevenson where the exchange takes place with a general in Barcelona.

Names

4 I remember your name perfectly; but I just can't think of your face.

Revd William Spooner, English clergyman and academic (1844–1930). Quoted in *The Penguin Dictionary of Quotations* (1960).

5 I've got Bright's Disease. And he's got mine.

S. J. Perelman, American humorist (1904–79). Caption to cartoon in *Judge* (16 November 1929).

6 No, Groucho is not my real name. I'm breaking it in for a friend.

Groucho Marx, American comedian (1895–1977). Quoted in *The Penguin Dictionary of Modern Quotations* (1971).

On having an inflatable life-jacket named after her:

7 I've been in *Who's Who*, and I know what's what, but it'll be the first time I ever made the dictionary.

Mae West, American vaudeville and film actress (1893–1980). Letter to the RAF in the early 1940s. Quoted in Fergus Cashin, *Mae West* (1981).

8 The Holy Roman Empire was neither holy, nor Roman, nor an empire.

Voltaire, French writer and philosopher (1694–1778). Quoted in *The Treasury of Humorous Quotations*, ed. Evan Esar & Nicolas Bentley (1951).

Of Sir Alfred Bossom MP:

9 Bossom? What an extraordinary name. Neither one thing nor the other!

Winston S. Churchill (later Sir Winston), British Conservative Prime Minister and writer (1874–1965). Quoted in Willans & Roetter, *The Wit of Winston Churchill* (1954).

At Christmas 1944, Churchill paid a visit to Athens. This resulted in the appointment of Archbishop Damaskinos as Regent of Greece and General Plastiras as Prime Minister. Of the latter, Churchill commented:

10 Well, I hope he doesn't have feet of clay, too.

Winston S. Churchill. Quoted in Leon Harris, *The Fine Art of Political Wit* (1966). In *Geoffrey Madan's Notebooks* (1981 – but Madan died in 1947), Churchill's remark is quoted as:

'A bewhiskered ecclesiastic, and a certain General Plastiras. I hope his feet are not of clay.'

1 He (who has tried to catch his companion's name, and wishes to find it out indirectly): 'By the way, how do you *spell* your name?' She: 'J-O-N-E-S'.

Anonymous (cartoonist). Caption to cartoon in *Punch*, Vol. 122 (8 January 1902).

Navy

2 We joined the Navy to see the world, And what did we see? We saw the sea.

Irving Berlin, American composer and lyricist (1888–1989). 'We Saw the Sea', *Follow the Fleet* (1936).

When a naval officer objected that a wartime operation the Prime Minister was supporting ran against the traditions of the Royal Navy:

3 Don't talk to me about naval tradition. It's nothing but rum, sodomy, and the lash.

Winston S. Churchill (later Sir Winston), British Conservative Prime Minister and writer (1874–1965). Quoted in Sir Peter Gretton, *Former Naval Person* (1968). In Harold Nicolson's diary (17 August 1950), this appears as: 'Naval tradition? Monstrous. Nothing but rum, sodomy, prayers and the lash.' Hence, *Rum, Bum and Concertina*, the title of a volume of George Melly's autobiography (1977) which he prefers to derive from 'an old naval saying': 'Ashore it's wine, women and song, aboard it's rum, bum and concertina.'

Necking

4 Whoever called it necking was a poor judge of anatomy.

Groucho Marx, American comedian (1895–1977). In 1970. Quoted in Bob Chieger, *Was It Good For You Too?* (1983).

Negotiation

5 Negotiating with [Eamon] de Valera [Irish politician] ... is like trying to pick up mercury with a fork.

David Lloyd George (1st Earl Lloyd George of Dwyfor), British Liberal Prime Minister (1863–1945). Quoted in M. J. MacManus,

Eamon de Valera (1944). [To which de Valera replied: 'Why doesn't he use a spoon?']

Neighbours

6 It is an offence to have a wireless on too loud these still summer evenings. It can annoy your neighbour. An even better way is to throw a dead cat on the lawn ...

Ronald Fletcher, English broadcaster (1910–96). Quoted in Bernard Braden, *The Kindness of Strangers* (1990). From Braden radio shows of the 1950s. Scripts by various.

7 Philosophy may teach us to bear with equanimity the misfortunes of our neighbours.

Oscar Wilde, Irish playwright, poet and wit (1854–1900). *The English Renaissance of Art* (Lecture in New York, 9 January 1882).

Mr Bennet speaking:

8 For what do we live, but to make sport for our neighbours, and laugh at them in our turn?

Jane Austen, English novelist (1775–1817). *Pride and Prejudice*, Chap. 57 (1813).

9 For my part I keep the commandments, I love my neighbour as myself, and to avoid coveting my neighbour's wife I desire to be coveted by her; which you know is quite another thing.

William Congreve, English playwright (1670–1729). Letter to Mrs Edward Porter (27 September 1700).

Neurotics

10 Neurotics build castles in the air. Psychotics live in them. Psychiatrists charge the rent.

Anonymous graffito from Birmingham University, included in the book *Graffiti 2* (1980). In Laurence J. Peter, *Quotations for Our Time* (1977), this observation is ascribed to Jerome Lawrence (1916–). Sometimes 'Psychotics smash the windows' is inserted.

Never-never

11 Live now, pay later.

Anonymous graffito in Los Angeles (1970) quoted in Reisner & Wechsler, *The Encyclo-*

pedia of Graffiti (1974). Earlier, however, it had been the title of a screenplay (1962) based on the novel *All On the Never Never* by Jack Lindsay.

New York City

1 New York is not the centre of the goddamn universe. I grant you it's an exciting, vibrant, stimulating, fabulous city, but it is not Mecca. It just smells like it.

Neil Simon, American playwright (1927–). *California Suite* (1976).

2 Baghdad-on-the-Subway.

O. Henry, American writer (1862–1910). *A Madison Square Arabian Night* (*c*.1913) and in other stories.

3 If ever there was an aviary overstocked with jays it is that Yaptown-on-the-Hudson, called New York.

O. Henry. 'A Tempered Wind', *Gentle Grafter* (1908).

4 The wonderful, cruel, enchanting, bewildering, fatal great city.

O. Henry. 'The Duel', *Strictly Business* (1910).

5 New York is a small place when it comes to the part of it that wakes up just as the rest is going to bed.

P. G. Wodehouse (later Sir Pelham), English-born novelist and lyricist (1881–1975). 'The Aunt and the Sluggard', *My Man Jeeves* (1919).

6 The city of dreadful height.

James Bone (untraced). In *Manchester Guardian* (undated). Quoted in *The Travellers' Dictionary of Quotations*, ed. Peter Yapp (1988).

7 New York ... that unnatural city where everyone is an exile, none more so than the American.

Charlotte Perkins Gilman, American novelist and social reformer (1860–1935). *The Living of Charlotte Perkins Gilman*, Chap. 20 (1935).

8 In New York people don't go to the theatre – they go to see hits.

Louis Jourdan, French-born actor (1921–). In *The New York Herald Tribune* (1 January 1950).

9 I'm the end of the line; absurd and appalling as it may seem, serious New York theatre has died in my lifetime.

Arthur Miller, American playwright (1915–). In *The Times* (11 January 1989).

10 In Manhattan, every flat surface is a potential stage and every inattentive waiter an unemployed, possibly unemployable, actor.

Quentin Crisp, English professional personality (1908–). 'Love Lies Bleeding', Channel 4 TV (6 August 1991).

11 New York is like being at some terrible late-night party. You're tired, you've had a headache since you arrived, but you can't leave because then you'd miss the party.

Simon Hoggart, English journalist (1946–). *America: A User's Guide*, Chap. 1 (1990).

12 New York is what Paris was in the twenties ... the centre of the art world. And we want to be in the centre. It's the greatest place on earth ... I've got a lot of friends here and I even brought my own cash.

John Lennon, English singer and songwriter (1940–80). NBC TV *The Tomorrow Show* (April 1975), quoted in *Imagine*, ed. Andrew Solt and Sam Egan (1988).

13 New York is the perfect town for getting over a disappointment, a loss, or a broken heart.

Shirley MacLaine, American film actress (1934–). *You Can't Get There From Here* (1975).

14 New York is like a disco, but without the music.

Elaine Stritch, American actress (1926–). Quoted in *The Observer*, 'Sayings of the Week' (17 February 1980).

15 There's no more crime in New Ysork – there's nothing left to steal.

Henny Youngman, British-born American comedian (1906–98). Quoted in Barbara Rowes, *The Book of Quotes* (1979).

16 If a man can live in New York, he can live anywhere.

(Sir) Arthur C. Clarke, English science fiction

writer (1917–). Quoted in Barbara Rowes, *The Book of Quotes* (1979).

1 If they had as much adultery going on in New York as they said in the divorce courts, they … would never have a chance to make the beds at the Plaza.

Zsa Zsa Gabor, Hungarian-born film actress (1919–). Quoted in Barbara Rowes, *The Book of Quotes* (1979).

2 A city where wise guys peddle gold bricks to each other and Truth, crushed down to earth, rises again as phoney as a glass eye.

Ben Hecht, American critic and screenwriter (1893–1964). In the film *Nothing Sacred* (US, 1937). Quoted in *The Penguin Dictionary of Modern Quotations* (1980 edn).

3 I think that New York is not the cultural centre of America, but the business and administrative centre of American culture.

Saul Bellow, Canadian-born novelist (1915–). Radio interview, in *The Listener* (22 May 1969).

4 New York is the perfect model of a city, not the model of a perfect city.

Lewis Mumford, American writer, editor and critic (1895–1990). *My Work and Days: A Personal Chronicle* (1979).

5 I don't like the life here in New York. There is no greenery. It would make a stone sick.

Nikita S. Khruschev, Soviet Communist Party leader (1894–1971). Quoted in the *Barnes and Noble Book of Quotations*, ed. Robert I. Fitzhenry (1987).

6 To Europe she was America, to America she was the gateway of the earth. But to tell the story of New York would be to write a social history of the world.

H. G. Wells, English novelist and writer (1866–1946). *The War in the Air*, Chap. 6 (1908).

7 Last Sunday afternoon
I took a trip to Hackensack
But after I gave Hackensack
  the once-over
I took the next train back.
I happen to like New York.

Cole Porter, American composer and lyricist (1891–1964). Song, 'I Happen to Like New York' (1931).

8 New York, New York, – a helluva town,
The Bronx is up but the Battery's down,
And people ride in a hole in the ground:
New York, New York, – It's a helluva town.

Betty Comden and Adolph Green, American songwriters (1919–) and (1915–). Song, 'New York, New York' (1945).

9 Nearly all th' most foolish people in th' country an' manny iv th' wisest goes to Noo York. Th'wise people ar-re there because th' foolish wint first. That's th' way th'wise men make a livin'.

Finley Peter Dunne, American writer (1867–1936). *Mr Dooley's Opinions* (1902).

10 Many a New Yorker spends a lifetime within the confines of an area smaller than a country village. Let him walk two blocks from his corner and he is in a strange land and will feel uneasy till he gets back.

Elwyn Brooks White, American humorist (1899–1985). Quoted in Herbert V. Prochnow, Snr & Jnr, *A Treasury of Humorous Quotations* (1969).

11 No other city in the United States can divest the visitor of so much money with so little enthusiasm. In Dallas, they take it away with gusto; in New Orleans, with a bow; in San Francisco, with a wink and a grin. In New York, you're lucky if you get a grunt.

Fletcher Knebel, American writer (undated). Quoted in Prochnow & Prochnow, *Treasury of Humorous Quotations* (1969).

12 Most of the people living in New York have come here from the farm to try to make enough money to go back to the farm.

Don Marquis, American writer (1878–1937). Quoted in Herbert V. Prochnow, Snr & Jnr, *A Treasury of Humorous Quotations* (1969).

13 There is more sophistication and less sense in New York than anywhere else on the globe.

Don Herold, American humorist and artist (1889–1966). Quoted in Herbert V. Prochnow, Snr & Jnr, *A Treasury of Humorous Quotations* (1969).

1 There is nothing distinctive about living in New York; over eight million other people are doing it.

Don Herold. Quoted in Herbert V. Prochnow, Snr & Jnr, *A Treasury of Humorous Quotations* (1969).

2 Broadway is a main artery of New York life – the hardened artery.

Walter Winchell, American journalist and broadcaster (1897–1972). Quoted in Herbert V. Prochnow, Snr & Jnr, *A Treasury of Humorous Quotations* (1969).

3 Coney Island, where the surf is one-third water and two-thirds people.

John Steinbeck, American writer (1902–68). Quoted in Herbert V. Prochnow, Snr & Jnr, *A Treasury of Humorous Quotations* (1969).

4 Why, if you're not in New York you are camping out.

Thomas W. Dewing, American writer (undated). Quoted in Herbert V. Prochnow, Snr & Jnr, *A Treasury of Humorous Quotations* (1969).

5 Buildings will collapse, power plants will stop generating electricity. Generals will drop atomic bombs on their own populations. Mad revolutionaries will run in the streets, crying fantastic slogans. I have often thought it would begin in New York. This metropolis has all the symptoms of a mind gone berserk.

Isaac Bashevis Singer, Polish-born American writer (1904–91). 'Cafeteria', *Collected Stories* (1986).

6 New York makes one think of the collapse of civilisation, about Sodom and Gomorrah, the end of the world. The end wouldn't come as a surprise here. Many people already bank on it.

Saul Bellow, Canadian-born novelist (1915–). *Mr Sammler's Planet*, Pt 1, Chap. 6 (1970).

7 The only credential the city [New York] asked was the boldness to dream. For

those who did, it unlocked its gates and its treasures, not caring who they were or where they came from.

Moss Hart, American theatrical playwright and director (1904–61). *Act One*, Pt 2 (1959).

8 When it's three o'clock in New York, it's still 1938 in London.

Bette Midler, American entertainer (1945–). Quoted in *The Times* (21 September 1978). However, in Vanessa Letts, *New York* (1991), 'When it's 9.30 in New York, it's 1937 in Los Angeles' is ascribed to Groucho Marx.

9 I always claim the mission workers came out too early to catch any sinners on this part of Broadway. At such an hour the sinners are still in bed resting up from their sinning of the night before, so they will be in good shape for more sinning a little later on.

Damon Runyon, American novelist (1884–1946). 'The Idyll of Miss Sarah Brown', *Collier's* Magazine (28 January 1933).

10 When I had looked at the lights of Broadway by night, I said to my American friends: what a glorious garden of wonders this would be to anyone who was lucky enough to be unable to read.

G. K. Chesterton, English poet, novelist and critic (1874–1936). Quoted in *The Treasury of Humorous Quotations*, ed. Evan Esar & Nicolas Bentley (1951).

11 New York is a fabulous place. The whole population, all 20 million of them, should be investigated by a committee for being so jolly.

Brendan Behan, Irish playwright (1923–64). Quoted in Rae Jeffs, *Man and Showman* (1966).

12 Lenin said that communism is socialism with electricity. New York is Paris with the English language.

Brendan Behan. Quoted in Ulick O'Connor, *Brendan Behan* (1970).

A writer writing:

13 'Chapter One. He adored New York City. He idolized it all out of proportion.' No, make that, 'he romanticized it all out of proportion.' Better. 'To him,

no matter what the season was, this was still a town that existed in black and white and pulsated to the great tunes of George Gershwin.' No, let me start this over. 'Chapter One. He was too romantic about Manhattan, as he was about everything else. He thrived on the hustle bustle of the crowds and the traffic. To him New York meant beautiful women and street-smart guys who seemed to know all the angles.' Ah ... too corny for my taste. Let me try and make it more profound. 'Chapter One. He adored New York City. To him it was a metaphor for the decay of contemporary culture. The same lack of individual integrity that caused so many people to take the easy way out was rapidly turning the town of his dreams ...' It's going to be too preachy. I mean, you know, let's face it, I want to sell some books here. 'Chapter One. He adored New York City, although to him it was a metaphor for the decay of contemporary culture. How hard it was to exist in a society desensitized by drugs, loud music, television, crime, garbage ...' Too angry. I don't want to be angry. 'Chapter One. He was as tough and romantic as the city he loved. Behind his black-rimmed glasses was the coiled sexual power of a jungle cat ...' I love this! 'New York was his town and it always would be ...'

Woody Allen, American film actor, writer and director (1937–). Opening scene of the film *Manhattan* (US, 1979).

New Zealand

1 I went to New Zealand but it was closed.

Anonymous. A line that gets rediscovered every so often. The Beatles found it in the 1960s; slightly before then, Anna Russell, the musical comedienne, said it on one of her records. It has also been attributed to Clement Freud. But William Franklyn, son of the Antipodean actor, Leo Franklyn, says that his father was saying it in the 1920s. Perhaps W. C. Fields began it all by saying 'Last week, I went to Philadelphia, but it was closed' about the same

time (if indeed he did). This last attribution comes from Richard J. Anobile, *Godfrey Daniels* (1975).

Newspapers

2 Editorial is what keeps the ads apart.

Roy Thomson (later Lord Thomson), Canadian-born industrialist (1894–1976). Attributed remark.

3 I read the newspaper avidly. It is my one form of continuous fiction.

Aneurin Bevan, Welsh Labour politician (1897–1960). Quoted in *The Times* (29 March 1960).

Of the Daily Mail:

4 By office boys for office boys.

Robert Cecil, 3rd Marquess of Salisbury, British Conservative Prime Minister (1830–1903). Quoted in H. Hamilton Fyfe, *Northcliffe, an Intimate Biography* (1930).

5 He was as shy as a newspaper is when referring to its own merits.

Mark Twain, American writer (1835–1910). *Following the Equator* (1897).

Niagara

6 Every American bride is taken there, and the sight of the stupendous waterfall must be one of the earliest, if not the keenest, disappointments in American married life.

Oscar Wilde, Irish playwright, poet and wit (1854–1900). *Impressions of America* (1906). Sometimes rendered as 'Niagara is only the second biggest disappointment of the standard honeymoon' and '[Niagara] is the first disappointment in the married life of many Americans who spend their honeymoon there.' Wilde visited Niagara in February 1882.

Nightmares

7 Have you noticed ... there is never any third act in a nightmare? They bring you to a climax of terror and then leave you there. They are the work of poor dramatists.

Sir Max Beerbohm, English writer and caricaturist (1872–1956). Quoted in S. N. Behrman, *Conversations with Max* (1960).

Nincompoops

Someone described the late wealthy actor Raymond Massey as a nincompoop. When asked why, he said:

1 Because he's a poop with an income.

Anonymous. Quoted in *The 'Quote ... Unquote' Newsletter* (January 1997).

Nixon, Richard M.

American Republican President (1913–94)

2 President Nixon's motto was, if two wrongs don't make a right, try three.

Norman Cousins, American writer (1915–). Quoted by Christie Davies in *The Daily Telegraph* (17 July 1979).

Nonsense

3 I dreamt I dwelt in marble halls,
And each damp thing that creeps
  and crawls
Went wobble-wobble on the walls.

Lewis Carroll (C. L. Dodgson), English writer (1832–98). *Lays of Mystery, Imagination, and Humour* (1855).

Norwegians

4 The Norwegian language has been described as German spoken underwater.

Anonymous. Quoted by Christopher Hampton in programme note to his translation of Ibsen's *An Enemy of the People*, Royal National Theatre, London (1997).

5 I don't like Norwegians at all. The sun never sets, the bar never opens, and the whole country smells of kippers.

Evelyn Waugh, English novelist (1903–66). Letter to Lady Diana Cooper (13 July 1934).

Nostalgia

6 Nostalgia isn't what it used to be.

Anonymous graffito in New York City. Used as the title of the autobiography (1978) of Simone Signoret, French film actress (1921–85). As 'Nostalgia ain't what it used to be', the remark has been attributed to the American novelist Peter de Vries.

Notes

When Miller was an undergraduate at Cambridge, he called on a friend whom he found in flagrante. So he left a note saying:

7 Called to see you but you were in.

Karl Miller, Scottish editor and academic (1931–). Quoted in *Cosmopolitan* (UK) (*c.*1979).

Notoriety

8 There is only one thing in the world worse than being talked about, and that is not being talked about.

Oscar Wilde, Irish playwright, poet and wit (1854–1900). *The Picture of Dorian Gray*, Chap. 1 (1891).

Novels

9 The trouble began with [E. M.] Forster. After him it was considered ungentlemanly to write more than five or six [novels].

Anthony Burgess, English novelist and critic (1917–93). In *The Guardian* (24 February 1989).

On the 'classic formula' for a novel:

10 A beginning, a muddle, and an end.

Philip Larkin, English poet (1922–85). In *New Fiction* (January 1978).

Nudity

On David Storey's play The Changing Room *which included a male nude scene:*

11 I didn't pay three pounds fifty just to see half a dozen acorns and a chipolata.

Noël Coward (later Sir Noël), English entertainer and writer (1899–1973). Quoted in Ned Sherrin, *Cutting Edge* (1984). See also 216:11.

When asked if she had really posed for a 1947 calendar with nothing on:

12 I had the radio on.

Marilyn Monroe, American film actress (1926–62). Quoted in *Time* Magazine (11 August 1952).

Nuns

On reading Monica Baldwin's book I Leap Over the Wall *(1949) about her return to the world after twenty-eight years in a convent:*

13 Very interesting, I must say. It has strengthened my decision not to become a nun.

Noël Coward (later Sir Noël), English entertainer and writer (1899–1973). *The Noël Coward Diaries* (1982) – entry for 1 December 1949.

Nursery rhymes

1 Little Miss Muffet
Sat on her tuffet,
So nobody could get at it.
There came a big spider,
Who sat down beside her –
But he couldn't get at it either.

Anonymous (1966).

2 The Grand Old Duchess of York,
She had ten thousand men.
She'd march them up to the top
 of the hill,
Then say, 'Go on, do it again!'

Anonymous (1966).

Nurses

3 And always keep a hold of Nurse
For fear of finding something worse.

Hilaire Belloc, French-born English poet and writer (1870–1953). 'Jim', *Cautionary Tales* (1907).

O

Oafs

1 Great oafs from little ikons grow.

Anonymous fake Russian-style proverb concerning Nikita Khruschev. Contributed to BBC Radio *Quote ... Unquote* (1 June 1977) by Benny Green. Richard Boston attributed to S. J. Perelman the similar 'Great oafs from little infants grow.'

Oats

2 A grain, which in England is generally given to horses, but in Scotland supports the people.

Samuel Johnson, English writer and lexicographer (1709–84). *A Dictionary of the English Language* (1755).

Obituaries

3 I always wait for *The Times* each morning. I look at the obituary column, and if I'm not in it, I go to work.

A. E. Matthews, English actor (1869–1960). Quoted in Leslie Halliwell, *The Filmgoer's Book of Quotes* (1973). Matthews's own obituary appeared on 26 July 1960. Several people have used the line subsequently. In *The Observer* (16 August 1987), William Douglas-Home, the playwright, was quoted as saying: 'Every morning I read the obits in *The Times*. If I'm not there, I carry on.'

After he reappeared having been reported dead during the Cyprus coup of 1974:

4 You should have known that it was not easy for me to die – but tell me, were my obituaries good?

Archbishop Makarios, Cypriot priest and President (1913–77). Quoted in *The Observer* (29 December 1974).

5 He loved shooting, hunting, horses, and above all dogs. The smell of a wet dog was delicious to him, and his devoted wife never let him know that, to her, it was abominable.

Anonymous obituarist in *The Times* (7 August 1963), of Sir Hereward Wake, English soldier (1876–1963).

Obscenity

6 Obscenity can be found in every book except the telephone directory.

Bernard Shaw, Irish playwright and critic (1856–1950). Quoted in *The Treasury of Humorous Quotations*, ed. Evan Esar & Nicolas Bentley (1951).

Obviousness

7 Well, he would, wouldn't he?

Mandy Rice-Davies, English 'model and show girl' (1944–). Magistrates Court hearing, London (28 June 1963). An innocuous enough phrase but one still used allusively because of the way it was spoken by Rice-Davies during the Profumo affair in 1963 (Secretary of State for War John Profumo carried on with Rice-Davies's friend Christine Keeler who was allegedly sharing her favours with the Soviet military attaché). Rice-Davies was called as a witness when Stephen Ward was charged under the Sexual Offences Act. During the preliminary hearing she was questioned about the men she had had sex with. When told by Ward's defence counsel that Lord Astor – one of the names on the list – had categorically denied any involvement with her, she chirpily made this reply. The court burst into laughter and the expression passed into the language.

Miss Rice-Davies' elevation to the quotation books has occasioned a good deal of humorous prevarication when it comes to giving her a job description. In *A Dictionary of Twentieth Century Quotations* (1987) I led the way with the neutral 'British woman'. *The Bloomsbury Dictionary of Quotations* (1987) boldly went for 'British call-girl'. *The Oxford Dictionary of Quotations* quaintly had 'English courtesan' in 1992. I switched to 'British "model and show girl"' for *Brewer's Quotations* (1994). *Collins Dictionary of Quotations* (1995) interestingly opted for 'Welsh model, nightclub performer and owner'. Somehow I still don't think that any of us has quite got it right.

Offensiveness

1 JUDGE: You are extremely offensive, young man.
F. E. SMITH: As a matter of fact, we both are, and the only difference between us is that I am trying to be, and you can't help it.

F. E. Smith (1st Earl of Birkenhead), English Conservative politician and lawyer (1872–1930). Quoted in 2nd Earl of Birkenhead, *The Earl of Birkenhead* (1933).

Old age

2 'Old age is coming on me rapidly,' as the urchin said when he was stealing apples from an old man's garden, and saw the owner coming.

Anonymous Wellerism. In *Ballou's Dollar Magazine*, Vol. 1 (US, 1855).

3 Old age is the outpatients' department of Purgatory.

Hugh Cecil (Lord Quickswood), English Conservative politician (1869–1956). Quoted by John Betjeman in a letter to Tom Driberg (21 July 1976).

4 Speak, you who are older, for it is fitting that you should,
but with accurate knowledge, and do not interrupt the music.

Bible, Ecclesiasticus, 32:3 (Apocrypha).

5 I prefer old age to the alternative.

Maurice Chevalier, French entertainer (1888–1972). Remark (1960), on his 72nd birthday. Or 'Growing old isn't so bad when you consider the alternative' – quoted in Laurence J. Peter, *Quotations for Our Time* (1977).

6 You only have to survive in England and all is forgiven you ... if you can eat a boiled egg at ninety in England they think you deserve a Nobel Prize.

Alan Bennett, English playwright and actor (1934–). On ITV's *South Bank Show* (1984). In his TV film *An Englishman Abroad* (1989), this reappears as: 'In England, you see, age wipes the slate clean ... If you live to be ninety in England and can still eat a boiled egg they think you deserve the Nobel Prize.'

On Max Beerbohm:

7 The gods bestowed on Max the gift of perpetual old age.

Oscar Wilde, Irish playwright, poet and wit (1854–1900). Quoted in Vincent O'Sullivan, *Aspects of Wilde* (1936). If this was said in the 1890s, Beerbohm would then have been in his twenties.

On seeing a pretty girl in the Champs-Elysées on his eightieth birthday:

8 Oh, to be seventy again!

Georges Clemenceau, French Prime Minister (1841–1929). Quoted in James Agate, *Ego 3* (1938). The same remark is ascribed to Oliver Wendell Holmes Jr (1841–1935), the American jurist, on reaching his eighty-seventh year (by Fadiman & van Doren in *The American Treasury*, 1955). Bernard de Fontenelle (1657–1757), the French writer and philosopher, is said in great old age to have attempted with difficulty to pick up a young lady's fan, murmuring, 'Ah, if I were only eighty again!' (Pedrazzini & Gris, *Autant en apportent les mots*, 1969).

On his hundredth birthday:

9 If I'd known I was gonna live this long, I'd have taken better care of myself.

Eubie Blake, American jazz musician (1883–1983). Quoted in *The Observer* (13 February 1983). Unfortunately, five days after marking his centennial, Blake died. Even so, his felicitous remark was not original. In *Radio Times* (17 February 1979), Benny Green quoted Adolph Zukor, founder of Paramount Pictures, as having said on the approach to his hundredth birthday: 'If I'd known how old I was going to be I'd have taken better care of myself.' Zukor died in 1976, having been born in 1873.

10 I will never be an old man. To me, old age is always fifteen years older than I am.

Bernard Baruch, American financier (1870–1965). Quoted in *The Observer* (21 August 1955).

Towards the end of his life, Churchill was sitting in the House of Commons smoking room with his fly-buttons undone. When this was pointed out to him, he said:

1 Dead birds don't fall out of nests.

Winston S. Churchill (later Sir Winston), British Conservative Prime Minister and writer (1874–1965). Quoted in *The Lyttelton Hart-Davis Letters*, Vol. 2 (1979) (from a letter dated 5 January 1957, where the reply is: 'No matter. The dead bird does not leave the nest.')

Resolutions when old:

2 Not to be fond of children, or let them come near me hardly ... Not to talk much, nor of myself. Not to boast of my former beauty, or strength, or favour with ladies, &c.

Jonathan Swift, Anglo-Irish writer and clergyman (1667–1745). *When I Come to be Old* (1699).

3 Every man desires to live long but no man would be old.

Jonathan Swift. *Thoughts on Various Subjects* (1706).

Old maids

4 Being an old maid is like death by drowning, a really delightful sensation after you cease to struggle.

Edna Ferber, American writer (1887–1968). Quoted in R. E. Drennan, *Wit's End* (1973).

Older women

5 Older women are best because they always think they may be doing it for the last time.

Ian Fleming, English novelist and journalist (1908–64). Quoted in John Pearson, *The Life of Ian Fleming* (1966). Compare Benjamin Franklin's *Reasons for Preferring an Elderly Mistress* (1745): '8th and lastly. They are so grateful!'

One-upmanship

Defining 'One-Upmanship':

6 How to be one up – how to make the other man feel that something has gone wrong, however slightly.

Stephen Potter, English humorist (1900–69). *Lifemanship* (1950).

Opera

7 How wonderful opera would be if there were no singers.

Gioachino Rossini, Italian composer (1792–1868). Quoted in *The Treasury of Humorous Quotations*, ed. Evan Esar & Nicolas Bentley (1951).

Quoting a supposed maxim concerning Italian opera:

8 That nothing is capable of being well set to music that is not nonsense.

Joseph Addison, English essayist and politician (1672–1719). In *The Spectator*, No. 18 (21 March 1711).

9 Opera in English is, in the main, just about as sensible as baseball in Italian.

H. L. Mencken, American journalist and linguist (1880–1956). Quoted in *The Treasury of Humorous Quotations*, ed. Evan Esar & Nicolas Bentley (1951).

10 Opera is when a guy gets stabbed in the back and instead of bleeding he sings.

Ed Gardner, American broadcaster (1901–63). In the 1940s radio show *Duffy's Tavern*, quoted in *The Frank Muir Book* (1976). Has also been ascribed to Robert Benchley.

11 An unalterable and unquestioned law of the musical world required that the German text of French operas sung by Swedish artists should be translated into Italian for the clearer understanding of English-speaking audiences.

Edith Wharton, American novelist (1862–1937). *The Age of Innocence* (1920).

12 People are wrong when they say that the opera isn't what it used to be. It is what it used to be – that's what's wrong with it.

Noël Coward (later Sir Noël), English entertainer and writer (1899–1973). *Design for Living* (1933).

Opposition

On why he kept J. Edgar Hoover at the FBI:

1 I'd much rather have that fellow inside my tent pissing out, than outside my tent pissing in.

Lyndon B. Johnson, American Democratic President (1908–73). Quoted in David Halberstam, *The Best and the Brightest* (1972). The same sentiment is attributed to Laurence Olivier about employing Kenneth Tynan, a critic, at the National Theatre, in John Dexter, *The Honourable Beast* (1993).

Optimism

2 I'm an optimist, but I'm an optimist who takes his raincoat.

Harold Wilson (later Lord Wilson of Rievaulx), British Labour Prime Minister (1916–95). Quoted in *The Observer* (18 January 1976).

3 Cheer up! The worst is yet to come.

Mark Twain, American writer (1835–1910). In a letter to his wife (1893/4) included in *The Love Letters of Mark Twain*. Also to be found in *Those Extraordinary Twins* (1894). The most usual attribution, though, is to the American writer Philander Johnson (1866–1939) in his *Shooting Stars* (c.1920). The similar expression, 'Cheer up ... you'll soon be dead!' appears in several British entertainments in the period 1909–18.

4 An optimist is a girl who mistakes a bulge for a curve.

Ring Lardner, American humorist (1885–1933). Quoted in *The Treasury of Humorous Quotations*, ed. Evan Esar & Nicolas Bentley (1951).

Orators

On Lord Charles Beresford:

5 He is one of those orators of whom it was well said, 'Before they get up, they do not know what they are going to say; when they are speaking, they do not know what they are saying; and when they have sat down, they do not know what they have said.'

Winston S. Churchill (later Sir Winston), British Conservative Prime Minister and writer (1874–1965). Speech, House of Commons (20 December 1912).

Organization

6 This island is made mainly of coal and surrounded by fish. Only an organizing genius could produce a shortage of coal and fish at the same time.

Aneurin Bevan, Welsh Labour politician (1897–1960). Speech at Blackpool (24 May 1945).

Orgasm

7 I finally had an orgasm ... and my doctor told me it was the wrong kind.

Woody Allen, American film actor, writer and director (1937–). Film, *Manhattan* (US, 1979).

8 In the case of some women, orgasms take quite a bit of time. Before signing on with such a partner, make sure you are willing to lay aside, say, the month of June, with sandwiches having to be brought in.

Bruce Jay Friedman, American writer (1930–). 'Sex and the Lonely Guy' in *Esquire* (1977).

9 Since most men can't keep it up long enough to fulfil woman's God-given – and soon to be Constitutioned – right to orgasm, the vibrator can take over while the man takes a leak.

Gore Vidal, American novelist, playwright and critic (1925–). In *Rolling Stone* (1980) – quoted in Bob Chieger, *Was It Good For You Too?* (1983).

Orgies

10 You get a better class of person at orgies, because people have to keep in trim more. There is an awful lot of going round holding in your stomach, you know. Everybody is very polite to each other. The conversation isn't very good but you can't have everything.

Gore Vidal, American novelist, playwright and critic (1925–). Interviewed on London Weekend Television, *Russell Harty Plus* (1972).

Originality

1 What a good thing Adam had – when he said a good thing he knew nobody had said it before.

Mark Twain, American writer (1835–1910). *Mark Twain's Notebook*, ed. A. B. Paine (1935).

2 Most people are other people. Their thoughts are someone else's opinions, their life a mimicry, their passions a quotation.

Oscar Wilde, Irish playwright, poet and wit (1854–1900). *De Profundis* (1905).

3 Damn those who have made my remarks before me!

Aelius Donatus, Roman grammarian (4th century AD). Quoted in this form in *The Treasury of Humorous Quotations*, ed. Evan Esar & Nicolas Bentley (1951). Quoted originally by St Jerome, *Commentary on Ecclesiastes*: 'The same idea is said by the comic poet [Terence, in *Prolog. Eunuchi*]: "Nothing is said which has not been said before." Whence my teacher Donatus when he was speaking of that verse, said, "Confound those who have said our remarks before us."'

4 As usual, the Liberals offer a mixture of sound and original ideas. Unfortunately none of the sound ideas is original and none of the original ideas is sound.

Harold Macmillan (later 1st Earl of Stockton), British Conservative Prime Minister (1894–1986). Speech to London Conservatives (7 March 1961). Compare what is ascribed to Dr Samuel Johnson: 'Your manuscript is both good and original; but the part that is good is not original, and the part that is original is not good.' Quoted in *The Treasury of Humorous Quotations*, ed. Evan Esar & Nicolas Bentley (1951). Has also been loosely ascribed to 'Samuel Johnson, *Letters* 1777'.

5 Nothing has yet been said that's not been said before.

Terence, Roman playwright (*c.*190–159 BC). *Eunuchus*.

6 Nothing should ever be done for the first time.

Francis Cornford, English academic (1874–1943). *Microcosmographia Academica* (1908).

The precise context is: 'Every public action, which is not customary, either is wrong, or, if it is right, is a dangerous precedent. It follows that nothing should ever be done for the first time.' Compare: 'The conservative in financial circles I have often described as a man who thinks nothing new ought ever to be adopted for the first time' – Frank A. Vaderlip, *From Farm Boy to Financier* (1935).

Outspokenness

When told that she was 'very outspoken':

7 Outspoken by whom?

Dorothy Parker, American writer (1893–1967). Quoted by Ralph L. Marquard, *Jokes and Anecdotes for All Occasions* (1977).

Overheard remarks

8 Walking one day in Oxford, I saw two elderly dons coming towards me engrossed apparently in some weighty discourse. As they passed me, I overheard just two words: 'And ninthly ...'

Anonymous. Quoted by S. H. Jarvis of Bristol in the book *Eavesdroppings* (1981).

9 Two American women were observing and admiring the statue of Achilles in Park Lane, London. One was overheard saying to the other, 'No, dear – Big Ben is a clock.'

Anonymous. Quoted by Norman Mitchell of Weybridge in *ibid*. The origins of this are said to lie in a cartoon (by 1965) but, if this is the case, it has not yet been found.

10 A young artist saw an eminent critic and a noble lord standing in front of one of his paintings, so he crept nearer to hear what they were saying about it. The noble lord said to the critic: 'Of the two, I prefer washing up.'

Anonymous. Quoted in *ibid*. T. H. White discussed a comic story current just after the Second World War in *The Age of Scandal* (1950): 'It said that there was some conference or other at Lambeth, thronged with Archbishops, Cardinals, Patriarchs, Moderators and so forth. The Archbishops of Canterbury and York were seen to be in earnest consultation in one corner of the room. Were they discussing a reunion with Rome or a revision of the Prayer Book? Thrilled with the ecclesiastical possibilities of such a meeting, one of the stripling curates managed to edge himself within earshot of these princes of the Church. They were discussing whether it was worse to wash-up or dry-up.'

Overheard at a hospital:

1 I don't mind dying; the trouble is, you feel so bloody stiff the next day.

Anonymous. Quoted on BBC Radio *Quote ... Unquote* (13 September 1979).

After a performance of Vivat! Vivat Regina! *which he directed at Chichester and which ends with the execution of Mary Queen of Scots, Peter Dews overheard a female member of the audience say:*

2 Do you know, it's extraordinary – exactly the same thing happened to Monica.

Anonymous. In a letter to me dated 10 January 1980, Dews called this anecdote 'absolutely true. I heard it with my own ears.'

3 During the First World War, my mother heard someone say, 'My husband has been wounded in the Dardanelles ... and they cannot find his whereabouts.'

Anonymous. Contributed to BBC Radio *Quote ... Unquote* (25 August 1984) by Mrs V. Lewis of Handsworth, Birmingham. However, in BBC TV *The Dawson Watch* (Christmas 1980), Les Dawson spoke the line 'During the war, I was shot in the Dardanelles' – with similar implications – and in the BBC Radio show *Beyond Our Ken* (15 July 1960) there was the line, 'The Turks pinned the Australians in the Dardanelles.' Compare:

4 GRANNY GROWL: Me tired husband, poor ould Paddins, he was shot in the Dardanelles.
   GRANNY GRUNT: And a most painful part of the body to be shot!

Brendan Behan, Irish playwright (1923–64). *Brendan Behan's Island* (1962).

5 Alfred Deller, the celebrated counter-tenor, was walking behind two women when he overheard one say to the other, 'Ow's Flo? Ow's 'er feet?' The second woman replied, 'Well, of course, they're not much use to 'er now. Not as feet, that is ...'

Anonymous. Contributed to BBC Radio *Quote ... Unquote* (5 June 1979) by Paul Fincham of Suffolk – who heard it from Paul Jennings who had it from Deller. Denis Norden recalled (1996) that he had first heard it from Nancy Spain at a recording of *My Word* in Cambridge in that programme's early years (it began in 1956).

Of a well-meant but rather pretentious play at Brighton:

6 Well, Emily, all I can say is, I hope the dogs haven't been sick in the car.

Anonymous woman. Quoted by Patrick Garland, the theatre and TV director, on BBC Radio *Quote ... Unquote* (1979).

Owning up

Asked how many of the Hill's Angels dancing troupe he had been to bed with:

7 Off the record, I haven't made love to one of those girls. I think her name was Sandra.

Benny Hill, English television comedian (1924–92). Quoted in David Lister's obituary of Hill in *The Independent* (22 April 1992).

Oxford

8 I was not unpopular [at school] ... It is Oxford that has made me insufferable.

Sir Max Beerbohm, English writer and caricaturist (1872–1956). 'Going Back to School', *More* (1899).

9 Very nice sort of place, Oxford, I should think, for people that like that sort of place.

Bernard Shaw, Irish playwright and critic (1856–1950). *Man and Superman*, Act 2 (1903).

P

Paintings

1 Buy old masters. They fetch a better price than old mistresses.

Maxwell Aitken (1st Baron Beaverbrook), Canadian-born English politician and newspaper proprietor (1879–1964). Quoted in *The Bloomsbury Dictionary of Quotations* (1987).

2 Painting is saying 'Ta' to God.

Sir Stanley Spencer, English painter (1891–1959). Quoted in letter to *The Observer* from his daughter Shirin (7 February 1988).

3 Every time I paint a portrait I lose a friend.

John Singer Sargent, American painter (1856–1925). Quoted in *The Treasury of Humorous Quotations*, ed. Evan Esar & Nicolas Bentley (1951).

Pakistan

4 The sort of place everyone should send his mother-in-law for a month, all expenses paid.

Ian Botham, English cricketer (1955–). In BBC Radio interview (March 1984). The following month he was fined £1,000 by the Test and County Cricket Board for making the comment.

Pants

An old Nonconformist minister chose as his text Psalm 42 v.1: 'As the hart panteth after the waterbrooks, so panteth my soul after Thee, O God.' His discourse, the minister said, would be divided into three parts:

5 The pants of the hart, the pants of the Psalmist, and, finally, pants in general.

Anonymous (by 1978). Source unrecorded.

Paranoia

6 Margaret said: 'Has it ever struck you that when people get persecution mania, they usually have a good deal to feel persecuted about?'

C. P. Snow (later Lord Snow), English novelist and scientist (1905–80). *The Affair*, Chap. 11 (1960). An early example of this observation.

7 I wouldn't be paranoid if people didn't pick on me.

Anonymous (graffito). Quoted in *Graffiti Lives OK* (1979).

8 Just because you're paranoid, it doesn't mean they're not out to get you.

Anonymous (graffito). Quoted in *Graffiti 2* (1980). In the 1976 biography of Rodgers and Hart written by Clayton and Marx, it is claimed that in preparing the 1943 revival of the musical *A Connecticut Yankee*, the line 'Just because you're paranoid doesn't mean they're not out to get you' became a running joke between Lorenz Hart, the lyricist, and librettist Herbert Fields. The line is not, however, apparently spoken in the show. Other formulations of this idea include:

9 Even a paranoid can have enemies.

Henry Kissinger, American Republican politician (1923–). Quoted in *Time* Magazine (24 January 1977). Has also been ascribed to Delmore Schwartz.

Parents

10 The thing that impresses me most about America is the way parents obey their children.

Edward VIII (later Duke of Windsor), British King (1894–1972). Quoted in *Look* Magazine (5 March 1957).

1 Some people seem compelled by unkind fate to parental servitude for life. There is no form of penal servitude much worse than this.

Samuel Butler, English author (1835–1902). Quoted in Herbert V. Prochnow, Snr & Jnr, *A Treasury of Humorous Quotations* (1969).

2 LADY BRACKNELL: To lose one parent, Mr Worthing, may be regarded as a misfortune; to lose both looks like carelessness.

Oscar Wilde, Irish playwright, poet and wit (1854–1900). *The Importance of Being Earnest*, Act 1 (1895).

3 Mom and Pop were just a couple of kids when they got married. He was eighteen, she was sixteen, and I was three.

Billie Holiday, American singer (1915–59). *Lady Sings the Blues* (1958). Opening words.

4 The question of who are the best people to take charge of children is a very difficult one; but it is quite certain that the parents are the very worst.

William Morris, English poet and craftsman (1834–96). Quoted in Shaw's *Everybody's Political What's What?*, Chap. 19 (1944). An unverified suggestion is that 'Parents are the last people on earth who ought to have children' appears in Samuel Butler's *Notebooks*. This is according to *Medical Quotations* (1989).

5 Parentage is a very important profession, but no test of fitness for it is ever imposed in the interest of the children.

Bernard Shaw, Irish playwright and critic (1856–1950). *Everybody's Political What's What?* (1944).

6 Children begin by loving their parents; after a time they judge them. Rarely, if ever, do they forgive them.

Oscar Wilde, Irish playwright, poet and wit (1854–1900). *A Woman of No Importance*, Act 4 (1893).

Parking

Alvy to Annie who has just parked the motor somewhat eccentrically:

7 That's OK, we can walk to the kerb from here.

Woody Allen, American film actor, writer and director (1937–). Film, *Annie Hall* (US, 1977). Also quoted in the form: 'After she's parked the car, it's normally just a short walk to the pavement.'

Parliament

8 The only man who had a proper understanding of Parliament was old Guy Fawkes.

Bernard Shaw, Irish playwright and critic (1856–1950). *On the Rocks*, Act 2 (1933).

Parodies

Parody of Time *Magazine style:*

9 Backward ran sentences until reeled the mind.

Wolcott Gibbs, American writer (1902–58). 'Time ... Fortune ... Life ... Luce', in *The New Yorker* (28 November 1936), reprinted in *More in Sorrow* (1958), which concludes with: 'Where it will all end, knows God.'

Of T. S. Eliot:

10 As we get older we do not get any
   younger.
Seasons return, and today I am fifty-five,
And this time last year I was fifty-four,
And this time next year I shall be
   sixty-two.

Henry Reed, English poet and playwright (1914–86). 'Chard Whitlow', *A Map of Verona* (1946).

Of the verses from 'My Mother' by Ann and Jane Taylor in Original Poems for Infant Minds *(1804):*

11 Who took me from my bed so hot
And placed me shivering on the pot,
Nor asked me whether I should or not?
My Mother!

Anonymous. Known by 1978.

12 The farmer's daughter hath soft
   brown hair;
(Butter and eggs and a pound of cheese)
And I met with a ballad, I can't say
   where,
Which wholly consisted of lines
   like these.

C. S. Calverley, English poet and parodist (1831–84). 'Ballad' (1872).

*Of 'In the Workhouse – Christmas Day'
(1879) by George R. Sims:*

1 It was Christmas day in the cookhouse,
The happiest day of the year,
Men's hearts were full of gladness
And their bellies full of beer,
When up spoke Private Shorthouse,
His face as bold as brass,
Saying, 'We don't want your
    Christmas pudding
You can stick it up your ... '

Anonymous from the First World War (and
included in the stage show *Oh What a
Lovely War*, 1963).

Of the same:

2 It was Christmas Day in the cookhouse.
The troops had all gone to bed.
None of them had any Christmas
    pudding
'Cause the sergeant had done what
    they said.

Billy Bennett, English music-hall comedian
(d.1942). Quoted in *The Penguin Dictionary
of Modern Quotations* (1980 edn).

Of A. E. Housman, A Shropshire Lad,
No. 21 (1896):

3 'Tis Summer Time on Bredon,
And now the farmers swear;
The cattle rise and listen
In valleys far and near,
And blush at what they hear.
But when the mists in autumn
On Bredon top are thick,
The happy hymns of farmers
Go up from fold and rick,
The cattle then are sick.

Hugh Kingsmill, English writer (1889–1949).
One of 'Two Poems after A. E. Housman',
The Table of Truth (1933).

Of A. A. Milne, 'Vespers', in When We
Were Very Young *(1924):*

4 Hush, hush
Nobody cares!
Christopher Robin
Has
Fallen
Down –
Stairs.

J. B. Morton (Beachcomber), English

humorous writer (1893–1979). 'Now We are
Sick', *By the Way* (1931).

Of J. W. Burgon's poem 'Petra' (1845):

5 Broadbosomed, bold, becalm'd, benign
Lies Balham foursquare on the Northern
    Line.
Matched by no marvel save in Eastern
    scene,
A rose-red city half as gold as green.

Frank Muir and Denis Norden, English writers
(1920–98) and (1922–). 'Balham – Gateway
to the South', BBC Third Programme comedy
show *Third Division* (1948). In 1959, this
was re-recorded by Peter Sellers on his album
The Best of Sellers.

*Of poet Ted Hughes and how he would have
celebrated the Queen's Silver Jubilee in 1977:*

6 The sky split apart in malice
Stars rattled like pans on a
Crow shat on Buckingham Palace
God pissed Himself ...

Philip Larkin, English poet (1922–85).
Included in *Selected Letters of Philip Larkin*
(1992).

Of W. B. Yeats's 'The Lake Isle of Innisfree':

7 I will arise and go now, and go
    to Innisfree,
And tell them, at the little Inn,
That there'll be twenty-four for tea.
Twenty-four ladies of the Band of Hope,
United in their hatred of the Pope,
Each one declaring loudly she would
    rather
Serve the Devil than the Holy Father.
The bee-loud glade may hum with
    sounds, I fear,
Other than the murmur of the bee.
I do not fancy they'll be very welcome
    there –
At Innisfree.

Lord (Gerald) Berners, English writer, com-
poser, painter and eccentric (1883–1950).
Quoted by Philip Lane of Cheltenham (1984).
Unverified.

Of Rudyard Kipling's 'Recessional':

8 The tumult and the shouting dies,
The captains and the kings depart,
And we are left with large supplies
Of cold blancmange and rhubarb tart.

Ronald Knox, English priest and writer (1888–1957). 'After the Party', included in Laurence Eyres, *In Three Tongues* (1959).

Of Jane Taylor's 'The Star' ('Twinkle, twinkle, little star ...'):

1 Scintillate, scintillate, globule vivific,
Fain would I fathom thy nature specific.
Loftily poised in the ether capacious,
Strongly resembling a gem
  carbonaceous.

Anonymous. Current by the mid-1940s.

Parthenon

2 The Parthenon without the [Elgin] marbles is like a smile with a tooth missing.

Neil Kinnock, Welsh Labour politician (1942–). Quoted in *The Observer*, 'Sayings of the Week' (8 January 1984).

Party-goers

On a frequent first-nighter and party-goer:

3 Sylvia Miles would go to the opening of an envelope.

Anonymous. Quoted by Christopher Mathew on BBC Radio *Quote ... Unquote* (12 June 1979).

Patience

4 *Con la patciencia et la saliva l'elephante la metio a la formiga* [With patience and saliva, the elephant screws the ant].

Anonymous saying. Quoted by Valerie Bornstein in *Proverbium Yearbook of International Proverb Scholarship* (1991). The original language may have been Mexican Spanish or Catalan: it does not appear to be regular Spanish or Italian.

Patriotism

5 'My country, right or wrong' is a thing no patriot would ever think of saying except in a desperate case. It is like saying, 'My mother, drunk or sober.'

G. K. Chesterton, English poet, novelist and critic (1874–1936). *The Defendant* (1901).

Paunches

6 F. E. Smith, 1st Earl of Birkenhead, taunted Lord Chief Justice Hewart about the size of his stomach. 'What's it to be –

a boy or a girl?' Replied Hewart: 'If it's a boy I'll call him John. If it's a girl I'll call her Mary. But if, as I suspect, it's only wind, I'll call it F. E. Smith.'

Gordon Hewart (later Viscount Hewart), British lawyer and politician (1870–1943). Quoted in the book *Quote ... Unquote* (1978). The story had come to me the previous year from a *Quote ... Unquote* listener who said it had been told to her brother 'by a stranger in a bus queue in Harrogate in 1923'. Smith died in 1930, Hewart in 1943.

According to Humphrey McQueen in *Social Sketches of Australia* (1978), the Antipodean version has Sir George Houstoun Reid (1845–1918) replying, in answer to the question, apropos his stomach, 'What are you going to call it, George?': 'If it's a boy, I'll call it after myself. If it's a girl, I'll call it Victoria after our Queen. But if, as I strongly suspect, it's nothing but piss and wind, I'll call it after you.'

According to *Pass the Port Again* (1981 edn) the exchange occurred between Lord Haldane and Winston Churchill, as also in John Parker, *Father of the House* (1982), in which the exchange is specifically located at the Oxford Union in 1926. *The Faber Book of Anecdotes* (1985) has the US version: President Taft (d.1930) making the retort to Senator Chauncey Depew (d.1929).

Pauses

On being telephoned by the Evening News *and asked if he had a comment on Harold Pinter's fiftieth birthday:*

7 I don't; it's only later I realize I could have suggested two minutes' silence.

Alan Bennett, English playwright and actor (1934–). *Writing Home* (1994) – diary entry for 1 October 1980.

Pavarotti, Luciano
Italian tenor (1935–)

8 Only slightly smaller than Vermont.

Anonymous (American). Quoted in Norman Lebrecht, *When the Music Stops* (1996).

Peace

9 Peace: in international affairs, a period of cheating between two periods of fighting.

Ambrose Bierce, American journalist (1842–
?1914). Quoted in *The Treasury of Humorous
Quotations*, ed. Evan Esar & Nicolas Bentley
(1951).

Pedantry

1 'Whom are you?' said he, for he had
been to night school.

George Ade, American playwright (1866–
1944). 'The Steel Box', in the *Chicago Record*
(16 March 1898).

*Correcting the proofs of his last parliament-
ary speech (31 March 1881):*

2 I will not go down to posterity talking
bad grammar.

Benjamin Disraeli (1st Earl of Beaconsfield),
British politician and writer (1804–81).
Quoted in Robert Blake, *Disraeli* (1966).

3 'You smell!'
'No, *you* smell, I stink.'

Anonymous, though it has been attributed,
inevitably, to Dr Samuel Johnson because, as a
lexicographer, he would be thought fastidious
about usage.

4 Noah Webster, the famous lexicographer, was discovered by his wife as
he embraced one of the maidservants:
'Why, Noah, I am surprised!' she said.
'No, dear,' replied Webster, 'You are
astonished; it is I who am surprised.'

Noah Webster, American lexicographer
(1758–1843). Quoted in Ralph L. Marquard,
Jokes and Anecdotes for All Occasions (1977).
A version with 'amazed/surprised' was quoted
by William Safire in *The New York Times*
(15 October 1973).

5 'Who was the leader of the Pedants'
Revolt?'
'Which Tyler.'

Anonymous. Quoted in *The 'Quote …
Unquote' Newsletter* (July 1995).

Pedestrians

6 [There are] only two classes of pedestrians in these days of reckless motor
traffic – the quick, and the dead.

Lord (Thomas Robert) Dewar, Scottish
distiller (1864–1930). Quoted in George
Robey, *Looking Back on Life* (1933).

A *Times* leader in April that same year merely
ventured: 'The saying that there are two
sorts of pedestrians, the quick and the dead,
is well matured.'

Peerage

7 You should study the Peerage, Gerald …
it is the best thing in fiction the English
have ever done.

Oscar Wilde, Irish playwright, poet and wit
(1854–1900). *A Woman of No Importance*,
Act 3 (1893).

Pelicans

8 Oh, a wondrous bird is the pelican!
His beak holds more than his belican.
He takes in his beak
Food enough for a week.
But I'll be darned if I know how
   the helican.

Dixon Lanier Merritt, American writer
(1879–1972). In the *Nashville Banner*
(22 April 1913).

Penises

9 I'm sixty-one today,
A year beyond the barrier,
And what was once a Magic Flute
Is now a Water Carrier.

Anonymous. Quoted in *The Penguin
Dictionary of Modern Quotations* (1971).

*Little girl to little boy when he dropped
his trousers for her to have a look:*

10 My, that's a handy little gadget.

Anonymous, before 1941. Quoted in book
Babes and Sucklings (1983).

Pensioners

11 Pensioner: a kept patriot.

H. L. Mencken, American journalist and
linguist (1880–1956). Quoted in Herbert
V. Prochnow, Snr & Jnr, *A Treasury of
Humorous Quotations* (1969).

Perfection

*To 'Daphne' (Jack Lemmon, in drag) who has
just confessed that he is not a woman and is
thus unable to marry the wealthy Osgood:*

12 Well, nobody's perfect.

Dialogue from film, *Some Like It Hot* (US, 1959). Script by Billy Wilder and I. A. L. Diamond. With Joe E. Brown as Osgood E. Fielding III. Last line of the film.

1 Revd Chasuble: Charity, dear Miss Prism, charity! None of us are perfect. I myself am peculiarly susceptible to draughts.

Oscar Wilde, Irish playwright, poet and wit (1854–1900). *The Importance of Being Earnest*, Act 2 (1895).

Perseverance

2 By perseverance, the snail reached the Ark.

Revd C. H. Spurgeon, English Baptist preacher (1834–92). Attributed.

Pets

3 I can train any dog in five minutes. It's training the owner that takes longer.

Barbara Woodhouse, English animal trainer (1910–88). Quoted in *Handbook of 20th Century Quotations*, ed. Frank S. Pepper (1984).

Explaining his penchant for taking a lobster for a walk in the gardens of the Palais Royal, Paris, on a long blue leash (pink, in some versions):

4 Well, you see, he doesn't bark and he knows the secrets of the sea.

Gérard de Nerval, French poet (1808–55). Quoted in Théophile Gautier, *Portraits et Souvenirs Littéraires* (1875), which has an elaborate version of the explanation, which translates as: 'Why should a lobster be any more ridiculous than a dog? Or any other animal that one chooses to take for a walk? I have a liking for lobsters; they are peaceful, serious creatures; they know the secrets of the sea; they don't bark, and they don't gnaw upon one's *monadic* privacy like dogs do. And Goethe had an aversion to dogs, and he wasn't mad.'

Philately

5 I don't know much about philately, but I know what I lick.

Philip French, English film critic (1933–). In *The Observer Review* (20 October 1985).

Philosophy

6 I expect to pass through this world but once and therefore if there is anybody that I want to kick in the crutch I had better kick them in the crutch *now*, for I do not expect to pass this way again.

(Sir) Maurice Bowra, English academic (1898–1971). Quoted in Arthur Marshall, *Life's Rich Pageant* (1984). Bowra was lunching at the Reform Club where there was a bishop sitting at the next table.

Photography

7 Most things in life are moments of pleasure and a lifetime of embarrassment; photography is a moment of embarrassment and a lifetime of pleasure.

Tony Benn, English Labour politician (1925–). Quoted in *The Independent* (21 October 1989).

8 If you look like your passport photo, in all probability you need the holiday.

Earl Wilson, American journalist (1907–87). In *Ladies' Home Journal* (1961). As 'If I look like this, I need the trip', ascribed to Gloria Swanson in Herbert V. Prochnow, Snr & Jnr, *A Treasury of Humorous Quotations* (1969).

Physicians

9 He had had much experience of physicians, and said 'the only way to keep your health is to eat what you don't want, drink what you don't like, and do what you'd druther not.'

Mark Twain, American writer (1835–1910). *Following the Equator* (1897).

Picasso, Pablo
Spanish artist (1881–1973)

On being asked what he would do if he saw Picasso walking ahead of him down Piccadilly:

10 I would kick him up the arse, Alfred.

Winston S. Churchill (later Sir Winston), British Conservative Prime Minister and writer (1874–1965). Attributed by Sir Alfred Munnings in a speech at the Royal Academy dinner (1949). Alas, the BBC recording of the event fails to confirm that Munnings ever said this. Not a born speaker, to put it mildly, what he said was, 'Once he said to me, "Alfred, if you met Picasso coming down the street, would you join with me in kicking his something-something?" I said, "Yes, sir, I would!"'

Pigeons

1 *Il y avait un jeune homme de Dijon*
Qui n'avait que peu de religion.
Il dit: 'Quant à moi,
Je déteste tous les trois,
Le Père, et le Fils, et le Pigeon.'
[There was a young man of Dijon
Who had only a little religion,
He said, 'As for me,
I detest all the three,
The Father, the Son and the Pigeon.']

Anonymous. Quoted in the introduction to *Some Limericks* (1928), privately printed by Norman Douglas (published 1969 as *The Norman Douglas Limerick Book*). To talk of the Holy Ghost in these terms seems to have been nothing new, even in the 1920s. Lord Berners, describing his time at Eton in the 1890s in *A Distant Prospect* (1945), tells of a friend called Manston: 'At first I was inclined to be shocked by his irreverence – for instance, when he had said that the Trinity put him in mind of a music-hall turn – the Father, the Son and the Performing Pigeon.'

Pilgrim Fathers

2 How much better it would have been if the Plymouth Rock had landed on the Pilgrim Fathers.

Anonymous. Quoted in H. L. Mencken's *Dictionary of Quotations* (1942).

Pilloried

3 I did not know then [when I was young], though I do now, that there is no suffering comparable with that which a private person feels when he is for the first time pilloried in print.

Mark Twain, American writer (1835–1910). *Life on the Mississippi* (1883).

Pipe-smoking

4 If you want to be happy for a day, go fishing. If you want to be happy for a week, get married. If you want to be happy for a month, kill a pig. If you want to be happy and contented for all time, smoke a pipe.

Anonymous. Quoted by Lord Mason, convenor of the Lords and Commons Pipe smokers' Club in March 1995, but untraced. On the other hand, this version described as a 'Chinese proverb' was heard in 1993: 'If you wish to be happy for an hour, drink wine; if you wish to be happy for three days, get married; if you wish to be happy for eight days, kill your pig and eat it; but if you wish to be happy for ever, become a gardener.'

Place names

5 MAD MARGARET: When I am lying awake at night, and the pale moonlight streams through the latticed casement, strange fancies crowd upon my poor mad brain, and I sometimes think that if we could hit upon some word for you to use whenever I am about to relapse – some word that teems with hidden meaning – like 'Basingstoke' – it might recall me to my saner self.

(Sir) W. S. Gilbert, English writer and lyricist (1836–1911). *Ruddigore* (1887).

Plagiarism

6 If you steal from one author, it's plagiarism; if you steal from many, it's research.

Wilson Mizner, American playwright (1876–1933). Quoted in Alva Johnston, *The Legendary Mizners* (1953).

7 The difference between my quotations and those of the next man is that I leave out the inverted commas.

George Moore, Irish novelist (1852–1933). Quoted in Laurence J. Peter, *Quotations for Our Time* (1977).

8 Taking something from one man and making it worse is plagiarism.

George Moore. Quoted in *The Treasury of Humorous Quotations*, ed. Evan Esar & Nicolas Bentley (1951).

9 I do borrow from other writers, *shamelessly*! I can only say in my defense,

like the woman brought before the judge on a charge of kleptomania, 'I do steal; but, Your Honor, only from the very best stores.'

Thornton Wilder, American novelist and playwright (1897–1975). Quoted in Barbara Rowes, *The Book of Quotes* (1979).

1 If I should die, think only this of me – That in some corner of a foreign field There lies a plagiarist.

Derek Alder (untraced). Quoted in book *Quote ... Unquote 3* (1983).

Platitudes

2 *Travels* by Edward Heath is a reminder that *Morning Cloud*'s skipper is no stranger to platitude and longitude.

Christopher Wordsworth, English journalist and critic (1914–). In *The Observer* (18 December 1977). The conjunction had been made earlier by Christopher Fry in his play *The Lady's Not For Burning* (1949): 'Where in this small-talking world can I find/A longitude with no platitude?'

Plays

The most important ingredients of a play are life, death, food, sex and money:

3 But not necessarily in that order.

Noël Coward (later Sir Noël), English entertainer and writer (1899–1973). Quoted in Dick Richards, *The Wit of Noel Coward* (1968).

Plonking

4 If you have nothing to say, or, rather, something extremely stupid and obvious, say it, but in a 'plonking' tone of voice – i.e. roundly, but hollowly and dogmatically.

Stephen Potter, English humorist (1900–69). *Lifemanship* (1950). Although 'plonking' had been used in Yorkshire dialect for 'large', this would appear to be the first appearance of the term, as defined.

Poets and Poetry

5 Publishing a volume of verse is like dropping a rose petal down the Grand Canyon and waiting for the echo.

Don Marquis, American writer (1878–1937). Quoted in *The Treasury of Humorous Quotations*, ed. Evan Esar & Nicolas Bentley (1951). E. Anthony, *O Rare Don Marquis* (1962), has it as: 'Writing a book of poetry is ...'

6 If there's no money in poetry, neither is there poetry in money.

Robert Graves, English poet (1895–1985). Speech at the London School of Economics (6 December 1963).

Of Ezra Pound:

7 A village explainer, excellent if you were a village, but if you were not, not.

Gertrude Stein, American poet (1874–1946). Quoted in Janet Hobhouse, *Everyone Who Was Anybody* (1975).

8 Wordsworth went to the lakes, but he was never a lake poet. He found in stones the sermons he had already hidden there.

Oscar Wilde, Irish playwright, poet and wit (1854–1900). 'The Decay of Lying', *Intentions* (1891).

9 WITWOUD: Madam, do you pin up your hair with all your letters?
MILLAMANT: Only with those in verse, Mr Witwoud. I never pin up my hair with prose.

William Congreve, English playwright (1670–1744). *The Way of the World* (1700).

10 Peotry is sissy stuff that rhymes. Weedy people sa la and fie and swoon when they see a bunch of daffodils.

Geoffrey Willans, English writer (1911–58) and Ronald Searle, English artist (1920–). *Down with Skool!* (1953).

11 I like a man with poetry in him, but not a poet.

Marilyn Monroe, American film actress (1926–62). Attributed, from 1956, in *The Oxford Dictionary of Literary Quotations*, ed. Peter Kemp (1997).

12 Dr Donne's verses are like the peace of God; they pass all understanding.

James I, English King (1566–1625). Quoted by Archdeacon Plume (1630–1704).

1 The poetic spirit ... is capable of flourishing in even the most barren and unpromising soil. Simon, for whom poetry is a closed book in a locked cupboard in a high attic in a lonely house in a remote hamlet in a distant land, kept saying to his friends, 'This is Uncle Ted. He's a famous poet.'

Stephen Fry, English novelist and actor (1957–). *The Hippopotamus*, Chap. 4 (1995).

Point

On being told over the telephone that he had been awarded the Nobel Prize for Literature in 1923:

2 Stop babbling, man! How much?

W. B. Yeats, Irish poet (1865–1939). Quoted in *A Dictionary of Literary Quotations* (1990). Another version: on being told how great an honour it was for himself and for the country, he asked, 'How much is it, Smyllie, how much is it?' – attributed in W. R. Rodgers (ed.), *Irish Literary Portraits* (1972).

Poker

3 As elaborate a waste of human intelligence as you could find outside an advertising agency.

Raymond Chandler, American novelist (1888– 1959). Quoted in *The Observer* (16 September 1990).

Poles

4 There are few virtues that the Poles do not possess – and there are few mistakes they have ever avoided.

Winston S. Churchill (later Sir Winston), British Conservative Prime Minister and writer (1874–1965). Speech, House of Commons (16 August 1945).

Police

On the supposed youthfulness of the Irish police force:

5 A thing of duty is a boy forever.

Flann O'Brien, Irish novelist and journalist (1911–66). Quoted in *The Listener* (24 February 1977).

6 I never came across a situation so dismal that a policeman couldn't make it worse.

Brendan Behan, Irish playwright (1923–64). On New York's *Open End* TV show (1959) and quoted in *The Sayings of Brendan Behan*, ed. Aubrey Dillon-Malone (1997).

On being awoken at 6.30 a.m. and assuming the men were reporters, Pandora Maxwell told them to 'piss off' and said that she would call the police if they did not leave. The reply came back:

7 Madam, we are the police.

Anonymous. Quoted in *The Independent* (19 June 1992). The police had come to arrest Kevin Maxwell on fraud charges.

Political correctness

On political correctness in book publishing:

8 'You old scrubber' came back as 'You ex-cleaning woman you'.

Jilly Cooper, English novelist and journalist (1937–). Quoted in *The Observer*, 'Sayings of the Week' (5 March 1995).

Politicians

9 Being an MP is a good job, the sort of job all working-class parents want for their children – clean, indoors and no heavy lifting. What could be nicer?

Diane Abbott, English Labour politician (1953–). In *The Independent* (18 January 1994). Much the same claim had earlier been made by Senator Robert Dole about the US vice-presidency (ABC TV broadcast, 24 July 1988): 'It is inside work with no heavy lifting.'

10 He knows nothing and he thinks he knows everything. That points clearly to a political career.

Bernard Shaw, Irish playwright and critic (1856–1950). *Major Barbara*, Act 3 (1905).

11 I am on the right wing of the middle of the road and with a strong radical bias.

Tony Benn, English Labour politician (1925–). Remark, from the 1950s, quoted by Robin Day in a radio interview (1977) when asked about his own political position.

12 A politician is an animal who can sit on a fence and yet keep both ears to the ground.

Anonymous. Quoted in H. L. Mencken's

Dictionary of Quotations (1942). A commonly-evoked criticism – from *The Observer* (8 September 1996): '[Archbishop Robert Runcie] was once described in a speech in the General Synod by the then Bishop of Leicester as a man who enjoyed "sitting on the fence with both ears to the ground". It helped him to accommodate both sides in every argument, but in the long term had the effect of destroying trust in his own statements.'

1 Politicians are the same all over. They promise to build a bridge even when there is no river.

Nikita Khruschev, Soviet Communist Party leader (1894–1971). Remark, Glen Cove, New York (1960).

2 A politician is a person who approaches every subject with an open mouth.

Anonymous – variously ascribed. Quoted in Leon A. Harris, *The Fine Art of Political Wit* (1966), where it is attributed to Adlai Stevenson. *The Penguin Dictionary of Modern Quotations* (1980 edn) gives it to Arthur Goldberg on the subject of diplomats.

3 a politician is an arse upon which everyone has sat except a man.

e. e. cummings, American poet (1894–1962). 'a politician', *1 x 1* (1944).

Politics

4 I was told when a young man ... that the two occupational hazards of the Palace of Varieties [Westminster] were alcohol and adultery. 'The Lords,' [a Knight of the Shires] said severely, 'has the cup for adultery' ... The hurroosh that follows the intermittent revelation of the sexual goings-on of an unlucky MP has convinced me that the only safe pleasure for a parliamentarian is a bag of boiled sweets.

(Sir) Julian Critchley, English Conservative politician and writer (1930–). In *The Listener* (10 June 1982).

5 Politics should be fun – politicians have no right to be pompous or po-faced. The moment politics become dull, democracy is in danger.

Quintin Hogg (Lord Hailsham), English Conservative politician (1907–). Quoted in

1966 and re-quoted in *The Observer*, 'Sayings of the Decade' (1970).

6 I know what is going on. I am going on.

Harold Wilson (later Lord Wilson of Rievaulx), British Labour Prime Minister (1916–95). Quoted in 1969 and re-quoted in *The Observer*, 'Sayings of the Decade' (1970).

Pollution

7 Pollution is cirrhosis of the river.

Anonymous (Australian). Quoted in the book *Graffiti 4* (1982).

Pomposity

A pompous woman, complaining to Berners that the head waiter of a restaurant had not shown her and her husband immediately to a table, said, 'We had to tell him who we were.' Berners, interested, inquired:

8 And who were you?

Lord Berners, English writer and composer (1883–1950). Quoted in Edith Sitwell, *Taken Care Of* (1965). Also told about John Betjeman. However, Patrick Balfour in *Society Racket* (1933) noted: 'I discovered the other day that [this] remark, attributed to a modern wit (and a true wit), Lord Berners, was in fact made by Lord Charles Beresford.' On 11 January 1933, *Punch* carried a cartoon by Fred Pegram, with the caption: 'They had the cheek to say there wasn't a single room in the whole blasted place. We were simply furious, and so we told 'em who we were.' – 'Really, and who were you?'

Pooterism

9 I left the room with silent dignity, but caught my foot in the mat.

George and Weedon Grossmith, English humorous writers (1847–1912) and (1854–1919). *The Diary of a Nobody*, Chap. 12 (1894). The nobody in question is Charles Pooter, an assistant in a mercantile firm, whose mundane doings and thoughts, described with a total lack of humour, gave rise to the term 'Pooterish' for anyone who displays similar characteristics coupled with a lack of awareness. From Chap. 13: 'I am a poor man, but I would gladly give ten shillings to find out who sent me the insulting Christmas card I received this morning.'

Popes

1 It often happens that I wake at night and begin to think about a serious problem and decide I must tell the Pope about it. Then I wake up completely and remember I am the Pope.

John XXIII, Italian-born Pope (1881–1963). Quoted in H. Fesquet, *The Wit and Wisdom of Good Pope John* (1964).

2 Anybody can be Pope; the proof of this is that I have become one.

Ibid.

3 Oho! The Pope! How many divisions has he got?

Joseph Stalin, Soviet Communist Party leader (1879–1953). Quoted in Winston Churchill, *The Second World War*, Vol. 1 (1948). Pierre Laval, French Foreign minister, asked Stalin in 1935, 'Can't you do something to encourage religion and the Catholics in Russia? It would help me so much with the Pope.' This was Stalin's reply.

On the Pope's attitude to birth control, 1974:

4 He no play-a da game. He no make-a da rules!

Earl Butz, American politician (1909–). A joke of the time. Butz lost his job as President Ford's Secretary of Agriculture after making another similar but racist remark.

Popularity

Of the poet W. E. Henley:

5 He has fought a good fight and has had to face every difficulty except popularity.

Oscar Wilde, Irish playwright, poet and wit (1854–1900). In an unpublished sketch, quoted in William Rothenstein, *Men and Memories* (1931). In Wilde's *The Duchess of Padua*, Act 1 (1883), the Duke remarks: 'Popularity/Is the one insult I have never suffered.'

Pornography

Of Oh! Calcutta!*:*

6 This is the kind of show that gives pornography a dirty name.

Clive Barnes, English-born theatre and ballet critic (1927–). Review in *The New York Times* (18 June 1969).

Posh

7 L'Avenue Foch
Is for people who are posh,
L'Avenue Victor Hugo
Is where people like me and you go.

Chas Henessey (untraced). Quoted in *The 'Quote … Unquote' Newsletter* (January 1995).

Positive thinking

8 RIGHT REVEREND HOST: I'm afraid you've got a bad egg, Mr Jones.
NERVOUS YOUNG CURATE: Oh no, my Lord, I assure you! Parts of it are excellent.

George Du Maurier, French-born artist (1834–96). Cartoon in *Punch* (9 November 1895).

Posterity

9 'We are always doing,' says he, 'something for Posterity, but I would fain see Posterity do something for us.'

Joseph Addison, English essayist and politician (1672–1719). In *The Spectator*, No. 583 (20 August 1714).

10 Why should we put ourselves out of our way to do anything for posterity; for what has posterity done for us? (Laughter). I apprehend you gentlemen have entirely mistaken my words, I assure the house that by posterity I do not mean my ancestors but those who came immediately after them.

Sir Boyle Roche, Irish politician (1743–1807). Quoted in *A Book of Irish Quotations* (1984). *Benham's Book of Quotations* (1948), claiming that it is 'erroneously attributed' to Roche, notes that the words occur in John Trumbull's poetic work *McFingal* (1775) and that Mrs Elizabeth Montagu had earlier written in a letter (1 January 1742): 'The man was laughed at as a blunderer who said in a public business "We do much for posterity; I would fain see them do something for us".' Stevenson's *Book of Quotations* (1974) has Thomas Gray writing in a letter to Dr Warton (8 March 1758): 'As to posterity, I may ask (with somebody whom I have forgot) what has it ever done to oblige me?' Inevitably, Oscar Wilde is also credited with the words. All these references obviously allude to the true originator, Addison, above.

1 Why should I write for posterity?
What, if I may be free
To ask a ridiculous question,
Has posterity done for me?

E. Y. Harburg, American lyricist (1898–1981). Song, 'Posterity is Right Around the Corner' (1976).

2 Posterity is capable of infinite vulgarity.

Noël Coward (later Sir Noël), English entertainer and writer (1899–1973). In *The Daily Telegraph* (1969).

3 After being turned down by numerous publishers, he had decided to write for posterity.

George Ade, American humorist and playwright (1866–1944). *Fables in Slang* (1900).

Potatoes

Spitting out a hot potato at dinner:

4 Madam, a fool would have swallowed that.

Anonymous – though Dr Samuel Johnson is often credited with the remark. In *The 'Quote … Unquote' Newsletter* (July 1996). Leonard Miall, the BBC's first post-war Washington correspondent, recalled attending a Dean Acheson press conference at the State Department when he was asked a very cleverly loaded question. 'None of us could imagine how the Secretary of State could answer it without getting himself into trouble. Acheson stroked his guardsman's moustache for a moment and then replied, "My late law partner, Judge Covington, once attended an oyster roast on the Eastern shore of Maryland. He was given a very hot oyster which he immediately spat on to the floor, remarking, 'A bigger damn fool would have swallowed that one'." There were no supplementaries.'

Poverty

5 Poverty is an anomaly to rich people; it is very difficult to make out why people who want dinner do not ring the bell.

Walter Bagehot, English political writer (1826–77). Quoted in *The Treasury of Humorous Quotations*, ed. Evan Esar & Nicolas Bentley (1951).

6 We were so poor that if we woke up on Christmas day without an erection, we had nothing to play with.

Frank McCourt, Irish writer. *Angela's Ashes* (1996).

7 I wasn't always rich. There was a time I didn't know where my next husband was coming from.

Mae West, American vaudeville and film actress (1893–1980). Film, *She Done Him Wrong* (US, 1933).

8 My children didn't have my advantages: I was born into abject poverty.

Kirk Douglas, American film actor (1916–). Remark, in several interviews, early 1980s. Quoted again in *Sunday Today*, 'Quotes of the Week' (26 April 1987).

9 Men of small incomes have often very acute feelings; and a Curate trod on feels a pang as great as when a Bishop is refuted.

Revd Sydney Smith, English clergyman, essayist and wit (1771–1845). In *Edinburgh Review* (1822).

Power

10 I see nothing wrong with power as long as I am the fellow who has it.

Cecil King, English newspaper proprietor (1901–87). Quoted in *The Observer*, 'Sayings of the Decade' (1970). When Chairman of the *Daily Mirror*.

On what it is like not to be President:

11 Well, for one thing, I find I no longer win every golf game I play.

George Bush, American Republican President (1924–). Quoted in *The Independent*, 'Quote Unquote' (15 January 1994).

Pragmatism

12 Alfred Lunt has his head in the clouds and his feet in the box-office.

Noël Coward (later Sir Noël), English entertainer and writer (1899–1973). Quoted in *The Treasury of Humorous Quotations*, ed. Evan Esar & Nicolas Bentley (1951).

Praise

1 Among the smaller duties of life, I hardly know one more important than that of not praising where praise is not due.

Revd Sydney Smith, English clergyman, essayist and wit (1771–1845). Quoted in Saba, Lady Holland, *Memoir* (1855).

Prayers

2 Behold thy votaries submissive beg,
That thou will deign to grant them all
   they ask;
Assist them to accomplish all their ends,
And sanctify whatever means they use
To gain them!

Richard Brinsley Sheridan, English dramatist and politician (1751–1816). *The Critic*, Act 2, Sc. 2 (1779).

3 Dear God, as you will undoubtedly have read in the leader column of *The Times* this morning...

Anonymous Anglican clergyman. Quoted by Anna Ford on BBC Radio *Quote ... Unquote* (29 June 1977). Richard Ingrams, *Muggeridge: The Biography* (1995), has, rather: 'A story was current at the time [1930s] of a clergyman who began an impromptu prayer with the words "Oh God, as thou wilt have read in the *Manchester Guardian* this morning..."'

4 Vouchsafe, O Lord, to keep us this day without being found out.

Samuel Butler, English author (1835–1902). Quoted in *The Treasury of Humorous Quotations*, ed. Evan Esar & Nicolas Bentley (1951).

5 O God, send me some good actors – cheap.

Lilian Baylis, English theatre manager and producer (1874–1937). Quoted in R. & S. Thorndike, *Lilian Baylis* (1938).

6 I am just going to pray for you in St Paul's, but with no very lively hope of success.

Revd Sydney Smith, English clergyman, essayist and wit (1771–1845). Quoted in Hesketh Pearson, *The Smith of Smiths* (1934).

7 Think of what our Nation stands for,
Books from Boots' and country lanes,
Free speech, free passes, class distinction
Democracy and proper drains.
Lord, put beneath thy special care
One eighty-nine Cadogan Square.

(Sir) John Betjeman, English poet (1906–84). 'Westminster Abbey' (1940).

8 When the Gods wish to punish us they answer our prayers.

Oscar Wilde, Irish playwright, poet and wit (1854–1900). *An Ideal Husband*, Act 2 (1895).

At a village kirk in the Scottish Highlands, the minister was much given to interminable impromptu prayer but occasionally lost his train of thought, 'Oh Lord,' he entreated, 'Thou that paintest the crocus purple ...' Here, his inspiration failing him, he rapidly concluded:

9 Paint us purple, too.

Anonymous. Quoted on BBC Radio *Quote ... Unquote* (8 June 1984).

10 Sudden prayers make God jump.

Eric Thacker and Anthony Earnshaw, *The Book of Musrum* (1968).

Predictions

11 I have determined that there is no market for talking pictures.

Thomas Alva Edison, American inventor (1847–1931). In 1926. Quoted in Stuart Berg Flexner, *Listening to America* (1982).

12 The phonograph is not of any commercial value.

Thomas Alva Edison. Quoted in *Time* Magazine (13 August 1984).

Pregnancy

On going into hospital for an abortion:

13 It serves me right for putting all my eggs in one bastard.

Dorothy Parker, American writer (1893–1967). Quoted in John Keats, *You Might as Well Live* (1970).

Presidency

14 When I was a boy I was told that

anybody could become President; I'm beginning to believe it.

Clarence Darrow, American lawyer (1857–1938). Quoted in Irving Stone, *Clarence Darrow for the Defence* (1941).

1 The pay is good and I can walk to work.

John F. Kennedy, American Democratic President (1917–63). Attributed.

2 Scrubbing floors and emptying bedpans has as much dignity as the Presidency.

Richard M. Nixon, American Republican President (1913–94). Quoted in Laurence J. Peter, *Quotations for Our Time* (1977).

Press

3 Freedom of the press in Britain is freedom to print such of the proprietor's prejudices as the advertisers don't object to.

Hannen Swaffer, English journalist (1879–1962). In conversation with Tom Driberg, *c*.1928 (recalled in Driberg's *Swaff*, 1974). Driberg suspected that Swaffer began to take this view in *c*.1902.

4 Have you heard? The Prime Minister has resigned and Lord Northcliffe has sent for the King.

Anonymous (member of the *Daily Mail* staff, 1919). Quoted in Hamilton Fyfe, *Northcliffe: An Intimate Biography* (1930).

5 On the whole I would not say that our Press is obscene. I would say that it trembles on the brink of obscenity.

Francis Pakenham, 7th Earl of Longford, English writer and politician (1905–). Quoted in *The Observer*, 'Sayings of the Week' (2 June 1963).

Presumption

6 I and my rhinoceros, said the tick-bird.

Anonymous (Sotho proverb). Quoted in Ruth Finnegan, *Oral Literature in Africa* (1970).

Pretentiousness

7 Two London taxi drivers were having a heated dispute. Said one, 'You know what you are, don't you? – pretentious!' And the other adopted a tone of hurt pride. 'Pretentious?' he replied. *'Moi?'*

Anonymous. Quoted by Anna Ford on BBC Radio *Quote ... Unquote* (recorded 5 December 1978). This joke featured also in the form:

8 So Harry says, 'You don't like me any more. Why not?' And he says, 'Because you've got so terribly pretentious.' And Harry says, 'Pretentious? *Moi?'*

John Cleese, English actor and writer (1939–) and Connie Booth, American actress and writer (1941–). 'The Psychiatrists', BBC TV *Fawlty Towers* (1979). Probably repeating an established joke of the time. It may have originally been uttered by Miss Piggy in TV's *The Muppet Show* at some time in the late 70s.

Pricks

9 A stiff prick hath no conscience.

Anonymous. Ascribed confidently by John Osborne in *Almost a Gentleman* (1991), to St Augustine, but dubiously so. The proverbial status of the remark was, however, evident by the 1880s when 'Walter' in *My Secret Life* (Vol. 1, Chap. 12) wrote: 'I thought how unfair it was to her sister, who was in the family way by me ... but a standing prick stifles all conscience.' Indeed, 'a *standing* prick has no conscience' is an equally well-known variant. Earlier, in his diary (15 May 1663), Samuel Pepys writes of hearing from Sir Thomas Crew that: 'The King [Charles II] doth mind nothing but pleasures and hates the very sight or thoughts of business. That my Lady Castlemayne rules him; who he says hath all the tricks of Aretin [erotic writer Pietro Aretino] that are to be practised to give pleasure – in which he is too able, hav[ing] a large —— [Pepys's blank]; but that which is the unhappiness is that, as the Italian proverb says, *"Cazzo dritto non vuolt consiglio"*.' This may be translated as 'A stiff prick doesn't want any advice.' Compare: 'Another writer whom [Wilde] did not spare was his old teacher J. P. Mahaffy, two of whose books Wilde reviewed ... [he] might have treated Mahaffy nostalgically, but the erect pen has no conscience' – Richard Ellman, *Oscar Wilde* (1987).

Priests

10 A priest is a man who is called Father by everyone except his own children who are obliged to call him Uncle.

Anonymous. Quoted in *The Lyttelton Hart-Davis Letters*, Vol. 1 (1978), in which Rupert Hart-Davis says he came across this 'Italian saying' in 'a French novel, read in the train', but gives no further information.

Priestley, J. B.
English novelist and playwright (1894–1984)

1 Playing on a fuddled fiddle, somewhere in the muddled middle.

Aneurin Bevan, Welsh Labour politician (1897–1960). Attributed, during the Second World War.

Principles

2 'Would you sleep with me if I gave you £10,000?' he asked her. She thought about it and acknowledged that, theoretically, she would. 'Good,' said Shaw, 'so would you also sleep with me for sixpence?' The lady became indignant. 'What sort of woman do you think I am?' she exploded. 'We've established what sort of woman you are,' the writer pointed out, 'we're merely haggling over the price.'

Bernard Shaw, Irish playwright and critic (1856–1950). Quoted in *The Sunday Times* (13 May 1990). The origin of this exchange remains untraced. This is the earliest citation found so far, ascribing it to Shaw. Compare, from William Rushton, *Superpig* (1976): 'This is from the same stable as a Lord Curzon asking some duchess or other whether she'd bed down with him for a million pounds and saying upon her eager nod, "Having established the principle, now let's get down to the hard bargaining."'

Priorities

3 You mustn't take out a man's appendix while he's moving a grand piano.

Anonymous. Quoted as a 'favourite aphorism' of Denis Healey's in Philip Ziegler, *Mountbatten* (1985).

Privilege

On being made Poet Laureate in 1850:

4 In the end I accepted the honour, because during dinner Venables told me, that, if I became Poet Laureate, I should always when I dined out be offered the liver-wing of a fowl.

Alfred, Lord Tennyson, English poet (1809–92). Quoted in *Alfred Lord Tennyson: a Memoir by his Son*, Vol. 1 (1897).

Producers

5 An associate producer is the only guy in Hollywood who will associate with a producer.

Fred Allen, American comedian (1894–1956). Quoted in *The Treasury of Humorous Quotations*, ed. Evan Esar & Nicolas Bentley (1951).

Productions

On the Emperor Gordian:

6 Twenty-two acknowledged concubines, and a library of sixty-two thousand volumes, attested the variety of his inclinations, and from the productions which he left behind him, it appears that the former as well as the latter were designed for use rather than ostentation.

Edward Gibbon, English historian (1737–94). *The Decline and Fall of the Roman Empire*, Chap. 7 (1776–88). An example of Gibbon's stony-faced sense of humour. In a footnote, Gibbon adds: 'By each of his concubines, the younger Gordian left three or four children. His literary productions were by no means contemptible.'

Professionals

7 Professionals built the *Titanic*; amateurs built the Ark.

Anonymous. Quoted by Richard Needham MP in seconding the Loyal Address in the House of Commons (6 November 1984).

8 Amateurs [musicians] practise until they can get it right; professionals practise until they can't get it wrong.

Anonymous. Quoted by Harold Craxton, one-time professor at the Royal Academy of Music, and re-quoted in *The 'Quote ... Unquote' Newsletter* (April 1994).

9 A professional is a man who can do his job when he doesn't feel like it; an amateur is one who can't [do his job] when he does feel like it.

James Agate, English drama critic (1877–1947). *Ego* (1935) – entry for 17 September 1933. The context was a lunch with the actor Cedric Hardwicke, who said: 'My theory of acting is that it is so minor an art that the only self-respect attaching to it is to be able to reproduce one's performance with mathematical accuracy.' The above was Agate's concurrence. Hardwicke added: 'It shouldn't make a hair's breadth of difference to an actor if he has a dead baby at home and a wife dying.'

Professions

1 The Actor and the Streetwalker ... the two oldest professions in the world – ruined by amateurs.

Alexander Woollcott, American writer and critic (1887–1943). *Shouts and Murmurs* (1922).

2 KITTY: The guy said that machinery is going to take the place of every profession?

CARLOTTA: That's something you need never worry about.

Dialogue from film, *Dinner At Eight* (US, 1933). Script by Frances Marion and Herman J. Mankiewicz. Jean Harlow as Kitty, Marie Dressler as Carlotta Vance.

Professors

3 A professor is one who talks in someone else's sleep.

W. H. Auden, Anglo-American poet (1907–73). Quoted in *The Treasury of Humorous Quotations*, ed. Evan Esar & Nicolas Bentley (1951).

4 Old professors never die, they merely lose their faculties.

Stephen Fry, English author and actor (1957–). *The Liar*, Chap. 2 (1991). But quoting an established line.

Promiscuity

5 There's a lot of promiscuity around these days and I'm all for it.

Ben Travers, English playwright (1886–1980). Remark, *c*.1980, quoted in the *Telegraph Sunday Magazine*.

6 What is a promiscuous person? It's usually someone who is getting more sex than you are.

Victor Lownes, American Playboy Club manager (1928–). Quoted in Bob Chieger, *Was It Good For You Too?* (1983).

Pronunciation

7 I take it you already know
Of tough and bough and cough
    and dough?
Others may stumble, but not you
On hiccough, thorough, laugh
    and through.
Well done! And now you wish perhaps
To learn of less familiar traps.
Beware of heard, a dreadful word
That looks like beard and sounds
    like bird.
And dead. It's said like bed, not bead –
For goodness sake don't call it deed.
Watch out for meat and great and threat
(They rhyme with suite and straight
    and debt.)
A moth is not a moth in mother
Nor both in bother, broth in brother.
And here is not a match for there
Nor dear and fear for bear and pear.
And then there's does and rose
    and lose –
Just look them up – and goose
    and choose,
And cork and work and card and ward,
And font and front and word and sword
And do and go and thwart and cart –
And yet I've hardly made a start!

Anonymous (by March 1980). *This England's Book of Parlour Poetry* (1989) adds a final couplet: 'A dreadful language? Man alive,/I'd mastered it when I was five!'

8 They spell it Vinci and pronounce it Vinchy; foreigners always spell better than they pronounce.

Mark Twain (Samuel Langhorne Clemens), American writer (1835–1910). *The Innocents Abroad* (1869).

To an American actor who returned from London pronouncing 'skedule' in the English way – 'schedule':

9 If you don't mind my saying so, I think you're full of skit.

Dorothy Parker, American writer (1893–1967). Quoted in Ned Sherrin, *Cutting Edge* (1984).

Prose

1 Good heavens! For more than forty years I have been speaking prose without knowing it.

Molière, French playwright (1622–73). *Le Bourgeois Gentilhomme*, Act 2, Sc. 4 (1671).

2 Meredith is a prose Browning, and so is Browning.

Oscar Wilde, Irish playwright, poet and wit (1854–1900). 'The Critic as Artist', Pt 1, *Intentions* (1891).

3 ACQUAINTANCE: How are you today? YEATS: Not very well. I can only write prose today.

William Butler Yeats, Irish poet (1865–1939). Attributed in *The Oxford Dictionary of Literary Quotations*, ed. Peter Kemp (1997).

4 Poetry is to prose as dancing is to walking.

John Wain, English novelist and critic (1925–94). On BBC Radio (13 January 1976).

Prosperity

5 There is an old time toast which is golden for its beauty. 'When you ascend the hill of prosperity may you not meet a friend.'

Mark Twain, American writer (1835–1910). *Following the Equator* (1897).

Proverbs

A dachshund-comforting proverb:

6 No leg is too short to touch the ground.

Lyndon Irving, English writer (1905–). Contributed to a *New Statesman* competition and included in the anthology *Salome, Dear, Not In the Fridge* (1968).

7 If you start throwing hedgehogs under me, I shall throw a couple of porcupines under you.

Nikita Khruschev, Soviet Communist Party leader (1894–1971). Quoted in *The New York Times* (7 November 1963).

Providence

8 JUDGE: What do you suppose I am on the bench for, Mr Smith?
F. E. SMITH: It is not for me, your honour, to attempt to fathom the inscrutable workings of Providence.

F. E. Smith (1st Earl of Birkenhead), English politician and lawyer (1872–1930). Quoted in Winston Churchill, *Great Contemporaries* (1937).

Psychiatrists

9 A psychiatrist is a man who goes to the Folies-Bergère and looks at the audience.

Mervyn Stockwood, English Anglican Bishop (1913–95). Quoted in *The Observer* (15 October 1961).

Public schools

10 Any one who has been to an English public school will always feel comparatively at home in prison. It is the people brought up in the gay intimacy of the slums, Paul learned, who find prison soul-destroying.

Evelyn Waugh, English novelist (1903–66). *Decline and Fall*, Prelude (1928).

Publicity

11 I don't care what you say about me, as long as you say *something* about me, and as long as you spell my name right.

George M. Cohan, American songwriter and entertainer (1878–1942). Quoted in J. McCabe, *George M. Cohan* (1973).

12 If you want to keep a secret, tell it to the BBC Press Office.

John Cleese, English actor and writer (1939–). Quoted in *A Year of Stings and Squelches* (1985).

13 There's no such thing as bad publicity except your own obituary.

Brendan Behan, Irish playwright (1923–64). Quoted in the *Sunday Express* (5 January 1964) and in Dominic Behan, *My Brother Brendan* (1965).

1 Publicity is justly commended as a remedy for social and industrial diseases. Sunlight is said to be the best of disinfectants; electric light the most efficient policeman.

Louis D. Brandeis, American jurist (1856–1941). Quoted in *Harper's Weekly* (20 December 1913). Compare the saying, 'Rain is the best policeman of all', heard from a senior police officer after London's Notting Hill Carnival had been rained off on the Late Summer Bank Holiday in August 1986. Meaning that the incidence of crime falls when the rain does (as it also does in very cold weather).

2 Publicity is easy to get. Just be so successful you don't need it, and then you'll get it.

Anonymous (American). Quoted in Herbert V. Prochnow, Snr & Jnr, *A Treasury of Humorous Quotations* (1969).

3 Will somebody please explain to me why public relations people are almost invariably 'associates'? Whom do they associate with, and who can stand it?

George Dixon (American). Quoted in Herbert V. Prochnow, Snr & Jnr, *A Treasury of Humorous Quotations* (1969).

4 [Dryden] has often said to me in confidence, that the world would have never suspected him to be so great a poet, if he had not assured them so frequently in his Prefaces that it was impossible they could either doubt or forget it.

Jonathan Swift, Anglo-Irish writer and clergyman (1667–1745). *A Tale of a Tub*, 5 (1704).

5 I don't care what is written about me so long as it isn't true.

Katharine Hepburn, American film actress (1909–). Quoted in Laurence J. Peter, *Quotations for Our Time* (1977).

Publishers

6 Now Barabbas was a publisher.

Lord Byron, English poet (1788–1824). The story has it that when John Murray, Byron's publisher, sent the poet a copy of the Bible in return for a favour, Byron sent it back with the words 'Now Barabbas was a robber' (John 18:40) altered to, 'Now Barabbas was a publisher ...' This story was included in Kazlitt Arvine's *Cyclopedia of Anecdotes of Literature and the Fine Arts,* published in Boston, Massachussetts, in 1851. In 1981, the then head of the firm, John G. (Jock) Murray, told me that those involved were in fact the poet Coleridge and his publishers, Longmans. But when I asked for evidence in 1988, he could only say that, 'I have satisfied myself that it was not Byron.' The copy of Byron's Bible which exists has no such comment in it. He also drew my attention to the fact that in Byron's day publishers were more usually called booksellers.

H. L. Mencken's Dictionary of Quotations (1942), on the other hand, gives Thomas Campbell (1777–1844) as the probable perpetrator. Certainly, Campbell seems to have taken the required attitude. At a literary dinner he once toasted Napoleon with the words: 'We must not forget that he once shot a bookseller' (quoted in G. O. Trevelyan, *The Life and Letters of Lord Macaulay,* 1876 – diary entry for 12 December 1848). Mark Twain wrote in a letter: 'How often we recall, with regret, that Napoleon once shot at a magazine editor and missed him and killed a publisher. But we remember with charity, that his intentions were good.'

7 As repressed sadists are supposed to become policemen or butchers, so those with an irrational fear of life become publishers.

Cyril Connolly, English critic (1903–74). *Enemies of Promise* (1938).

8 Being published by the Oxford University Press is rather like being married to a duchess: the honour is almost greater than the pleasure.

G. M. Young, English historian (1882–1959). Quoted by Rupert Hart-Davis in letter to George Lyttelton (29 April 1956).

Publishing

Of poems:

9 You shall see them on a beautiful quarto page where a neat rivulet of text shall meander through a meadow of margin.

Richard Brinsley Sheridan, English dramatist and politician (1751–1816). *The School for Scandal*, Act 1, Sc.1 (1777).

Punch Magazine

When asked why his organ wasn't as funny or as good as it used to be:

1 It never was.

F. C. Burnand (later Sir Francis), English editor (1836–1917). Quoted in R. G. G. Price, *A History of Punch* (1957).

2 Very much like the Church of England. It is doctrinally inexplicable but it goes on.

Malcolm Muggeridge, English writer and broadcaster (1903–90). Attributed in A. Andrews, *Quotations for Speakers and Writers* (1969).

Punctuality

3 The only way of catching a train I ever discovered is to miss the train before.

G. K. Chesterton, English poet, novelist and critic (1874–1936). Quoted in *The Treasury of Humorous Quotations*, ed. Evan Esar & Nicolas Bentley (1951). P. Daninos, 'Le Supplice de l'heure', *Vacances à tous prix* (1958), has: 'Chesterton taught me this: the only way to be sure of catching a train was to miss the one before it.'

When criticized for continually arriving late for work in the City in 1919:

4 But think how early I go.

Lord Castlerosse, English eccentric (1891–1943). Quoted in Leonard Mosley, *Castlerosse* (1956). Also attributed to Howard Dietz at MGM.

On being told that he was seven minutes late arriving at Dublin Castle on 16 January 1922 for the handing-over ceremony by British forces:

5 We've been waiting seven hundred years. You can have the seven minutes.

Michael Collins, Irish politician (1880–1922). Quoted in Tim Pat Coogan, *Michael Collins* (1990).

Punishment

When sewing mail-bags in prison and being greeted by a visitor with the words, 'Ah, Bottomley, sewing?':

6 No, reaping.

Horatio Bottomley, English journalist, financier and politician (1860–1933). Quoted in S. T. Felstead, *Horatio Bottomley* (1936). In 1922, Bottomley (an MP) was found guilty of fraudulent conversion and sent to prison.

Punning

7 A man who would make so vile a pun would not scruple to pick a pocket.

John Dennis, English playwright and critic (1657–1734). Editorial note in *The Gentleman's Magazine* (1781). Possibly said *of* Dennis rather than by him.

8 Hanging is too good for a man who makes puns. He should be drawn and quoted.

Fred Allen, American comedian (1894–1956). Quoted in Laurence J. Peter, *Quotations for Our Time* (1977).

9 I have very little to say about puns; they are in very bad repute, and so they ought to be. The wit of language is so miserably inferior to the wit of ideas that it is very deservedly driven out of good company.

Revd Sydney Smith, English clergyman, essayist and wit (1771–1845). *Sketches of Moral Philosophy* (1849).

Puns

10 'Do you know Sir Arthur Evans's reported remark on finding a fragment of pottery in Crete – "an ill-favoured thing, but Minoan"?'

Anonymous. Quoted in *The 'Quote … Unquote' Newsletter* (April 1995). 'A Small Thing But Minoan' is ascribed as a title to Alan Coren in Frank Muir, *The Oxford Book of Humorous Prose* (1992).

11 TEACHER: And who was JOAN OF ARC? SCHOLAR: Please, sir, NOAH'S WIFE.

Anonymous. *Punch*, Vol. 122 (29 January 1902). 'Noah's wife was called Joan of Ark' was listed as one of 'British children's answers to church school questions' in a US publication called *Speaker's Idea File* (1993). But how old did the compilers think it to be? About as old as the Ark itself is the fact of the matter.

12 *Peccavi* – I have Sindh.

Punch, Vol. 6 (18 May 1844). *Punch* suggested that Caesar's *'Veni, vidi, vici'* was beaten for brevity by 'Napier's dispatch to Lord Ellenborough, *Peccavi.*' *The Oxford Dictionary of*

Quotations credits the joke to Catherine Wink-worth (1827–78). She was a young girl, so it was sent into *Punch* on her behalf. Later, she became a noted translator of hymns.

It seems, however, that the supposed remark was soon taken as genuine, even at *Punch* itself. On 22 March 1856, the magazine (confusing sender and receiver in the original) included the couplet: "'*Peccavi* – I've Scinde,' wrote Lord Ellen, so proud. More briefly Dalhousie wrote – '*Vovi* – I've Oude.'" '*Peccavi*' is the Latin phrase for 'I have sinned'.

1 The quality of Mersea is not strained.

Anonymous. *Punch*, Vol. 181 (19 August 1931). Writing to James Agate from Liverpool on 17 April 1942, John Gielgud, the actor, who was touring in Macbeth, noted: 'There was a very nice misprint in the *Liverpool Echo* on Wednesday, paying tribute to our broad comedian George Woodbridge, who plays the Porter, as "an engaging Portia". I could not forbear to murmur that the quality of Mersey is not strained.' Well, this was an early appearance of the 'Mersey' joke, in *Ego 5* (1942). It had already appeared, though, in *Punch* (19 August 1931).

2 A water bison is what yer wash yer face in.

Roger McGough, English poet (1937–). *An Imaginary Menagerie* (1988).

3 Dada wouldn't buy me a Bauhaus.

Anonymous graffito by students at local art college, spotted by Finlay Bates of Norwich (1981).

4 Are you a spy?
Yes.
Then why are you covered in mint?
I'm a mint-spy!

Spike Milligan, English entertainer and writer (1918–). 'The Jet-Propelled Guided NAAFI', BBC Radio *The Goon Show* (24 January 1956).

5 Life's a binge and then you diet.

Anonymous. Caption to an article in the London *Observer* (23 September 1990) about frozen food.

Promoting sun-tan products with a window-display under the slogan:

6 Life's a beach – and then you fry.

Anonymous slogan for the Body Shop chain in the UK (summer of 1991).

To a waiter at Buckingham Palace who had spilled soup on her new dress:

7 Never darken my Dior again!

Beatrice Lillie, Canadian-born actress (1898–1989). *Every Other Inch a Lady* (1973).

8 And I'll stay off Verlaine, too; he was always chasing Rimbauds.

Kenneth Tynan, English critic (1927–80). Quoted in James Agate, *Ego 8*, for 20 July 1945, who wrote: 'To say that "Verlaine was always chasing Rimbauds" is just common. Like cheap scent.' Whether the schoolboy Tynan knew it or not, he had been anticipated by Dorothy Parker who wrote the 'chasing Rimbauds' line, in 'The Little Hours', *Here Lies* (1939).

9 I remember once having made this observation to Edmund Burke, that it would be no bad definition of one sort of epitaphs, to call them grave epigrams. He repeated the words '*grave* epigrams', and gave me the credit of a pun, which I never intended.

Sir Joshua Reynolds, English painter (1723–92). Letter (31 May 1791).

10 Like Webster's Dictionary
We're Morocco bound.

Johnny Burke, American songwriter (1908–64). Song, 'Road to Morocco', with music by Jimmy van Heusen. In film, *Road To Morocco* (US, 1942). Performed by Bob Hope and Bing Crosby.

11 MACBULL: I shall be a gay grass widower for the next two months – wife's gone for a holiday to the West Indies.
O'BEAR: Jamaica?
MACBULL: No, it was her own idea.

Anonymous (cartoonist). Caption to cartoon in *Punch* (25 February 1914).

Puritanism

12 That kind of so-called housekeeping where they have six Bibles and no corkscrew.

Mark Twain, American writer (1835–1910). *Mark Twain's Notebook*, ed. A. B. Paine (1935).

Purity

1 I'm as pure as the driven slush.

Tallulah Bankhead, American actress (1903–68). Quoted in the *Saturday Evening Post* (12 April 1947).

2 I used to be Snow White ... but I drifted.

Mae West, American vaudeville and film actress (1893–1980). Quoted in Joseph Weintraub, *Peel Me a Grape* (1975).

Purpose

3 If people want a sense of purpose they should get it from their archbishops. They should not hope to get it from their politicians.

Harold Macmillan (later 1st Earl of Stockton), British Conservative Prime Minister (1894–1986). Quoted in Henry Fairlie, *The Life of Politics* (1968). Said to Fairlie in 1963.

Put-downs

To her husband Walter, who had asked a starlet with thick legs how old she was:

4 For God's sake, Walter, why don't you chop off her legs and count the rings?

Carol Matthau, American writer (1932–). Quoted in Truman Capote, *Answered Prayers* (1986). This was a well-known Hollywood joke by this stage. George Axelrod had told it on BBC Radio *Quote ... Unquote* (11 September 1979).

On William F. Buckley Jnr:

5 Looks and sounds not unlike Hitler, but without the charm.

Gore Vidal, American novelist, playwright and critic (1925–). Quoted in *The Observer* (26 April 1981).

On David Frost:

6 He rose without trace.

Kitty Muggeridge, English writer (1903–94). Remark made *c.*1965, quoted in book *Quote ... Unquote* (1978). Curiously delighting in it, Frost provides the context in the first volume of his autobiography (1993). Malcolm Muggeridge (Kitty's husband) had predicted that after *That Was The Week That Was*, Frost would sink without trace. She said, 'Instead, he has risen without trace.'

When Ned Sherrin claimed that Laugh-In *was a spin-off of* That Was The Week That Was:

7 Like Concorde is a spin-off of the Tiger Moth, darling.

Germaine Greer, Australian-born writer and feminist (1939–). On BBC Radio *Quote ... Unquote* (7 March 1976).

To a man who came up to her at a party and exclaimed, effusively, 'Tallulah! I haven't seen you for 41 years!':

8 I thought I told you to wait in the car.

Tallulah Bankhead, American actress (1903–68). Quoted by Clement Freud on BBC Radio *Quote ... Unquote* (1979).

To Lady Astor who had said, 'If you were my husband, I'd poison your coffee', (c.1912):

9 If you were my wife, I'd drink it.

Winston S. Churchill (later Sir Winston), British Conservative Prime Minister and writer (1874–1965). Quoted in Consuelo Vanderbilt Balsan, *Glitter and Gold* (1952).

To Bessie Braddock MP who had told him he was drunk:

10 And you, madam, are ugly. But I shall be sober in the morning.

Winston Churchill. Quoted in Sykes & Sproat, *The Wit of Sir Winston* (1965), without naming Braddock. She was named in Leslie Frewin, *Immortal Jester* (1973).

Katharine Hepburn, sighing with relief after she had completed filming A Bill of Divorcement *with John Barrymore in 1932, said, 'Thank goodness I don't have to act with you any more.' Replied he:*

11 I didn't know you ever had, darling.

John Barrymore, American actor (1882–1942). Quoted in Leslie Halliwell, *The Filmgoer's Book of Quotes* (1973).

Pyjamas

12 One morning I shot an elephant in my pyjamas. How he got in my pyjamas I'll never know.

Groucho Marx, American comedian (1895–1977). Film, *Animal Crackers* (US, 1930). Script by Morrie Ryskind, from a musical by himself and George S. Kaufman.

Q

Quakers

1 Did you say 'a Quaker baby'? Impossible! there is no such thing; there never was; they are always born broadbrimmed and in full quake.

Revd Sydney Smith, English clergyman, essayist and wit (1771–1845). Quoted in Saba, Lady Holland, *Memoir* (1855).

Qualifications

2 My only qualification for being put at the head of the Navy is that I am very much at sea.

Edward Carson (later Lord Carson), Irish-born lawyer and politician (1854–1935). Quoted in Ian Colvin, *Life of Lord Carson* (1936).

Queerness

On breaking up with his business partner, W. Allen, at New Lanark (1828):

3 All the world is queer save thee and me, and even thou art a little queer.

Robert Owen, Welsh-born socialist reformer (1771–1858). Quoted in *The Penguin Dictionary of Quotations* (1960).

Questions

4 Ah, what is man? Wherefore does he why? Whence did he whence? Whither is he withering?

Dan Leno, English music-hall entertainer (1860–1904). *Dan Leno Hys Booke* (1901).

5 Well, if I Called the Wrong Number, Why Did You Answer the Phone?

James Thurber, American cartoonist and writer (1894–1961). Caption to cartoon in *Men, Women and Dogs* (1943).

6 'Pray, my dear,' quoth my mother, 'have you not forgot to wind up the clock?' – 'Good G—?' cried my father, making an exclamation, but taking care to moderate his voice at the same time, – 'Did ever woman, since the creation of the world, interrupt a man with such a silly question?'

Laurence Sterne, Irish novelist and clergyman (1713–68). *Tristram Shandy*, Bk 1, Chap.6 (1760–67). Accordingly, Walter Shandy attributed most of his son's misfortunes to the fact that at a highly critical moment his wife had asked him if he had wound the clock, a question so irrelevant that he despaired of the child's ever being able to pursue a logical train of thought.

Quiet

In the wilds:

7 It's so quiet up here you can hear a mouse get a hard-on.

Dialogue in film, *Continental Divide* (US, 1981). Quoted in Bob Chieger, *Was It Good For You Too?* (1983). Script by Lawrence Kasdan. Spoken by John Belushi.

Quiz

When an excitable Fellow rushed up to announce that a member of the college had killed himself:

8 Pray don't tell me who. Allow me to guess.

Martin Routh, President of Magdalen College, Oxford (1755–1854). Quoted in Dacre Balsdon, *Oxford Life* (1957).

On being told, when he was a housemaster at Eton, that a murder had been committed in the College and one of the boys killed:

9 What dangerous clown has done this?

A. C. Benson, English writer (1862–1925). Quoted by Humphrey Lyttelton (an Old Etonian) on BBC Radio *Quote ... Unquote* (1988). Two years earlier it had been told on the show by Steve Race who happened to have the headmaster of Eton sitting next to him (and who did not dispute the tale). However, Kenneth Tynan in a 1948 theatre review (included in *A View of the English Stage*) gives it as an 'Alexander Woollcott story' of merely 'a schoolmaster' who, coming upon a mutilated torso in the Lower Third dormitory, remarked: 'Some dangerous clown has been here.' Humphrey Lyttelton's father, George, apparently resolves the matter in *The Lyttelton Hart-Davis Letters* (for 23 February 1956): 'Woollcott records in one of his books his high appreciation when my colleague [at Eton] Booker was summoned one Sunday afternoon to his kitchen where his cook had been murdered, and on seeing the body, asked "What dangerous clown has done this?"'

Quotations

1 Quotation, *n*. The act of repeating erroneously the words of another. The words erroneously repeated.

Ambrose Bierce, American journalist (1842–?1914). *The Cynic's Word Book* (later retitled *The Devil's Dictionary*) (1906).

2 You see I have the common folly of quoting myself.

Jonathan Swift, Anglo-Irish writer and clergyman (1667–1745). Letter to Charles Ford (9 December 1732).

3 What though his head be empty, provided his commonplace book be full.

Jonathan Swift. 'Digression in Praise of Digressions', *A Tale of a Tub* (1704).

Reviewing a book by Edmund Blunden:

4 Mr Blunden is no more able to resist a quotation than some people are to refuse a drink.

George Orwell, English novelist and journalist (1903–50). In the *Manchester Evening News* (20 April 1944).

5 He liked those literary cooks
Who skim the cream of other's books;
And ruin half an author's graces
By plucking bon-mots from their places.

Hannah More, English writer (1745–1833). *Florio* (1786).

6 Ah, yes! I wrote the 'Purple Cow' –
I'm sorry, now, I wrote it!
But I can tell you anyhow,
I'll kill you if you quote it.

Gelett Burgess, American writer (1866–1951). 'Confessional' (1914).

When asked for his favourite quotation:

7 My favourite quotation is eight pounds ten for a second-hand suit.

Spike Milligan, English entertainer and writer (1918–). On BBC Radio *Quote... Unquote* (1 January 1979).

8 Everything I've ever said will be credited to Dorothy Parker.

George S. Kaufman, American playwright (1889–1961). Quoted in Scott Meredith, *George S. Kaufman and the Algonquin Round Table* (1974).

9 OSCAR WILDE: I wish I had said that.
WHISTLER: You will, Oscar, you will.

James McNeill Whistler, American painter (1834–1903). Quoted in L. C. Ingleby, *Oscar Wilde* (1907) and Douglas Sladen, *Twenty Years of My Life* (1915). Sladen says that it was of a remark by a woman that Wilde had rather taken a fancy to, but Hesketh Pearson, *The Life of Oscar Wilde* (1946) has it, more convincingly, that it was something said by Whistler himself that Wilde was obviously going to make his own.

When asked for 'a good quote' by a French journalist on a cold night:

10 If I had a good quote, I'd be wearing it.

Bob Dylan, American singer and songwriter (1941–). Quoted in *The Times* (July 1981).

11 I don't want to be quoted, and don't quote me that I don't want to be quoted.

Winston Burdett, American journalist (twentieth century). Quoted in Barbara Rowes, *The Book of Quotes* (1979).

1 Quotes, unquotes and quotes. That's three quotes. And another quote'll make it a gallon.

Groucho Marx, American comedian (1895–1977). Film, *Animal Crackers* (US, 1930). Script by Morrie Ryskind, from a musical by himself and George S. Kaufman.

2 When I'm talking to people I like to stop and quote myself. My quotes have a way of spicing up a conversation.

Brendan Behan, Irish playwright (1923–64). *With Brendan Behan* (1981).

R

Rabbits

1 The rabbit has a charming face:
Its private life is a disgrace.
I really dare not name to you
The awful things that rabbits do.

Anonymous. 'The Rabbit' (1925). Quoted in
The Week-End Book (1925).

Radicals

2 A radical is a man with both feet firmly
planted in the air.

Franklin D. Roosevelt, American Democratic
President (1882–1945). Radio broadcast
(26 October 1939).

Railways

*In a letter to the station master at Baker Street
station, London, on the Metropolitan Line:*

3 Sir, Saturday morning, although recur-
ring at regular and well-foreseen
intervals, always seems to take this
railway by surprise.

(Sir) W. S. Gilbert, English writer and lyricist
(1836–1911). Quoted in John Julius Norwich,
A Christmas Cracker (1973).

Rain

4 The rain, it raineth on the just
And also on the unjust fella:
But chiefly on the just, because
The unjust steals the just's umbrella.

Lord Bowen, English judge (1835–94).
Quoted in Walter Sichel, *The Sands of Time*
(1923).

5 If God had intended man to live in
England, he'd have given him gills.

David Renwick, English writer (1951–),
with Andrew Marshall. BBC Radio *The
Burkiss Way* (11 November 1980).

Rape

*Appearing before a military tribunal to
put his case as a conscientious objector, he
was asked by the chairman what, in
view of his beliefs, he would do if he
saw a German soldier trying to violate
his sister:*

6 I would try to get between them.

Lytton Strachey, English biographer (1880–
1932). Quoted in Robert Graves, *Goodbye
To All That* (1929).

Rats

7 Even if you win the rat-race, you're
still a rat.

William Sloane Coffin, American clergyman (1924–). When consulted at his home
in Vermont (July 1995), the Revd Coffin
said that to the best of his knowledge he did
originate this statement in the above form.
He thought up the quip 'in the 1950s or
1960s' when he was chaplain either at
Williams College or at Yale University. He
added the caveat that he originated the statement 'as far as I know'. The line is often
attributed to the American actress Lily
Tomlin who, in turn, ascribes it to the writer,
Jane Wagner.

*On 'crossing the floor' of the House of
Commons (i.e. changing political alleg-
iance) more than once:*

8 They say you can rat, but you
can't re-rat.

Winston S. Churchill (later Sir Winston),
British Conservative Prime Minister and
writer (1874–1965). Quoted in John Colville,
The Fringes of Power, Vol.1 (1985) – entry for
26 January 1941. The remark may date from
1923/4 when Churchill rejoined the Conservatives, having earlier left them to join
the Liberals.

On Air Vice-Marshal Bennett, who had joined the Liberals:

1 It [is] the first time that [I have] heard of a rat actually swimming out to join a sinking ship.

Winston Churchill. Quoted in Malcolm Muggeridge, *Like It Was* (1981) – diary entry for 14 February 1948. Later, Ralph Yarborough said of John B. Connally's 1973 switch from Democratic to Republican party in pursuit of the presidential nomination: 'It is the only case on record of a man swimming toward a sinking ship' (quoted in *The Washington Post*, 18 January 1988).

On puppet Roland Rat's success in reversing the fortunes of TV-am, a rival breakfast television station (1983):

2 This must be the first time a rat has come to the aid of a sinking ship.

Anonymous BBC spokesman. Quoted on BBC Radio *Quote...Unquote* (25 August 1984).

Ravishment

3 It is impossible to ravish me I'm so willing.

John Fletcher, English playwright (1579–1625). *The Faithful Shepherdess*, Act 3, Sc. 1 (1610).

4 I have been more ravished myself than any body since the Trojan war.

Lord Byron, English poet (1788–1824). Letter to Hoppner (1819).

5 He in a few minutes ravished this fair creature, or at least would have ravished her, if she had not, by a timely compliance, prevented him.

Henry Fielding, English novelist and judge (1707–54). *Jonathan Wild*, Bk 3, Chap.7 (1743).

6 Some things can't be ravished. You can't ravish a tin of sardines.

D. H. Lawrence, English novelist and poet (1885–1930). *Lady Chatterley's Lover*, Chap. 8 (1928).

Reading

To an author who had sent him an unsolicited manuscript:

7 Many thanks; I shall lose no time in reading it.

Benjamin Disraeli (later 1st Earl of Beaconsfield), British Conservative Prime Minister and writer (1804–81). Quoted in Wilfrid Meynell, *The Man Disraeli* (1903).

Of Aldous Huxley:

8 You could always tell by his conversation which volume of the *Encyclopedia Brittanica* he'd been reading. One day it would be Alps, Andes and Apennines, and the next it would be the Himalayas and the Hippocratic Oath.

Bertrand Russell (3rd Earl Russell), English philosopher and mathematician (1872–1970). Letter to R. W. Clark (July 1965).

To Melvyn Bragg when no one in the audience admitted to having read any of his novels:

9 You're going to have to slow down. We can't keep up with you!

Dame Edna Everage (Barry Humphries, Australian entertainer, 1934–). TV show *An Audience With Dame Edna Everage* (1980/1).

Reagan, Ronald
American film actor and Republican President (1911–)

10 A triumph of the embalmer's art.

Gore Vidal, American novelist, playwright and critic (1925–). Quoted in *The Observer* (26 April 1981).

11 He does not dye his hair – he bleaches his face.

Gore Vidal. Quoted in *A Year of Stings and Squelches* (1985).

12 He doesn't dye his hair. He's just prematurely orange.

Gerald Ford, American Republican President (1913–). Quoted in Ned Sherrin, *Cutting Edge* (1984).

13 After carefully watching Ronald Reagan, he is attempting a great break-through in political technology – he has been

perfecting the Teflon-coated Presidency. He sees to it that nothing sticks to him.

Patricia Schroeder, American Democratic politician (1940–). Speech in the US House of Representatives (2 August 1983).

1 We've got the kind of President who thinks arms control means some kind of deodorant.

Patricia Schroeder. Quoted in *The Observer*, 'Sayings of the Week' (9 August 1987).

When it was announced that Ronald Reagan was going to stand for the governorship of California:

2 All wrong. Jimmy Stewart for governor, Reagan for best friend.

Jack L. Warner, American film producer (1892–1978). Quoted in Max Wilk, *The Wit and Wisdom of Hollywood* (1972) and Edmund G. & Bill Brown, *Reagan: The Political Chameleon* (1976).

Doing a microphone test prior to a brodcast:

3 My fellow Americans, I am pleased to tell you that I have signed legislation to outlaw Russia for ever. We begin bombing in five minutes.

Ronald Reagan. Audio recording (13 August 1984).

Reality

4 Reality is a delusion created by an alcohol deficiency.

Anonymous (graffito). Quoted on BBC Radio *Quote . . . Unquote* (7 June 1979).

Recession

5 It's a recession when your neighbour loses his job: it's a depression when you lose yours.

Harry S Truman, American Democratic President (1884–1972). Quoted in *The Observer* (13 April 1958).

Recordings

6 Phonograph, *n*. An irritating toy that restores life to dead noises.

Ambrose Bierce, American journalist (1842–?1914). *The Cynic's Word Book* (later retitled *The Devil's Dictionary*) (1906).

7 Sir, I have tested your machine [a gramophone]. It adds new terror to life and makes death a long-felt want.

Sir Herbert Beerbohm Tree, English actor-manager (1853–1917). Quoted in Hesketh Pearson, *Beerbohm Tree* (1956).

Rectification

8 Once the toothpaste is out of the tube, it is awfully hard to get it back in.

H. R. Haldeman, American government official (1926–93). Remark to John Dean on the Watergate affair (8 April 1973) and reported in *Hearings Before the Select Committee on Presidential Campaign Activities: Watergate and Related Activities* (Vol. 4, 1973). The remark has been wrongly attributed to his colleague, John D. Ehrlichman, and to President Nixon, but it is probably not an original expression in any case.

Reform

9 Any reform that does not result in the exact opposite of what it was intended to do must be considered a success.

Anonymous. Quoted by Katharine Whitehorn in letter to the author (21 January 1992).

10 Every reform, however necessary, will by weak minds be carried to an excess which will itself need reforming.

Samuel Taylor Coleridge, English poet and writer (1772–1834). *Biographia Literaria* (1815–16).

Regent, Prince (later George IV)
British prince (1762–1830)

11 Tell me, Alvanley, who is your fat friend?

Beau Brummell, English dandy (1778–1840). Quoted in Capt. Jesse, *Life of George Brummell* (1844). A famous question to Lord Alvanley about the Prince Regent. Brummell, almost a dandy by profession, had fallen out with the Prince of Wales. He is said to have annoyed the Prince by ridiculing his mistress and also by saying once to his royal guest at dinner, 'Wales, ring the bell, will you?' When they met in London in July 1813, the Prince cut Brummell but greeted his companion. As the Prince walked off, Brummell put his question in ringing tones.

Regimen

1 Early to rise and early to bed makes
a male healthy and wealthy and dead.

James Thurber, American cartoonist and writer
(1894–1961). 'The Shrike and the Chipmunks',
Fables for Our Time (1940).

Regrets

When asked if he had any regrets:

2 Yes, I haven't had enough sex.

(Sir) John Betjeman, English poet (1906–84).
On BBC TV, *Time With Betjeman* (February
1983).

Rejection

Rejection slip when editor of The American
Mercury:

3 Mr Mencken has just entered a trappist
monastery in Kentucky and left strict
instructions that no mail was to be
forwarded. The enclosed is returned
therefore for your archives.

H. L. Mencken, American journalist and
linguist (1880–1956). Quoted on BBC Radio
Quote . . . Unquote (19 January 1982).

4 Look here, Steward, if this is coffee,
I want tea; but if this is tea, then I wish
for coffee.

G. D. Armour, English cartoonist. *Punch*,
Vol. 123 (23 July 1902). Robert Byrne in *The
637 Best Things Anybody Ever Said* (1982)
ascribes the line to Abraham Lincoln, as does
The Treasury of Humorous Quotations, ed. Evan
Esar & Nicolas Bentley (1951).

Relations

5 [Friends are] God's apology for relations.

Hugh Kingsmill, English writer (1889–1949).
Quoted in Michael Holroyd, *The Best of Hugh
Kingsmill* (1970). The origin of the saying has
been said to lie in a Spanish proverb.

Relativity

6 When a man sits with a pretty girl for
an hour, it seems like a minute. But let
him sit on a hot stove for a minute –
and it's longer than any hour. That's
relativity.

Albert Einstein, German-born physicist

(1879–1955). Quoted in Barbara Rowes, *The
Book of Quotes* (1979).

Religion

7 It is the test of a good religion whether
you can joke about it.

G. K. Chesterton, English poet, novelist and
critic (1874–1936). Quoted in Herbert
V. Prochnow, Snr & Jnr, *A Treasury of Humorous Quotations* (1969).

Repartee

*When a woman said to him, 'I could give
you tit for tat any time':*

8 Tat!

Calvin Coolidge, American Republican
President (1872–1933). Quoted on BBC
Radio *Quote . . . Unquote* (2 March 1982).

Replies

*Message telegraphed to the Prince of Wales
(presumably the future Edward VII), on
receiving a dinner invitation at short notice:*

9 VERY SORRY CAN'T COME. LIE
FOLLOWS BY POST.

Lord Charles Beresford, English politician
(1846–1919). Quoted in Ralph Nevill,
The World of Fashion 1837–1922 (1923).
The same joke occurs in Marcel Proust,
Le Temps Retrouvé (published in 1927 after his
death in 1922), in the form: 'One of those
telegrams of which M. de Guermantes has
wittily fixed the formula: "Can't come, lie
follows [*Impossible venir, mensonge suit*]."'

Reports

10 The report of my death was an
exaggeration.

Mark Twain, American writer (1835–1910).
Twain's reaction to a false report, quoted in the
New York Journal (2 June 1897). Frequently
over-quoted and paraphrased ever since, this
has become the inevitable remark to invoke
when someone's death has been wrongly
reported (most usually one's own). Twain's own
version of the incident appears in A. B. Paine,
Mark Twain: A Biography (1912): [when a
reporter called regarding reports of his death
with an order to write 5,000 words if very ill,
1,000 if dead] 'You don't need as much as that.
Just say the report of my death has been grossly
exaggerated.'

Research

1 In that state of resentful coma that they dignified by the name of research.

Harold Laski, English political scientist (1893– 1950). In one of his letters to Oliver Wendell Holmes Jr (dated 10 October 1922, published 1953).

Resemblance

Of Anna Pavlova, Russian ballerina (1885– 1931) when making her last appearance in Edinburgh:

2 She's awfully like Mrs Wishart ...

Anonymous Scotswoman. Eric Maschwitz in *No Chip on My Shoulder* (1957) pinpoints the originator of the tale as Walford Hyden, a conductor who accompanied Pavlova on her world tours. His version: when she gave a performance of 'The Dying Swan' in Glasgow and finally sank to the floor in her feathered costume, Hyden heard a woman in the front row observe to her companion, 'Aye, she is awfu' like Mrs Wishart.'

Responsibility

3 Do you realize the responsibility I carry? I'm the only person standing between Nixon and the White House.

John F. Kennedy, American Democratic President (1917–63). Remark (13 October 1960), quoted in Arthur M. Schlesinger Jr, *A Thousand Days* (1965).

Restaurants

4 Avoid approaching horses and restaurants from the rear.

Anonymous. Quoted in *The 'Quote ... Unquote' Newsletter* (October 1994). A modern proverb contributed by Miss O. E. Burns of Stourbridge.

Revelations

On Earl Haig:

5 With the publication of his Private Papers in 1952, he committed suicide twenty-five years after his death.

David Lloyd George (1st Earl Lloyd George of Dwyfor), British Liberal Prime Minister (1863–1945). *Men and Power* (1956).

Reviews

6 A bad review is even less important than whether it is raining in Patagonia.

Iris Murdoch (later Dame Iris), English novelist and philosopher (1919–). Quoted in a profile in *The Times* (6 July 1989).

7 A bad review may spoil your breakfast but you shouldn't allow it to spoil your lunch.

(Sir) Kingsley Amis, English novelist, poet and critic (1922–95). Quoted in the *Independent on Sunday* (6 September 1992).

Revolution

8 Come the revolution, everyone will eat strawberries and cream.
But, Comrade, I don't like strawberries and cream.
Come the revolution, everyone will eat strawberries and cream!

Willis Howard, American vaudeville comedian (1899–?). Attributed. Also included as an anonymous Jewish joke in Leo Rosten, *The Joys of Yiddish* (1968).

Rewrites

Alterations ordered to the script of The Bed-Sitting Room *(1963) by John Antrobus and Spike Milligan:*

9 Omit 'You get all the dirt off the tail of your shirt.' Substitute 'You get all the dirt off the front of your shirt' ... Omit the song 'Plastic Mac Man' and substitute 'Oh you dirty young devil, how dare you presume to wet the bed when the po's in the room. I'll wallop your bum with a dirty great broom when I get up in the morning.'

Office of the Lord Chamberlain, British theatre censor until 1968. Quoted in Kenneth Tynan, *Tynan Right and Left* (1967).

10 Ah, did you once see Shelley plain? And was he such a frightful pain ...?

Anonymous. With apologies to Browning. Quoted in *The 'Quote ... Unquote' Newsletter* (January 1993). Most of the following are 'deflating additions' as they were called in *New Statesman* competitions of yesteryear:

1 When you are old and grey and full
   of sleep
You haven't got to bother counting
sheep.

W. B. Yeats, done over by H. A. C. Evans.

2 When lovely woman stoops to folly
The evening can be awfully jolly.

Oliver Goldsmith, done over by Mary
Demetriadis.

3 Yet once more, O ye Laurels, and once
   more,
I deliver the 'Telegraph' under the door.

John Milton, altered by Edward Blishen,
English writer (1920–96).

4 Full fathom five thy father lies,
His aqualung was the wrong size.

Shakespeare, seen to by June Mercer Langfield.

5 Birds in their little nests agree
With Chinamen but not with me.

Hilaire Belloc once capped a line by Isaac
Watts, thus.

6 Earth has not anything to show
   more fair
Than Auntie Mabel since she bleached
her hair.

Harold Ollerenshaw. Quoted in The 'Quote …
Unquote' Newsletter (April 1993). With
apologies to Wordsworth.

Rhodes, Cecil
**English-born South African colonialist
(1853–1902)**

7 I admire him, I frankly confess it. When
his time comes I shall buy a piece of
rope for a keepsake.

Mark Twain, American writer (1835–1910).
Following the Equator (1897).

Rich and Poor

8 F. SCOTT FITZGERALD: The very rich
are different from you and me.
HEMINGWAY: Yes, they have more
money.

Ernest Hemingway, American novelist (1899–
1961). In Tom Burnam, More Misinformation
(1980), the facts are neatly established about
this famous exchange. In his short story 'The
Rich Boy' (1926) Fitzgerald had written:

'Let me tell you about the very rich. They are
different from you and me.' Twelve years later
in his short story 'The Snows of Kilimanjaro'
(1938) Hemingway had the narrator remember 'poor Scott Fitzgerald', his awe of the rich
and that 'someone' had said, 'Yes, they have
more money'.

When Fitzgerald read the story, he protested
to Hemingway who dropped Fitzgerald's
name from further printings. In any case, the
put-down 'Yes, they have more money' had
not been administered to Fitzgerald but to
Hemingway himself. In 1936, Hemingway
said at a lunch with the critic Mary Colum:
'I am getting to know the rich.' She replied:
'The only difference between the rich and
other people is that the rich have more money.'
Also discussed in Scott and Ernest (1978) by
Mathew J. Bruccoli. Compare: 'The Rich
aren't like us – they pay less taxes' – Peter de
Vries, in The Washington Post (30 July 1989).

9 I've been rich and I've been poor.
Believe me, honey, rich is better.

Sophie Tucker, Russian-born American
entertainer (1884–1966). Attributed but un-
sourced. However, 'I've been rich and I've been
poor; believe me rich is better' is definitely
spoken by Gloria Grahame in the film The
Big Heat (US, 1953), screenplay by Sydney
Boehm from the story by William P.
McGivern.

Riddles

10 Why is a raven like a writing desk?

Lewis Carroll (C. L. Dodgson), English writer
(1832–98). Alice's Adventures in Wonderland,
Chap. 7 (1865). The Hatter poses this riddle
at the 'Mad Tea-Party', but Carroll stated positively that there was no answer. Nevertheless,
various people have tried to supply one:
'a quill' – what a raven and a writing desk
would have had in common in the last century
(Christopher Brown of Portswood, Southampton); 'they both begin with the letter R' (Leo
Harris); 'because it can produce a few notes,
tho they are very flat; and it is never put with
the wrong end in front' – these were Lewis
Carroll's own possible solutions (1896
edition); 'because the notes for which they are
noted are not noted for being musical notes'
(Sam Loyd); 'Edgar Allan Poe' – he wrote on
both a raven and a writing desk (Sam Loyd);
'because bills and tales (tails) are among their
characteristics; because they both stand on

their legs; conceal their steels (steals); and ought to be made to shut up' (Sam Loyd); 'because it slopes with a flap' (A. Cyril Pearson); 'because there is a "B" in "both"' (Dr E. V. Rieu). Some of these solutions are included in *The Annotated Alice*, ed. Martin Gardner (1960).

Right

1 Always do right. This will gratify some people, and astonish the rest.

Mark Twain, American writer (1835–1910). Talk to young people, Brooklyn (16 February 1901), included as 'Frontispiece', *Mark Twain in Eruption*, ed. Bernard de Vote (1940). President Truman kept this saying on his desk.

Ripostes

2 EARL OF SANDWICH: 'Pon my soul, Wilkes, I don't know whether you'll die upon the gallows or of the pox.
   WILKES: That depends, my Lord, whether I first embrace your Lordship's principles, or your Lordship's mistresses.

John Wilkes, English politician (1727–97). Quoted in Sir Charles Petrie, *The Four Georges* (1935).

Mother at table saying: 'It's broccoli, dear.' Her little girl replies:

3 'I say it's spinach, and I say the hell with it.'

Elwyn Brooks White, American humorist (1899–1985). Caption devised for a cartoon by Carl Rose in *The New Yorker* (8 December 1928).

In answer to a heckler who cried, 'I wouldn't vote for you if you were the Archangel Gabriel':

4 If I were the Archangel Gabriel, madam, I'm afraid you would not be in my constituency.

Sir Robert Menzies, Australian Liberal Prime Minister (1894–1978). Quoted in R. Robinson, *The Wit of Sir Robert Menzies* (1966).

Replying to Mr Dundas in the House of Commons:

5 The Right Honourable Gentleman is

indebted to his memory for his jests, and to his imagination for his facts.

Richard Brinsley Sheridan, English dramatist and politician (1751–1816). Quoted in T. Moore, *Life of Sheridan* (1825).

One Saturday night, the actor playing the lead in Shakespeare's Richard III *had taken rather too much drink with a fellow cast member prior to the performance. This fact communicated itself to the audience when he came on swaying like a ship at sea. Someone shouted, 'Get off – you're drunk!' At which the actor, steadying himself, replied:*

6 Who, me? Drunk? Just wait till you see Buckingham!

Anonymous. Quoted by Sir Cedric Hardwicke in *A Victorian in Orbit* (1961). Sometimes told as though involving Wilfred Lawson, a noted tippler, though he does not appear to have played either part.

A magazine writer preparing a profile of Cary Grant sent a cable to his agent inquiring, 'HOW OLD CARY GRANT?' Grant sent the reply himself:

7 CARY GRANT FINE. HOW YOU?

Cary Grant, English-born American film actor (1904–86). Quoted in Leslie Halliwell, *The Filmgoer's Book of Quotes* (1973).

When interviewing Mae West and encouraged by her PR man to try and sound a bit more 'sexy':

8 If, sir, I possessed the power of conveying unlimited sexual attraction through the potency of my voice, I would not be reduced to accepting a miserable pittance from the BBC for interviewing a faded female in a damp basement.

Gilbert Harding, English radio and TV personality (1907–60). Quoted by Wynford Vaughan-Thomas in *Gilbert Harding By His Friends* (1961).

On being asked if he had ever smoked a marijuana cigarette in the permissive Sixties:

9 Only when committing adultery.

Senator Wyche Fowler, American politician. Quoted in *The Oxford Dictionary of Humorous Quotations*, ed. Ned Sherrin (1995).

Rise and Fall

1 [Always] be nice to people on your way up, because you'll meet 'em on your way down.

Wilson Mizner, American playwright (1876– 1933). Quoted in Alva Johnston, *The Legendary Mizners* (1953). Also ascribed to Jimmy Durante and others.

Rivalry

2 Every time Mr Macmillan comes back from abroad, Mr Butler goes to the airport and grips him warmly by the throat.

Harold Wilson (later Lord Wilson of Rievaulx), British Labour Prime Minister (1916–95). Quoted in Leslie Smith, *Harold Wilson* (1964).

Roads

3 Before the Roman came to Rye or out to Severn strode,
The rolling English drunkard made the rolling English road.

G. K. Chesterton, English poet, novelist and critic (1874–1936). 'The Rolling English Road', *The Flying Inn* (1914).

Roses

4 A rose by any other name
As sweet would smell –
A rhododendron, by any other name,
Would be much easier to spell.

Anonymous. Quoted in book *Quote ... Unquote* (1978).

Rosebery, Archibald Primrose, 5th Earl of
British Liberal Prime Minister (1847–1929)

5 A man who never missed an occasion to let slip an opportunity.

Bernard Shaw, Irish playwright and critic (1856–1950). Quoted in Robert Rhodes James, *Rosebery* (1963), as the 'man who never missed a chance of missing an opportunity'.

Royal jokes

6 No more coals to Newcastle, no more Hoares to Paris.

George V, British King (1865–1936). Quoted in the Earl of Avon, *Facing the Dictators* (1962). This rare example of a royal joke comes from the period just before George V's death. In December 1935, it was revealed that Sir Samuel Hoare, the Foreign Secretary, had come to an arrangement with Pierre Laval, his French counterpart, whereby Abyssinia was virtually to be consigned to the Italians behind the League of Nations' back. The Hoare-Laval Pact had been concluded in Paris when Sir Samuel was passing through on his way to a holiday in Switzerland. In the furore that followed he had to resign. The King may have been repeating a remark that was current anyway and it is surely unlikely that he made it direct to Hoare himself, despite Lord Avon's recollection of what the King told him.

When a fishbone lodged in her throat:

7 The salmon are striking back.

Queen Elizabeth the Queen Mother. Quoted in Compton Miller, *Who's Really Who* (1983).

To her daughter, when the Queen accepted a second glass of wine at lunch:

8 Do you think it's wise, darling? You know you've got to rule this afternoon.

Queen Elizabeth the Queen Mother. Quoted in Compton Miller, *Who's Really Who* (1983).

Rule

9 The golden rule is that there are no golden rules.

Bernard Shaw, Irish playwright and critic (1856–1950). 'Maxims for Revolutionists', *Man and Superman* (1903).

Running

The Red Queen:

10 Now, here, you see, it takes all the running you can do, to keep in the same place. If you want to get somewhere else, you must run at least twice as fast as that.

Lewis Carroll (C. L. Dodgson), English writer (1832–98). *Through the Looking-Glass and What Alice Found There*, Chap. 2 (1872).

S

Sack

On being replaced in the Shadow Cabinet by a man four years his senior:

1 There comes a time in every man's life when he must make way for an older man.

Reginald Maudling, English Conservative politician (1917–77). Reported in *The Guardian* (20 November 1976). He also said at that time: 'I have never been sacked before. I was appointed by Winston Churchill and I am now being dismissed by Margaret Thatcher. Life goes on. The world changes.'

Sackville-West, Vita
English novelist and poet (1892–1962)

2 She looked like Lady Chatterley above the waist and the gamekeeper below.

Cyril Connolly, English writer and critic (1903–74). Attributed. Alluded to in Peter Quennell, *Customs and Characters* (1982): the poet's appearance was 'strange almost beyond the reach of adjectives ... she resembled a puissant blend of both sexes – Lady Chatterley and her lover rolled into one, I recollect a contemporary humorist observing ... her legs, which reminded [Virginia] Woolf of stalwart tree trunks, were encased in a gamekeeper's breeches and top-boots laced up to the knee.' By 'contemporary humorist' he probably meant Connolly, who went with him on a joint visit to Sackville-West at Sissinghurst in 1936.

Safety

3 When I take a gun in hand, the safest place for a pheasant is just opposite the muzzle.

Revd Sydney Smith, English clergyman, essayist and wit (1771–1845). Quoted in *The Treasury of Humorous Quotations*, ed. Evan Esar & Nicolas Bentley (1951).

Salaries

4 The salary of the chief executive of the large corporation is not a market award for achievement. It is frequently in the nature of a warm personal gesture by the individual to himself.

John Kenneth Galbraith, Canadian-born American economist (1908–). *Annals of an Abiding Liberal* (1979).

Sang-froid

On being found drinking a glass of wine in the street, when watching the Drury Lane Theatre, which he owned, burning down (24 February 1809):

5 A man may surely be allowed to take a glass of wine by his own fireside.

Richard Brinsley Sheridan, English dramatist and politician (1751–1816). Reported in T. Moore, *Life of Sheridan* (1825).

Sarcasm

6 Sarcasm is the lowest form of wit.

Anonymous proverbial saying. Quoted in Greville Janner, *Janner's Complete Letter-writer* (1989). Origin obscure. Thomas Carlyle remarked in *Sartor Resartus*, II.iv (1834) that, 'Sarcasm is the language of the devil'. The more usual observation is that 'Punning is the lowest form of wit', which probably derives from Dryden's comment on Ben Jonson's 'clenches' – 'the lowest and most grovelling kind of wit'.

Satire

7 Satire is what closes Saturday night.

George S. Kaufman, American playwright (1889–1961). Quoted in Scott Meredith, *George S. Kaufman and the Algonquin Round Table* (1974).

1 Well, it was satire, wasn't it? ...You can say bum, you can say po, you can say anything ... Well, he said it! The thin one! He said bum one night. I heard him! Satire!

Keith Waterhouse and Willis Hall, English writers (1929–) and (1929–). Sketch, 'Close Down', BBC TV *That Was the Week That Was* (1962–3).

2 Satire is a kind of glass, wherein beholders do generally discover everybody's face but their own.

Jonathan Swift, Anglo-Irish writer and clergyman (1667–1745). Preface, *The Battle of the Books* (1704).

3 To hear some people talk, you would think humour was an aspect of satire, instead of the other way round. Satire is simply humour in uniform.

Paul Jennings, English humorist (1918–90). Quoted in his obituary in *The Guardian* (1 January 1990).

4 The purpose of satire it has been rightly said is to strip off the veneer of comforting illusion and cosy half-truth and our job, as I see it, is to put it back again.

Michael Flanders, English writer and entertainer (1922–75). *At the Drop of Another Hat* (1963).

Saving

5 Saving is a very fine thing especially when your parents have done it for you.

Winston S. Churchill (later Sir Winston), British Conservative Prime Minister and writer (1874–1965). Quoted in Fred Metcalf, *The Penguin Dictionary of Modern Humorous Quotations* (1987).

Schedule

6 There cannot be a crisis next week. My schedule is already full.

Henry Kissinger, American Republican politician (1923–). Quoted in *The New York Times* Magazine (1 June 1969).

Scientists

7 When I find myself in the company of scientists, I feel like a shabby curate who has strayed by mistake into a drawing room full of dukes.

W. H. Auden, Anglo-American poet (1907–73). 'The Poet and the City', in *The Dyer's Hand* (1962).

Scotsmen and Scottishness

8 Sir, let me tell you, the noblest prospect which a Scotsman ever sees, is the high road that leads him to England!

Samuel Johnson, English writer and lexicographer (1709–84). In James Boswell, *Life of Johnson* (1791) – for 6 July 1763. Johnson no doubt enjoyed baiting the Scotsman Boswell in this fashion, but his biographer records how 'this unexpected and pointed sally produced a roar of applause'.

9 It requires a surgical operation to get a joke well into a Scotch understanding. Their only idea of wit, or rather that inferior variety of the electric talent which prevails occasionally in the North, and which, under the name of WUT, is so infinitely distressing to people of good taste, is laughing immoderately at stated intervals.

Revd Sydney Smith, English clergyman, essayist and wit (1771–1845). Quoted in Saba, Lady Holland, *A Memoir of Sydney Smith* (1855). In J. M. Barrie's play *What Every Woman Knows* (1908), this remark is built upon further to undermine a humourless Scotsman, John Shand: 'I remember reading of someone that said it needed a surgical operation to get a joke into a Scotsman's head.' 'Yes, that's been said.' 'What beats me, Maggie, is how you could insert a joke with an operation.'

10 I proposed that we should set up a Review, and I remained long enough in Edinburgh to edit the first number. The motto I proposed for the Review was *Tenui musam meditamur avena* – 'we cultivate literature on a little oatmeal'. But this was too near the truth to be admitted.

Revd Sydney Smith. Quoted in Saba, Lady Holland, *A Memoir of Sydney Smith* (1855).

Said by a Scotsman who has just been on a visit to London:

1 Mun, a had na' been the-ere abune twa hoours when – *Bang* – went *Saxpence*!

Anonymous (caption to cartoon). *Punch*, Vol. 54 (5 December 1868).

2 I never met with any one Scotchman but what was a man of sense ... everybody of that country who has any leaves it as fast as they can.

Francis Lockier, English divine and essayist (1667–1740). Quoted in *The Treasury of Humorous Quotations*, ed. Evan Esar & Nicolas Bentley (1951).

3 I have been trying all my life to like Scotchmen, and am obliged to desist from the experiment in despair.

Charles Lamb, English writer (1775–1834). Quoted in *The Treasury of Humorous Quotations*, ed. Evan Esar & Nicolas Bentley (1951).

Screenwriting

4 'Oh, son, I wish you hadn't become a scenario writer!' she sniffed.
  'Aw, now, Moms,' I comforted her, 'it's no worse than playing the piano in a call house.'

S. J. Perelman, American humorist (1904–79). 'Strictly from Hunger' – which later became the title of his second book (1937).

Screwing

On her lover Johnny Stompanato's use of her money in 1958:

5 I wonder if the screwing I'm getting is worth the screwing I'm getting.

Lana Turner, American film actress (1920–). Quoted in Bob Chieger, *Was It Good For You Too?* (1983).

Sculptors

6 Patriotism is the last refuge of the sculptor.

William Plomer, English writer and poet (1903–73). Quoted in *The Lyttelton Hart-Davis Letters*, Vol. 2 (1979 – for 13 October 1956).

Sea

On the state of England:

7 Everything's at sea – except the Fleet.

Horace Walpole (4th Earl of Orford), English writer (1717–97). Quoted by Malcolm Muggeridge on BBC Radio *Quote ... Unquote* (21 June 1978).

Seals

8 All right, have it your way – you heard a seal bark.

James Thurber, American cartoonist and writer (1894–1961). Caption to cartoon 'The Seal in the Bedroom' in *The New Yorker* (1932).

Secrets

9 Three may keep a secret, if two of them are dead.

Benjamin Franklin, American politician and scientist (1706– z90). *Poor Richard's Almanack* (July 1735) – a work in which Franklin often revised already existing sayings.

Self-indulgence

After Lord Hailsham's comments on John Profumo's frailties in 1963:

10 From Lord Hailsham we have had a virtuoso performance in the art of kicking a fallen friend in the guts ... When self-indulgence has reduced a man to the shape of Lord Hailsham, sexual continence requires no more than a sense of the ridiculous.

Reginald Paget (later Lord Paget), English lawyer and Labour politician (1908–90). Quoted in Ned Sherrin, *Cutting Edge* (1984).

Self-made

11 Self-made men are most alwus apt tew be a leetle too proud ov the job.

Josh Billings (Henry Wheeler Shaw), American humorist (1818–85). 'Koarse Shot' in *Everybody's Friend*; and in *Josh Billing's Encyclopedia and Proverbial Philosophy of Wit and Humor* (1874).

Of Benjamin Disraeli:

12 He is a self-made man and worships his creator.

John Bright, English Radical politician

(1811–89). Attributed. *H. L. Mencken's Dictionary of Quotations* (1942) has, rather, Henry Clapp saying this (*c.*1858) about Horace Greeley, and dates Bright's use of the saying about Benjamin Disraeli ten years later, to *c.*1868. Leon Harris, in *The Fine Art of Political Wit* (1965), has Disraeli saying it about Bright.

1 The trouble with self-made men is that they're working with inferior materials.

Anonymous. Quoted in *Picking on Men*, compiled by Judy Allen (1985).

2 Self-made men are very apt to usurp the prerogative of the Almighty and overwork themselves.

Edgar Wilson ('Bill') Nye, American humorist (1850–96). Quoted in Herbert V. Prochnow, Snr & Jnr, *A Treasury of Humorous Quotations* (1969).

3 He was a self-made man who owed his lack of success to nobody.

Joseph Heller, American novelist (1923–). *Catch-22*, Chap. 3 (1961).

4 Self-made man, you know. They know how to talk. They do deserve more credit than any other breed of men, yes, that is true, and they are among the very first to find it out, too.

Mark Twain, American writer (1835–1910). *A Connecticut Yankee in King Arthur's Court* (1889).

Self-regard

5 That favourite subject, Myself.

James Boswell, Scottish lawyer, biographer and diarist (1740–95). Letter to William Temple (26 July 1763), quoted in Boswell's *Life of Johnson* (1791).

On being awarded the Order of Merit in 1977:

6 I've only two things to say about it. First I deserve it. Second, they've been too long about giving me it. There'll be another vacancy very soon.

J. B. Priestley, English playwright, novelist and author (1894–1984). In radio interview (October 1977), quoted in John Braine, *J. B. Priestley* (1978).

7 Faith, that's as well said, as if I had said it myself.

Jonathan Swift, Anglo-Irish writer and clergyman (1667–1745). *Polite Conversation* (1738) – a compendium of traditional conversational expressions.

Of her former husband, George Sanders:

8 We were both in love with George Sanders.

Zsa Zsa Gabor, Hungarian-born film actress (1919–). Quoted in *A Year of Stings and Squelches* (1985).

9 To love oneself is the beginning of a lifelong romance.

Oscar Wilde, Irish playwright, poet and wit (1854–1900). *An Ideal Husband*, Act 3 (1895).

10 He that falls in love with himself, will have no rivals.

Benjamin Franklin, American politician and scientist (1706–90). *Poor Richard's Almanack* (May 1738) – a work in which Franklin often revised already existing sayings.

11 Sal laughs at every thing you say. Why? Because she has fine teeth.

Benjamin Franklin in *ibid.*

When President Eisenhower's death prevented her from being on the cover of Newsweek *Magazine:*

12 Fourteen heart attacks and he had to die in my week. In MY week.

Janis Joplin, American rock musician (1943– 70). In *New Musical Express* (12 April 1969).

To George Gershwin:

13 Tell me, George, if you had to do it all over would you fall in love with yourself again?

Oscar Levant, American pianist and actor (1906–72). Quoted in David Ewen, *The Story of George Gershwin* (1943). In the Gershwin biopic *Rhapsody in Blue* (1945) Levant (playing himself) got to repeat the line. He is also reputed to have told Gershwin once: 'George, why don't you sit down and play us a medley of your hit.'

Sequels

On the vogue for sequels:

1 It adds a new terror to the death of the novelist.

Peter Ackroyd, English novelist (1949–).
In *The Independent on Sunday* (22 September 1996).

Serendipity

2 Serendipity means searching for a needle in a haystack and instead finding a farmer's daughter.

Anonymous. Quoted by the scientist Sir Herman Bondi and reported in *The 'Quote ... Unquote' Newsletter* (July 1995).

Seriousness

Of Lincoln Steffens:

3 Everything serious that he says is a joke and everything humorous that he says is dead serious.

Clarence Darrow, American lawyer (1857–1938). Quoted in *A Year of Stings and Squelches* (1985).

4 The one serious conviction that a man should have is that nothing is to be taken seriously.

Samuel Butler, English author (1835–1902). Quoted in *The Treasury of Humorous Quotations*, ed. Evan Esar & Nicolas Bentley (1951).

Sermons

5 Preaching to some people is like eating custard with a fork. It goes in one ear and out the other.

Anonymous (curate). Quoted on BBC Radio *Quote ... Unquote* (2 February 1982).

Servants

6 *Vivre? les serviteurs feront cela pour nous* [Living? The servants will do that for us].

Philippe-Auguste Villiers de l'Isle Adam, French poet, novelist and playwright (1838–89). Play, *Axël*, Act 4, Sc. 2 (1890).

When told that he looked as though he had slept in his clothes, he is said to have replied:

7 Don't be ridiculous. I pay someone to do that for me.

Victor Mature, American film actor (1915–). Quoted by William Franklyn on BBC Radio *Quote ... Unquote* (20 July 1985).

8 The difference between a man and his valet: they both smoke the same cigars, but only one pays for them.

Robert Frost, American poet (1874–1963). Quoted in *The Treasury of Humorous Quotations*, ed. Evan Esar & Nicolas Bentley (1951).

In the course of a routine house-to-house inquiry in Belgravia, a highly-placed old lady was told of the murder of Sandra Rivett, the nanny it is believed Lord Lucan mistakenly killed instead of his wife. Said she:

9 Oh dear, what a pity. Nannies are so hard to come by these days.

Anonymous. Quoted in *The Sunday Times* Magazine (8 June 1975).

Sex

Written on a photograph that she gave to her fiancé, Harry Richman:

10 To my gorgeous lover, Harry. I'll trade all my It for your that.

Clara Bow, American film actress (1905–65), known as the 'It Girl' – to describe her vivacious sex appeal – after appearing in the film *It* (1928). Quoted in Bob Chieger, *Was It Good for You Too?* (1983).

To Laurence Olivier's five-year-old daughter, Tamsin, when she asked what two dogs were doing together:

11 The doggie in front has suddenly gone blind, and the other one has very kindly offered to push him all the way to St Dunstan's.

Noël Coward (later Sir Noël), English entertainer and writer (1899–1973). Quoted by Kenneth Tynan in *The Observer* (1 April 1973).

12 Cannes is where you lie on the beach and stare at the stars – or vice versa.

Rex Reed, American critic (1938–). Quoted in *Playboy* Magazine (*c.*1980).

13 Sexual intercourse began
In nineteen sixty-three
(Which was rather late for me) –
Between the end of the Chatterley ban
And the Beatles' first LP.

Philip Larkin, English poet (1922–85). 'Annus Mirabilis', *High Windows* (1974).

1 You were born with your legs apart. They'll send you to the grave in a Y-shaped coffin.

Joe Orton, English playwright (1933–67). *What the Butler Saw* (1967).

2 He's got – I don't mean to be – well, he looks like he's got a cheese danish stuffed down his pants!

Tom Wolfe, American novelist and journalist (1931–). *The Bonfire of the Vanities* (1984).

3 This sublime age reduces everything to its quintessence; all periphrases and expletives are so much in disuse, that I suppose soon the only way to making love will be to say 'Lie down'.

Horace Walpole (4th Earl of Orford), English writer (1717–97). Letter to H. S. Conway (23 October 1778).

When asked whether the first person he had experienced sex with was male or female:

4 I was far too polite to ask.

Gore Vidal, American novelist, playwright and critic (1925–). Remark in interview (*c.*1971), quoted in *Forum* (1987).

5 Mad men and lame men copulate best.

Anonymous proverb. Quoted in Walter Redfern, *Clichés and Coinages* (1989). Compare, from the Greek poet Mimnermus (7th century BC): 'The lame copulate best.' Also, Byron may have expressed this thought, for understandable reasons.

6 Sex – the poor man's polo.

Clifford Odets, American playwright (1906– 63). Quoted in *The Penguin Dictionary of Modern Humorous Quotations*, ed. Fred Metcalf (1987).

7 Sex is one of the nine reasons for reincarnation ... The other eight are unimportant.

Henry Miller, American writer (1891–1980). Quoted in *The Penguin Dictionary of Modern Humorous Quotations*, ed. Fred Metcalf (1987).

8 My own belief is that there is hardly anyone whose sexual life, if it were

broadcast would not fill the whole world at large with surprise and horror.

W. Somerset Maugham, English writer (1874– 1965). Quoted in *The Penguin Dictionary of Modern Humorous Quotations*, ed. Fred Metcalf (1987).

9 He had ambitions, at one time, to become a sex maniac, but he failed his practical.

Les Dawson, English comedian (1934–93). Quoted in *The Penguin Dictionary of Modern Humorous Quotations*, ed. Fred Metcalf (1987).

10 At certain times I like sex – like after a cigarette.

Rodney Dangerfield, American comedian (1921–). Quoted in *The Penguin Dictionary of Modern Humorous Quotations*, ed. Fred Metcalf (1987).

11 It has to be admitted that we English have sex on the brain, which is a very unsatisfactory place to have it.

Malcolm Muggeridge, English writer and broadcaster (1903–90). 'Ideas and Men', in *The New York Times* (11 October 1964).

On sex in the age of AIDS:

12 These days, you fuck someone, your arm drops off.

Bette Midler, American actress (1944–). Quoted in *The Independent* (12 November 1988).

13 As I grow older and older
And totter towards the tomb,
I find that I care less and less
Who goes to bed with whom.

Dorothy L. Sayers, English novelist (1893– 1957). 'That's Why I Never Read Modern Novels', quoted in Janet Hitchman, *Such a Strange Lady* (1975).

14 Sex between a man and a woman can be wonderful – provided you get between the right man and the right woman.

Woody Allen, American film actor, writer and director (1937–). Attributed. Compare 'I believe that sex is a beautiful thing between two people. Between five, it's fantastic ...' on Allen's record album *The Nightclub Years 1964–1968* (1972).

15 The psychiatrist asked me if I thought

sex was dirty and I said, 'It is if you're doing it right'.

Woody Allen. Film, *Take the Money and Run* (US, 1969). Compare: 'Is sex dirty? Only if it's done right' – film, *Everything You Always Wanted to Know About Sex* (1972).

1 Fun? That was the most fun I've ever had without laughing.

Woody Allen. Film, *Annie Hall* (US, 1977), written with Marshall Brickman. Alvy speaking. Also attributed to Humphrey Bogart in the form 'It was the most fun I ever had without laughing.'

2 Bed is the poor man's opera.

Anonymous (Italian proverb). Quoted in Aldous Huxley, *Heaven and Hell* (1956). Sometimes given as 'Sex is ...' Compare Charles Baudelaire, *Journaux intimes* (1887): 'Sexuality is the lyricism of the masses.'

On reading Lady Chatterley's Lover *by D. H. Lawrence:*

3 Surely the sex business isn't worth all this damned fuss? I've met only a handful of people who cared a biscuit for it.

T. E. Lawrence, English soldier and writer (1888–1935). Quoted in Christopher Hassall, *Edward Marsh* (1959).

To an admirer:

4 I'll come and make love to you at five o'clock. If I'm late start without me.

Tallulah Bankhead, American actress (1903–68). Quoted in Ted Morgan, *Somerset Maugham* (1980).

5 A little still she strove, and much repented,
And whispering 'I will ne'er consent' – consented.

Lord Byron, English poet (1788–1824). *Don Juan*, Canto 1, St. 117 (1819–24).

6 Prostitutes for pleasure, concubines for service, wives for breeding ... A melon for ecstasy.

Anonymous. The first part was quoted by Pearl Binder (Lady Elwyn-Jones) when she appeared with octogenarian aplomb on BBC Radio *Quote ... Unquote* in 1984. She claimed that Sir Richard Burton had 'borrowed it from Demosthenes'. Alan Brien, who was in attendance, chimed in with, 'And a melon for ecstasy.' This is a separate saying, used as the title of a novel (1971) by John Fortune and John Wells. Apparently, the novelist John Masters once ascribed to a 'Pathan tribesman' the saying 'A woman for duty, a boy for pleasure, a goat for ecstasy' whereas Stephen Fry in *Paperweight* (1992) credits this to the Greeks. Apropos the main quotation, compare John Gay, 'The Toilette' (1716): 'A miss for pleasure, and a wife for breed.'

7 It doesn't matter what you do, as long as you don't do it in the street and frighten the horses.

Mrs Patrick Campbell, English actress (1865–1940). Variously worded. Quoted in Daphne Fielding, *The Duchess of Jermyn Street* (1964), as: 'It doesn't matter what you do in the bedroom as long as you don't do it in the street and frighten the horses.' *The Oxford Dictionary of Quotations* (1979) had, 'I don't mind where people make love, so long as they ...' Margot Peters, in her otherwise painstakingly-footnoted biography Mrs Pat (1984), gives no reason for stating her belief that it was 'when told of a homosexual affair between actors' that the actress uttered: 'I don't care what people do, as long as they don't do it in the street and frighten the horses.'

8 The pleasure is momentary, the position ridiculous, the expense damnable.

Philip Dormer Stanhope, 4th Earl of Chesterfield, English politician and writer (1694–1773). Usually attributed to Chesterfield – though it has not been found in his works – as in *Nature*, Vol. 227 (22 August 1970). An earlier unattached allusion is contained in a letter from Evelyn Waugh to Nancy Mitford (5 May 1954): 'Of children as of procreation – the pleasure momentary, the posture ridiculous, the expense damnable.'

On sex scandal in the newspapers in the age of AIDS:

9 The more you don't do it, the more it's fun to read about.

Caryl Churchill, English playwright (1938–). *Serious Money* (1987).

10 I am always looking for meaningful one-night stands.

Dudley Moore, English musician and actor

(1935–). In 1982 – quoted in Bob Chieger, *Was It Good For You Too?* (1983).

1 The thing that takes the least amount of time and causes the most amount of trouble is sex.

John Barrymore, American actor (1882–1942). Quoted in *The Treasury of Humorous Quotations*, ed. Evan Esar & Nicolas Bentley (1951).

2 My dad told me, 'Anything worth having is worth waiting for.' I waited until I was fifteen.

Zsa Zsa Gabor, Hungarian-born film actress (1919–). In 1981 – quoted in Bob Chieger, *Was It Good For You Too?* (1983).

3 I met my love in the graveyard
I did her before we were wed
I laid her on top of the tombstone
We did it to cheer up the dead.

Brendan Behan, Irish playwright (1923–64). Attributed.

4 I like to wake up feeling a new man.

Jean Harlow, American film actress (1911–37). Quoted in book *Nudge Nudge, Wink Wink* (1986).

On Henry Kissinger:

5 Henry's idea of sex is to slow down to thirty miles an hour when he drops you off at the door.

Barbara Howar, American one-time companion of Kissinger. Quoted in Barbara Rowes, *The Book of Quotes* (1979).

6 Do you think that sex ought to take place before the wedding?
No, not if it delays the ceremony ...

Anonymous. Quoted in the sketch 'Sex' in the Kenneth Williams revue, *One Over the Eight*, London (1961).

7 MRS SWABB: Me, I don't bother with sex. I leave that to the experts.

Alan Bennett, English playwright and actor (1934–). *Habeas Corpus*, Act 1 (1973).

8 When Eve said to Adam
'Start calling me Madam'
The world became far more exciting;
Which turns to confusion,
The modern delusion
That sex is a question of lighting.

Noël Coward (later Sir Noël), English entertainer and writer (1899–1973). Introduction on the album 'Marlene Dietrich at the Café de Paris' (a recording of her London cabaret performance, 1954). Misquoted as 'sex is a question of liking' in *The Observer* (24 March 1992).

9 I caught a thin bat's squeak of sexuality, inaudible to any but me.

Evelyn Waugh, English novelist (1903–66). *Brideshead Revisited*, Chap. 3 (1945).

Sexes

10 This world consists of men, women and Herveys.

Lady Mary Wortley Montagu, English writer (1689–1762). Quoted by Lord Wharncliffe in *The Letters and Works of Lady Mary Wortley Montagu* (1837). Alluding to John Harvey, Baron Hervey of Ickworth (1696–1743), with whom she had some sort of literary friendship. According to the *Dictionary of National Biography*, Hervey had loose morals, was 'effeminate in appearance as well as in habits', but had eight children.

Sexual orientation

11 He was into animal husbandry – until they caught him at it.

Tom Lehrer, American songwriter and entertainer (1928–). On record album *An Evening Wasted with Tom Lehrer* (1953).

When asked, 'Why have you come to America, Mr Thomas?':

12 In pursuit of my life-long quest for naked women in wet mackintoshes.

Dylan Thomas, Welsh poet (1914–53). Quoted in Constantine Fitzgibbon, *Dylan Thomas*, Chap. 8 (1965). Another version from the *Evening Standard* (2 May 1995): 'Asked by the hack pack the reason for his visit to [New York] his succinct reply was: "Naked women in wet macs".'

On being asked by Ian McKellen if he was homosexual:

13 [That's] a bit like asking a man crawling across the Sahara whether he would prefer Perrier or Malvern Water.

Alan Bennett, English playwright and actor (1934–). Quoted in *The Observer* (12 June 1988).

1 I'm all for bringing back the birch,
   but only between consenting adults in
   private.

   Gore Vidal, American novelist, playwright
   and critic (1925–). Interviewed on TV by
   David Frost and quoted in *The Sunday Times*
   Magazine (16 September 1973).

Shakespeare, William
English playwright and poet
(1564–1616)

2 The Devil can quote Shakespeare for
   his own purposes.

   Bernard Shaw, Irish playwright and critic
   (1856–1950). Quoted in *The Treasury of
   Humorous Quotations*, ed. Evan Esar &
   Nicolas Bentley (1951).

3 With the single exception of Homer,
   there is no eminent writer, not even Sir
   Walter Scott, whom I can despise so
   entirely as I despise Shakespear when
   I measure my mind against his ... It
   would positively be a relief to me to dig
   him up and throw stones at him.

   Bernard Shaw. *Dramatic Opinions and Essays*,
   Vol. 2 (1907).

*Contribution to the debate as to whether
Shakespeare or Bacon wrote Shakespeare's
plays:*

4 Beerbohm Tree should play Hamlet.
   Then they should dig up both Shakespeare and Bacon and see which one
   had turned over.

   Bernard Shaw. Quoted on BBC Radio
   Quote ... Unquote (1985), but probably a
   misattribution. Alexander Woollcott wrote in
   While Rome Burns (1934) of a bad actor's
   performance of Hamlet: 'Scholars should
   have kept watch beside the graves of Shakespeare and Bacon to see which one of them
   turned over.'

5 Shakespeare is so tiring. You never
   get a chance to sit down unless you're
   a king.

   Josephine Hull, American actress (1886–
   1957). Quoted in *Time* Magazine
   (16 November 1953).

6 Now we sit through Shakespeare in
   order to recognise the quotations.

Orson Welles, American film director, writer
and actor (1915–85). Quoted in *The Treasury
of Humorous Quotations*, ed. Evan Esar &
Nicolas Bentley (1951). In Prochnow &
Prochnow, *Treasury of Humorous Quotations*
(1969), the remark is ascribed to Oscar Wilde.
Easy to confuse the two, of course ...

7 The remarkable thing about Shakespeare is that he is really very good –
   in spite of all the people who say he is
   very good.

   Robert Graves, English poet (1895–1985).
   Quoted in *The Observer* (6 December 1964).

8 Shake was a dramatist of note;
   He lived by writing things to quote.

   Henry Cuyler Bunner, American humorous
   writer (1855–96). Said to be in 'Shake,
   Mulleary and Go-ethe' (untraced). Quoted in
   The Treasury of Humorous Quotations, ed.
   Evan Esar & Nicolas Bentley (1951).

9 I thought I'd begin with a sonnet by
   Shakespeare but then I thought why
   should I? He never reads any of mine.

   Spike Milligan, English entertainer and writer
   (1918–). Remark at Poetry and Jazz concert,
   Hampstead Town Hall (1961), quoted in
   The Oxford Dictionary of Literary Quotations,
   ed. Peter Kemp (1997).

10 Brush up your Shakespeare,
    Start quoting him now.
    Brush up your Shakespeare
    And the women you will wow ...
    If she says your behaviour is heinous
    Kick her right in the 'Coriolanus'.
    Brush up your Shakespeare
    And they'll all kowtow.

    Cole Porter, American composer and lyricist
    (1891–1964). 'Brush Up Your Shakespeare',
    Kiss Me Kate (1948).

Shaw, (George) Bernard
Irish playwright and critic
(1856–1950)

11 He hasn't an enemy in the world – and
    none of his friends like him.

    Oscar Wilde, Irish playwright, poet and wit
    (1854–1900). Shaw himself quoted this
    remark in *Sixteen Self Sketches* (1949). An early
    appearance occurs in Irvin S. Cobb, *A Laugh
    a Day Keeps the Doctor Away* (1921), in which

someone says of Shaw, 'He's in a fair way to make himself a lot of enemies.' 'Well,' replies Wilde, 'as yet he hasn't become prominent enough to have any enemies. But none of his friends like him.'

1 He writes like a Pakistani who has learned English when he was twelve years old in order to become a chartered accountant.

John Osborne, English playwright (1929–94). Letter to *The Guardian* (undated), quoted in Ned Sherrin, *Cutting Edge* (1984).

2 The first man to have cut a swathe through the theatre and left it strewn with virgins.

Frank Harris, Irish writer and journalist (1856–1931). Quoted in Nancy McPhee, *The Second Book of Insults* (1981).

3 When you were quite a little boy somebody ought to have said 'hush' just once!

Mrs Patrick Campbell, English actress (1865–1940). Letter to Bernard Shaw (1 November 1912).

On the grounds that he was a vegetarian:

4 You are a terrible man, Mr Shaw. One day you'll eat a beefsteak and then God help all women.

Mrs Patrick Campbell. Quoted in Arnold Bennett, *The Journals* (18 June 1919). Alexander Woollcott, *While Rome Burns* (1934), has a slightly different version: 'Some day you'll eat a pork chop, Joey, and then God help all women.'

5 That Bernadette Shaw? What a chatterbox! Nags away from asshole to breakfast-time but never sees what's staring her in the face.

Peter Nichols, English playwright (1927–). *Privates on Parade*, Act 1 Sc. 5 (1977).

Shepherd's pie

6 Shepherd's pie and peppered
With genuine shepherds on top.

Stephen Sondheim, American songwriter (1930–). *Sweeney Todd* (1979). Compare this cartoon caption from *Punch* (30 January 1918): '*Bobbie (who is eating shepherd's pie, and has been told not to be wasteful)* "Mummie,

must I eat this? It's such a *partickerly* nasty bit of the shepherd?"'

Shopkeepers

7 CUSTOMER: D'you serve lobsters?
FISHMONGER: Yessir, we serve anybody.

Charles Graves (untraced). Caption to cartoon in *Punch* (11 January 1933).

Shortcomings

After a streaker disrupted the 1973 Oscar awards ceremony:

8 The only laugh that man will probably ever get is for stripping off and showing his shortcomings.

David Niven, English actor (1910–83). Quoted in *A Year of Stings and Squelches* (1985).

Show business

Stopped at the stage door and asked if he was 'with the show':

9 Well, let's say I'm not against it …

George S. Kaufman, American playwright (1889–1961). Quoted in Scott Meredith, *George S. Kaufman and the Algonquin Round Table* (1974).

Sickness

When told that his boss, whom he disliked, was off sick:

10 Nothing trivial, I trust?

Irvin S. Cobb, American humorist and writer (1876–1944). Recounted in Ralph L. Marquard, *Jokes and Anecdotes* (1977). When Cobb was a reporter on the New York *World*, he had to work under Charles E. Chapin, whom he found to be a difficult boss. Arriving at the office one day, Cobb was told that Chapin was off sick and made this inquiry. Recalled earlier as 'I've just learned about his illness; let's hope it's nothing trivial' in *The Treasury of Humorous Quotations*, ed. Evan Esar & Nicolas Bentley (1951). In Ulick O'Connor's *Oliver St John Gogarty* (1964), John Pentland Mahaffy is quoted as having said of the illness of Traill who had beaten him for the Provostship of Trinity College Dublin (in 1904): 'Nothing trivial, I hope.'

Signs

Warning notice near Milan cathedral:

1 The Sisters, so called, of Mercy solicit tender alms. They harbour all kinds of diseases and have no respect for religion.

Anonymous. Said to have been observed by Mark Twain, but untraced. In John G. Murray, *A Gentleman Publisher's Commonplace Book* (1996), this version is said to have appeared outside an Italian hospital run by nuns: 'These little sisters solicit gentle alms, they do not respect religion and harbour all manner of disease.'

2 When she saw the sign 'Members only' she thought of him.

Spike Milligan, English entertainer and writer (1918–). *Puckoon*, Chap. 3 (1963).

3 ANYONE THROWING STONES AT THIS NOTICE WILL BE PROSECUTED.

Lord Berners, English writer and composer (1883–1950). Quoted in *The Independent on Sunday* (25 July 1993). At least he is said to have had this sign put up at his home, Faringdon House, in Oxfordshire. Compare David Frost's narration from BBC TV's *The Frost Report* (*c*.1966): 'For many of us, authority is summed up by the sign that one of the team found on the Yorkshire Moors which said simply, "It is forbidden to throw stones at this notice".' However, even earlier, *Punch* (22 March 1939) contained a drawing of a notice which stated: 'IT IS FORBIDDEN TO THROW STONES AT THIS NOTICE BOARD.'

Sign from a pub:

4 LADIES UNACCOMPANIED ARE RESPECTFULLY REQUESTED TO USE THE TABLES FOR THEIR REFRESHMENTS AND NOT TO STAND AT THE BAR AND OBLIGE.

Anonymous. Quoted in James Agate. *Ego 3* (1938).

5 It is no good putting up notices saying 'Beware of the bull' because very rude things are sometimes written on them. I have found one of the most effective notices is 'Beware of the Agapanthus'.

Lord Massereene and Ferrard, English politician (1914–93). Speech, House of Lords, on the Wildlife and Countryside Bill (16 December 1980).

Silence

6 The soldier ... of today is ... a quiet, grave man ... perhaps like Count Moltke, 'silent in seven languages'.

Walter Bagehot, English constitutional historian (1826–77). 'Checks and Balances', *The English Constitution* (1867). Referring to the taciturn German, Helmuth Graf von Moltke (1800–91). 'Moltke' is, in consequence, a name given to a taciturn, unsmiling person. Michael Wharton ('Peter Simple' columnist in *The Daily Telegraph*) described in *The Missing Will* (1984) how he was so nicknamed, as a child, by his German grandfather after the famous general, 'who seldom spoke and was said to have smiled only twice in his life'. *Geoffrey Madan's Notebooks* (1981) recorded that these two occasions were 'once when his mother-in-law died, and once when a certain fortress was declared to be impregnable'.

7 Better to keep your mouth shut and appear stupid than to open it and remove all doubt.

Mark Twain, American writer (1835–1910). Attributed but not verified. Quoted in *The Sayings of Mark Twain*, ed. James Munson (1992).

Similes

8 Jeeves coughed one soft, low, gentle cough like a sheep with a blade of grass in its throat.

P. G. Wodehouse (later Sir Pelham) English-born novelist and lyricist (1881–1975). *The Inimitable Jeeves* (1923).

9 I turned to Aunt Agatha, whose demeanour was now rather like that of one who, picking daisies on the railway, has just caught the down express in the small of the back.

P. G. Wodehouse. *The Inimitable Jeeves* (1923).

10 I wish I could shimmy like my sister Kate,
She shivers like the jelly on a plate.

Armand J. Piron and Peter Bocage, American songwriters (1888–1943 and 1887–1967). Song, 'I Wish I Could Shimmy Like My Sister Kate' (1919).

1 Like using a guillotine to cure dandruff.

Clare Boothe Luce, American writer and diplomat (1903–87). Quoted in Laurence J. Peter, *Quotations for Our Time* (1977).

Sin

When asked what a clergyman had said in his sermon on sin:

2 He was against it.

Calvin Coolidge, American Republican President (1872–1933). Quoted in John Hiram McKee, *Coolidge Wit and Wisdom* (1933). Mrs Coolidge said it was just the sort of thing he would have said. Coolidge himself said it would be funnier if it were true.

3 To err is human – but it feels divine.

Mae West, American vaudeville and film actress (1893–1980). Quoted in *The Penguin Dictionary of Modern Humorous Quotations*, ed. Fred Metcalf (1987).

Sincerity

4 A little sincerity is a dangerous thing, and a great deal of it is absolutely fatal.

Oscar Wilde, Irish playwright, poet and wit (1854–1900). *The Critic As Artist* (1890).

Singers

Of Barry Manilow's singing voice:

5 [It sounds like] a bluebottle caught in the curtains.

Jean Rook, English journalist (1932–91). Quoted in Lynn Barber, *Mostly Men* (1991).

6 Swans sing before they die; 'twere no bad thing
Should certain persons die before they sing.

Samuel Taylor Coleridge, English poet and writer (1772–1834). 'On a Volunteer Singer' (1834).

Singing

7 What is too silly to be said can be sung.

Pierre Augustin Caron de Beaumarchais, French playwright (1732–99). Quoted by Philip Larkin in letter to Barbara Pym (22 July 1975).

Sitwell, Edith (Dame Edith)
English poet (1887–1964)

8 She's genuinely bogus.

Christopher Hassall, English writer (1912–63). Quoted in *The Penguin Dictionary of Modern Quotations* (1971).

Sixties, The

9 If you can remember the sixties you weren't really there.

Anonymous. Quoted as said by 'a guy from Jefferson Airplane' – *Today* (2 June 1987); 'The best quote about the period came from a leading American hippie – now, I think, something huge on Wall Street – who said: "If you can remember the sixties, you weren't there." There's a lot of truth in that, though I think he's pointing at certain kinds of substance' – *The Independent* (11 March 1989). This hippie might well have been Jerry Rubin.

Size

Two women were discussing a man, when one of them said:

10 God, he was so small, he had turn-ups in his underpants.

Anonymous. Quoted by Julian Mitchell on BBC Radio *Quote ... Unquote* (5 January 1982).

On the unimpressively physical cast of David Storey's rugby play The Changing Room*:*

11 No, fifteen acorns is hardly worth the price of admission.

Noël Coward (later Sir Noël), English entertainer and writer (1899–1973). Quoted by Kenneth Tynan in *The New York Times* (1970). *See also* 163:11.

On his film Titanic*:*

12 Does this prove once and for all that size does matter?

James Cameron, Canadian-born film director (1954–). Quoted in *The Observer* (25 January 1998).

Slander

To the editors of Confidential *Magazine:*

13 If you continue to publish slanderous pieces about me, I shall feel compelled to cancel my subscription.

Groucho Marx, American comedian (1895–1977). In *The Groucho Letters*, Introduction (1967).

Sleaze

1 I got fed up with all the sex and sleaze and backhanders of rock'n'roll so I went into politics.

Tony Blair, British Labour Prime Minister (1953–). Quoted in *The Observer*, 'Sayings of the Week' (13 November 1994).

Sleep

2 Don't go to sleep, so many people die there.

Mark Twain, American writer (1835–1910). Attributed but not verified. Quoted in *The Sayings of Mark Twain*, ed. James Munson (1992).

Slough (England)

3 Come, friendly bombs, and fall on Slough.
It isn't fit for humans now.

(Sir) John Betjeman, English poet (1906–84). 'Slough' (1937).

Sluggards

4 Up, sluggards, and waste no life; in the grave will be sleeping enough.

Benjamin Franklin, American politician and scientist (1706–90). *Poor Richard's Almanack* (September 1741) – a work in which Franklin often revised already existing sayings.

Smiles

Of Sir Robert Peel:

5 [The Right Honourable Gentleman's smile is] like the silver plate on a coffin.

John Philpot Curran, Irish judge (1750–1817), quoted by Daniel O'Connell in the House of Commons (26 February 1835). Also mistakenly ascribed to Benjamin Disraeli (later 1st Earl of Beaconsfield), British Conservative Prime Minister and writer (1804–81).

6 It takes seventy-two muscles to frown, but only thirteen to smile.

Anonymous. Quoted in Celia Haddon, *The Yearbook of Comfort and Joy* (1991).

Smoking

7 A cigarette is the perfect type of a perfect pleasure. It is exquisite, and it leaves one unsatisfied. What more can one want?

Oscar Wilde, Irish playwright, poet and wit (1854–1900). *The Portrait of Dorian Gray*, Chap. 6 (1891).

Non-smoker to smoker in restaurant:

8 Thank you for not smoking: I hope my food isn't interfering with your cigar.

Mel Calman, English cartoonist (1931–94). Caption to cartoon. Quoted in Nigel Rees, *Best Behaviour* (1992).

9 Cancer cures smoking.

Anonymous. Quoted in Reisner & Wechsler, *Encyclopedia of Graffiti* (1974).

10 I kissed my first woman and smoked my first cigarette on the same day; I have never had time for tobacco since.

Arturo Toscanini, Italian-born operatic and symphonic conductor (1867–1957). Quoted in Herbert V. Prochnow, Snr & Jnr, *A Treasury of Humorous Quotations* (1969).

11 It has always been my rule never to smoke when asleep and never to refrain when awake.

Mark Twain, American writer (1835–1910). Quoted in *The Treasury of Humorous Quotations*, ed. Evan Esar & Nicolas Bentley (1951).

Smoothness

Of a certain Conservative MP:

12 With him, one just has to learn to take the smooth with the smooth.

Anonymous. Quoted by Susan Hill on BBC Radio *Quote … Unquote* (29 August 1980).

Snobbery

13 Sapper, Buchan, Dornford Yates, practitioners in that school of Snobbery with Violence that runs like a thread of good-class tweed through twentieth-century literature.

Alan Bennett, English playwright and actor (1934–). *Forty Years On*, Act 2 (1969). In his preface to the published text of *Forty Years On and Other Plays* (1991), Bennett states that he thought he had invented the phrase but was then told it had been used before: it was the title of a pamphlet by the New Zealand eccentric, Count Potocki de Montalk. *Snobbery with Violence. A Poet in Gaol* was published in 1932.

Snoring

1 Laugh and the world laughs with you; Snore and you sleep alone.

Anthony Burgess, English novelist (1917–93). *Inside Mr Enderby* (1963) – though he did not claim this as original, despite its appearance as such in *The Penguin Dictionary of Modern Quotations* (1971). Based on the earlier anonymous parody of Ella Wheeler Cox, 'Solitude' (1883) ending '... Weep and you sleep alone.' This last was quoted by the architectural historian James Lees-Milne and recorded by him in his diary on 6 June 1945 (published in *Prophesying Peace*, 1977).

Snubs

2 DEDICATED GRATEFULLY TO THE WARDEN AND FELLOWS OF ST ANTONY'S COLLEGE, OXFORD. EXCEPT ONE.

Jan Morris, Welsh writer (1926–). Dedication of *The Oxford Book of Oxford* (1978).

3 A Merry Christmas to all my friends except two.

W. C. Fields, American comedian (1879–1946). Quoted in *The Oxford Dictionary of Humorous Quotations*, ed. Ned Sherrin (1995).

Sobriety

4 I drink little, miss my glass often, put water in my wine, and go away before the rest, which I take to be a good receipt for sobriety. Let us put it into rhyme, and so make a proverb:
　　Drink little at a time:
　　Put water with your wine;
　　Miss your glass when you can;
　　And go off the first man.

Jonathan Swift, Anglo-Irish writer and clergyman (1667–1745). *Journal to Stella* – for 21 April 1711.

Socialism and Socialists

5 Why is it always the intelligent people who are socialists?

Alan Bennett, English playwright and actor (1934–). *Forty Years On*, Act 2 (1969).

Of Paul Johnson, socialist journalist, before his swing to the right:

6 He eats more oysters than the dukes.

Anonymous waiter at London club. Quoted in the 'William Hickey' column of the *Daily Express* (c.1977).

7 There is nothing in Socialism that a little age or a little money will not cure.

Will Durant, American writer (1885–1981). Quoted in *A Dictionary of Twentieth Century Quotations* (1987).

Society

8 Mrs So-and-So, a well-known figure in Café. (Pause). Nescafé Society.

Noël Coward (later Sir Noël), English entertainer and writer (1899–1973). Quoted in Alec Guinness, *Blessings in Disguise* (1985). Remark made to Guinness in Jamaica prior to the filming of *Our Man In Havana* (released 1959).

9 Never speak disrespectfully of Society ... Only people who can't get into it do that.

Oscar Wilde, Irish playwright, poet and wit (1854–1900). *The Importance of Being Earnest*, Act 2 (1895).

Soixante-neuf

10 As for that topsy-turvy tangle known as soixante-neuf, personally I have always felt it to be madly confusing, like trying to pat your head and rub your stomach at the same time.

Helen Lawrenson, American writer. Quoted in *Esquire* (1977) and then in Bob Chieger, *Was It Good For You Too?* (1983).

Soviet Union

11 Gaiety is the most outstanding feature of the Soviet Union.

Joseph Stalin, Soviet Communist leader (1879–1953). Quoted in *The Observer* (24 November 1935).

12 Miles of cornfields, and ballet in the evening.

Alan Hackney, English comedy writer (1924–). *Private Life* (1958) – filmed as *I'm All Right, Jack* (UK, 1959).

Spades

1 CECILY: When I see a spade I call it
a spade.
GWENDOLEN: I am glad to say that
I have never seen a spade.

Oscar Wilde, Irish playwright, poet and wit
(1854–1900). *The Importance of Being Earnest*,
Act 2 (1895).

Spam

2 I'm pink therefore I'm spam.

Anonymous graffito. Contributed by
J. O'Grady of Longford, Coventry, to
Granada TV *Cabbages and Kings* (18 Nov-
ember 1979).

Speculation

3 October. This is one of the peculiarly
dangerous months to speculate in
stocks in. The others are July, January,
September, April, November, May,
March, June, December, August, and
February.

Mark Twain, American writer (1835–1910).
Puddn'head Wilson (1894).

4 There are two times in a man's life when
he should not speculate: when he can't
afford it, and when he can.

Mark Twain. *Following the Equator* (1897).

Speech-making

5 The head cannot take in more than the
seat can endure.

Winston S. Churchill (later Sir Winston),
British Conservative Prime Minister and
writer (1874–1965). Quoted in Jock Murray,
A Gentleman Publisher's Commonplace Book
(1996).

6 I have always been a bit shy of the
really extemporary speech ever since
I heard it said that an extemporary
speech was not worth the paper
it was written on.

Winston Churchill. Speech in his constituency (18 November 1955).

7 I do not object to people looking at
their watches when I am speaking.
But I strongly object when they start
shaking them to make sure they are
still going.

Norman Birkett (later Lord Birkett), English
barrister and judge (1883–1962). Quoted in
The Observer (30 October 1960). However,
in *Joyce Grenfell Requests the Pleasure* (1976),
Grenfell writes: 'It made me think of my
father's story of Edward Marsh, who said he
didn't mind if anyone looked at his watch
when he was lecturing, but he didn't much like
it when they looked at it a second time and
shook it to see if it was still going.' As Eddie
Marsh died in 1953 and Joyce Grenfell's
father died in 1954, there may be grounds
for wondering if Birkett really originated
the joke.

8 If I am to speak for ten minutes,
I need a week for preparation; if fifteen
minutes, three days; if half an hour,
two days; if an hour, I am ready
now.

Woodrow Wilson, American Democratic
President (1856–1924). Quoted in Josephus
Daniels, *The Wilson Era* (1946).

Opening a Red Cross bazaar in Oxford:

9 Desperately accustomed as I am to
public speaking...

Noël Coward (later Sir Noël), English entertainer and writer (1899–1973). Quoted in
Dick Richards, *The Wit of Noël Coward*
(1968).

10 We often say a speaker needs no introduction: what most of them need is
a conclusion. In my view, an after-
dinner speech – and I've experienced
40,000 of them – needs a good beginning, a good ending, and not much
space in between.

Ivor Spencer, English President, Guild
of Professional Toastmasters (1924–).
Quoted in *The Observer*, 'Sayings of
the Week' (24 November 1991).

11 There is but one pleasure in life equal
to that of being called on to make
an after-dinner speech, and that is not
being called on to make one.

Charles Dudley Warner, American editor and
writer (1829–1900). Quoted in *The Treasury
of Humorous Quotations*, ed. Evan Esar &
Nicolas Bentley (1951).

1 A speech is a solemn responsibility. The man who makes a bad thirty-minute speech to two hundred people wastes only a half-hour of his own time. But he wastes one hundred hours of the audience's time – more than four days – which should be a hanging offense.

Jenkin Lloyd Jones (untraced). Quoted in Laurence J. Peter, *Quotations for Our Time* (1977).

Spoonerisms

Announcing a hymn in New College Chapel (1879):

2 Kinquering congs their titles take.

William Spooner, English clergyman and academic (1844–1930). Quoted in the Oxford *Echo* (4 May 1892).

3 A half-warmed fish.

William Spooner. Quoted on BBC Radio *Quote...Unquote* (15 June 1977).

4 Sir, you have tasted two whole worms; you have hissed all my mystery lectures and been caught fighting a liar in the quad; you will leave Oxford by the next town drain.

William Spooner. Quoted in *The Oxford University What's What* (1948). Surely aprocryphal.

5 Let us drink a toast to the queer old dean.

William Spooner. Quoted in *The Penguin Dictionary of Quotations* (1960).

The most remarkable sight in Egypt:

6 The Minx by Spoonlight.

William Spooner. Quoted in Julian Huxley, *Memories* (1970).

Of a cat falling from a window:

7 It popped on its little drawers.

William Spooner. Quoted in William Hayter, *Spooner* (1977).

8 Yes indeed, the Lord is a shoving leopard.

William Spooner. Quoted in *Brewer's Dictionary of Phrase & Fable* (1989 edn).

9 Through a dark glassly...

William Spooner. Attributed by James Laver, in conversation with the author (5 December 1969).

Introducing radio broadcast by President Herbert Hoover:

10 Ladies and gentlemen – the President of the United States, Hoobert Herver.

Harry Von Zell, American broadcaster and actor (1906–81). Quoted in *Current Biography* (1944).

Spoons

11 The louder he talked of his honour, the faster we counted our spoons.

R. W. Emerson, American poet and essayist (1803–82). 'Worship', *The Conduct of Life* (1860).

Of James Macpherson:

12 If he does really think that there is no distinction between virtue and vice, why, Sir, when he leaves our houses let us count our spoons.

Samuel Johnson, English writer and lexicographer (1709–84). In James Boswell, *Life of Johnson* (1791) – 14 July 1763.

Sportsmen

Of a rowing eight:

13 Eight minds with but a single thought – if that!

Sir Max Beerbohm, English writer and caricaturist (1872–1956). Attributed.

Standards

14 Standards are always out of date. That is what makes them standards.

Alan Bennett, English playwright and actor (1934–). *Forty Years On*, Act 2 (1969).

Standing

15 There are seventy stanzas in the Uruguay national anthem, which fact may account for the Uruguay standing army.

Franklin P. Adams, American humorist (1881– 1960). Quoted in *The Treasury of Humorous Quotations*, ed. Evan Esar & Nicolas Bentley (1951).

Stars

On swimming film star Esther Williams:

1 Wet, she was a star – dry she ain't.

Joe Pasternak, Hungarian-born film producer (1901–91). Quoted (except for the last three words) in Leslie Halliwell, *The Filmgoer's Book of Quotes* (1973).

2 Being a star has made it possible for me to get insulted in places where the average Negro could never hope to go and get insulted.

Sammy Davis Jnr, American entertainer (1925–90). *Yes I Can* (1965).

Statesmen

3 A statesman is a successful politician who is dead.

Thomas B(rackett) Reed, American politician (1839–1902). Quoted in Henry Cabot Lodge, *The Democracy of the Constitution* (1915). Remark c.1880. Reed was in the House of Representatives.

4 A politician is a person with whose politics you don't agree; if you agree with him he is a statesman.

David Lloyd George (1st Earl Lloyd George of Dwyfor), British Liberal Prime Minister (1863–1945). Speech at Central Hall, Westminster (2 July 1935).

5 A politician is a man who understands government, and it takes a politician to run a government. A statesman is a politician who's been dead ten or fifteen years.

Harry S Truman, American Democratic President (1884–1972). In the *New York World Telegram and Sun* (12 April 1958).

Of David Steel, leader of the Liberal Party:

6 I say this in the utmost affection … he has passed from rising hope to elder statesman without any intervening period whatsoever.

Michael Foot, English journalist and Labour politician (1913–). Speech in the House of Commons (28 March 1979) – taken from a recording rather than Hansard. Foot, as Leader of the House, was ending the debate which resulted in the Labour Government's defeat on a motion of no confidence (and led to its general election defeat the following month). The Liberals, led by the youngish David Steel, had until quite recently been part of the 'Lib-Lab' pact which had helped keep Labour in office. But then it collapsed.

7 The first requirement of a statesman is that he be dull. This is not always easy to achieve.

Dean Acheson, American Democratic politician (1893–1971). Quoted in *The Observer* (8 March 1998).

Statistics

8 It is now proved beyond doubt that cigarettes are the biggest single cause of statistics.

Anonymous graffito. Contributed to BBC Radio *Quote … Unquote* (19 June 1980) by Mr R. F. Crosher of London N4. In *Reader's Digest* (December 1961), a similar observation was attributed to Fletcher Knebel (1911–).

9 He uses statistics as a drunken man uses lamp-posts – for support rather than illumination.

Andrew Lang, Scottish poet and scholar (1844–1912). Quoted in *The Treasury of Humorous Quotations*, ed. Evan Esar & Nicolas Bentley (1951).

Statisticians

10 A statistician is someone who is good with figures but who doesn't have the personality to become an accountant.

Anonymous (known by 1994). Another version: 'An actuary is someone who is too boring to be an accountant.' Also: 'An actuary is someone who finds accountancy too exciting' – quoted by Richard Boston in *The Guardian* (20 July 1987).

11 A statistician is a person who draws a mathematically precise line from an unwarranted assumption to a foregone conclusion.

Anonymous. Quoted in *The Guinness Dictionary of Jokes* (1995).

Statues

12 I had rather men should ask why no statue has been erected in my honour, than why one has.

Marcus Porcius Cato ('the Censor'), Roman politician (234–149 BC). Quoted in *The Treasury of Humorous Quotations*, ed. Evan Esar & Nicolas Bentley (1951).

Stein, Gertrude
American poet (1866–1936)

1 The mama of dada.

Clifton Fadiman, American writer (1904–). *Party of One* (1955).

Stigma

2 Any stigma, as the old saying is, will serve to beat a dogma.

Philip Guedalla, English writer (1889–1944). 'Patriotism', *Outspoken Essays: First series* (1923).

Strangers

3 Who's 'im, Bill?
A stranger!
'Eave 'arf a brick at 'im.

Anonymous. Caption to cartoon in *Punch*, Vol.26 (1854).

Streisand, Barbra
American singer and actress (1942–)

In the film What's Up, Doc?*:*

4 She's playing herself – and it's awfully soon for that.

Pauline Kael, American film critic (1919–). 'Collaboration and Resistance', *Deeper into Movies* (1973).

5 I am a nice person. I care about my driver having lunch, you know ...

Barbra Streisand. Quoted in *The Sunday Times*, 'Words of the Week' (1 April 1984).

Strength

On Lady Desborough:

6 She's as strong as an ox. She'll be turned into Bovril when she dies.

Margot Asquith (later Countess of Oxford and Asquith) (1864–1945). Quoted by her stepdaughter Baroness Asquith in BBC TV programme *As I Remember* (30 April 1967).

Striking

7 AMANDA: I've been brought up to believe that it's beyond the pale, for a man to strike a woman.
ELYOT: A very poor tradition. Certain women should be struck regularly, like gongs.

Noël Coward (later Sir Noël), English entertainer and writer (1899–1973). *Private Lives*, Act 3 (1930).

Stroking

8 'Why are you stroking the shell?', said my father. 'Oh, to please the turtle.' 'Why, child, you might as well stroke the dome of St Paul's, to please the Dean and Chapter.'

Revd Sydney Smith, English clergyman, essayist and wit (1771–1845). Quoted in Saba, Lady Holland, *Memoir* (1855).

Struggle

To the actor Victor Spinetti:

9 Ah, Victor, still struggling to keep your head below water.

Emlyn Williams, Welsh actor and playwright (1905–87). Quoted in Ned Sherrin, *Cutting Edge* (1984).

Students

10 Undergraduates owe their happiness chiefly to the consciousness that they are no longer at school. The nonsense which was knocked out of them at school is all put gently back at Oxford or Cambridge.

Sir Max Beerbohm, English writer and caricaturist (1872–1956). 'Going Back to School', *More* (1899).

Style

11 As a general rule, run your pen through every other word you have written; you have no idea what vigour it will give your style.

Revd Sydney Smith, English clergyman, essayist and wit (1771–1845). Quoted in Saba, Lady Holland, *Memoir* (1855).

Defining style:

12 A candy-striped jeep, Jane Austen, Cassius Clay, *The Times* before it

changed, Danny La Rue, Charleston in South Carolina, 'Monsieur de Givenchy', a zebra (but not a zebra crossing), evading boredom, Gertrude Lawrence, the Paris Opera House, white, a seagull, a Brixham trawler, Margot Fonteyn, any Cole Porter song, English pageantry, Marlene's voice ... and ... Lingfield has a tiny bit.

Noël Coward (later Sir Noël), English entertainer and writer (1899–1973). Copy for Gillette razor blade advertisement, shortly before he died. Quoted in Kenneth Tynan article in *The Observer* (1 April 1973).

1 Proper words in proper places, makes the true definition of a style.

Jonathan Swift, Anglo-Irish writer and clergyman (1667–1745). *Letter to a young gentleman lately entered into Holy Orders* (1720).

2 I affected a combination of the styles of Macaulay and Gibbon, the staccato antithesis of the former, and the rolling sentences and genitival endings of the latter: and I stuck in a bit of my own from time to time.

Winston S. Churchill (later Sir Winston), British Conservative Prime Minister and writer (1874–1965). Quoted in Herbert V. Prochnow, Snr & Jnr, *A Treasury of Humorous Quotations* (1969).

3 Her hat is a creation that will never go out of style; it will just look ridiculous year after year.

Fred Allen, American comedian (1894–1956). Quoted in *The Treasury of Humorous Quotations*, ed. Evan Esar & Nicolas Bentley (1951).

Substitution

When forbidden to sing 'She sits among the cabbages and peas,' she substituted:

4 She sits among the cabbages and leeks.

Marie Lloyd, English music-hall entertainer (1870–1922). Quoted by John Trevelyan, the British film censor, in *TV Times* (23 April– 9 May 1981). The reputed song (untraced) was reportedly censored by a local 'watch' committee before being performed by her in a theatre.

Suburbs

On the city of Salisbury (now Harare) when capital of Rhodesia (now Zimbabwe):

5 All suburb and no urb.

Alan Coren, English humorist (1938–). Quoted in *The Sunday Times* Magazine (27 November 1977).

6 Los Angeles is seventy-two suburbs in search of a city.

James Gleason, American actor (1886–1959). Quoted in Leslie Halliwell, *The Filmgoer's Book of Quotes* (1973).

Subversion

Scrawled on interminable US immigration questionnaire that had asked, 'Is it your intention to subvert the government of the United States?':

7 Sole purpose of visit!

Gilbert Harding, English radio and TV personality (1907–60). Quoted by Wallace Reyburn, *Gilbert Harding: A Candid Portrayal* (1978) – he sets the story in the American consulate in Toronto.

Success

8 Success smells like Brighton.

Sir Laurence Olivier (later Lord Olivier), English actor (1907–89). Quoted in *Peter Hall's Diaries* (1983) in an entry for 1977. Unless it was a remark Olivier was fond of making, this quotation comes from a TV interview he gave to Kenneth Tynan in the BBC series *Great Acting* (26 February 1966). Talking of the tumultuous reception of his stage *Richard III* (1944), Olivier said: 'There was something in the atmosphere ... There is a phrase "the sweet smell of success" ... I have had two experiences like that and it just smells like Brighton and oyster bars and things like that.'

9 On the door to success it says: push and pull.

Anonymous (Yiddish proverb). Quoted in Herbert V. Prochnow, Snr & Jnr, *A Treasury of Humorous Quotations* (1969).

10 It is not enough to succeed. Others must fail.

Gore Vidal, American novelist, playwright and critic (1925–). This was quoted as 'the cynical maxim of a clever friend' by the Revd Gerard

Irvine during his 'anti-panegyric' for Tom Driberg (Lord Bradwell) after a requiem mass in London on 7 December 1976. 'It's not enough that I should succeed – others should fail,' was attributed to David Merrick, the Broadway producer, in Barbara Rowes, *The Book of Quotes* (1979).

1 To succeed pre-eminently in English public life it is necessary to conform either to the popular image of a bookie or of a clergyman; Churchill being a perfect example of the former, Halifax of the latter.

Malcolm Muggeridge, English writer and broadcaster (1903–90). *The Infernal Grove* (1973). To James Callaghan (Lord Callaghan) has, however, been ascribed the view: 'Prime Ministers tend either to be book-makers or bishops, and they take it in turn.'

2 The higher the monkey climbs, the more he shows his tail.

Anonymous proverbial saying. Discussed in *Notes and Queries* (1887). Applied to anyone in any profession who has achieved high rank, as for example in the version, 'The egotistical surgeon is like a monkey; the higher he climbs the more you see of his less attractive features.' On BBC Radio *Quote... Unquote* (29 March 1994), John Oaksey recalled that his father, Geoffrey Lawrence (Lord Oaksey) (1880–1971) had said the same sort of thing about judges and other high-ups in the legal profession, drawing a parallel rather with orang-utangs.

3 The critical laurels that had been so confidently prophesied for me in the Twenties never graced my brow, and I was forced throughout the Thirties to console myself with the bitter pallia-tive of commercial success – which I enjoyed very much indeed.

Noël Coward (later Sir Noël), English enter-tainer and writer (1899–1973). Introduction, *Play Parade*, Vol. 4 (1954).

Suicide

On being told that a certain person he knew had just blown his brains out:

4 He must have been an incredibly good shot.

Noël Coward (later Sir Noël), English enter-tainer and writer (1899–1973). Quoted in Dick Richards, *The Wit of Noël Coward* (1968).

On the Labour Party's 1983 General Election manifesto:

5 The longest suicide note [ever penned] in history.

Gerald Kaufman, English Labour politician (1930–). Quoted in Denis Healey, *The Time of My Life* (1989). Kaufman was a member of the Labour Shadow Cabinet at the time.

Sullivan, Ed
American journalist and broadcaster (1902–74)

6 Ed Sullivan will be around as long as someone else has talent.

Fred Allen, American comedian (1894–1956). Quoted in Laurence J. Peter, *Quotations for Our Time* (1977).

Summer

7 An English summer – three fine days and a thunderstorm.

Anonymous. Quoted in *The 'Quote... Unquote' Newsletter* (January 1992). John Aiton's *Manual of Domestic Economy for Clergymen* (1842) has: 'Our [Scotch] summers are said to consist of 3 hot days and a thunder-storm', which would seem to suggest it is a saying by no means restricted to English summers.

8 The English winter – ending in July, To recommence in August.

Lord Byron, English poet (1788–1824). *Don Juan*, Canto 13, St. 42 (1819–24).

9 The coldest winter I ever spent was a summer in San Francisco.

Mark Twain, American writer (1835–1910). Attributed but not verified. Quoted in *The Sayings of Mark Twain*, ed. James Munson (1992).

Sunshine

10 Thank heavens, the sun has gone in, and I don't have to go out and enjoy it.

Logan Pearsall Smith, American writer (1865–1946). These are sometimes quoted as though they were Logan Pearsall Smith's last (dying) words – as in *A Dictionary of Famous Quotations* (1962), for example. They are not, though the misunderstanding is understandable. They appear in 'Last Words' in his *All Trivia* (1933). Smith did not die until 1946 when, according to James Lees-Milne, *Caves of Ice* (1983), his actual last words were, 'I must telephone to the Pope-Hennesseys'.

Superiority

When accused by a member of Parliament of harbouring a superiority complex:

1 Considering the company I keep in this place, that is hardly surprising.

Sir Robert Menzies, Australian Liberal Prime Minister (1894–1978). Quoted in *Time* Magazine (29 May 1978).

In reply to the comment 'Anyway, she's always very nice to her inferiors':

2 Where does she find them?

Dorothy Parker, American writer (1893–1967). Quoted in *The Lyttelton Hart-Davis Letters*, Vol. 1 (1978). Told sometimes regarding Clare Boothe Luce – as in Marion Meade, *What Fresh Hell is This?* (1988).

3 He was not brought by the stork; he was delivered by a man from the Audubon Society personally.

Fred Allen, American comedian (1894–1956). Quoted in *The Treasury of Humorous Quotations*, ed. Evan Esar & Nicolas Bentley (1951).

Support

4 Every great man has a woman behind him ... And every great woman has some man or other in front of her, tripping her up.

Dorothy L. Sayers, English novelist and playwright (1893–1957). In *Love All*, a little known-play that opened at the Torch Theatre, Knightsbridge, London (9 April 1940) and closed before the end of the month.

5 Behind every good man is a good woman – I mean an exhausted one.

Sarah, Duchess of York (1959–). Speech (September 1987).

6 As usual there's a great woman behind every idiot.

John Lennon, English singer and songwriter (1940–80). Quoted 1979.

7 Behind every successful man you'll find a woman who has nothing to wear.

L. Grant Glickman (untraced). Quoted 1977. Also attributed to James Stewart, the film actor (quoted 1979).

8 We in the industry know that behind every successful screenwriter stands a woman. And behind her stands his wife.

Groucho Marx, American comedian (1895–1977). Quoted 1977.

9 The road to success is filled with women pushing their husbands along.

Lord (Thomas Robert) Dewar, British distiller (1864–1930). Quoted in Burton Stevenson, *The Home Book of Quotations* (1967).

10 And behind every man who is a failure there's a woman, too!

John Ruge (untraced). Cartoon caption in *Playboy* (March 1967).

11 Behind every successful man stands a surprised mother-in-law.

Hubert Humphrey, American Democratic Vice-President (1911–78). Speech (1964). Attributed to Brooks Hays in the form 'Back of every achievement is a proud wife and a surprised mother-in-law', in Herbert V. Prochnow, Snr & Jnr, *A Treasury of Humorous Quotations* (1969).

12 Behind every great woman is a man telling her she's ignoring him.

Anonymous. Quoted in Nan Tucket, *The Dumb Men Joke Book*, Vol. 2 (1994).

Suspicion

13 ELIZA: My aunt died of influenza: so they said ... But it's my belief (as how) they done the old woman in.

Bernard Shaw, Irish playwright and critic (1856–1950). *Pygmalion*, Act 3 (1914). The words 'as how' were inserted by Mrs Patrick Campbell in her performances as Eliza Doolittle and were also incorporated in the 1938 film.

Swans

1 What happened when Leda was seduced by that swan in classical mythology? Well, for one thing, she got down in the dumps.

Anonymous. A version was quoted in BBC Radio *The Burkiss Way* c.1979. Script by Andrew Marshall and David Renwick.

Switzerland

2 I look upon Switzerland as an inferior sort of Scotland.

Revd Sydney Smith, English clergyman, essayist and wit (1771–1845). Letter to Lord Holland (1815).

Of a beautiful maiden:

3 She's like Switzerland – beautiful but dumb.

Anonymous. Quoted in *A Year of Stings and Squelches* (1985).

4 You know what the fellow said – in Italy, for thirty years under the Borgias, they had warfare, terror, murder and bloodshed, but they produced Michelangelo, Leonardo da Vinci and the Renaissance. In Switzerland, they had brotherly love; they had five hundred years of democracy and peace – and what did that produce? The cuckoo clock.

Orson Welles, American film director, writer and actor (1915–85). So says Harry Lime (played by Welles) in Carol Reed's film *The Third Man* (1949). It soon got around that Welles had added this speech to the basic script which was written by Graham Greene and Carol Reed. Indeed, it appears only as a footnote in the published script of the film. In a letter, dated 13 October 1977, Greene confirmed to me that it *had* been written by Welles: 'What happened was that during the shooting of *The Third Man* it was found necessary for the timing to insert another sentence and the speech you mention was put in by Orson Welles.'

Whether the idea was original to Welles is another matter. After all he introduces the speech with, 'You know what the fellow said . . .' In James McNeill Whistler, *Mr Whistler's 'Ten O'Clock'* (1888), the text of a lecture he gave on art in 1885, he spoke of: 'The Swiss in their mountains . . . What more worthy people! . . . yet, the perverse and scornful [goddess, Art] will none of it, and the sons of patriots are left with the clock that turns the mill, and the sudden cuckoo, with difficulty restrained in its box! For this was Tell a hero! For this did Gessler die!'

Sympathy

5 My nose bleeds for you.

Sir Herbert Beerbohm Tree, English actor-manager (1853–1917). Quoted in Hesketh Pearson, *Beerbohm Tree* (1956).

T

Taciturnity

A woman sat down next to him at a dinner party and said, 'You must talk to me, Mr Coolidge. I made a bet with someone that I could get more than two words out of you.' Coolidge replied:

1 You lose.

Calvin Coolidge, American Republican President (1872–1933). Quoted in Gamaliel Bradford, *The Quick and the Dead* (1931).

When a girl said to Coolidge that her father had bet her she could not get more than two words out of him:

2 Poppa wins.

Calvin Coolidge. Quoted on BBC Radio *Quote ... Unquote* (7 June 1978).

3 None preaches better than the ant, and she says nothing.

Benjamin Franklin, American politician and scientist (1706–90). *Poor Richard's Almanack* (July 1736) – a work in which Franklin often revised already existing sayings.

Taj Mahal

On refusing to see the Taj Mahal when staying nearby:

4 I'd seen it on biscuit boxes and didn't want to spoil the illusion.

Noël Coward (later Sir Noël), English entertainer and writer (1899–1973). Quoted in *The Observer* (1969).

Tastes

5 There's no accounting for tastes, as the woman said when somebody told her her son was wanted by the police.

Franklin Pierce Adams, American humorist (1881–1960). Quoted in *The Treasury of Humorous Quotations*, ed. Evan Esar & Nicolas Bentley (1951).

6 What sight is sadder than the sight of a lady we admire admiring a nauseating picture.

Logan Pearsall Smith, American writer (1865–1946). Quoted in Laurence J. Peter, *Quotations for Our Time* (1977).

Taxation

7 All money nowadays seems to be produced with a natural homing instinct for the Treasury.

Prince Philip, Greek-born consort of Queen Elizabeth II (1921–). In 1963. Quoted in Herbert V. Prochnow, Snr & Jnr, *A Treasury of Humorous Quotations* (1969).

8 He's spending a year dead for tax reasons.

Douglas Adams, English novelist (1952–). Untraced.

9 The hardest thing in the world is to understand income tax.

Albert Einstein, German-born physicist (1879–1955). Attributed.

10 The avoidance of taxes is the only pursuit that still carries any reward.

John Maynard Keynes (later Lord Keynes), English economist (1883–1946). Untraced.

11 The one thing that hurts more than paying an income tax is not having to pay an income tax.

Lord (Thomas Robert) Dewar, British distiller (1864–1930). Quoted in *The Treasury of Humorous Quotations*, ed. Evan Esar & Nicolas Bentley (1951).

Taxis

1 I have done almost every human activity inside a taxi which does not require main drainage.

Alan Brien, English journalist (1925–). In *Punch* (1972).

Teachers

2 He who can, does. He who cannot, teaches.

Bernard Shaw, Irish playwright and critic (1856–1950). 'Maxims for Revolutionists', *Man and Superman* (1903).

3 ... And those who can't teach lecture on the sociology of education degrees.

Anonymous graffito. Quoted in *Graffiti 2* (1980), from Middlesex Polytechnic in 1979.

4 No teacher I of boys or smaller fry,
No teacher I of teachers, no, not I.
Mine was the distant aim, the longer reach,
To teach men how to teach men how to teach.

A. B. Ramsay, English writer (*fl.* 1930s/40s). 'Epitaph on a Syndic', *Frondes Salicis* (1935).

Tebbit, Norman (later Lord Tebbit)
English Conservative politician (1931–)

5 Is it always his desire to give his imitation of a semi-house-trained polecat?

Michael Foot, English journalist and Labour politician (1913–). Speech, Ebbw Vale in 1983. He noted that he had said it first in the House of Commons 'a few years ago' – indeed, on 2 March 1978.

Teeth

6 She could eat an apple through a tennis racquet.

Noël Coward (later Sir Noël), English entertainer and writer (1899–1973). *Come Into the Garden, Maud* (1966). Coward's inspiration for this line is apparent from a note in his diary for 10 December 1954: 'Lunched and dined with Darryl Zannuck who, David Niven wickedly said, is the only man who can eat an apple through a tennis racquet!'

Telegrams

Telegram to Gertrude Lawrence on her marriage to Richard S. Aldrich:

7 Dear Mrs A., hooray hooray,
At last you are deflowered
On this as every other day
I love you. Noël Coward.

Noël Coward (later Sir Noël), English entertainer and writer (1899–1973). Quoted in Sheridan Morley, *A Talent to Amuse* (1969).

First night cable of congratulations to Gertrude Lawrence:

8 A WARM HAND ON YOUR OPENING.

Noël Coward. Quoted in *The Sayings of Noël Coward*, ed. Philip Hoare (1997).

Telegram to Cole Lesley after a visit to Turkey:

9 AM BACK FROM ISTANBUL WHERE I WAS KNOWN AS ENGLISH DELIGHT.

Noël Coward. Quoted in Cole Lesley, *The Life of Noël Coward* (1976).

While ill in Italy, telegram to Cole Lesley:

10 HAVE MOVED TO HOTEL EXCELSIOR COUGHING MYSELF INTO A FIRENZE.

Noël Coward. Quoted in Cole Lesley, *The Life of Noël Coward* (1976).

Telegram to Mrs Robert Sherwood, when delivered of a baby after a pregnancy that had been long and/or one that she had made much of:

11 GOOD WORK, MARY. WE ALL KNEW YOU HAD IT IN YOU.

Dorothy Parker, American writer (1893–1967). Quoted in Alexander Woollcott, *While Rome Burns* (1934).

Telegram to a couple who were marrying after living together:

12 WHAT'S NEW?

Dorothy Parker. Quoted in *The Sayings of Dorothy Parker*, ed. S. T. Brownlow (1992).

When Cantor heard that Norma Shearer, the actress wife of Irving Thalberg, had produced a son, he sent a telegram of the utmost point to the noted Jewish film producer:

1 CONGRATULATIONS ON YOUR LATEST PRODUCTION. AM SURE IT WILL LOOK BETTER AFTER IT'S BEEN CUT.

Eddie Cantor, American comedian, in vaudeville and films (1892–1964). Quoted by Max Wilk in *The Wit and Wisdom of Hollywood* (1972).

Telegram received by Sir Alec Douglas-Home:

2 TO HELL WITH YOU. OFFENSIVE LETTER FOLLOWS.

Anonymous. Quoted in William Safire, *Safire's Political Dictionary* (1978).

Television

3 Never miss a chance to have sex or be on television.

Gore Vidal, American novelist, playwright and critic (1925–). Quoted in Bob Chieger, *Was It Good For You Too?* (1983).

4 Television's got so bad they're scraping the top of the barrel.

Gore Vidal. Attributed, by 1979.

5 Television is more interesting than people. If it were not, we should have people standing in the corners of our rooms.

Alan Coren, English humorist (1938–). In *The Times*, quoted in *The Penguin Dictionary of Modern Quotations* (1980 edn).

6 The bland leading the bland.

Anonymous. Quoted in Leslie Halliwell, *The Filmgoer's Book of Quotes* (1973).

7 Television? No good will come of this device. The word is half Greek and half Latin.

C. P. Scott, English editor (1846–1932). Quoted in *The Penguin Dictionary of Modern Quotations* (1971).

8 I have had my [TV] aerials removed – it's the moral equivalent of a prostate operation.

Malcolm Muggeridge, English writer and broadcaster (1903–90). Quoted in the *Radio Times* (April 1981).

9 Some television programmes are so much chewing gum for the eyes.

John Mason Brown, American critic (1900–69). In interview (28 July 1955) with James B. Simpson, in *Best Quotes of '54, '55, '56* (1957). This was not his own remark – he was, in fact, quoting a young friend of his son.

10 TV … is our latest medium – we call it a medium because nothing's well done.

Goodman Ace, American writer (1899–1982). In letter (1954) to Groucho Marx, quoted in *The Groucho Letters* (1967). However, Leslie Halliwell, *The Filmgoer's Book of Quotes* (1973) ascribes, 'A medium, so called because it is neither rare nor well done' to Ernie Kovacs, the American entertainer (1919–62).

Of TV chat shows:

11 The kind of show I do consists of two consenting adults performing unnatural acts in public.

Michael Parkinson, English broadcaster and journalist (1935–). Quoted in *Sunday Today*, 'Quotes of the Week' (29 March 1987).

12 An audience doesn't know what it wants; it only knows when it sees it.

William G. Stewart, English TV producer (1935–). Quoted in *The Observer*, 'Sayings of the Week' (30 September 1990).

On television:

13 It is for appearing on, not for looking at.

Noël Coward (later Sir Noël), English entertainer and writer (1899–1973). On *The Ed Murrow Show*, US TV (1956). Quoted in Wallace Raeburn, *Gilbert Harding* (1978).

Temperance

On a dinner given by President Rutherford B. Hayes, who occupied the White House 1877–81 and was also a temperance advocate:

14 It was a brilliant affair; the water flowed like champagne.

William Maxwell Evarts, American lawyer and politician (1818–1901). Quoted in George F. Hoar, *Autobiography of Seventy Years* (1906).

Temptation

15 I can resist everything except temptation.

Oscar Wilde, Irish playwright, poet and wit (1854–1900). *Lady Windermere's Fan*, Act 1 (1892).

Texas

1 [Texas is] the place where there are the most cows and the least milk and the most rivers and the least water in them, and where you can look the furthest and see the least.

Anonymous. Quoted in *H. L. Mencken's Dictionary of Quotations* (1942).

A child asks a stranger where he comes from, whereupon his father rebukes him gently:

2 Never do that, son. If a man's from Texas, he'll tell you. If he's not, why embarrass him by asking.

Anonymous. Quoted in John Gunther, *Inside U.S.A.* (1947). Roy Hattersley reworked this on BBC Radio *Quote ... Unquote* (27 October 1984) as though said by Sydney Smith to the French Ambassador. 'Never asks a man if he comes from Yorkshire. If he does, he'll already have told you. If he does not, why humiliate him?'

Thatcher, Margaret (later Baroness Thatcher)

British Conservative Prime Minister (1925–)

3 Mrs Thatcher is doing for monetarism what the Boston Strangler did for door-to-door salesmen.

Denis Healey (later Lord Healey), English Labour politician (1917–). Speech, House of Commons (15 December 1979).

4 The great she-elephant, she who must be obeyed, the Catherine the Great of Finchley.

Denis Healey. Quoted in *The Observer*, 'Sayings of the Week' (4 March 1984).

5 She cannot see an institution without hitting it with her handbag.

(Sir) Julian Critchley, English Conservative politician (1930–). In *The Times* (21 June 1982).

6 *Prima donna inter pares.*

Julian Critchley. Interviewed in *The Guardian* (5 September 1987).

Asked why he thought Baroness Thatcher disapproved of him:

7 I am not a doctor.

Sir Edward Heath, British Conservative Prime Minister (1916–). Quoted in *The Independent on Sunday* (30 October 1994).

Theatre

8 You know, I go to the theatre to be entertained ... I don't want to see plays about rape, sodomy and drug addiction ... I can get all that at home.

Peter Cook, English humorist (1937–95). Caption to cartoon by Roger Law in *The Observer* (8 July 1962). However, the words 'I go to the theatre to be entertained. I want to be taken out of myself. I don't want to see lust and rape, incest and sodomy – I can get all that at home' also occur in the sketch 'Frank Speaking' credited to Cook and Alan Bennett in *Beyond the Fringe*. This sketch is also described as 'Lord Cobbold/The Duke' and credited to Cook and Jonathan Miller. By the time of Leslie Halliwell, *The Filmgoer's Book of Quotes* (1973), this was being quoted as:'I don't like watching rape and violence at the cinema. I get enough of that at home!'

Theatrical criticism

On the first night of J. M. Barrie's play Peter Pan *(1904):*

9 Oh, for an hour of Herod!

Anthony Hope (Sir Anthony Hope Hawkins), English novelist (1863–1933). Quoted in Denis Mackail, *The Story of JMB* (1941). Compare: 'There are moments when one sympathizes with Herod' – Saki, 'Reginald on House-Parties' (1904). An even earlier outing for this remark occurred when 'Master Betty', the child acting prodigy, was all the rage in London theatre. Dorothea Jordan, the actress mistress of the Duke of Clarence, surveying the throng of juvenile would-be imitators of 'Master Betty', exclaimed,'Oh, for the days of King Herod!' – Anne Matthews, *Anecdotes of Actors* (1844).

On being bored with J. M. Barrie's play The Admirable Crichton*:*

10 Well, for Crichton out loud.

Walter Winchell, American journalist and broadcaster (1892–72). Reported by Dorothy

Parker and quoted in *The Sayings of Dorothy Parker*, ed. S. T. Brownlow (1992).

On Lionel Bart's musical Blitz! *(1962) – which was all about London in the Second World War and chiefly notable for the elaborate moving scenery by Sean Kenny:*

1 Just as long as the real thing and twice as noisy.

Noël Coward (later Sir Noël), English entertainer and writer (1899–1973). Quoted in Sheridan Morley, *Spread a Little Happiness* (1987).

Of the musical Camelot *on Broadway, in December 1960:*

2 It's like *Parsifal* without the jokes.

Noël Coward. Or 'It's about as long as *Parsifal*, and not as funny', in Dick Richards, *The Wit of Noël Coward* (1968). In *The Noël Coward Diaries* (entry for 16 December 1960) he merely relates how he took Marlene Dietrich to the first night and found the show 'disappointing ... music and lyrics uninspired and story uninteresting'.

On a revival of the musical Godspell *in 1981:*

3 Heralded by a sprinkling of glitter-dust and much laying on of microphones, *Godspell* is back in London at the Young Vic. For those who missed it the first time, this is your golden opportunity: you can miss it again.

Michael Billington, English theatre critic (1939–). Quoted in Diana Rigg, *No Turn Unstoned* (1982).

Review of play in The New Yorker *(1933):*

4 *House Beautiful* is play lousy.

Dorothy Parker, American writer (1893–1967). Quoted in Phyllis Hartnoll, *Plays and Players* (1984).

To Anton Chekhov, after seeing Uncle Vanya*:*

5 Shakespeare's plays are bad enough, but yours are even worse.

Leo Tolstoy, Russian novelist (1828–1910). Quoted in Henri Troyat, *Tolstoy* (1965).

On a play he disliked:

6 Its impact was like the banging together of two damp dish-cloths.

Brendan Behan, Irish playwright (1923–64). Attributed in *The Sayings of Brendan Behan*, ed. Aubrey Dillon-Malone (1997).

7 The play left a taste [in the mouth] of lukewarm parsnip juice.

Alexander Woollcott, American writer and critic (1887–1943). Quoted in H. Techman, *Smart Alex* (1976).

A comedy by Kenneth Horne with the title Yes and No *featuring Steve Geray and Magda Kun opened at the Ambassadors Theatre, London, in the autumn of 1938. It occasioned probably the shortest theatrical notice of all time:*

8 *Yes and No* – No!

Hannen Swaffer, English journalist (1879–1962). Attributed in letter from Bill Galley to *The Sunday Telegraph* (24 March 1970).

Reviewing a 'modern' production of a Shakespeare play in Sheffield:

9 [It should be titled] Twelfth Night, or What the Hell.

Anonymous. In *The Guardian* (11 February 1987).

Of an off-Broadway revue in the 1920s called A Good Time*:*

10 No.

Anonymous. Quoted in *The Observer* (18 January 1998). Ascribed dubiously to C. A. Lejeune.

Of Oscar Wilde's shortlived play Vera, *or* The Nihilists *(1882),* Punch *opined:*

11 It must have been vera, vera bad.

Anonymous. Quoted in Diana Rigg, *No Turn Unstoned* (1982).

Of a 1946 Chekhov production:

12 If you were to ask me what *Uncle Vanya* is about, I would say about as much as I can take.

Robert Garland (untraced). In *Journal American* (1946). Quoted in Diana Rigg, *No Turn Unstoned* (1982).

13 *Hook and Ladder* is the sort of play that gives failures a bad name.

Walter Kerr, American critic (1913–). Quoted in *The Frank Muir Book* (1976).

On a play called The Nerd *by Larry Shue:*

1 The lesson of the evening is that writing comedy is quite a serious business, and Mr Shue is much too small for his boots.

John Peter, English theatre critic (1938–). In *The Sunday Times*. Quoted in *A Year of Stings and Squelches* (1985).

Of Creston Clarke as King Lear:

2 He played the King as though under momentary apprehension that someone else was about to play the ace.

Eugene Field, American critic (1850–95). In the *Denver Tribune* (*c*.1880).

3 I have knocked everything but the knees of the chorus-girls, and Nature has anticipated me there.

Percy Hammond, American theatre critic (1873–1936). Quoted in *The Frank Muir Book* (1976).

On the nude revue Oh! Calcutta!*:*

4 Smithfield with songs.

Anonymous. Quoted by Barry Cryer on BBC Radio *Quote . . . Unquote* (29 January 1979).

Reviewing Dustin Hoffman's performance as Willy Loman in Arthur Miller's Death of a Salesman*:*

5 I was overwhelmed by the tragic small-ness of Dustin Hoffman's Willy.

Frank Rich, American theatre critic (of *The New York Times*). Quoted in *The Observer* (28 May 1989).

On costume drama:

6 Audiences don't like plays where people write letters with feathers.

Lee Shubert, American impresario (1875–1953). Attributed. Ascribed, regarding film costume epics, to a Missouri cinema owner of the mid-1930s – by Robin Bailey on BBC Radio *Quote . . . Unquote* (27 July 1985). Also ascribed to Max Gordon, Broadway producer, by Arthur Miller – in Ned Sherrin, *Theatrical Anecdotes* (1991).

On the London production of The World of Suzie Wong *in 1959:*

7 It is . . . a lot of Chinese junk . . . To pay it a visit would be to enter the world of choosy wrong.

Bernard Levin, English journalist and critic (1928–). In the *Daily Express* (November 1959).

8 A dramatic critic is a man who leaves no turn unstoned.

Bernard Shaw, Irish playwright and critic (1856–1950). Attributed in *The New York Times* (5 November 1950). According to E. Short, *Fifty Years of Vaudeville*, Arthur Wimperis (1874–1953) said of a vaudeville show: 'My dear fellow, a unique evening! I wouldn't have left a turn unstoned.'

Reviewing The Lake *(1933):*

9 Go to the Martin Beck Theatre and watch Katharine Hepburn run the whole gamut of emotions from A to B.

Dorothy Parker, American writer (1893–1967). Quoted in G. Carey, *Katharine Hepburn* (1985) – but only as a remark made in the intermission on the first night, not in a written review. Some would say that Parker went on and stated that Hepburn put some distance 'between herself and a more experienced colleague [Alison Skipworth] lest she catch acting from her'.

Of an actor called Guido Nadzo:

10 Guido Nadzo is nadzo guido.

George S. Kaufman, American playwright (1889–1961). Quoted in Scott Meredith, *George S. Kaufman and the Algonquin Round Table* (1974). Also attributed to Brooks Atkinson.

11 I acted so tragic the house rose like magic,
The audience yelled 'You're sublime.'
They made me a present of Mornington Crescent –
They threw it a brick at a time.

William Hargreaves, English songwriter (1846–1919). Song, 'The Night I Appeared as Macbeth' (1922).

On an inadequate portrayal of Queen Victoria in a play:

12 It made me feel that Albert had married beneath his station.

Noël Coward (later Sir Noël), English entertainer and writer (1899–1973). Quoted in

Kenneth Tynan, *Tynan on Theatre* (1964) and in *The Wit of Noël Coward* (ed. Dick Richards, 1968). However, James Agate has this in *Ego 6* (for 17 August 1943): 'At a luncheon party to-day I heard two women discussing historical films. One said, "My dear, they have a certain social value. Until I saw Anna Neagle and Anton Walbrook in the film about Queen Victoria [*Sixty Glorious Years*, 1938] I had no idea that the Prince Consort married beneath him!"' This may be no more than Agate purposely obscuring a source which was known to him, if indeed Coward was the originator. Coward makes no comment on the film in his published diaries.

On an American production of Chekhov's The Cherry Orchard *set in the Deep South:*

1 A Month in the Wrong Country.

Noël Coward. In *The Noël Coward Diaries* (1982) – entry for 4 September 1950.

Going backstage after a particularly disastrous opening night, Beerbohm is supposed to have reassured the leading lady with the compliment:

2 My dear, good is not the word.

Sir Max Beerbohm, English writer and caricaturist (1872–1956). Quoted on BBC Radio *Quote ... Unquote* (1979), but later also ascribed to Bernard Shaw.

When the play Abie's Irish Rose *ran for so long on Broadway (1922–7), Benchley found that he was incapable of saying anything new about it in the capsule criticisms that he had to supply each week, so he put:*

3 See Hebrews 13:8.

Robert Benchley, American humorist and drama critic for *Life* and *The New Yorker* (1889–1945). Quoted in Diana Rigg, *No Turn Unstoned* (1982). The text he alluded to reads: 'Jesus Christ the same yesterday, and today, and for ever.'

On the play Aglavaine and Selysette *by Maurice Maeterlinck on 3 January 1922:*

4 There's less in this than meets the eye.

Tallulah Bankhead, American actress (1903–68). Remark to Alexander Woollcott. However, in his journal, James Boswell attributed a version to Richard Burke, son of Edmund (1 May 1783): 'I suppose here *less* is meant than meets the ear.'

On a less than adequate performance in King Lear*:*

5 Quite a sweet little Goneril, don't you think?

Lilian Baylis, English theatrical manager (1874–1937). Quoted in *The Guardian* (1 March 1976).

On Bankhead as Shakespeare's Cleopatra:

6 Tallulah Bankhead barged down the Nile last night and sank. As the Serpent of the Nile she proves to be no more dangerous than a garter snake.

John Mason Brown, American critic (1900–69). In the *New York Post* (11 November 1937).

Theft

7 Thieves respect property; they merely wish the property to become their property that they may more perfectly respect it.

G. K. Chesterton, English poet, novelist and critic (1874–1936). *The Man Who Was Thursday* (1908).

8 See how the rascals use me! They will not let my play run and yet they steal my thunder!

John Dennis, English playwright (1657–1734). Quoted in William S. Walsh, *A Handy-Book of Literary Curiosities* (1893). Hence the expression 'to steal a person's thunder' meaning 'to get in first and do whatever the other wanted to make a big impression with', particularly with regard to ideas and policies. It is said to derive from an incident involving Dennis who had invented a device for making the sound of thunder in plays and had used it in an unsuccessful one of his own at the Drury Lane Theatre, London (*c.*1700). Subsequently, at the same theatre, he saw a performance of *Macbeth* and noted that the thunder was being produced in his special way. Another version of his remark is: 'That is my thunder, by God; the villains will play my thunder, but not my play.'

9 Lady Dorothy Nevill, so Sir Edmund Gosse tells, preserved her library by pasting in each volume the legend: 'This book has been stolen from Lady Dorothy Nevill.'

Lady Dorothy Nevill (untraced). Quoted in *The Week-End Book* (1955).

1 The people of Zaïre are not thieves. It merely happens that they move things, or borrow them.

Sese Seko Mobutu, Zaïrean President (1930–). Quoted in *The Sunday Times* (28 May 1978).

Theory

2 It is a good thing not to put confidence in observations until they have been checked against theory.

Anonymous. Quoted in *The 'Quote ... Unquote' Newsletter* (October 1994). Also known in a French form, sarcastically applied by graduates of the Napoleonic *Grandes Écoles* to the graduates of the post-war, Gaullist *École Nationale d'Administration* (ENA): *Ça marche en pratique, mais en théorie ... ?* [Well, it works in practice, but will it work in theory?]'

Thinness

3 Outside every thin girl there is a fat man trying to get in.

Katharine Whitehorn, English journalist (1928–). Revived by her on BBC Radio *Quote ... Unquote*, BBC Radio (27 July 1985).

4 You can never be too rich or too thin.

Duchess of Windsor, American-born wife of the Duke of Windsor (1896–1986). Quoted in *The Penguin Dictionary of Modern Quotations* (1980 edn).

Threats

When asked what was the greatest threat to the Beatles – the H-Bomb or dandruff:

5 The H-Bomb. We've already got dandruff.

Ringo Starr, English pop musician and singer (1940–). Quoted in Michael Braun, *Love Me Do: the Beatles' Progress* (1964).

Time

6 At my back I often hear Time's winged chariot changing gear.

Eric Linklater, Scottish writer (1899–1974). *Juan in China* (1937).

7 The Duke of Newcastle did everything by halves and nothing well. He invariably lost half an hour in the morning and spent the rest of the day trying to find it.

Philip Dormer Stanhope, 4th Earl of Chesterfield, English politician and writer (1694–1773). Quoted in *The 'Quote ... Unquote' Newsletter* (October 1992).

Titanic

On the sinking of the Titanic *in 1912:*

8 I am sorry to hear there has been a bad boating accident.

Mrs Edmund Warre, wife of the Headmaster of Eton at that time. Quoted by George Lyttelton in *The Lyttelton Hart-Davis Letters* (for 7 December 1955). He adds, 'She came in, quivering slightly with age and dottiness ... An odd but very characteristic way of describing the sinking of the largest ship in the world and the death of 1400 people.'

Titles (honours)

9 Titles distinguish the mediocre, embarrass the superior, and are disgraced by the inferior.

Bernard Shaw, Irish playwright and critic (1856–1950). 'Maxims for Revolutionaries', *Man and Superman* (1903).

Titles (literary)

Advice to a young writer who did not know what title to give his work. 'Are there any trumpets in it?' 'No'. 'Are there any drums in it?' 'No':

10 Then why not call it *Without Drums or Trumpets*?

(Sir) J. M. Barrie, Scottish playwright (1860–1937). Untraced, but when quoted by Ludovic Kennedy (1991), the title suggested was, rather, *No Horses, No Trumpets*. A similar story is told about the French playwright, Tristan Bernard (1866–1947) in Cornelia Otis Skinner's *Elegant Wits and Grand Horizontals* (1962). Somebody did take the advice: the English translation of Alec Le Vernoy's Second World War memoir was entitled *No Drums, No Trumpets* (1983).

Toasts

1 'Gentlemen, lift the seat' ... perhaps
it's a loyal toast?

Jonathan Miller, English entertainer, writer
and director (1934–). 'The Heat-Death
of the Universe', *Beyond the Fringe*
(1961).

2 Here's to pure scholarship. May
it never be of any use to anyone!

Anonymous. Quoted in *The 'Quote ...
Unquote' Newsletter* (July 1993). John
Julius Norwich commented that his father,
Duff Cooper (1890–1954), used to
quote this as a toast specifically to higher
mathematics.

Tobacco

3 Tobacco is a dirty weed. I like it.
It satisfies no normal need. I like it.
It makes you thin, it makes you lean,
It takes the hair right off your
     bean [= head].
It's the worst darn stuff I've ever seen.
I like it.

Graham L. Hemminger (untraced).
Quoted in Herbert V. Prochnow, Snr & Jnr,
A Treasury of Humorous Quotations (1969).
Another version follows:

Tobacco is an ugly weed, I like it!
It can fulfil no earthly need, I like it!
Its smell is neither nice nor clean,
It takes the hair hair right off your bean.
It's the foulest weed I've ever seen,
     I like it!

Tolkien, J. R. R.
**English scholar and novelist
(1892–1973)**

4 Tolkien is Hobbit-forming.

Anonymous (graffito), by the 1980s. In
a letter to Roger Lancelyn Green (8 January 1971) and included in *The Letters of
J. R. Tolkien* (1981), Tolkien himself
noted: 'A review appeared in *The Observer*
16 Jan[uary] 1938, signed "Habit" (inciden-
tally thus long anticipating [Nevill] Coghill's
perception of the similarity of the words
in his humorous adj. "hobbit-forming"
applied to my books).'

Tourists

*Suggestion to tourists visiting Britain for
the first time:*

5 Have you tried the famous echo in the
Reading Room of the British Museum?

Gerard Hoffnung, English cartoonist and
musician (1925–59). Speech, Oxford Union
debating society (4 December 1958).

6 If it's Tuesday it must be Belgium.

Anonymous saying (the kind of thing fast-
moving American tourists would say).
Enshrined in the title of a film (US,
1969).

Tragedy

7 The bad ended unhappily, the good
unluckily. That is what tragedy means.

(Sir) Tom Stoppard, English playwright
(1937–). *Rosencrantz and Guildenstern Are
Dead*, Act 2 (1966).

Translation

8 Edward III had very good manners.
One day at a royal dance he noticed
some men-about-court mocking a lady
whose garter had come off, whereupon
to put her at her ease he stopped the
dance and made the memorable
epitaph: *'Honi soie qui mal y pense'*
('Honey, your silk stocking's hanging down').

W. C. Sellar & R. J. Yeatman, English
humorists (1898–1951) and (1897–1968).
1066 and All That (1930). Byron is
said to have re-translated the motto as,
'On his walk he madly puns.'

9 Nothing is improved by translation,
except a Bishop.

Philip Dormer Stanhope, 4th Earl of
Chesterfield, English politician and
writer (1694–1773). Quoted in *The
'Quote ... Unquote' Newsletter* (October
1992).

10 I have a prejudice against people who
print things in a foreign language and
add no translation. When I am the
reader, and the author considers me
able to do the translating myself,
he pays me quite a nice compliment –

but if he would do the translating for me I would try to get along without the compliment.

Mark Twain, American writer (1835–1910). *A Tramp Abroad*, Chap. 16 (1880).

1 Translations (like wives) are seldom strictly faithful if they are in the least attractive.

Roy Campbell, South African poet and journalist (1901–57). In *Poetry Review* (June–July 1949).

Travel

2 I have found out that there ain't no surer way to find out whether you like people or hate them than to travel with them.

Mark Twain, American writer (1835–1910). *Tom Sawyer Abroad* (1894).

3 It is not travel that narrows the mind but travel writing.

James Buchan, British writer (1916–). In *The Spectator* (11 August 1990).

4 Definition: I am a traveller, you are a tourist, they are trippers.

Anonymous. Quoted in about 1974 by John Julius Norwich. It may have originated in a *New Statesman* competition.

Trousers

5 You should never have your best trousers on when you go out to fight for freedom and truth.

Henrik Ibsen, Norwegian playwright (1828–1906). *An Enemy of the People* (1882).

In November 1982 when Sir Geoffrey Howe, British Chancellor of the Exchequer, had his trousers stolen when travelling by rail on an overnight sleeper:

6 I am thrilled about the loss of your trousers because it revealed your human face.

Anonymous colleague – probably a fellow member of the Cabinet. Quoted by Lady Howe in *The Observer* Magazine (12 January 1984).

Trust

7 In God we trust, all others [must] pay cash.

Anonymous (American). Quoted by US Secretary of State George Schulz after the Washington summit between Mikhail Gorbachev and Ronald Reagan in December 1987. Listed in *H. L. Mencken's Dictionary of Quotations* (1942) as an 'American saying'.

8 Would you buy a used car from me?

John De Lorean, American businessman. Quoted in *The Observer*, 'Sayings of the Week' (19 August 1984).

Truth

9 There was things he stretched, but mainly he told the truth.

Mark Twain, American writer (1835–1910). *The Adventures of Huckleberry Finn* (1884).

10 The truth is rarely pure, and never simple.

Oscar Wilde, Irish playwright, poet and wit (1854–1900). *The Importance of Being Earnest*, Act 1 (1895).

11 Truth is always duller than fiction.

Piers Paul Read, English writer (1941–). In *The Observer* (1981).

Turpentine

12 Two farmers met and one said to the other: "Ere, you remember telling me you gave your 'oss turpentine when 'e 'ad colic.' The other said: 'Ay!' The first farmer went on: 'Well, I gave my 'oss turpentine, an' 'e died.' Said the other: 'Well, mine died too!'

Craven Hill, English cartoonist. Version of caption to cartoon in *Punch* Magazine (24 November 1909).

Typewriters

13 I wrote all my formal communications to the press in longhand. I have never had the secret knack of typewriters. Typewriters can't spell, you know.

Sir Max Beerbohm, English writer and caricaturist (1872–1956). Quoted in S. N. Behrman, *Conversations with Max* (1960).

Typhoid

1 Typhoid is a terrible disease; it can kill you or damage your brain. I know what I'm talking about, I've had typhoid.

Marshal MacMahon, French soldier and statesman (1808–93). Quoted in Bechtel & Carrière, *Dictionnaire de la Bêtise* (1983).

U

Ugliness

1 I was so ugly when I was born, the doctor slapped my mother.

Henny Youngman, British-born American comedian (1906–98). Quoted in *The Times* (26 February 1998).

Umbrellas

2 All men are equal – all men, that is to say, who possess umbrellas.

E. M. Forster, English novelist (1879–1970). *Howard's End*, Chap. 6 (1910).

Uncompromising

3 I've met a lot of hardboiled eggs in my time, but you're twenty minutes.

Billy Wilder, American film director and writer (1906–). Line from the film *Ace in the Hole* (US, 1951). Co-written with Lesser Samuels and Walter Newman.

Unexpurgated

4 We have long passed the Victorian Era when asterisks were followed after a certain interval by a baby.

W. Somerset Maugham, English writer (1874–1965). *The Constant Wife* (1926).

Uniforms

5 He [Benchley] came out of a night club one evening and, tapping a uniformed figure on the shoulder, said, 'get me a cab.' The uniformed figure turned round furiously and informed him that he was not a doorman but a rear admiral. 'O.K.,' said Benchley, 'Get me a battleship.'

Robert Benchley, American humorist (1889–1945). Quoted in *The New Yorker* (5 January 1946).

Usefulness

Remark by a small boy to his mother about a man carrying a bag of golf clubs:

6 Mummy, what's that man for?

F. H. Townsend, English illustrator. Caption to cartoon in *Punch*, Vol. 131 (14 November 1906).

On Prince Andrew:

7 He's the only one who knows how to work the video.

Elizabeth II, British Queen (1926–). Quoted in *The Observer*, 'Sayings of the Week' (11 August 1985).

One old woman is reported to have said to another:

8 Yes, I had him cremated and his ashes made into an eggtimer. He never did any work while he was alive, so he might as well do some now he's dead.

Anonymous. In J. B. Priestley's *English Journey* (1934), he recounts attending a lunch club in Manchester where commercial travellers told stories. He repeats one: 'A weaver up Blackburn way had just lost her husband. "Where yer going to bury 'im?" a neighbour asked her. "Ah'm not going to bury 'im," she replied. "Ah'm going to 'ave 'im creamated," she replied. The neighbour was impressed. "But whatever will yer do wi' th'ashes?' she inquired. "Ah'll tell yer what Ah'm going to do wi' th'ashes,"said the widow. "Ah'm going to 'ave 'em put into an eggtimer. Th'owd devil wouldn't ever work when 'e wer alive, so 'e can start doing a bit now 'e's deead."' Priestley comments: 'That still seems to me a very good story, even though I am no longer under the influence of beer and Bury Black Puddings. It is a fair sample of Lanca-shire's grimly ironic humour.' The line was also quoted by Alan Bennett in 'The English Way of Death', *Beyond the Fringe*, Broadway version (1964).

V

Van Gogh

To actor Cliff Osmond:

1 You have Van Gogh's ear for music.

Billy Wilder, American film director and writer (1906–). Quoted in Leslie Halliwell, *The Filmgoer's Book of Quotes* (1973). Appearing on BBC Radio *Quote... Unquote* in 1977, the comic actor Kenneth Williams came up with a rather good showbiz story. He quoted the above as what Orson Welles had reputedly said of the singing of Donny Osmond (then a popular young star). In fact, Orson Welles did not say it, nor was it about Donny Osmond, but the reasons why the joke had been reascribed and redirected are instructive. It was in fact Billy Wilder who made the original remark. He has a notably waspish wit but is, perhaps, not such a household name as Orson Welles. He lacks, too, Welles's Falstaffian stature and his, largely unearned, reputation in the public mind for having said witty things. And Wilder said it about Cliff Osmond, an American comedy actor who had appeared in the film director's *Kiss Me Stupid*, *The Fortune Cookie* and *The Front Page*. As far as one knows, he is not related to Donny Osmond but, apparently, he had to be replaced in the anecdote because he lacked star status. Tom Stoppard included something very similar in *The Real Inspector Hound* (1968): 'An uncanny ear that might [have] belonged to a Van Gogh.'

Vanity

2 You're so vain, you probably think this song is about you.

Carly Simon, American singer and song-writer (1945–). Song, 'You're So Vain' (1972). It is usually assumed that the subject of the song was, in fact, the film actor Warren Beatty.

Vasectomy

3 A vasectomy means never having to say you're sorry.

Anonymous (graffito). Quoted in Reisner & Wechsler, *The Encyclopedia of Graffiti* (1974). Ascribed to Rubin Carson (untraced) in Laurence J. Peter, *Quotations for Our Time* (1977).

Vendettas

On Peter Cook:

4 For a man linked with satire he was without malice to anyone, although he did admit to pursuing an irrational vendetta against the late great Gracie Fields.

Richard Ingrams, English editor and writer (1937–). Quoted in *The Independent* 'Quote Unquote' (6 May 1995).

Venice

5 The most striking thing about the City of Venice is the complete absence of the smell of horse dung.

Alphonse Allais, French humorist (1854–1905). Quoted in *The World of Alphonse Allais*, selected, translated and introduced by Miles Kington (1976).

Telegram to The New Yorker *on arriving in Venice:*

6 STREETS FLOODED. PLEASE ADVISE.

Robert Benchley, American humorist (1889–1945). Quoted in R. E. Drennan, *Wit's End* (1973).

7 Venice is like eating an entire box of chocolate liqueurs at one go.

Truman Capote, American writer (1924–84).

Quoted in *The Observer* (26 November 1961).

1 We have often heard Cork called the Venice of Ireland, but have never heard Venice called the Cork of Italy.

Anonymous. Quoted by John Betjeman in a letter to Michael Rose (25 September 1955).

Venus de Milo

2 See what'll happen if you don't stop biting your finger-nails.

Will Rogers, American humorist (1879–1935). Quoted in Bennett Cerf, *Shake Well Before Using* (1948).

Vice-Presidency

3 [The Vice-Presidency] isn't worth a pitcher of warm piss.

John Nance Garner, American Democratic Vice-President (1868–1967). Quoted in O. C. Fisher, *Cactus Jack* (1978). Usually bowdlerized to 'warm spit', as apparently it was by the first journalist who reported it and (invariably) by Alistair Cooke. Garner was Vice-President (1933–41) during F. D. Roosevelt's first two terms. Furthermore, Garner said, in 1963, that the job 'didn't amount to a hill of beans' (also in Fisher). Theo Lippman Jr in the *San Francisco Chronicle* (25 December 1992) provided this further Garner story: he was walking down the halls of the Capitol one day when the circus was in Washington. A fellow came up to him and introduced himself. 'I am the head clown in the circus,' he said. Very solemnly, Garner replied, 'And I am the Vice-President of the United States. You'd better stick around here a while. You might pick up some new ideas.'

4 Once there were two brothers: one ran away to sea, the other was elected Vice-President – and nothing was ever heard from either of them again.

Thomas R. Marshall, American Democratic Vice-President (1854–1925). Quoted in Laurence J. Peter, *Quotations for Our Time* (1977).

Views

5 Oh it really is a wery pretty garden, and Chingford to the eastward can be seen;

Wiv a ladder and some glasses
You could see to 'Ackney Marshes,
If it wasn't for the 'ouses in between.

Edgar Bateman, English songwriter (*fl.*1900). Song, 'The 'Ouses In Between' (1894), popularized by Gus Elen (d.1940), which had music by George Le Brunn (1862–1905).

Violence

6 Violence is the repartee of the illiterate.

Alan Brien, English writer and journalist (1925–). In *Punch* (7 February 1973). When Brien was asked to source this quotation on BBC Radio *Quote . . . Unquote* (10 August 1985) he said: 'I don't think I've heard it before . . . modernish? . . . it can't be very old. Bernard Shaw would be too good for it . . . but it's approaching Bernard Shaw. Perhaps it's Chesterton, is it?'

7 AMANDA: I've been brought up to believe that it's beyond the pale, for a man to strike a woman.
ELYOT: A very poor tradition. Certain women should be struck regularly, like gongs.

Noël Coward (later Sir Noël), English entertainer and writer (1899–1973). *Private Lives*, Act 3 (1930).

Virginity

8 Romance on the High Seas was Doris Day's first picture; that was before she became a virgin.

Oscar Levant, American pianist and actor (1906–72). *Memoirs of an Amnesiac* (1965).

To unsuitable American actresses who had been assembled to play ladies-in-waiting to a queen:

9 Ladies, just a little more virginity, if you don't mind.

Sir Herbert Beerbohm Tree, English actor-manager (1853–1917). Quoted in Alexander Woollcott, *Shouts and Murmurs* (1923).

Visitors

10 Fish and visitors smell in three days.

Anonymous. Quoted in Benjamin Franklin, *Poor Richard's Almanack* (1736). *The Concise Oxford Dictionary of Proverbs* (1982) finds the idea (without the fish) in Plautus and the first English reference (with the fish) in Lyly's *Euphues* (1580).

On American troops in Britain during the Second World War:

1 Overpaid, overfed, oversexed and over here.

Anonymous, though sometimes attributed to Tommy Trinder, English comedian (1909–89).

Vultures

2 If there's one thing above all a vulture can't stand, it's a glass eye.

Frank McKinney ('Kin') Hubbard, American humorist (1868–1930). Attributed. Possibly from *Abe Martin's Sayings and Sketches* (1915). 'Abe Martin' was a folksy humorous character whose sayings, originally published in the *Indianapolis News* from 1892, were later collected annually.

W

Wagner, Richard
German composer (1813–83)

1 Wagner is the Puccini of music.

J. B. Morton (Beachcomber), English humorous writer (1893–1979). Quoted in the *Lyttelton Hart-Davis Letters* (for 5 February 1956). Rupert Hart-Davis comments that the announcement 'summed up the jargon-bosh of art- and music-critics beautifully.' On the other hand, James Agate in *Ego 6* (for 13 October 1943) has: 'I do not doubt the sincerity of the solemn ass who, the other evening, said portentously: "Wagner is the Puccini of music!"' As Agate was addressing a group of 'school-marms' and as he generally had an after-dinner speaker's way with attribution, it may well still have been a Beachcomber coinage.

2 Wagner has beautiful moments but awful quarters of an hour.

Gioacchino Rossini, Italian composer (1792–1868). Letter (April 1867), quoted in E. Naumann, *Italiensiche Tondichter* (1883). In his *Reminiscences, Inscriptions & Anecdotes* (1913), the musician Francesco Berger attributed this to the pianist Hans von Bülow: 'Some one observed, "Well, you must admit that he has some heavenly moments." "I don't dispute the heavenly moments," said he, "but he has some devilish ugly half-hours."'

3 One can't judge Wagner's opera *Lohengrin* after a first hearing, and I certainly don't intend hearing it a second time.

Gioacchino Rossini. Quoted in *The Frank Muir Book* (1976).

Lady Henry commenting on a performance of Lohengrin:

4 I like Wagner's music better than anybody's. It is so loud that one can talk the whole time without other people hearing what one says. That is a great advantage.

Oscar Wilde, Irish playwright, poet and wit (1854–1900). *The Picture of Dorian Gray*, Chap. 4 (1891).

5 I have been told that Wagner's music is better than it sounds.

Edgar Wilson 'Bill' Nye, American humorist (1850–96). In Mark Twain's *Autobiography* (published posthumously in 1924) he ascribes this to Nye who had predeceased him in 1896. Given the dates involved here, it is curious that Lewis Baumer was providing this caption to a *Punch* cartoon (20 November 1918): (Two women talking) – 'Going to hear some Wagner.' 'What! – do you like the stuff?' 'Frankly, no; but I've heard on the best authority that his music's very much better than it sounds.'

6 *Parsifal* is the kind of opera that starts at six o'clock. After it has been going three hours, you look at your watch and it says 6.20.

David Randolph, American conductor and writer (1914–). Quoted in *The American Treasury*, ed. Clifton Fadiman (1955).

On hearing Wagner's Lohengrin:

7 The banging and slamming and booming and crashing were something beyond belief. The racking and pitiless pain of it remains stored up in my memory alongside the memory of the time that I had my teeth fixed.

Mark Twain, American writer (1835–1910). *A Tramp Abroad*, Chap. 9 (1880).

Waiters

8 Diner: I'd complain about the service if I could find a waiter to complain to.

Mel Calman, English cartoonist (1931–94). Caption to cartoon in *How to Survive Abroad* (1971).

1 I vividly recall one story [Compton Mackenzie] told. He was sitting in the Café Royal, dining alone. Near him, leaning against a pillar, was a waiter. A second waiter approached the first waiter, looked surreptitiously all round, then whispered confidentially: '*Well* ... He's eaten it.'

Anonymous. Quoted in Michael Pertwee, *Name Dropping* (1974). The real original probably lies in a *Punch* cartoon by G. L. Stampa that appeared on 16 May 1934. 'He's eaten it!' was the caption below a picture of two waiters and a diner.

Of a dead waiter:

2 God finally caught his eye.

George S. Kaufman, American playwright (1889–1961). Quoted in Scott Meredith, *George S. Kaufman and the Algonquin Round Table* (1974). As 'By and by/God caught his eye' this epitaph is attributed to David McCord (1897– ?), in 'Remainders' from *Bay Window Ballads* (1935).

Wales and the Welsh

3 The land of my fathers – my fathers can have it.

Dylan Thomas, Welsh poet (1914–53). Quoted in *Adam* (December 1953). 'Land of My Fathers' (1860) is the Welsh national anthem.

4 There are still parts of Wales where the only concession to gaiety is a striped shroud.

Gwyn Thomas, Welsh novelist, playwright and humorist (1913–81). In *Punch* (18 June 1958).

5 We can trace nearly all the disasters of English history to the influence of Wales.

Evelyn Waugh, English novelist (1903–66). *Decline and Fall* (1928).

6 Welshmen prize their women so highly that they put a picture of their mother-in-law on the national flag.

Anonymous. Quoted by Canon Don Lewis on BBC Radio *Quote ... Unquote* (16 July 1983).

7 A Welshman is a man who prays on his knees on Sundays and preys on his neighbours all the rest of the week.

Anonymous. Quoted in *The Penguin Dictionary of Modern Humorous Quotations*, ed. Fred Metcalf (1987).

8 The Welsh are the Italians in the rain.

Anonymous. Quoted by the writer Elaine Morgan on BBC Radio *Quote ... Unquote* (25 April 1983). An earlier version spoken, though probably not coined, by the journalist René Cutforth was: 'The Welsh are the Mediterraneans in the rain', which was quoted by Nancy Banks-Smith in *The Guardian* (17 October 1979).

War

9 The Falklands thing was a fight between two bald men over a comb.

Jorge Luis Borges, Argentinian novelist (1899–1986). Quoted in *Time* Magazine (14 February 1983). The basic expression is proverbial, however. It is quoted in *H. L. Mencken's Dictionary of Quotations* (1942), as 'Two bald-headed men are fighting over a comb' (listed as a 'Russian saying') and in Champion's *Racial Proverbs* (1938).

10 The late unpleasantness.

Petroleum V. Nasby (David Ross Locke), American humorist (1833–88). *Ekkoes from Kentucky* (1868). A euphemism for a previous war or recent hostilities. 'Nasby' referred to the recently ended Civil War as 'the late onpleasantniss'.

11 Non-combatant, *n.* A dead Quaker.

Ambrose Bierce, American journalist (1842–?1914). *The Cynic's Word Book* (later retitled *The Devil's Dictionary*) (1906).

12 They are rolling up the maps all over Europe. We shall not see them lit again in our lifetime.

Alan Bennett, English playwright and actor (1934–). *Forty Years On*, Act 1 (1969).

13 As long as war is regarded as wicked, it will always have its fascination. When it is looked upon as vulgar, it will cease to be popular.

Oscar Wilde, Irish playwright, poet and wit (1854–1900). *The Critic As Artist* (1890).

Water

1 Water taken in moderation cannot hurt anybody.

Mark Twain, American writer (1835–1910). *Mark Twain's Notebook*, ed. A. B. Paine (1935).

We

2 Only presidents, editors, and people with tapeworms have the right to use the editorial 'we'.

H. L. Mencken, American journalist and linguist (1880–1956). Attributed, sometimes in the form: 'There are two kinds of people entitled to refer to themselves as "we". One is an editor, the other is a fellow with a tapeworm.' Also attributed to Edgar Wilson 'Bill' Nye and Mark Twain.

Wealth

3 If you would know what the Lord God thinks of money, you have only to look at those to whom He gave it.

Maurice Baring, English writer (1874–1945). Attributed by Dorothy Parker, according to Malcolm Cowley (ed.), *Writers at Work*, First Series (1958).

4 A rich man's joke is always funny.

T(homas) E(dward) Brown, English poet and schoolmaster (1830–97). Poem, 'The Doctor' (1887) – and preceded by the line, 'Money is honey, my little sonny'.

5 Lord Finchley tried to mend the Electric Light
Himself. It struck him dead: And serve him right!
It is the business of the wealthy man
To give employment to the artisan.

Hilaire Belloc, French-born English poet and writer (1870–1953). 'Lord Finchley', *More Peers* (1911).

6 He does not possess wealth; it possesses him.

Benjamin Franklin, American politician and scientist (1706–90). *Poor Richard's Almanack* (July 1735) – a work in which Franklin often revised already existing sayings.

7 I don't know how much money I've got ... I did ask the accountant how much it came to. I wrote it down on a bit of paper. But I've lost the bit of paper.

John Lennon, English singer and songwriter (1940–80). Quoted in Hunter Davies, *The Beatles* (1968).

Weariness

8 After three days men grow weary, of a wench, a guest and weather rainy.

Benjamin Franklin, American politician and scientist (1706–90). *Poor Richard's Almanack* (June 1733) – a work in which Franklin often revised already existing sayings.

Weather

9 Everybody talks about the weather but nobody does anything about it.

Charles Dudley Warner, American journalist (1829–1900). It first appeared in an unsigned editorial in the *Hartford Courant* (24 August 1897) in the form – 'A well-known American writer said once that, while everybody talked about the weather, nobody seemed to do anything about it' – but the quip has often been assigned to Mark Twain who lived in Hartford (Connecticut) at the time and was a friend and collaborator of Warner's.

10 If you don't like the weather in New England now, just wait a few minutes.

Mark Twain, American writer (1835–1910). Quoted in Herbert V. Prochnow, Snr & Jnr, *A Treasury of Humorous Quotations* (1969).

11 Some are weather-wise, some otherwise.

Benjamin Franklin, American politician and scientist (1706–90). *Poor Richard's Almanack* (February 1735) – a work in which Franklin often revised already existing sayings.

12 A woman rang to say she'd heard there was a hurricane on the way. Well, don't worry. There isn't.

Michael Fish, English TV weather forecaster (1933–). On BBC TV, on the eve of the Great Storm in which devastation laid waste a swathe of southern England. Quoted in *The Observer*, 'Sayings of the Week' (19 October 1987).

13 I was measured for a cork jacket yesterday. Walking is out of the question just now. We can only get from place to place by swimming.

Revd Sydney Smith, English clergyman, essayist and wit (1771–1845). Quoted in Saba, Lady Holland, *Memoir* (1855).

Webb, Sidney and Beatrice
English socialist thinkers
(1859–1947 and 1858–1943)

1 Two of the nicest people if ever there was one.

Alan Bennett, English playwright and actor (1934–). *Forty Years On,* Act 2 (1969). This line does not appear in the published script of Bennett's play, though it was spoken in the original production.

Wellerisms

2 SAM WELLER: It's over, and can't be helped, and that's one consolation, as they always say in Turkey, ven they cut the wrong man's head off.

Charles Dickens, English novelist (1812–70). *Pickwick Papers*, Chap. 23 (1837).

3 'That's an antelope,' observed the small boy when he heard that his mother's sister had run away with the coachman.

Anonymous. In *The Wasp* (California), Vol.3, No.144 (1879). Quoted in *A Dictionary of Wellerisms*, ed. Mieder & Kingsbury (1994).

4 'Every little helps,' quoth the wren when she pissed in the sea.

Anonymous. Quoted in William Camden, *Remains Concerning Britaine* (1605).

5 Far from it, as the private said when he aimed at the bulls-eye and hit the gunnery instructor.

Dorothy L. Sayers, English novelist (1893–1957). *Unnatural Death* (1927).

6 *'Au contraire',* as the man said when asked if he'd dined on the boat.

G. K. Chesterton, English poet, novelist and critic (1874–1936). *The Man Who Was Thursday* (1907/8).

Wembley

7 Wembley, adj. Suffering from a vague *malaise.* 'I feel a bit w. this morning.'

Paul Jennings, English humorist (1918–89). 'Ware, Wye, Watford', *The Jenguin Pennings* (1963).

Westerns

8 I wouldn't say when you've seen one Western you've seen the lot: but when you've seen the lot you get the feeling you've seen one.

Katharine Whitehorn, English journalist (1928–). 'Decoding the West', *Sunday Best* (1976).

Wetness

9 I must get out of these wet clothes and into a dry martini.

Robert Benchley, American humorist (1889–1945). Variously used line, as in the film, *The Major and the Minor* (US, 1942) – spoken by Benchley to Ginger Rogers in the form 'Why don't you get out of that wet coat and into a dry Martini?', according to Harry Haun, *The Movie Quote Book* (1980). Sometimes also attributed to Alexander Woollcott, the line may actually have originated with Benchley's press agent in the 1920s or with his friend Charles Butterworth. In any case, apparently, Mae West also adopted the line, as screenwriter, in *Every Day's a Holiday* (1937).

Whims

10 King Barumph has a whim of iron.

Oliver Herford, American humorist (1863–1935). 'Impossible pudding', *Excuse It Please* (1929).

Widows

11 He had heard that one is permitted a certain latitude with widows, and went in for the whole 180 degrees.

George Ade, American humorist (1866–1944). Quoted in *The Treasury of Humorous Quotations*, ed. Evan Esar & Nicolas Bentley (1951).

Letter from a Tyrolean landlord:

12 Standing among savage scenery, the hotel offers stupendous revelations. There is a French widow in every bedroom (affording delightful prospects).

Gerard Hoffnung, English cartoonist and musician (1925–59). Speech, Oxford Union debating society (4 December 1958).

Wilde, Oscar

**Irish playwright, poet and wit
(1854–1900)**

1 If, with the literate, I am
Impelled to try an epigram,
I never seek to take the credit;
We all assume that Oscar said it.

Dorothy Parker, American writer (1893–1967).
'A Pig's Eye View of Literature' (1937).

2 He had nothing to say and he said it.

Ambrose Bierce, American journalist (1942–
?1914). Attributed. In Wilde's own *The Picture
of Dorian Gray*, there is: 'Women ... never have
anything to say, but they say it charmingly.'
Similarly, a review in *The Times* (5 May 1937)
of a book by A. A. Milne said: 'When there is
nothing whatever to say, no one knows better
than Mr Milne how to say it.' Compare also:
'Berlioz says nothing in his music but he says
it magnificently' – James Gibbons Huneker,
Old Fogy (1913).

Wills

3 I think it will be a clash between the political will and the administrative won't.

Jonathan Lynn and Antony Jay, English writers
(1943– and 1930–). *Yes Prime Minister*,
Vol. 2 (1987).

Willies

*Fat man with an enormous stomach (or
'corporation') that prevents him from seeing
the small boy seated at his feet:*

4 Can't see my little Willy.

Donald McGill, English comic postcard artist
(1875–1962). Caption to postcard *c.*1910. 'I've
lost my little Willie!' (which rather obscures
the joke) was used as the title of a 'celebration
of comic postcards' (1976) by Benny Green.
This book title may have been taken from the
caption to a re-drawing of the idea by another
cartoonist.

Wilson, Harold
(later Lord Wilson of Rievaulx)

**British Labour Prime Minister
(1916–95)**

5 If ever he went to school without any
boots it was because he was too big
for them.

Ivor Bulmer-Thomas (formerly Ivor Thomas),
Welsh Labour, then Conservative, MP
(1905– 93). Speech at Conservative Party
Conference (12 October 1949) – a remark
often wrongly ascribed to Harold Macmillan.
It followed a press dispute involving Wilson
the previous year.

Wine snobbery

6 It's a Naive Domestic Burgundy without
Any Breeding, But I Think You'll be
amused by its Presumption.

James Thurber, American cartoonist and
writer (1894–1961). Caption to cartoon in
Men, Women and Dogs (1943).

7 ONE DRINKER TO ANOTHER: I keep
this port only for my best friends.
OTHER DRINKER: I don't blame you.

Anonymous. Quoted in *A Year of Stings and
Squelches* (1985).

*How to promote a Cockburn '97, clearly
past its best:*

8 Talk of the 'imperial decay' of your
invalid port. 'Its gracious withdrawal
from perfection, keeping a hint of former
majesty, withal, as it hovers between
oblivion and the divine *Untergang* of
infinite recession.'

Stephen Potter, English humorist (1900–69).
One-Upmanship (1952).

Winning

On the tortoise and hare myth:

9 In real life, of course, it is the hare who
wins. Every time. Look around you.
And in any case it is my contention
that Aesop was writing for the tortoise
market ... Hares have no time to read.
They are too busy winning the game.

Anita Brookner, English art historian and novelist (1928–). *Hotel du Lac*, Chap. 2 (1984).

Wisdom

*To a judge who had complained that he was no
wiser at the end than when he started
hearing one of Smith's cases:*

10 Possibly not, My Lord, but far better
informed.

F. E. Smith (1st Earl of Birkenhead), English

politician and lawyer (1872–1930). Quoted in 2nd Earl of Birkenhead, *The Earl of Birkenhead* (1933).

1 It hath been my opinion, that the French are wiser than they seem, and the Spaniards seem wiser than they are.

Francis Bacon (1st Baron Verulam and Viscount St Albans), English philosopher and politician (1561–1626). 'Of Seeming Wise', *Essays* (1625).

Wise

2 Some folks are wise, and some are otherwise.

Tobias Smollett, Scottish novelist (1721–71). *The Adventures of Roderick Random*, Chap. 6 (1748).

Wit

3 Wit is like caviar – it should be served in small portions, and not spread about like marmalade.

Noël Coward (later Sir Noël), English entertainer and writer (1899–1973). Quoted in *Newsweek* (1965).

On New York taxi drivers:

4 They try to live up to the reputation all taxi drivers have, of being a wit. As I am in the wit business myself, I object to competition.

Brendan Behan, Irish playwright (1923–64). *Brendan Behan's New York* (1964).

Wives

Explaining why he wasn't taking his wife on an official visit to Paris:

5 You don't take a ham sandwich to the Lord Mayor's banquet, do you?

J(ames) H(enry) Thomas, English trade unionist and politician (1874–1949). Quoted in the *Cassell Companion to Quotations* (1997).

6 Greater luck hath no man than this, that he lay down his wife at the right moment.

Samuel Butler, English author (1835–1902). *Notebooks* (c.1890).

7 They say a woman should be a cook in the kitchen and a whore in bed. Unfor-tunately, my wife is a whore in the kitchen and a cook in bed.

Anonymous. Quoted in Geoffrey Gorer, *Exploring English Character* (1955) – in which readers of the *Sunday People* were invited to take part in a survey about their sex lives. This was collected from a 'working class, Sunderland' man.

Notice outside fried-fish shop:

8 CLEANLINESS, ECONOMY AND CIVILITY. ALWAYS HOT AND ALWAYS READY.

Anonymous. A passer-by remarked that this was the motto for a perfect wife. The passer-by was possibly Edward Thomas and the remark was recorded by E. S. P. Haynes in his *Lawyer's Notebook* (1932).

9 Take my wife – please!

Henny Youngman, British-born American comedian (1906–98). His most famous joke. According to an obituary in *The Times* (26 February 1998), this 'most-repeated one-liner was, in fact, first delivered by accident. Nervous before a radio appearance, he had begged an usher to seat his wife with the words: "Take my wife – please!" Everyone laughed, and the line became his signature.' He used it as the title of his autobiography in 1973.

Women

10 A woman's mind is cleaner than a man's; she changes it more often.

Oliver Herford, American humorist (1863–1935). Quoted in *The Treasury of Humorous Quotations*, ed. Evan Esar & Nicolas Bentley (1951).

11 Men who do not make advances to women are apt to become victims to women who make advances to them.

Walter Bagehot, English political writer (1826–77). Quoted in *The Treasury of Humorous Quotations*, ed. Evan Esar & Nicolas Bentley (1951).

12 In a world without men, there would be no war – just intense negotiations every 28 days.

Robin Williams, American comic and actor (1951–). In *Robin Williams at the Met One-Man Show* (1986).

At an all-women college in Massachusetts:

1 Who knows, somewhere out there in the audience may even be someone who will one day follow in my footsteps and preside over the White House as the President's spouse. I wish him well.

Barbara Bush, American First Lady (1925–). Quoted in *The Independent* 'Quote Unquote' (9 June 1990).

2 A woman is like a teabag. It's only when she's in hot water that you realize how strong she is.

Nancy Reagan, American First Lady (1923–). Quoted in *The Observer*, 'Sayings of the Week' (29 March 1981).

3 Women should be obscene and not heard.

Anonymous (graffito) from New York. Quoted in Reisner & Wechsler, *Encyclopedia of Graffiti* (1974).

4 There is a tide in the affairs of women, Which, taken at the flood, leads – God knows where.

Lord Byron, English poet (1788–1824). *Don Juan*, Canto 6, St. 2 (1819–24).

5 A woman without a man is like a fish without a bicycle.

Anonymous (graffito). Contributed by Mrs C. Raikes of Moseley, Birmingham, to BBC Radio *Quote ... Unquote* (1977). She had found it written in German on a lavatory wall in Birmingham University. Indeed, the chances are that the saying may have originated in West Germany where it is known in the form, *'Eine Frau ohne Mann ist wie ein Fisch ohne Velo!'* Elaine Partnow's *The Quotable Woman 1800–1981* (1982) attributes the saying to the feminist writer Gloria Steinem but gives no hint as to why it makes such a dubious attribution. Compare, however, what Arthur Bloch in *Murphy's Law ...* (also 1977) calls 'Vique's Law': 'A man without religion is like a fish without a bicycle.' In 1979, Arthur Marshall contributed the interesting variant: 'A woman without a man is like a moose without a hatrack.' In Haan & Hammerstrom, *Graffiti in the Big Ten* (1981), is 'Behind every successful man is a fish with a bicycle.'

6 The female sex has no bigger fan than I, and I have the bills to prove it.

Alan Jay Lerner, American songwriter and playwright (1918–86). *The Street Where I Live* (1978).

7 She has a Rolls body and a Balham mind.

J. B. Morton (Beachcomber), English humorous writer (1893–1979). *Morton's Folly* (1933).

8 When women kiss, it always reminds me of prize-fighters shaking hands.

H. L. Mencken, American journalist and linguist (1880–1956). *A Mencken Chrestomathy* (1949).

9 My mother said it was simple to keep a man – you must be a maid in the living room, a cook in the kitchen and a whore in the bedroom. I said I'd hire the other two and take care of the bedroom bit.

Jerry Hall, American model (1956–). Quoted in *The Observer*, 'Sayings of the Week' (6 October 1985).

10 Can you imagine a world without men? No crime and lots of happy, fat women.

Nicole Hollander, American illustrator and cartoonist (late twentieth century). Syndicated comic strip 'Sylvia' (1981). It has also been attributed to Marion Smith.

11 Women never look so well as when one comes in wet and dirty from hunting.

R. S. Surtees, English novelist and journalist (1805–64). *Mr Sponge's Sporting Tour*, Chap. 21 (1853). A possibly ambivalent statement, but it is definitely from the man's point of view.

12 Do you know why God withheld the sense of humour from women? That we may love you instead of laughing at you.

Mrs Patrick Campbell, English actress (1865–1940). Quoted in Leslie Robert Missen, *Quotable Anecdotes* (1966). As 'Women were born without a sense of humour – so they could love men, not laugh at them', quoted from Amsterdam in the book *Graffiti 2* (1980).

13 Individually, men may present a more or less rational appearance, eating, sleeping and scheming. But humanity as

a whole is changeful, mystical, fickle and delightful. Men are men, but Man is a woman.

G. K. Chesterton, English poet, novelist and critic (1874–1936). *The Napoleon of Notting Hill*, Chap. 1 (1904).

1 Sir, a woman's preaching is like a dog's walking on his hinder legs. It is not done well; but you are surprised to find it done at all.

Samuel Johnson, English writer and lexicographer (1709–84). In James Boswell, *Life of Johnson* (1791) – relating to 31 July 1763, when Boswell mentions that, 'I had been that morning at a meeting of the people called Quakers, where I had heard a woman preach.'

2 Brigands demand your money or your life; women require both.

Samuel Butler, English author (1835–1902). Quoted in *The Treasury of Humorous Quotations*, ed. Evan Esar & Nicolas Bentley (1951).

Wordplay

Challenged to compose a sentence including the word 'horticulture':

3 You can a lead a whore to culture but you can't make her think.

Dorothy Parker, American writer (1893–1967). Quoted in John Keats, *You Might as Well Live* (1970).

Words

4 The trouble with words is that you never know whose mouths they've been in.

Dennis Potter, English playwright (1935–94). Quoted in *The Guardian* (15 February 1993).

5 Man does not live by words alone, despite the fact that sometimes he has to eat them.

Adlai Stevenson, American Democratic politician (1900–65). Quoted in Herbert V. Prochnow, Snr & Jnr, *A Treasury of Humorous Quotations* (1969).

6 'Well,' said Owl, 'the customary procedure in such cases is as follows.' 'What does Crustimoney Proseedcake mean?'

said Pooh. 'For I am a Bear of Very Little Brain, and long words Bother me.'

A. A. Milne, English writer (1882–1956). *Winnie-the-Pooh*, Chap. 4 (1926).

To two ladies who said they were glad there were no naughty words included in his Dictionary:

7 What, my dears! then you have been looking for them.

Samuel Johnson, English writer and lexicographer (1709–84). Quoted in *Johnsonian Miscellanies*, ed. Hill (1897).

8 In the beginning was the Word. It's about the only sentence on which I find myself in total agreement with God.

(Sir) John Mortimer, English author, playwright and lawyer (1923–). Quoted in *The Observer*, 'Sayings of the Week' (1 July 1984).

9 Short words are best and the old words when short are the best of all.

Winston S. Churchill (later Sir Winston), British Conservative Prime Minister and writer (1874–1965). Speech, London (2 November 1949).

Work

10 I go on working for the same reason that a hen goes on laying eggs.

H. L. Mencken, American writer and editor (1880–1956). Quoted in *The Treasury of Humorous Quotations*, ed. Evan Esar & Nicolas Bentley (1951).

11 The only way to enjoy life is to work. Work is much more fun than fun.

Noël Coward (later Sir Noël), English entertainer and writer (1899–1973). Quoted in Dick Richards, *The Wit of Noël Coward* (1968).

12 I like work: it fascinates me. I can sit and look at it for hours.

Jerome K. Jerome, English writer (1859–1927). *Three Men In a Boat*, Chap. 3 (1889).

13 Work is the curse of the drinking classes.

Oscar Wilde, Irish playwright, poet and wit (1854–1900). Quoted in Hesketh Pearson, *The Life of Oscar Wilde* (1946).

14 It's true hard work never killed

anybody, but I figure, why take the chance?

Ronald Reagan, American actor and Republican President (1911–). Speech (28 March 1987).

1 The only place where success comes before work is in a dictionary.

Anonymous. Quoted in *The Penguin Dictionary of Modern Quotations* (1980 edn).

2 Nothing is really work unless you would rather be doing something else.

(Sir) J. M Barrie, Scottish playwright (1860–1937). Quoted in Laurence J. Peter, *Quotations for Our Time* (1977).

Working life

3 Working for Warner Bros is like fucking a porcupine; it's a hundred pricks against one.

Wilson Mizner, American playwright (1876–1933). Quoted in David Niven, *Bring on the Empty Horses* (1975).

World

4 This world is a comedy to those that think, a tragedy to those that feel.

Horace Walpole (4th Earl of Orford), English writer (1717–97). Letter to the Countess of Upper Ossory (16 August 1776). However, Blaise Pascal (1623–1662) is reported to have said earlier: *'La vie, c'est une tragédie pour celui qui sent, mais une comédie pour celui qui pense.'*

Worship

Of Lord John Russell:

5 If a traveller were informed that such a man was Leader of the House of Commons, he might begin to comprehend how the Egyptians worshipped – AN INSECT.

Benjamin Disraeli (later 1st Earl of Beaconsfield), British Conservative Prime Minister and writer (1804–81). Pseudonymously in 'The Letters of Runnymede', *The Times* (January–May 1836).

Worst

6 Cheer up! the worst is yet to come!

Philander Chase Johnson, American writer (1866–1939). *Everybody's Magazine* (May 1920). This had been written earlier in a letter from Mark Twain to his wife (1893/4) included in *The Love Letters of Mark Twain*. Twain also used it in *Those Extraordinary Twins* (1894).

Wren, Sir Christopher
English architect (1632–1723)

7 Sir Christopher Wren
Said, 'I am going to dine with
    some men.
If anybody calls
Say I am designing St Paul's.'

E. Clerihew Bentley, English novelist, journalist and poet (1875–1956). *Biography for Beginners* (1905).

Writers

Of Ernest Hemingway:

8 He got hold of the red meat of the English language and turned it into hamburgers.

Richard Gordon, English novelist (1921–). Possibly quoting another on BBC Radio *Quote ... Unquote* (17 May 1978).

9 What does [Upton] Sinclair know about anything? He's just a writer.

Louis B. Mayer, American film producer (1885–1957). Quoted in Philip French, *The Movie Moguls* (1969).

10 Authors are easy enough to get on with – if you are fond of children.

Michael Joseph, English publisher (1897–1958). Quoted in *The Observer* (29 May 1949).

11 I love being a writer. What I can't stand is the paperwork.

Peter de Vries, American writer (1910–93). Quoted in Laurence J. Peter, *Quotations for Our Time* (1977).

12 When audiences come to see authors lecture, it is largely in the hope that we'll be funnier to look at than to read.

Sinclair Lewis, American novelist (1885–1951). Quoted in Laurence J. Peter, *Quotations for Our Time* (1977).

1 Some writers take to drink, others take to audiences.

Gore Vidal, American novelist, playwright and critic (1925–). In *The Paris Review* (1981).

2 If a third of all the novelists and maybe two-thirds of all the poets now writing dropped dead suddenly the loss to literature would not be great.

Charles Osborne, Australian-born writer and arts administrator (1927–). Quoted in *The Observer*, 'Sayings of the Week' (3 November 1985) from remarks he had made at a (British) Arts Council press conference. It was only later – as he confirmed in 1991 – that Osborne became aware Rebecca West had uttered a similar sentiment at the 1962 Edinburgh Festival Writers' Conference: 'It would be no loss to the world if most of the writers now writing had been strangled at birth' (a remark recorded, for example, in Stephen Spender, *Journals 1939–83*, 1985).

3 There's no greater bliss in life than when the plumber eventually comes to unblock your drains. No writer can give that sort of pleasure.

Victoria Glendinning, English biographer and novelist (1937–). Quoted in *The Observer* (3 January 1993).

Writing

4 To give an accurate and exhaustive account of the period would need a far less brilliant pen than mine.

Sir Max Beerbohm, English writer and caricaturist (1872–1956). In *The Yellow Book* (1894).

5 All good writing is *swimming under water* and holding your breath.

F. Scott Fitzgerald, American novelist (1896–1940). In undated letter to Frances Scott Fitzgerald. Quoted in *The Penguin Dictionary of Modern Quotations* (1971).

6 I never can understand how two men can write a book together; to me that's like three people getting together to have a baby.

Evelyn Waugh, English novelist (1903–66). Quoted in Laurence J. Peter, *Quotations for Our Time* (1977).

7 Writing a book was an adventure. To begin with it was a toy, an amusement; then it became a mistress, and then a master, and then a tyrant.

Winston S. Churchill (later Sir Winston), British Conservative Prime Minister and writer (1874–1965). Speech, London (2 November 1949).

Coral Browne appeared as herself in Alan Bennett's TV play An Englishman Abroad, *based on her encounter in Moscow with the exiled spy Guy Burgess. A Hollywood writer told her that although he had enjoyed the play, he didn't think the writing was up to scratch. Aghast at this slight, Browne put the American in his place on the question of writing:*

8 Listen, dear, you couldn't write 'fuck' on a dusty venetian blind.

Coral Browne, Australian-born actress (1913–91). Quoted by Alan Bennett in *The Sunday Times Magazine* (18 November 1984), and the story was confirmed by Browne in a Channel 4 documentary, December 1990.

9 I never understand anything until I have written about it.

Horace Walpole, English writer (1717–97). Quoted in *The Treasury of Humorous Quotations*, ed. Evan Esar & Nicolas Bentley (1951).

10 After writing for fifteen years it struck me I had no talent for writing. I couldn't give it up. By that time I was already famous.

Mark Twain, American writer (1835–1910). Quoted in *The Twainian* (May–June 1952). Robert Benchley, according to Nathaniel Benchley's *Robert Benchley* (1955), covered much the same ground with the reflection: 'It took me fifteen years to discover that I had no talent for writing, but I couldn't give it up because by that time I was too famous.'

11 The shelf life of the modern hardback writer is somewhere between the milk and the yoghurt.

(Sir) John Mortimer, English playwright and lawyer (1923–). Quoted in *The Observer* (28 June 1987). As he had, in fact, said at the time, Mortimer was quoting the American

humorous columnist Calvin Trillin (1935–)
who had spoken, rather, of 'A shelf life somewhere between butter and yoghurt' in *The
New York Times* on the 14 June.

*At a rehearsal of the Marx Brothers
film* Animal Crackers *for which
he wrote the script:*

1 Excuse me for interrupting but I
actually thought I heard a line
I wrote.

George S. Kaufman, American playwright
(1889–1961). Quoted in Scott Meredith,
*George S. Kaufman and the Algonquin Round
Table* (1974).

2 If you want to get rich from writing,
write the sort of thing that's read by
persons who move their lips when
reading.

Don Marquis, American writer (1878–1937).
Attributed in *The Oxford Dictionary of
Literary Quotations*, ed. Peter Kemp
(1997).

On the work of Jack Kerouac:

3 That's not writing, that's typing.

Truman Capote, American writer (1924–84).
Attributed remark (1959). In Gerald Clarke,
Capote (1988), '[It] isn't writing at all – it's
typing' is given as his view of Beat Generation
writers in general.

4 WAITER: Do you just do your writing
now – or are you still working?
CHARLIE: No ... I just do the writing.

Dialogue from film, *Charlie Bubbles* (UK,
1968). Script by Shelagh Delaney. With
Albert Finney as Charlie and Joe Gladwin as
the waiter.

YZ

Yes-persons

1 That woman speaks eighteen languages, and can't say No in any of them.

Dorothy Parker, American writer (1893–1967). Quoted in Alexander Woollcott, *While Rome Burns* (1934).

Characteristic remark to minions:

2 Don't say yes until I finish talking!

Darryl F. Zanuck, American film producer (1902–79). Hence, the title of Mel Gussow's biography of him (1971).

Youth

On a youthful presidential candidate:

3 Dewey has thrown his diaper into the ring.

Harold L. Ickes, American lawyer and administrator (1874–1952). Quoted in *The New York Times* (12 December 1939).

4 It were a real increase of human happiness, could all young men from the age of nineteen be covered under barrels, or rendered otherwise invisible; and there left to follow their lawful studies and callings; till they emerged, sadder and wiser, at the age of twenty-five.

Thomas Carlyle, Scottish historian and philosopher (1795–1881). *Sartor Resartus* (1838).

5 To get back my youth I would do anything in the world, except take exercise, get up early, or be respectable.

Oscar Wilde, Irish playwright, poet and wit (1854–1900). *The Picture of Dorian Gray*, Chap. 19 (1891).

6 Only the young die good.

Oliver Herford, American humorist (1863–1935). Quoted in *Quotations for Speakers and Writers*, ed. A. Andrews (1969).

7 No wise man ever wished to be younger.

Jonathan Swift, Anglo-Irish writer and clergyman (1667–1745). *Thoughts on Various Subjects* (1706).

8 Youth is too important to be wasted on the young.

Bernard Shaw, Irish playwright and critic (1856–1950). Quoted in Copeland (1939) in the form '[Youth is] far too good to waste on children'. Quoted as 'Youth is a wonderful thing; what a crime to waste it on children' – in *The Treasury of Humorous Quotations*, ed. Evan Esar & Nicolas Bentley (1951).

When Somerset Maugham left a dinner party early, saying, 'I must look after my youth':

9 Next time do bring him. We adore those sort of people.

Lady Tree, English aristocrat (1863–1937). Quoted in *The Oxford Dictionary of Humorous Quotations*, ed. Ned Sherrin (1995). In Daphne Fielding, *Emerald and Nancy* (1968), this is ascribed rather to Lady ('Emerald') Cunard, the American-born society figure in Britain: 'Then why didn't you bring him with you? I should be delighted to meet him.'

10 I suppose that the high-water mark of my youth in Columbus, Ohio,

was the night the bed fell on my father.

James Thurber, American writer and cartoonist (1894–1961). *My Life and Hard Times* (1933). The chapter in which this line occurs is simply called 'The Night the Bed Fell'.

Zoos

1 Zoo: a place devised for animals to study the habits of human beings.

Oliver Herford, American humorist (1863–1935). Quoted in Herbert V. Prochnow, Snr & Jnr, *A Treasury of Humorous Quotations* (1969).

Index

In the Index quotations are represented in capsule form under keyword headings
drawn from the one or two most significant words in the quotation.

A

aardvark: it's a. but it pays, 1:1
  reminds me of a.'s ass, 56:2
Aberdeen: exciting as A., 43:2
A-bomb is dynamite, 100:7
above: to the one a. him, 106:1
Abraham: safe in arms of A., 71:11
abroad is bloody, 87:8
  criticize when a., 49:1
abscess: brink of great a., 100:9
absence of body, 1:5
  shoot me in my a., 1:4
absent: two of whom are a., 42:6
absinthe makes heart grow fonder, 1:8
  makes tart grow fonder, 1:9
abstainer, defined, 2:2
abstinence thin end of pledge, 2:1
academic: no a. voted chair, 2:4
accent: speak English with a., 2:5
acceptable invitations only, 129:3
accident: bad boating a., 234:8
  died in gardening a., 53:3
accommodation unit, 108:4
accordion: gentleman plays a., 2:6
accountancy, idea of excitement, 2:8
  in chartered a., 2:7
accountant: personality to be a., 221:9
accustomed as I am to, 219:9
ace: about to play a., 4:7, 232:2
acorns: dozen a. and chipolata, 163:11
  fifteen a. hardly worth, 216:11
act: can't a. in any, 4:5
  don't have to a. with you, 191:11
  don't so much a., 4:11
acting gives trees bad name, 4:8
  secret of a. is, 4:13
  why not try a., 4:9
actor and the streetwalker, 186:1
  guy who ain't listening, 2:11
  scratch an a., 3:5
  when a. has money, 3:1
actors: send good a. cheap, 183:5

actress: bishop said to a., 24:7–11
  for an a. to succeed, 3:6
  you'll find an a., 3:5
actresses will happen, 4:2
Adam and Bruce, 109:2
  good thing A. had, 169:1
  when Eve said to A., 212:8
address: letter delivered to wrong a., 12:8
adequacy: delusions of a., 4:10
adjective: as to a., 5:5
admiral: kill an a. from time to time,
    67:8
  not doorman but rear a., 239:5
  still call me a., 157:3
admirals: three great a., 85:12
adolescence is stage between, 5:6
adored: he a. New York City, 161:13
adornment of his person, 56:10
adultery: autobiography like a., 18:3
  between puberty and a., 5:6
  going on in New York, 160:1
  Lords has cup for a., 180:4
  only when committing a., 203:9
adults: consenting a. in private, 213:1
advances: women who make a., 250:11
advantage of having been born, 13:7
advantages: children haven't my a., 182:8
adventure: writing book was a., 254:7
advertisement: good a., 5:7
advertisements: keeps a. apart, 162:2
  speak so well, 5:8
advertising: business without a., 6:6
  described, 6:2
  is confusion, 6:3
  most fun with clothes, 5:11
  rattling stick, 6:5
  money spent on a., 6:7
  outside an a. agency, 179:3
advice: doesn't want any a., 184:9
  to actors, 7:5, 6:10
  to persons about to marry, 143:2
aerials: had my TV a. removed, 229:8
afflict the comfortable, 41:6

C

D

dialogue of deaf, 59:2
snappy 19th century d., 98:8
diamond: imitation rough d., 12:6
diamonds hardest thing in world, 57:11
put d. on floor, 120:1
diaper: thrown d. in ring, 257:3
diaries: only good girls keep d., 58:1
diary like vomit, 58:3
never travel without d., 57:13
who would stuff d. with, 58:2
will keep you, 57:12
dictatorships: benevolent d., 58:4
dictionary: first time made d., 157:7
like Webster's d., 190:10
only place is in d., 253:1
die at the top, 149:2
before they sing, 216:6
beyond my means, 62:3
done my best to d., 81:4
good Americans d., 10:4
had to d. in my week, 208:12
had to die to prove, 52:9
if I should d., 178:1
not afraid to d., 53:11
old professors never d., 186:4
see anybody d., 53:10
so many people d. there, 217:2
will be last thing I do, 62:8
died a gentleman, 71:10
as lived at sea, 139:5
maintaining his right, 74:5
mine d. too, 236:11
would never have d., 60:1
dies: something in me d., 89:1
diet: Doctor D., 60:3
then you d., 190:5
differently: could have happened d.,
128:10
difficult do you call it, 154:13
Christianity found d., 36:10
every d. except, 181:5
dig up Shakespeare and Bacon, 213:4
digging: except ditch d., 20:11
nails in coffin, 140:5
when in hole stop d., 107:4
dignity: as much d. as presidency,
184:2
left room with silent d., 180:9
Dijon, young man of, 177:1
dined last night with Borgias, 110:2
more d. against,110:1
off her husband, 150:9
dinner: ask Him to d., 58:11
at d. party eat, 58:8

best number for d., 58:9
with Princess Michael, 96:4
Dior: never darken D., 190:7
diplomacy art of saying, 59:1
lying in state, 59:3
megaphone d., 59:2
diplomat like head waiter, 58:12
direction: didn't care about d., 96:1
directions: rode off in all d., 79:11
directory: except telephone d., 165:6
direful: something d. in sound, 23:12
dirt doesn't get any worse, 110:10
dirty days hath September, 51:8
if sex was d., 210:15
whether d. or not, 21:3
disappointments: earliest d., 162:6
disasters: English d. traced Wales,
246:5
disbelieve in God, 59:6
disciples: why only twelve d., 99:14
disco without music, 159:14
discothèque: winter of our d., 154:1
disease: foot and mouth d., 86:11
one d. haven't got, 112:1
while nature cures d., 145:3
diseases: all kinds of d., 215:1
disgruntled: if not actually d., 59:8
disguised: effectively d., 25:9
dish-cloths: banging two d., 231:6
dishwasher: only learned to stack d.,
30:2
disinfectant: sunlight is best d., 188:1
displeasing: something not d. to us,
89:5
Disraeli, Benjamin, described, 207:12
distinctive about New York, 161:1
ditch: except ditch digging, 20:11
ditching: failed at d., 121:5
divisions: how many d. has Pope, 181:3
divorce never, 142:9
divorces made in heaven, 59:12
do: do not d. unto others, 60:8
don't just d. something, 116:10
I am to d. what I please, 124:4
nothing to d., 9:11
we must d. something, 54:8
dobedobedo: 59:13
doctor: I am not a d., 230:7
performance as d., 85:7
slapped by mother, 239:1
doctors: best d. in world are, 60:3
doctrinally inexplicable, 189:2
does: he who can d., 228:2
dog: as d. is to lamppost, 121:9

E

F

found: from being f. out, 183:4
 thou shalt not be f. out, 41:7
four-letter: era of f. word, 69:4
France is country where, 88:8
 is only place where, 88:7
Fred: here lies F., 75:2
free: trouble with f. elections, 67:2
freedom: when fighting for f., 236:5
French: excess of F. Revolution, 82:1
 wiser than seem, 250:1
Freud never played Glasgow, 41:5
fricassee of dead dog, 134:10
fried: children boiled or f., 36:2
Friedman, Milton, described, 65:7
friend: breaking it in for f., 157:6
 I lose a f., 171:3
 if you want f., 88:12
 may you not meet a f., 187:5
 old f. fall from roof, 89:4
 Reagan for best f., 199:2
 save from candid f., 88:11
 who is fat f., 199:11
friends are God's apology, 200:5
 champagne for real f., 34:1
 God protect me from f., 88:9
 hat and few f., 129:11
 in both places, 105:7
 lay down f. for life, 89:2
 making and preserving g., 89:3
 money can't buy f., 150:10
 none of his f. likes him, 213:11
 only for my best f., 249:7
 with f. like that, 88:10
friendship recognised by police, 141:7
frighten: and f. horses, 211:7
frog: wonderful bird f. are, 89:6
frogs better than Huns, 87:8
Frost, David, described, 191:6
frown: seventy-two muscles to f., 217:6
frozen: few are f., 40:9
 God's f. people, 40:8
 this show is f., 34:3
fruit: melon is good f., 146:1
fry: and then you f., 190:6
fuck: couldn't write f., 254:8
 fish f. in it, 61:8
 have to f. to get out, 4:12
 if can't plug it in or f. it, 55:8
 you f. in age of AIDS, 210:12
fucking: like f. porcupine, 253:3
 too f. busy, 79:5
fuddled: playing on f. fiddle, 185:1
fun: more f. to read it, 211:9
 most f. with clothes, 5:11

most fun without laughing, 211:1.
 politics should be f., 180:5
 read Homer for f., 96:12
 this is where f. starts, 75:7
 work is much more f. than f., 252:11
funeral: approved of f., 54:2
 down on him for f. expenses, 152:3
 march of fried eel, 154:11
 nothing like morning f., 89:10
funerals: go to other men's f., 90:3
 of friends who exercise, 79:9
funnier to look at than read, 253:12
funny peculiar or f. ha-ha, 90:5–6
 rich man's joke is f., 247:4
 why not as f. as it used to be, 189:1
 without being vulgar, 103:5
furniture: all f. passes before them, 103:8
 don't bump f., 7:5
 no f. so charming, 26:7
 re-arrange f. on Titanic, 109:7
future behind one, 90:8–91:3

G

Gable, Clark, described, 93:1–2
Gabriel, Archangel, and votes, 203:4
gadget: handy little g., 175:10
gaiety feature of Soviet Union, 218:11
 only concession to g., 246:4
gallantry: what men call g., 40:2
gallon: another quote make g., 195:1
gallows: die upon g. or of pox, 203:2
game: he no play g., 181:4
 takes three days to reach, 48:4
 whole family can play, 114:9
gamekeeper: and g. below waist, 205:2
gamut: whole g. of emotions, 232:9
gapes: for if she g., 77:2
garden: come into g., 85:13
 is lovesome thing, 93:8–9
 looks as if laid out, 93:10
 man and woman in g., 23:6
gardening: died in g. accident, 53:3
gare: ce n'est pas la g., 13:11
garter: and Knight of the G., 16:1
generalizations: all g. dangerous, 94:2
generalizer learns less, 94:1
generalizes: he who g. lies, 93:11
genitals: breaking my g., 105:4
genius: better be a g., 94:6
 does what it must, 94:4–5
 except my g., 94:7
 is infinite capacity, 94:10
 organizing g., 168:6

H

Lawrence of Arabia, described, 129:6
laws: if you like l. and sausages, 127:7
lawyer: here lies honest l., 74:2
  man who is own l., 129:9
  with briefcase, 129:7
lawyers: scarce as l. in heaven, 129:8
lay down wife at right moment, 143:7
  space to l. hat, 129:11
lays: biting hand that l., 98:3
lead: with bit of l. piping, 82:10
leader: for I am their l., 129:12
leadership like swimming, 129:13
learning bagpipes, 19:9
  instrument as one goes, 131:13
leaves country as fast as he can, 207:2
leeks: sits among cabbages and l., 223:4
left: somewhere on L. Wing, 100:8
  what's l. of her, 20:10
leg: fly would break l., 17:1
  no l. is too short, 187:6
  which l. comes after which, 33:8
legend in own lunchtime, 121:13
legibility: with dawn of l., 104:3
legs: born with l. apart, 210:1
  chop off her l. and count, 191:4
  has between l., 154:2
Leica: me no L., 84:13
leisure tends to corrupt, 130:2
lemon: twelve miles from l., 47:3
lend: would l. money to poor risk, 130:5
Lennon, John, remains dead, 53:8
leopard: the Lord is shoving l., 220:8
less: about l. and l., 80:3
  can't take anything l., 99:17
  had he pleased us l., 135:2
  than meets eye, 233:4
letter: answered l. sooner, 130:9
  delivered to wrong address, 12:8
  offensive l. follows, 229:2
  wrote a very nice l., 54:2
letters: no l. in grave, 130:10
  pin your hair with l., 178:9
Levant, Oscar, necessary miracle, 149:5
levity: little judicious l., 131:3
lexicographer: to l. God is, 97:1
liberal is conservative who, 131:4
  no l. left in New York, 131:5
lick: know what I l., 176:5
lid: don't slam lid, 88:5
lie down: make love by saying l., 210:3
  follows by post, 200:9
  heavy on him earth, 75:4
  sent to l. abroad, 9:9
  where you l. on beach, 209:11

lies down with dogs, 43:1
  enough white l. to ice, 131:8
  he generally l., 93:11
  stop telling l. about, 131:7
life, as beach, 190:6
  as binge, 190:5
  before death, 132:6
  cycle of song, 59:5
  is terrible thing, 131:12
  just bowl of toenails, 131:9
  like opening tin, 132:10
  men in my l., 146:10
  part of l.'s rich, 131:11
  third of l. over, 8:7
  this is real l., 131:10
  too short to stuff, 153:4
lift: can't even l. them, 146:4
  while I give two a l., 28:6
lifting: no heavy l., 179:9
light at end of tunnel, 65:8, 109:8
  refrigerator with l. out, 56:4
lighting: sex question of l., 212:8
lightning: church not struck by l., 108:8
lights: switch off l., 126:6
  when l. went out, 151:4
like: I happen to l. New York, 160:7
  sort of thing they l., 49:4
  trying to l. Scotchmen, 207:3
limelight, 129:6
line: drawing a l. somewhere, 14:9
  heard l. I wrote, 255:1
  shortest l. moves slowest, 128:7
lines: consisted of l. like, 172:12
  know your l., 7:5
lingerie: brevity soul of l., 133:12
lining: crowd has silver l., 49:10
lion and calf lie down, 10:8
lips are moving, 131:6
  move l. when reading, 255:2
liquor is quicker, 61:2
lisp, defined, 134:1
listen carefully, 40:5
lit: not see l. again, 246:12
literary cooks, 194:5
literature about having sex, 135:9
  cultivate l. on oatmeal, 206:10
  loss to l. not great, 254:2
littered: come down and l., 13:10
Little Nell, death of, 127:1
little: every l. helps, 248:4
  it was very l. one, 79:7
  like being l. pregnant, 115:9
live: if man can l. in New York, 159:16
  I'm going to l. forever, 94:8

M

Q

R

S